PRAISE FOR *GUNSMITHING MODERN FIREARMS*

"Bryce Towsley is an icon in the industry and one of the most knowledgeable gun people of modern times. You will really enjoy reading his new book, *Gunsmithing Modern Firearms,* not only for the valuable information and his great stories but for the sense of personal connection he makes with gunsmithing."

—Pete Brownell

"This book is a treasure trove of information and has something for every gun enthusiast, from the raw novice to the grizzled shooter who picks lottery ticket numbers based on his favorite ballistic coefficients."

—Roy Hill, public relations, Brownells

"When we're looking for an expert to write an article on gun modifications for the 675,000 NRA members who get *Shooting Illustrated* each month, there's one scribe we turn to: Bryce M. Towsley. This book is further evidence that Towsley is the go-to man for clear, concise, and entertaining instructions for anyone looking to work on their firearms at home."

—Ed Friedman, editor-in-chief, *Shooting Illustrated*

"Bryce Towsley has forgotten more about guns and gunsmithing than most people could hope to learn in a lifetime. Through his writing he is keeping the art of gunsmithing alive, sharing knowledge not often shared willingly and leaving a guide for the generations to come."

—Jim Majoros, owner, Viktor's Legacy Custom Gunsmithing

"The new go-to DIY reference for the novice or a seasoned gun nut! Informative, precise—let's cut some threads. Well done!"

—Mark Bansner, Bansner & Co. LLC Riflemakers

"Bryce Towsley's knowledge of the historical development of small arms for American shooters and hunters is exhaustive. When I have a question about what makes a cartridge or a rifle tick, I know I can rely on him to provide an authoritative answer. When I need a thorough feature story on cartridge development, reloading, gunsmithing or shooting, I know he can deliver the goods."

—J. Scott Olmsted, editor-in-chief, *American Hunter*

GUNSMITHING
MODERN FIREARMS

GUNSMITHING MODERN FIREARMS

A GUN GUY'S GUIDE TO MAKING GOOD GUNS EVEN BETTER

BRYCE M. TOWSLEY

Skyhorse Publishing

Skyhorse Publishing books may be purchased in bulk at special discounts for sales promotion, corporate gifts, fund-raising, or educational purposes. Special editions can also be created to specifications. For details, contact the Special Sales Department, Skyhorse Publishing, 307 West 36th Street, 11th Floor, New York, NY 10018 or info@skyhorsepublishing.com.

Skyhorse® and Skyhorse Publishing® are registered trademarks of Skyhorse Publishing, Inc.®, a Delaware corporation.

Visit our website at www.skyhorsepublishing.com.

10 9 8 7 6 5

Library of Congress Cataloging-in-Publication Data is available on file.

Cover design by Tom Lau
Cover photo credit: Bryce Towsley

Print ISBN: 978-1-5107-1880-7
Ebook ISBN: 978-1-5107-1881-4

Printed in China

This book is dedicated to the memory of Bob Brownell.

If he had not started his company and sent out that first catalog in 1947, hobby gunsmithing would be much different today.

CONTENTS

Foreword by Pete Brownell   ix

Introduction   x

SECTION ONE: PRIMARY PROJECTS

FOREWORD

Gunsmithing is in our blood. My family has been in gunsmithing for the better part of three generations. We all started at home, on our kitchen table or work shop. Our passion drove us to learn more, to ask questions and to improve our skills.

The moment you started tinkering with your firearm you became a gunsmith. This is how Brownells started. My grandpa's passion for fixing his own guns and those of his neighbors turned into a business that would become Brownells.

From the do-it-yourself hobbyist to the most-skilled firearms artisans, it all starts with a spark to learn more about firearms. The hunter who wants to make his rifle as accurate he can. The competitor looking for the extra little edge. The shooter who wants to make his gun truly unique and special and wants to put his own stamp on it. We are all gunsmiths.

Those are the people who will get the most out of this book. The honest-to-goodness "gun people" who are passionate about not only guns and the Second Amendment lifestyle, but also about being as self-reliant as possible—to the point they can do most of their own gunsmithing.

And they've got an excellent guide in author Bryce Towsley.

We've known Bryce for years. He's been a professional gun writer and photographer since 1982, and was a field editor for NRA's American Rifleman, American Hunter and Shooting Illustrated. He's written articles and shot photos for just about all the major gun and hunting publications, and has appeared numerous times on TV.

More than that, Bryce is a true member of gun culture. He's a shooter, a hunter, a competitor, and a gunsmith. Bryce lives, breathes, and knows guns.

He shares some of his extensive knowledge and experience in this book. He shows the aspiring hobbyist gunsmith how to accomplish all sorts of important tasks. From changing a magazine spring on your favorite shotgun, to protecting and enhancing your gun's appearance with coatings like DuraCoat and Cerakote.

There's a section on how to modify one of the most-popular handguns on the planet—the Glock. And another on how to replace the trigger on a Remington 700.

For the more advanced hobbyist, Bryce lays out how to build the classic 1911 from parts, showing how to hand-fit the various pieces for maximum reliability. He demonstrates the tools and techniques to build a precision rifle from scratch; how to blueprint the action, fit and chamber the barrel, cut a crown, and even install a Sako or M-16 extractor on a bolt.

And he does it all with his trademark personal, fun-to-read style. Bryce not only tells you what to do, he also shows you what not to do, using the mistakes he's made as teaching moments. This is not a technical manual. It's a collection of personal stories told by a master story-teller, centered around guns and gunsmithing.

Guns are a very special part of our unique American heritage. Guns are useful tools. They can help feed us and protect us. They are used in competition. They are inherently interesting examples of engineering and human ingenuity. They are family heirlooms. They are physical embodiments of our constitutionally guaranteed freedoms and liberties. They help us maintain and protect those freedoms and liberties. And added to all of those amazing qualities, guns are also simply fun to both shoot and work on. You'll like this book. It's about guns, and how you can learn how to repair, maintain, customize, and even build them yourself.

—Pete Brownell
February 1, 2018

INTRODUCTION

While I was working on this book the news reported that Robert M. Pirsig had passed away. The current generation is probably responding, "Who?" But when I was a young man, he was a household name. He is best known for the book *Zen and the Art of Motorcycle Maintenance*. This was a huge, international best seller and for a while it was the primary topic with young people arguing late into the night.

Although I am an avid reader, I had somehow never read this book. Probably because it was so popular and I rebelled, but upon seeing the news I wondered what it was that I had missed in my stubbornness, so I ordered the paperback.

This book first came out in 1974 and I wish I had read it then as a wide-eyed kid a year out of high school, because I think it would have had more impact. While I don't mean to alienate its millions of fans, this book just didn't grab me. Reading it now, much later in life, I found it just drudgery to get through his philosophical ramblings. I never skip anything in any book, but I found myself jumping over pages in an attempt to get to the end. (Please don't do that with this book.)

Pirsig's descriptions of the motorcycle trip and the interactions with his friends and his son are quite interesting, but he continually runs off on philosophical rants that just make my eyes glaze over. However, he does have one passage that I think works well for any aspiring gunsmith. It's part of a multi-page discussion about the written instructions for an outdoor barbecue rotisserie. (This really is not an edge-of-your-seat kind of book.)

His friend has spent an ineffective afternoon trying to assemble the rotisserie and is looking for somebody or something to blame for his failure. Pirsig makes his living writing technical instruction manuals (which probably explains his less than exciting writing style) and his friend asks him to tell him that the instructions are the problem, not his inability to understand them. That launches a long and rather boring discussion about the classic-romantic split and how different minds interpret technology. I suppose a stoned-out eighteen-year-old would be mesmerized, but a 60-something jaded gun writer just wanted it to end.

Until I found this passage about the difference in how a novice or a bad worker will differ from the craftsman:

"The craftsman isn't ever following a single line of instruction. He's making decisions as he goes along. For that reason he'll be absorbed and attentive to what he's doing even though he doesn't deliberately contrive this. His motions and the machine are in a kind of harmony. He isn't following any set of written instructions because the nature of the material at hand determines his thoughts and motions, which simultaneously change the nature of the material at hand. The material and his thoughts are changing together in a progression of changes until his mind's at rest at the same time the material's right."

See what I mean about this book? Not exactly a tightly written thriller. Anyway, I think what he is saying is this: a true craftsman will use the instructions as a guideline, but he is always thinking and always very aware of what he is doing. A craftsman always adds his own personal touch to the work being performed even if it's not always evident to an outsider. A craftsman does not simply blindly follow the instructions like a robot, but instead develops a deep understanding of what is being performed with his actions. The instructions may say "do this" and the craftsman does exactly "this." But, at the same time he has an understanding of why he is doing "this" and what exactly "this" is.

A craftsman will always be thinking and often may be developing a better way to do "this." His mind will be deep into the processes so that he is always thinking, always learning, and always questioning what he is doing.

Maybe that questioning concludes that the processes he is using are exactly perfect, or perhaps he has a better idea. The point is that a craftsman doesn't just do something, he understands what he is doing and its importance and relevance to the entire job.

If I can inspire nothing else with this book, I would like the readers to develop into the kind of craftsmen I am describing. Use what I am writing here when working on guns, but try to develop a complete understanding of the processes and how they relate to the entire job and the entire firearm. Always be thinking, always be questioning, and always be looking for a better way. You may not find it and you may discover that the way described here is the best way, but at least you will understand why. If you do find a better way, then you know you are thinking as a craftsman, not just a parts assembler.

This book is not meant to be like the instruction sheet for an outdoor barbecue rotisserie where you insert bolt "A" into hole "B" and tighten with nut "C." Yes, there is some of that type of instruction in this book, but it slipped in when I wasn't looking. Overall, I tried to avoid that sort of mindedness. My goal here is to make you think about gunsmithing and to develop a deep understanding of how it all ties together. For example, when you set the headspace with a chamber reamer, install a new trigger, cut a new crown, or do any other process, I want you to understand not just how to do it, but why it's done the way it is and its relevance to the performance of the firearm.

My goal is for this book to be like that one great teacher we are lucky to find in a lifetime: not only do they instruct, they challenge and inspire you as well. I hope that by reading this book you will learn how make good guns even better and I hope you develop a thirst for learning and a creativity that allows you to add your personal signature to every job you do.

Most of all, I hope that you enjoy reading the book. Too often, "technical" books are boring and bland. I want you to have this one beside your bed to read at night. I want you to laugh out loud sometimes and I want you stop, go back, and reread some passages, just as I often do with any good book.

Gunsmithing is a great hobby. It brings a satisfaction that few others can achieve. There is the pride in fixing something that is broken and the feeling of artistic achievement when you modify a firearm to make it better or more unique. I like to think that the feeling of standing back and looking at a finished project, large or small, is the same as a great artist feels when looking at a finished painting or a completed sculpture.

There are other joys in this hobby. For me, it's therapy. When I can escape to my shop and my tools I can tune out a world that I often don't much like and enter one I enjoy. Walton had his fishing, I have my lathe. It's the journey that's important here and I hope to instill that understanding. It doesn't matter if you are just doing a small job at the kitchen table or if you go all out and start building custom guns, it's really all the same. You can tune out the world, become *absorbed and attentive* and immerse yourself in this wonderful hobby of gunsmithing and for a few hours life will be perfect.

—*Bryce M. Towsley*

SECTION ONE
PRIMARY PROJECTS

These are projects that a hobby gunsmith can do (mostly) without a lathe or milling machine. Let's call them "Projects for the bench, or even the kitchen table."

▲ Nathan Towsley shooting the Mosin-Nagant "Poor Man's Sniper Rifle."
We turned an old Russian Battle Rifle into a viable long-range rifle.

CHAPTER 1

TURNING A
MOSIN-NAGANT "TACTICAL"

Lipstick on a pig or a silk purse from a sow's ear?

HISTORY LESSON

The Mosin-Nagant bolt-action military rifle was developed by the Imperial Russian Army in 1891. It is one of the most common military bolt action rifles in history, with more than thirty-seven million units produced. Odds are you have one or know somebody who does. At the very least, you have seen them lined up on the rack at a gun shop in years past with a stupidly low price tag.

The 7.62X54R cartridge it fires is still used by the Russians and is the longest serving military cartridge in the world. It's the only rimmed cartridge still being used by any military.

Ed Freidman, editor of NRA's *Shooting Illustrated* magazine, and I were talking about these guns and he came up with the idea of taking a standard Mosin-Nagant, the rifle

▲ The Mosin-Nagant 91/30.

that's as common as dirt, and tricking it out into a "poor man's sniper rifle."

I am always up for a DIY project, so I started looking for a donor rifle. That turned out to be a bigger problem than I expected. With my usual knack for timing, I began this project about the same time the rifles started to become scarce. For years they were easy to find and very inexpensive to buy, often going for less than $100. That was before the Obama administration implemented policies negatively affecting the import of these rifles which drove the price up quite a bit. The market has stabilized a little now, but when I started this project they were hard to find. As I write this, it's early in Trump's administration. The guns are still hard to find and are drawing a premium price when compared to the price tags of the past. That may or may not change in the future.

I found a guy about 30 miles from me who had one for sale and he wanted something I had, so we worked out a trade. It would have been fine, except that it was late in a horrible winter and every driveway in Vermont was shrinking as the plows ran out of places to put the snow.

His wife came home while we were making the deal and parked her car tight beside my truck. The edge of a six-foot-tall snowbank protruded past the back of my truck and rather than find her to move her car and give the guy a chance to change his mind, I decided to back through the snowbank. It's what any native Vermonter would have done. It had been a cold winter and most snow banks were still soft, so it should have worked. The trouble was the telephone pole buried out of sight in the snow. I hit it so hard that most of the world noticed. I left with a new rifle, a badly crumpled bumper, and a truckload of embarrassment.

The bore looked good on the rifle and everything seemed to be in working order, so I took it apart. (The rule of thumb is you never shoot the donor gun for any build project. You risk falling in love and not completing the project.)

Full disclosure: I already had a Mosin-Nagant rifle. I got together with my shooting buddies a while before all this and we did a bulk buy of several rifles. We got great pricing and shared the shipping costs. My problem was that "falling in love" thing. I just couldn't bear to alter my rifle, so I got another one.

My buddies do not suffer from "Rifle Attachment Syndrome" like I do and after I finished my gun, they all wanted to do the same to their Mosin-Nagant rifles.

The smart thing to do in these circumstances is to use their rifles as the learning platform so your own comes out with fewer mistakes or do-overs. My signature catchphrase when working on my friends' guns for free is "No guarantees!" That keeps my butt covered in the event of a problem. Experimenting on their guns also lets me develop skills I can apply to my own guns later, but I reversed that process here and did mine first. Anything for my friends, right?

SCOPE MOUNTING ISSUES

If you are going to build a long-range sniper rifle you will need optics, which creates some problems as this gun was not designed to be fitted with a modern scope. Forget adding a Russian PU scope, the one used on the Sniper version of this gun. They are very expensive and to be honest, the optics suck. I have one of the Mosin-Nagant Sniper rifles and by today's standards the scope "ain't much." You are far better off with a modern scope.

There are a bunch of scope mounts on the market and they may or may not all be good. I honestly don't know,

as my experience is limited to the Advanced Technology International (ATI) mount. We all picked it because it has a scope mount and a replacement bolt handle in a kit that is designed to adapt the Mosin-Nagant for use with a modern rifle scope.

The scope mount is the trickiest part of the project and the most difficult step is getting the scope mount base located correctly before drilling holes in the receiver.

If you read chapter 2, "How We Learn," in my first gunsmithing book, *Gunsmithing Made Easy*, you know that I have some experience with this issue. I attempted to drill and tap a friend's .22 rifle for a scope mount back when I was in junior high school and I botched it big time. That lesson has stuck with me and nearly a half-century later I still think of it each time I start to drill a hole in a gun.

The old saying is "measure twice—cut once" and it applies even more in gunsmithing. Check, double-check and triple check. Measure everything multiple times before you turn on that power tool. It's easy to remove metal from a gun and extremely difficult to replace it if you do it wrong.

So don't do it wrong.

Here is what I discovered during the evolution of the process over multiple guns. The first method I used illustrates the creativity needed in gunsmithing when you do not have the expensive tools and fixtures that will make this job easier. This approach, while not ideal, will get the job done. It is classic "redneck gunsmithing," something I try to avoid in this book, but somehow it fits with these rifles.

THE REDNECK WAY

Line up the front of the scope mount with the front edge of the receiver. Just to be sure, measure inside the receiver to the back of the barrel. Then measure to the front screw hole in the mount. You should have plenty of clearance to drill through without hitting the barrel. If for some reason you were to drill through the chamber it would

▲ A Mosin–Nagant Sniper rifle with Russian PU Scope.

▲ A Mosin-Nagant action on a 1-2-3 block.

1-2-3 BLOCKS

Once I started buying machine tools all the big companies put me on their mailing lists for their flyers and catalogs, which make for wonderful bathroom reading.

1-2-3 blocks

When tools I am not familiar with show up over and over again in these catalogs I figure they must be good sellers and perhaps something I need, so I start looking into their use to see if they apply to what I am doing.

Something called 1-2-3 blocks showed up in every flyer and catalog. That made me think that maybe I needed some in my tool box, so I started investigating their use. I dug and dug and never could come up with anything more than they are used in "setup," but never how or why.

During my internet research one guy on a forum suggested, "They are about the right weight and size to hurl at someone if they enter the shop and goose you while you are running a machine."

Sadly, that's never happened to me even once, so I held off buying them.

The blocks usually come in pairs and are precision ground for dimension and parallel. They are one inch thick, two inches wide, and three inches long. Most have a bunch of holes drilled through and many of the holes are threaded. In other words, they are steel blocks with holes. I could not figure out where I would use them in "setup."

Still, I just could not stand it anymore: I had to try a set. With machine tools, the price can vary a lot and the prices on 1-2-3 blocks run from about ten bucks to several hundred dollars. Being a "monetarily challenged" writer I am usually looking at the cheapest tools if I am not sure whether I need them. That way, if something turns out to be useless, I haven't spent a ton of money and my wife won't start with all that crazy talk again. (You know, divorce, contract hit, involuntary commitment, all the usual stuff.) As you might imagine, though, it turns out that most of these tools do indeed have an important use and that "buy cheap" approach almost always results in buying the better-quality tool later. I remind myself that it only means I have a backup if the good one is lost, stolen, or broken, which is usually what I tell my wife happened to the first one.

One late night, in a fit of insomnia-induced boredom I ordered a cheap set of 1-2-3 blocks off the internet. They came from China, packed like they were being shipped to Mars. The metal was hidden someplace under layers of oiled paper and packing goo that stuck to and penetrated everything it touched. Cleaning these blocks to bare metal should have been a chapter in this book all on its own. Finally, after irreparable damage to a nice pair of jeans, two t-shirts, and one tablecloth (okay, I get it now, "Do that in the shop" is good advice), something metal emerged and split into two pieces. After I cleaned them up I started measuring, expecting to find that they were nothing more than a geometric mutant of a precision tool, sold to insomniac suckers looking for a bargain. (Been there, done that!) I was surprised to find that they are both dimensionally correct and parallel to the degree of accuracy that any of my tools can measure. (I have some very expensive and very accurate micrometers. And yes, I have some cheap ones too. For backup.)

Even after just a few months, I am absolutely amazed at how often I use these blocks. As mentioned in the chapter on tricking out old Russian rifles, I set one on a level surface and it was the perfect size to balance the Mosin-Nagant action to level the scope mount on top for the redneck gunsmithing approach to fitting a scope mount.

Another thing I struggled with was getting the tool holder on my lathe parallel with the chuck face when that was required, for example for threading operations. The dogs on the chuck are spaced so that the tool holder block will not fit between them. I messed with a machinist's square until I bought these 1-2-3 blocks. Now I put a 1-2-3 block against the chuck, loosen the nut on my tool holder, run the carriage back until the tool holder is flat against the 1-2-3 block and tighten the nut.

I also use a 1-2-3 block as a parallel in my milling machine to raise the work higher in the vise. This keeps the part exactly parallel with the bottom of the vise, which I have carefully trammed to the spindle.

It's an old vise with lots of scars and when tramming the vise I have trouble with my indicator reading off the rough surface. A 1-2-3 block lies flat on the bottom of the vise and gives me a smooth surface to measure from.

I have used the 1-2-3 blocks as spacers time and again. After all, they are pretty precise, so if you need an inch, you get an inch. Most recently I was welding some pieces to a plate where the pieces needed to be three inches apart. It was easy to put in the 1-2-3 block, slide the second piece to it and tack it in place.

I have used them as bench blocks when taking guns apart or putting them back together. Often when doing that you will have the part you are working on elevated so you can drive out pins. The part may need support on one

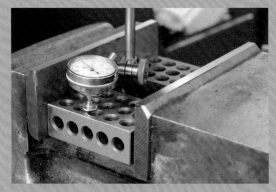

Using 1-2-3 blocks to ensure the milling machine vise is trammed to the spindle. The old vise is rough on the bottom and hard to get an accurate reading off. By laying the blocks on the base, they allow a smoother surface to use with the indicator.

end to keep it level. These blocks work perfectly. I can put one under the part, line up with a hole and drive out a pin. The blocks are steel, so you must be careful not to scar the surface of the gun with them.

I have also used the blocks to prop up guns while I am photographing them. If I allow the block to show in the photo it gives a "precision" look to photos of the guns I have built.

The uses for these 1-2-3 blocks are almost limitless. I have even used them for "setup." I discovered that they can be a big help in locating the work on a mill table before clamping it in place or for setting a stop on any machine.

Bottom line, these are handy tools and once you have them you will think of a lot of other uses. Mine were $14.95. They are most certainly the "cheap" version, but it was money well spent and so far I have not found any reason to buy the more expensive set!

At least until I lose one to hurling it at somebody bent on molesting me at my machine.

ruin the gun and render it unsafe and unusable, so make sure you are drilling through the receiver well behind the barrel.

Find a smooth, flat, and level surface. Lay the gun on top, making sure the flat on the bottom of the receiver is on the level surface. If the surface is too big, it may require the use of a support that is the correct size to fit the flat on the bottom of the receiver. The support must be square with parallel sides so that it holds the gun level. I used a 1-2-3 block, which was a good fit with the rifle's action and elevated the gun enough so that the other parts cleared the milling machine vise I was using as a level surface.

The flat on the bottom of the receiver will be the index point to ensure you have the scope mount on correctly. Based on suggestions on the internet, I have tried to index off other points on the gun, such as the rear sight flat, but none of them are ever correctly aligned. Clearly, the Russians were not about precision and on the guns I have

checked no two flat surfaces are parallel to each other. So it's necessary to pick one and the bottom of the receiver is the best option. Once the gun is exactly level, place the scope mount correctly aligned with the end of the receiver. Adjust the mount so it is also level. Make sure that the level reads exactly the same on the flat "index" surface and the scope mount, with no variation. Make sure the spacing on the bubble is exactly the same for the level surface as it is for the scope mount. Use a single level for this, moving it back and forth to reduce the chance of error.

Clamp the mount in place with a parallel jaw clamp. Check, double-check and triple check to make sure you have the mount exactly right. The centerline of the scope mount should be exactly the same as the centerline of the action/barrel and the top of the mount should be parallel with the flat on the bottom of the action.

You can often check that it's aligned to the center of the barrel with your eye. The human eye is pretty good

▲ It's important that the scope mount be aligned correctly before drilling the receiver.

for doing this. Step back and look down the barrel. Any misalignment should be apparent. Another approach is to stretch a thin string from each end, suspended just over the rifle and use it as a reference to ensure that the mount is correctly aligned.

The mount is self-centering with its concaved shape on the round receiver, so usually you just need to verify that the centerline of the mount follows exactly with the centerline of the bore. I suppose it would be better to use an indicator and find the center of the receiver and the center of the mount and then measure multiple points on each to verify they are on the same line. Doing that would probably take an elaborate setup that would allow you to run the indicator back and forth on a mill table. As mentioned a bit further on in this chapter, there may be better options in a fully equipped shop, but they cost money. Like I said, this is the "redneck gunsmithing" approach to this job. This approach works pretty well if you are careful and take your time. Any small misalignment can be compensated for with a rear scope mount ring that is adjustable for windage.

I had one mount that would not line up. After multiple attempts I opened the package on another mount, same brand and model, and substituted that base to do the alignment and drill the holes. That one fit perfectly. Because neither base belonged to me and it would be unfair to somebody to swap them out, I went back to the first base for installation. I stretched some emery cloth over the receiver and sanded the base to the shape of the receiver. That helped with the alignment and, using the properly placed screw holes I had drilled earlier using the other base, I screwed the mount to the gun. It worked out fine, with a good solid fit that was properly aligned, making zeroing the scope easy.

The point is, things are not always perfect. We had two mounts from the same manufacturer, one fit perfectly on that receiver, the other did not. I have no idea why, as I could not see any difference. If we did not have the option of the second mount, it might have been a

much tougher installation. The lesson is to stop and think through problems; there is always a solution, but it's not always obvious.

Clamp the action in a padded drill press or milling machine vise. I use two pieces of wood that are cut to fit my milling machine vise. I made them from strapping, which is soft pine and will crush a bit to grip the gun. If they get buggered up, I cut two new pieces and toss the old ones in the wood stove.

▲ When drilling, the hole in the scope mount guides the drill bit.

Find the larger of the two drills that are included with the mount, the #11 (.191-inch) and using the holes in the clamped mount as a guide, carefully spot the receiver with this drill to create a shallow, concave mark. The idea is that the drill diameter is the same diameter as the hole. This keeps the tip of the drill centered so it can mark the center on the receiver with a slight cone to guide the next drill. Repeat with the second hole to mark that center.

Switch to the smaller drill, size #21 (.159-inch). Make sure the drill is centered, using the dimple from the larger drill to guide the tip. Carefully drill through the receiver.

▲ When tapping the receiver, use cutting oil and work carefully to avoid breaking the brittle tap.

Use plenty of cutting oil. Repeat on the next hole. Keeping the mount clamped in place, use the supplied 10-32 tap to carefully cut threads in each of the holes.

Again, use lots of cutting oil and make sure the tap is started straight. Work carefully and reverse the tap often to break the chips. Taps are very brittle and break easily, so use a light touch. This old Russian steel can have hard spots, so work very slowly. If you break off the tap, you will have major problems. In fact, that's an understatement. In my never humble opinion, removing a broken tap from a rifle receiver is one of the worst jobs a gunsmith can encounter. I promise it will increase your knowledge of bad words exponentially. The best approach is to never do it and that means not breaking any taps. Work slowly, work carefully, and use caution. It's worth the extra time. Run the tap well past the end of the hole so you get past the tapered section of the tap's threads so that all the threads in the receiver are cut to full depth.

Once all the holes are tapped you can remove the clamp and scope mount. If you are going to coat the metal, the base will be installed later. If you are not going to coat the metal on the barreled action, you can install the mount now.

The screws that came with my kit were too short and too soft. They held by only a few threads and they stripped out after two or three shots. Nothing is more demoralizing than having the scope you just spent all that time installing fall off after a couple of shots. It will brutalize your ego and people at the range will laugh at you. Don't let it happen.

The mount is held by only two screws to start with. Toss the screws that shipped with the mount and replace them with high-quality 10-32 screws that you have cut to length for an exact fit. You want to use every single bit of the available threads, so make the screws an exact fit.

THIS IS "MORE BETTER"

Okay, so that's the "redneck gunsmithing" approach to mounting a scope mount base on a Mosin-Nagant. For a better result, or at least a much faster job when drilling the receiver, try using a fixture like the Universal Sight Mounting Fixture from Forster Products, available from Brownells.

I'll make a confession here. I had one the entire time. It was on a shelf less than four feet from me as I worked. I just blanked. I hadn't used it in a while and forgot I had it. I was talking with my buddy Jim Majoros, owner of Viktor's Legacy Gunsmithing, about how he does this job and he mentioned the Forster Fixture.

It was one of those slap your forehead moments. "Oh yeah," I said. "I have one of those and I feel like a real dumbass right now."

If you plan to do a lot of these upgrades on Mosin-Nagants or any scope mounting work for almost all other

▲ A Mosin-Nagant Rifle in a Forster Products Universal Sight Mounting Fixture. This fixture ensures that the screw holes are drilled top dead center on the receiver. Note the scope mount base on the vise.

actions, the Forster tool is an excellent investment. It will repair any misalignment in the original screw holes on existing actions and it can perfectly align the scope mount on almost any rifle action much faster than the approach detailed above. I use it a lot when building tactical rifles on a Remington Model 700 action to upgrade the scope mount screws from 6-48 to 8-40 screws.

The last Mosin-Nagant I fitted with a scope mount was for my friend Eric Reynolds. I used the Forster jig and discovered that it's pretty easy and a lot faster to get everything right on the first try. The Forster tool is a bit expensive and if you are just going to trick out your Mosin-Nagant and be done with it, go with the less expensive "redneck" approach. But, if you are serious about gunsmithing and will be doing scope mounting on multiple rifles, this jig is a good addition to any gunsmithing shop. There is more information about using the Forster jig in the chapter on tuning actions.

BOLT OPTIONS

The straight bolt handle on the Mosin-Nagant 91/30 rifle will not clear a scope, which is why a new bolt handle comes in the kit. I thought I would be smart and just bend the existing bolt. Before doing that, I chucked the bolt in a 4-jaw chuck in my lathe, turned off the bolt handle and threaded it to fit an oversized bolt knob. Then I heated the bolt handle with an oxy-acetylene torch and bent it to 90 degrees. I installed an oversized "tactical" bolt knob and it was a thing of beauty when I finished, until I put it back in the gun. It still would not clear the scope or scope mount.

This was the Mosin-Nagant model with the bolt handle coming off a raised table or platform on the bolt. As a result, I could not make it work because I could not make the bend close enough to the bolt body. All I lost was pride and time, so I cut the handle off and installed the bolt

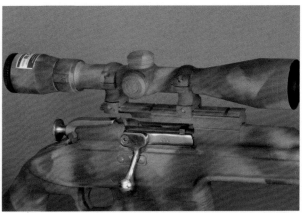

▲ The Mosin-Nagant Sniper with the PU 3.5X scope. Note the longer, bent down bolt handle common to the Model 91/30 Sniper rifle, compared to a standard-issue Mosin-Nagant 91/30 with the shorter, straight bolt handle. When converting the straight-handled Mosin-Nagant 91/30 to use a modern scope, the straight bolt handle must be replaced.

handle that came with the kit. It's a pity, as I had some great photos of the process for this book.

Before you take the bolt apart to start the modifications, take some photos from multiple angles so you can see how it all fits back together. You may think you can remember, but odds are you can't. Trust me, you will be glad you did.

Also, take note of the firing pin depth. It's important that it be returned to that exact point when reinstalling the firing pin. That is the slotted screw you can see centered at the very back of the bolt. Note its position and depth in the bolt so you can return it to the proper location. Misfires are not as demoralizing as the scope flying off and hitting you in the head, but they do suck. Keep in mind it's adjustable

for a reason, so if you do experience misfires, turn it in to extend the firing pin protrusion. Look at the dents in the primers to judge how much. Don't go so far that it pierces the primers, but just enough for a strong dent.

The best approach, of course, is to use the tool supplied with most rifles to adjust the firing pin depth as explained in the sidebar.

Take the bolt apart. Following the instructions included with the kit for the style of bolt handle you have (they are not all the same) mark a line and cut the handle off with a hacksaw. It's best to cut it a bit longer than needed so you can file or grind it to fit. I used a bench mounted disk grinder to take off a little bit at a time on the remaining nub, stopping often to try the fit. Make sure that you keep the ground surface square. The new bolt handle fits properly when it is tight against the bolt and just making contact with the part you ground.

Next, clamp the bolt handle in place and use the #11 drill to mark the center. Drill with the #21 drill, being very careful as it breaks through. Thread the hole with the 10-32 tap. Degrease everything and put a little Loctite on the screw and tighten into place. Make sure the screw is not protruding too far into the bolt.

▲ Note the scope mount and the new bolt handle, two major components of this conversion.

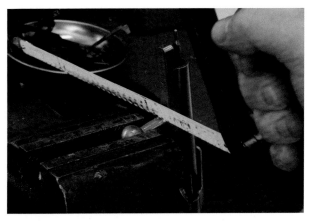

▲ Clamp the bolt in a vise and use a hacksaw to remove the bolt handle.

▲ Leave a little stump so that it can be ground to a perfect fit with the new bolt handle.

To be honest, this setup has always had me a bit puckered because it looks like it is not strong enough. I have never had one break, but as an insurance policy I have started gluing the bolt handles as well as screwing them in place. To do this, degrease all the metal and rough the surface with course sandpaper or a Dremel tool with a grinding attachment. Fill the bolt handle's back side with Brownell's Acraglas Gel (or J-B Weld) making sure you have all the recesses and gaps filled. Then, install and tighten the screw, using blue #242 Loctite on the threads. Clean up any excess epoxy that squeezed out and let the bolt set for a day or two.

Is this necessary? I don't know, but I don't think any part can be too strong. If for some odd reason you need to take the bolt off, heat will release the bedding compound.

(In retrospect, it might not be a bad idea to use Acraglas gel or J-B Weld to glue the scope mount into place as well, as two screws is a rather weak system for most modern and heavy scopes. I have not done that, but probably will on the next job.)

Take a deep breath and relax. It's all easy from here.

Okay, that's a lie.

You are out of the woods about things you can mess up beyond repair, but it's not all "easy."

Putting the bolt back together can make you scream in frustration, but the upside is you can't break anything now that you are done with the modifications. Unless you throw the bolt at the concrete floor in frustration, then stuff can break.

Or you can look at the sidebar on the Mosin-Nagant bolt. Then it's easy.

DISASSEMBLY AND REASSEMBLY OF A MOSIN-NAGANT BOLT

The Mosin-Nagant bolt is like a Chinese puzzle box. If you know how to take it apart and put it back together, it's simple. If you do not, it will make you howling-at-the-moon crazy.

I can say that most of the instruction and information about this process I have found on the web or in books is guilty of promoting that kind of crazy. It is confusing and much more difficult than it needs to be. Let me give you the simple approach.

If that's still too confusing, I have pictures.

Make sure the gun is unloaded.

Don't make me say this too many times. If you have to be reminded over and over, then maybe you are not well suited to be working on guns.

Just saying.

DISASSEMBLY
Remove the bolt from the rifle by opening the bolt and pulling the trigger as you pull the bolt out of the gun. Holding the trigger back will release the bolt stop and allow the bolt to exit the gun.

Hold the bolt by the rear cocking section with the bolt face pointing away from you. Rotate the bolt handle clockwise. This will uncock the bolt and release the bolt head, which you can now pull free.

The connector bar might be attached to the bolt head. Rotate the bolt head until you can pull it free from the connector bar. If the connector bar is still on the bolt body, pull it free.

There is a slot on the Mosin-Nagant bolt tool that fits the firing pin flats. Lacking that, use the fork on the

The Mosin-Nagant bolt shown with the Mosin-Nagant tool. Note the modified bolt handle.

connector bar as a wrench. Unscrew the firing pin from the cocking piece. Be careful, as it is spring loaded and may pop forward when it is released. Once released, pull the firing pin and the spring out of the bolt body. This should also release the cocking piece from the bolt.

You now have six pieces. The seventh piece of the bolt is the extractor, which is a press fit, so there is no reason to remove it now.

The Mosin-Nagant bolt in parts.

Using the M-N tool to unscrew the firing pin.

REASSEMBLY

Put the spring on the firing pin and insert both into the bolt body from the front. Align the cocking piece on the bolt with the decocked position. This allows it to fit against the bolt body. Put some pressure on the firing pin by pushing it against something non-damaging, like a wooden bench or a plastic bench block and using the bolt tool or the fork on the connector bar to turn the firing pin. Once the threads are started a few threads, it's no longer necessary to put pressure on the firing pin as the threads will hold. Screw the firing pin into the cocking piece until it's about one thread short of flush with the back of the cocking piece.

Fit the bolt head to the connector bar by lining up the slot in the bolt head with the stud on the connector bar. Insert and turn.

Slide this assembly onto the firing pin. You may need to adjust the orientation of the firing pin so that the bolt head will fit over the flats. Orient the small lug on the bolt head so it will slide into the slot on the bolt that is aligned with the bolt handle. The large lug on the connector bar piece will be oriented to the left and the fork on the connecting piece should line up with the lug on the cocking piece. Everything should slide into place, leaving the bolt assembled and in the uncocked position.

The next step is to set the firing pin protrusion. The bolt should be uncocked. The Mosin-Nagant bolt tool that typically comes with the rifle is easiest to use for this chore. There are several styles of tools. On mine, the two center notches are used for setting the firing pin protrusion.

Using the tool's go and no-go notches to check the firing pin protrusion.

To reassemble the bolt you must hold the firing pin in against the compressed spring until you can turn the firing pin with the wrench and start the threaded back end of the firing pin into the cocking piece.

The notches should be marked "75" and "95." They are go and no-go for the firing pin protrusion. I don't know what the hell those marks mean, but on my gauge the one marked 75 is .085 inch deep and the one marked 95 measures .100 inch. I plugged those numbers into a converter and nothing made a bit of sense upon trying to convert to metric. I started searching some internet forums, but when some fool said they are .75mm and .85mm (that's not a typo, he said .85mm), I quit thinking there was any chance of finding any meaningful or correct information from the web.

I have to assume that they are supposed to be .075 inch and .095 inch and, true to Russian faithfulness to precision, my gauge is just oversized.

(continued . . .)

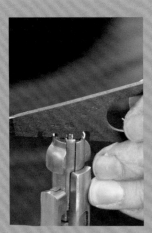

This bolt is correctly adjusted for a proper firing pin protrusion.

Measuring the firing pin protrusion with a dial caliper.

Cocking the bolt as the final step in reassembly of the bolt.

Without the tool it's possible to measure with a dial caliper by keeping the stem of the caliper tight to the firing pin and measuring off the bolt face.

Adjust by pulling the bolt head and connector bar off and turning the firing pin in or out until it's correct. Once you have the firing pin protrusion set, it's time to cock the bolt and put it back in the rifle.

Pull forward against the bolt handle and back on the cocking piece, while twisting the cocking piece clockwise to rotate the lug on the connector bar into the slot on the bolt body. That cocks the bolt. Insert the bolt into the rifle while holding the trigger back. Push forward until it stops and turn the bolt down to close.

The final test of the firing pin adjustment is at the range. The gun should fire with 100 percent reliability and never pierce a primer.

PAINTING IT UP REAL PRETTY

There is a large section on spray coatings for firearms in this book, so I won't go into deep detail here. However, if you plan to coat the gun, you must degrease it. I have a bluing tank to soak the barreled action with degreaser, or you can hang it outdoors and go to work with a brush and a couple of cans of Outers gun degreaser or CRC Brakleen. Make sure to use the kind of solvent that dries with no residue.

▲ Brownells Aluma-Hyde II is an easy-to-use, air-dry coating.

Once degreased, you can go really high tech and sand-blast the metal, but why bother? It's a lot of extra work and most folks don't have a blasting cabinet big enough to handle the length of the action and 29-inch barrel. Besides, the metal is likely already rough enough from the Russian machining anyway.

Brownells Aluma-Hyde is a good gun coating to use for this project as it comes in a rattle can, air dries and you can get all the tacticool colors. I found a can in my shop in Coyote Tan to match the Weaver scope I was going to mount on my gun.

◀ Outers gun degreaser is a good choice for preparing metal for a spray-on coating.

(Note to self. Next time, don't be so cheap; buy a new can of Aluma-Hyde. Or at least check the date on the can you use before spraying. Ten years past the expiration date is pushing it!) Once the coating cures (overnight for a new can, something much, much, much longer if it's a decade old) you can move on to the next step.

TRIGGER POINTS

Any rifle is only as good as its trigger. Back then, the Russians were not big advocates of precise triggers with anorexic pull weights. If you want your rifle to shoot to

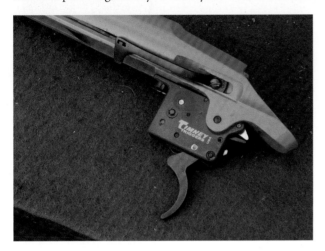

▲ Timney makes a replacement trigger for the Mosin-Nagant and it may well be one of the easiest in their catalog to install.

its potential, you will need to fix the trigger. You can tune and polish, but why? Hours later, when you are done, you will still have a Russian military trigger, just one that's shiny in places.

▲ The Timney trigger comes with a built-in safety, which is a huge improvement over the M-N safety system.

Timney makes an excellent drop-in replacement trigger. It comes with a safety on the side, much like a Remington 700. This is a vast improvement over the hard to use and perhaps dangerous Mosin-Nagant safety that requires you to pull the cocking piece back against the firing pin spring and turn it to lock against the back of the receiver. Releasing that safety can be extremely noisy, which is an issue if you plan to hunt with this rifle or use it for defense. It can also cause the gun to fire unexpectedly if the sear is not perfect on that antique Russian trigger. The Timney eliminates all those problems. It provides an outstanding trigger pull and a modern safety.

Installing the trigger is easy. Remove all the old trigger parts. Slide the new trigger into place and start the screw in front, leaving it loose. (Put a dab of blue #242 Loctite on it first.) Then insert the retaining pin through the receiver and the trigger. Tighten the screw and check function. My new trigger is clean and crisp and breaks at just under three pounds on my Lyman digital scale.

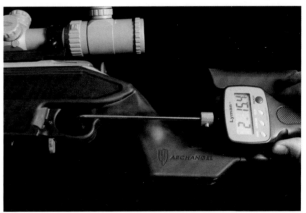

▲ The Timney trigger is a huge improvement in this Mosin-Nagant rifle. The pull weight is less than three pounds and it's clean and crisp. If the Russians had this Timney trigger on their rifles at Stalingrad the siege might have ended much sooner.

CLEAN UP THE RUSSIAN MESS

While you are at it, clean the bore. I have removed enough copper fouling from some of these old M-N rifles to sell for scrap. Mike Brookman's rifle had so much copper fouling I think the bore was reduced to a .270. Get some aggressive copper solvent, a lot of patches, and go to work. It might take a while, but it's the only way to make the gun shoot well.

A RUSSIAN BORE

Not a vodka-drunk at a party, but the bore of a Mosin-Nagant rifle. The key to success with any rifle, even an old Russian relic, is to be "boringly" clean.

If you want your rifle to perform to its potential you must clean it properly and often. That means any rifle, not just a one-hundred-year-old Russian battle rifle. I have found that most of these surplus Mosin-Nagant rifles are in desperate need of having the copper removed from the bore. I suspect the Russians shot them more than they cleaned them and most I have encountered are badly fouled. They will never shoot to their potential until you get the copper out and clean the bore back to bare steel.

There is a very detailed chapter on cleaning in my first gunsmithing book, *Gunsmithing Made Easy*, so I am

Years of neglect call for a strong copper solvent to dig out the copper fouling.

not going to go into as much depth here. I understand that's a bit of larcenous blackmail, designed to get you to buy the first book and I am quite comfortable with it. If you don't already own that book, please buy a copy. It's a great companion to this one and I need the royalties. You'll also find more information on bore cleaning in this book's chapter 2.

There are a couple of points about cleaning these old battle rifles that might bear notice. You can leave Hoppe's Copper Removing Benchrest solvent overnight to work at tough copper and powder fouling. Overnight soaks often find hidden caches of copper that are so small they go unnoticed with an aggressive cleaning approach. Is that important? Maybe. These old guns may have rough bores, giving the copper multiple places to hide.

Anytime there is copper fouling it attracts more copper fouling. Fouling tends to meld with the bullet jacket more than clean steel, so the fouling grows. That's one reason it's so important to clean completely every time.

With some of these old Mosin-Nagant guns you will swear there is no end to the copper or that the Russians must have substituted copper for steel when they made the barrel. Just keep at it and you will get it clean.

Or die of old age trying.

Either way, the problem is solved.

Barnes CR-10 is an aggressive copper solvent.

RE-CROWN THE RIFLE'S MUZZLE

Most surplus Mosin-Nagant rifles have been carried by soldiers who didn't much care about damage to the rifle, so the crowns are rarely in good shape. It's a good idea to recut the crown before installing the muzzle brake.

There are detailed instructions on how to repair the crown in chapter 7.

BADASS BRAKES

No "tactical" rifle is complete without a muzzle brake. Brakes mitigate recoil and just look badass on a Mosin-Nagant rifle. Many muzzle brakes require threading the barrel, which is beyond the scope of most hobby guys. There are a few brakes available for the Mosin-Nagant that

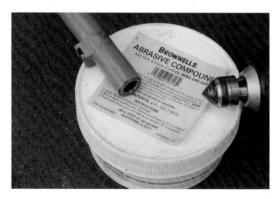

▲ The crown is the last place the rifle has any physical influence on the bullet and it is critical that it be perfect.

▲ The Texas Precision Products muzzle brake fits over the barrel and turns to lock on the front sight lug.

do not require threading. I used a Texas Precision Products muzzle brake which fits over the barrel and turns to lock on the front sight lug. Then you tighten two set screws and it's done. They say it reduces the felt recoil to that of a .243 Winchester. I don't know if it's true. It does reduce recoil, but I have no way to measure it scientifically. Who cares? It looks badass and that's what really matters, right?

▲ A Howling Raven muzzle brake on Mike Brookman's Mosin-Nagant.

Some of the muzzle brakes I have installed have been a very tight fit by design. Clamp the barrel in a barrel vise and use a big adjustable wrench to turn the brake into place. If you lack a barrel vise you may be able to clamp the action in a bench vise using wood to pad the jaws. Again, I use sections of strapping, which are inexpensive to buy at any lumber yard. Clamp across the flats of the bottom and the scope mount and carefully turn the muzzle brake into place.

NEW FURNITURE

Archangel offers a tactical replacement stock that also converts the rifle to use removable magazines. The stock comes with a five-round magazine and they offer 10-round magazines as well. This stock is a drop-in fit and free-floats the barrel. It also has a barrel tension module you can install to tune the rifle's accuracy if free floating isn't working.

▲ Using a Dremel and sanding disk to modify the Archangel stock for bolt clearance.

Important!

If you are using the ATI bolt handle, make sure you relieve the Archangel stock to clear the new bolt handle and that the bolt will close all the way. If you don't, the bolt will close part way before hitting the stock. These old guns were built back before lawyers designed guns and they can fire even when the bolt is not completely in battery. This can be a very dangerous situation as the bolt lugs are only partially engaged. If the bolt leaves the gun and passes through your head it's likely to be a bad day.

▲ You must make sure the bolt can close fully without contacting the stock. We used a thin strip of paper to pass behind the bolt handle to verify it was not in contact.

Cut the stock to provide clearance for the bolt handle and to let the bolt close completely. If you do this with a Dremel tool, be careful as the plastic in the stock will melt easily. Work slowly and carefully and keep the RPMs turned down. If you are using a file and/or handheld cutting tools, you cannot generate enough heat to get into trouble.

Do you see a hint here?

Good, take it.

Simply try to close the bolt and you will see where the handle hits the stock. Patiently cut away at that point until the bolt can close completely without the handle contacting the stock. There must be some clearance between the bolt handle and the stock when the bolt is fully closed. If you go slowly you will get a nice-looking job. If you try to rush it, it will look like you rushed it.

Care to guess which approach I took on my gun?

I did it after I discovered the problem at the range. The trouble was that I had fired the gun a bunch of times before I noticed the problem. I was upset and scared about cheating death by shooting with the bolt partially closed when I "attacked" the stock. I should have waited a while and calmed down, but that's just not my way. Take my advice: always do as I say, not as I do and you will thank me later.

The stock has an adjustable cheek piece and butt pad. This lets you adjust length of pull to fit the shooter and ensures a correct cheek weld with the optic and rings of your choice. There are pockets in the stock for pushbutton-style sling swivels. I also added the included swivel stud so I could mount a bipod. This was as easy as drilling through the guide inside the stock and then screwing in the swivel stud.

The instructions that accompany the stock are pretty clear, so I won't repeat them here.

ADDING GLASS

I installed a Weaver Kaspa 3-12X44 Tactical scope in Flat Dark Earth. This affordable tactical scope packs a lot of features, including dial-up turrets, an illuminated Mil-Dot reticle, and side-focus parallax adjustment.

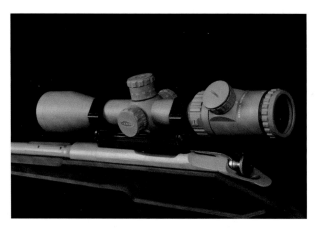

I mounted the scope in 30mm Weaver Tactical 4-screw Picatinny rings. One note on that: I tried to use the 6-screw rings, but they were too wide to mount this scope on the short base and maintain the correct eye relief. So, if you order, get the slimmer 4-hole rings, which are more than rugged enough for the application. Or better yet, order windage adjustable rings, particularly if you used the "redneck" approach. It's likely that your scope mount will not be centered perfectly, so having a little additional adjustment for windage in the mount can help keep the scope aligned correctly.

FINAL THOUGHTS

My gun is an eye catcher and gets a lot of attention at the range. Mike Brookman's is even better looking as he has an artistic flair that he applied to the gun with an interesting paint scheme. The current work was his second time around, though.

The first time he did a beautiful job of applying a black and white pattern with a flame motif to the stock. It was one of the best paint jobs I have seen on a rifle, very artistic and extremely well executed. It took him hours and hours, but the end result was worth it.

The trouble was the paint he used came off all over my hands when I was cleaning the bore on his rifle. He used heat resistant paint designed to be used on wood stoves and it was not even close to being solvent resistant. By the time I had the gun cleaned, the stock was a smeared, ugly mess that looked like the result of an unsupervised kindergarten art class.

While I figured I did him a favor by finding the flaw in his work, somehow he had a much different point of view. He reapplied the art using a better grade of materials and finally stopped threatening to rip my hands off at the wrist, so it's all good now.

These old war machines will never be tack drivers, but they can be surprisingly accurate. They all seem to shoot about 1.5 MOA with Hornady factory ammo and a little better with handloads. I suppose I could even mess with

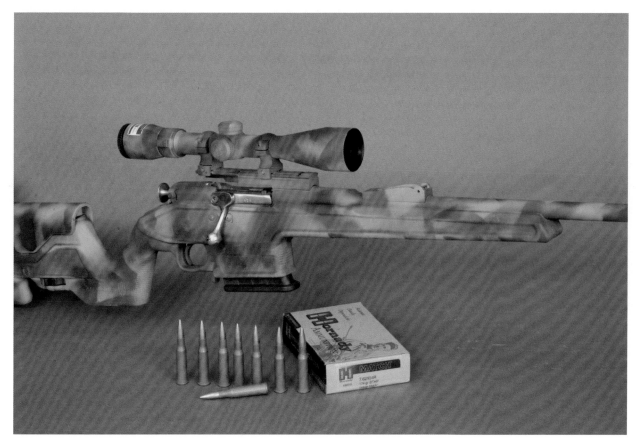

▲ This is Mike Brookman's Mosin-Nagant's second paint job.

the barrel tension module in the stock to see if that will improve the accuracy; and by tweaking the handloads I might expect one MOA is a possibility. But, to be honest, I don't think it's worth the trouble.

Even now, my Mosin-Nagant can easily keep all its shots on a 10-inch plate out past 500 yards, which is not too bad considering where this all started. Remember, this design is more than 125 years old and they are Russian military rifles which doesn't exactly shout "precision" to the heavens. I have been to some gun factories in Russia and have seen how they build modern rifles. A lot of it is not pretty: big, sweaty guys with large hammers doing the "precision" fitting work and castings made in sand on the floor just like it was done in King Arthur's time. If a lot of it is still that primitive today, I shudder to think about how war time production was in the 1930s and 1940s. My guess is that precision was not at the top of the priority list.

Our rifles were probably built during the WWII era to military specifications. The accuracy standard according to *The Soviet Mosin-Nagant Manual* is a four-shot group at 100 meters. Three of these must be in a 15cm circle, which is 5.9 inches. In other words, three out of four shots must hit a six-inch circle at 100 yards. Wow! Tough standard . . . for a musket using rocks instead of bullets, maybe.

Clearly the Russians just wanted to get guns on the battlefield and didn't want to take any chances that many would be rejected. Given that standard, the fact that we are even considering the possibility of achieving near MOA accuracy is pretty amazing.

No matter, this is one of the best DIY projects you can do. The guns are a lot of fun to shoot and will always draw attention at the range.

▲ This is what a target looks like after a good gun has gone bad.

CHAPTER 2
WHEN A GOOD GUN GOES BAD

I suppose I am dating myself, but I remember the public service commercials on television back in the late sixties. The gist was "lock up your car and take the keys." The tag line was, "Don't Make a Good Boy Go Bad." It would send my father into a rage to see that PSA and it was years before I understood why.

It actually happened to us. I was about fifteen years old and watching television when I heard a crash in front of our house. I looked out the window to see a guy exiting our car, which had just smashed into another car passing by on the main road through our small town. My father was at a Masonic meeting across the street and when I ran through the door hollering loud enough to shake the walls, the entire lodge, including the local game warden, got involved.

The game warden and I tracked the guy in the fresh snow and finally found him hiding in another car a mile from our house. The game warden was a big guy and a former Marine drill sergeant. I remember him holding the guy by the shirt collar and running him back down the snowy road to our house so fast I had trouble keeping up.

When the cops finally showed up the guy was arrested, but a liberal judge later let him off, because the keys were in our car. In effect, the judge said it was all Dad's fault for making that good boy go bad.

I pretty much grew up in a snowier version of Mayberry and nobody took their keys or locked their doors on their house. In fact, the house we lived in didn't even have working locks. Still, in the judge's mind we were the problem. I never would have believed it at the time, but as it turns out that ruling was a glimpse of Vermont's future.

Maybe it's some subliminal thing buried deep in my brain from that incident, but I have little tolerance for when a good rifle goes bad (or buttheads steal cars). In the rifle situation, the blame is always with the rifle and it's up to you to find the problem and fix it. As for fixing society, I think that's a cause that was lost long ago. Which might be construed as a good reason to have a properly working rifle.

No matter. This is a gunsmithing book. So, don't let a bad rifle off the hook. Make it take responsibility and start behaving again.

When you are the gun guy in the neighborhood it's amazing how many "friends" you have. It seems that my shop is the first stop when somebody is having gun troubles. All too often, it's an accurate rifle that suddenly started misbehaving and spraying the target with patterns instead of groups. I have a checklist of steps to correct that.

CLEAN THE GUN

I can't tell you how many times a fouled bore is the source of accuracy problems. I also can't tell you how many times the gun owner denies it. Almost without fail, they insist to the point of confrontation that they "already cleaned it and it still won't shoot!"

The key here is to clean it correctly, which is something few gun owners have the knowledge or temperament to do.

I had a precision rifle in the shop recently that had stopped shooting tiny groups. The guy was convinced it needed a new barrel. While the barrel was getting a little shot out, I managed to bring the gun around again and bought at least another season of competition before it needs a barrel. It had a few other problems, including some

▲ Cleaning the bore is the first step to correcting a rifle gone bad.

▲ Using the Lyman BoreCam Digital Bore Scope to check out the bore on a misbehaving rifle.

bedding issues introduced by the guy trying to make it shoot, but the root cause of the problem was fouling.

I ran a couple of wet patches through to get out the carbon fouling and then used one of the new Lyman BoreCam Digital Bore Scopes to look at the bore. The inside of the rifle bore looked like it was copper plated. The entire thing was coated like a copper-chromed trailer hitch ball. Yet, the guy insisted he had cleaned the rifle. I am certain that he had, but cleaning doesn't mean it's clean.

I try to explain, but it usually falls on deaf ears. So, when they pick up a rifle that is shooting well again, I don't bother to tell them what I did. I smile, hand them back the gun and let them think I am a miracle worker.

Lately I am seeing "experts" on the internet claiming that a rifle bore must be fouled to shoot well. They claim that a clean rifle will not shoot accurately.

I have tested hundreds, perhaps thousands, of rifles over my career as a gun writer and have shot countless groups with those rifles. There is one simple truth I have learned: clean barrels shoot better than fouled barrels.

Some of the internet experts brag about shooting thousands of rounds without cleaning and then insist that you must shoot dozens of fouling rounds after cleaning before the gun shoots well again. This is nothing but total crap. I have seen some guns that shoot well for a long time between cleanings. Usually, but not always, they are rifles with high-end, hand-lapped barrels that don't foul badly anyway. But I have never seen a rifle where accuracy failed to deteriorate as copper fouling increased. A rough bore fouls faster than a polished and lapped bore, but they all foul sooner or later and when they do, accuracy decays.

Let me say again, just to make sure the point is clear. When a good rifle suddenly goes bad, more often than not, bore fouling is the reason. So it's first on the checklist.

Many shooters run a few patches through the bore and maybe make a pass or two with a brush and assume that they have cleaned the rifle. That's the equivalent of running your car through a puddle and claiming you washed it. Even if they have scrubbed for days, it doesn't ensure the rifle is clean. Scrubbing with the wrong solvent accomplishes nothing and, even with the correct solvent, sometimes guns are so badly fouled it takes a while to hit bottom.

I once spent a week cleaning a badly fouled .17 Remington rifle and I was starting to think it was physically impossible for that much copper to be trapped in so small a bore. Another time, I had a .338 Winchester that was fouled so much it looked like a smoothbore. It took days to get all the copper out of the rifle that my long-range competition shooting friend brought to my shop. I am not saying I stood at the bench all that time, I didn't. But I worked on those rifles a few times every day.

Running a few patches with some solvent through the barrel is not enough. The key is to clean the bore down to bare steel and remove all powder and metal fouling. If you can accomplish that with a few patches, fine, but it doesn't happen often. I have a few high-end barrels on custom rifles that foul so little they clean up with a few patches, but they are very rare critters in the shooting world. Most rifle barrels will require some effort to clean.

I can't say how many patches or how many swipes of the brush will be required to clean any specific rifle, nobody

▲ Hoppe's Bench Rest 9 Copper Gun Bore Cleaner.

can. If you read something or saw a video of a "system" where "X" number of passes with a patch will clean your bore, you have witnessed the work of a charlatan or a fool. No two rifles are the same and there is no possible way to predict the number of patches needed to clean a fouled bore. It might be four or it might be four hundred and only somebody who can see the future can know. In that case, I'll just get the lottery numbers from them and hire somebody else to clean guns. I detest the chore, but I find that I spend a lot of time doing it anyway.

It sucks being poor.

Copper removing solvents are strong, so glove up, use eye protection and lots of ventilation. Start with a bore solvent that will remove both powder fouling and copper fouling such as Hoppe's Bench Rest 9. Clean from the breech end when possible and always use a rod guide to keep the rod centered and to keep the crud out of the action and trigger.

Make several passes with a new wet patch each time. It's best to use each patch for only one pass before replacing it with a new solvent-soaked patch, but I do sometimes use both sides of the patch at this stage of cleaning; one pass for each side. You may want to let the gun soak a few minutes between patches to allow the solvent to work.

Leaving the barrel wet with solvent, use a properly fitted bronze brush soaked with solvent to make several passes. Keep the brush wet with solvent, reapplying after every couple of passes. Don't dip the brush in the solvent bottle, as this will contaminate the remaining solvent. Instead put some solvent in a small container and dip in that. I keep a supply of small Dixie Cups in my shop for this use. Or at least that was my approach for years until Jamey Majoros gave me a box of pipettes. These are disposable tubes that will suck up the solvent, filling a bulb at the top, and allow you to drip it back out a little at a time. They work well for wetting the brush and actually use considerably less solvent than the Dixie Cup approach because there is no waste. Any leftover is still clean and can be returned to the bottle, where the leftover solvent in the Dixie Cup is contaminated and must be disposed of.

Never reverse the brush in the bore. Push it all the way out of the muzzle and then pull it back. After use, always

A pipette works well for dispensing solvent. ▶

clean the solvent from your brush with a spray of degreasing solvent, allowing it to run off the brush and flush away the gunk. This is to prevent abrasive debris from accumulating and to extend the life of the brush.

Let the gun sit for a few minutes to allow the solvent to work, then follow with a couple more wet patches. Wait a few more minutes and run a dry patch through.

Now remove all traces of the first solvent using dry patches, followed with a few patches soaked with a degreaser like acetone, and follow those with a final dry patch. The idea is to remove all the solvent, as some bore solvents do not mix well and we are about to get a lot more aggressive.

▲ These aggressive copper removing solvents will dig out the fouling fast.

Switch to an aggressive copper removing solvent like Sweet's 7.62, Montana X-Treme Copper Killer or Barnes CR10. Run a couple wet patches through the bore and let it sit for a few minutes. Follow with another wet patch, wait, and repeat. Use snug fitting patches so they will get down into the corners of the rifling, but not so tight that the solvent is squeezed out of them as they go down the bore. I often use the next smaller size jag and double up on the patches so there is thicker cotton that will shape to the lands and grooves better.

The goal is to get to the point where you can let the solvent sit in the bore for at least five minutes and have no blue stains on the next patch through, indicating that there is no remaining metal fouling.

Be aware that a brass jag can leave a "false" stain on the patch, although it's usually on the inside rather than the outside of the patch so it's easy to distinguish from stains from bore fouling. When in doubt use a plastic or stainless steel jag.

If it's just not happening fast enough, use a brush. Many sources recommend nylon brushes. They are useful, but I don't think they are aggressive enough for serious fouling. I prefer a bronze brush with the understanding that these strong solvents will eat the brush. Even when cleaning the brush with a degreasing spray immediately after use they are only good for a few cleaning sessions, so treat them as a consumable product just like the patches and solvents. Buy a few extra brushes to replace them as they are used up.

After scrubbing with a strong solvent and a bronze brush there will be a lot of blue gunk on the next patch through the bore. Some of that is from the dissolving brush, some of it is from the bore. It can be a lot, so don't be shocked. Also, don't think you have stumbled onto the secret to doing this fast. (If you actually do unlock the secret, please share.) All that blue gunk is a good thing to get out of the bore, but don't assume it means you are done.

For most aggressive copper solvents, it is recommended that they not be left in the bore for more than fifteen minutes. That doesn't mean you can stop cleaning after fifteen minutes, only that you need to keep removing the old solvent and replacing it with fresh. Keep working with wet patches and brushes to refresh the solvent often.

Even after the patches start coming out clean, it's possible to have copper fouling trapped between layers of powder or carbon fouling. Just to be sure, clean all the solvent out of the gun and switch solvents with the idea that one might get the fouling that the other does not.

The best approach is to return to a general use solvent like Hoppe's Bench Rest 9. Make sure to remove all traces of the first solvent before switching to another solvent.

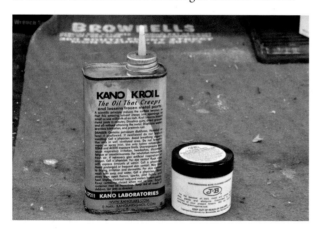

▲ Using Kroil and J-B paste is an old benchrest shooter's trick for cleaning out stubborn fouling from the bore.

If it's really fouled, the old benchrest shooter's trick of Kroil and J-B Bore Cleaning Compound can help to loosen things up. Kroil has excellent penetration qualities so it will work in under the fouling. The J-B Bore Cleaning Compound is slightly abrasive so it cleans the crud and copper out, but it's not abrasive enough to damage the bore. In fact, with regular use it helps smooth the bore.

Wet a few patches and saturate the bore with Kroil, then let it soak for a while. Wet a tight fitting patch with Kroil and then coat it with J-B Compound. Run it through the bore a bunch of times, at least 20 passes and twice that is better. Check the patch often and add more J-B and Kroil as needed. If the patch gets worn, replace it.

Switch to a clean patch wet with Kroil and clean all the goop out of the bore. Repeat until the bore is wiped clean. Then use a few dry patches. Follow with a couple of wet patches using an aggressive copper solvent. Let it stand five minutes, then run a clean patch. If it comes out with no blue stains, you are almost done. If there are blue stains indicating there is still copper fouling, keep repeating this process with both solvents and the J-B and Kroil in rotation until there is no sign of blue on any patches after letting the aggressive solvent work for five minutes.

▲ Clean until there are no more blue stains on the patch.

Like I said, sometimes it's a fast process and sometimes it seems like you will never get the darn thing clean, but until you can soak the bore with an aggressive copper removing solvent, wait a timed five minutes and then run a clean patch through without blue staining, the gun is not clean.

Once it's clean, you must remove all traces of any solvent or cleaning agents. Use patches soaked with acetone until the bore is clean and follow with dry patches. Wet a few patches with a CLP oil like Clenzoil and swab the bore. Follow with a clean patch to wipe out the excess, but leave a film.

Give the chamber the same treatment with a couple of swabs. One wet with oil, the other to dry. Clean up any solvent that has dripped into the action or other gun parts. Clean the bolt lug recesses in the receiver. Don't forget to wipe off the muzzle, then oil everything to prevent rust.

Very often this will correct the accuracy problems, but, even if it doesn't, cleaning at least eliminates one big issue on the checklist.

CHECK THE SCOPE

Make sure all the screws are tight and that the scope base screws are actually holding the base tight to the gun and not bottoming out. Shake the scope to see if it rattles. If it

▲ Make sure there isn't a screw loose.

does, clearly something inside is broken, which is more common than you might think.

Look through to see if the optics are clear edge to edge. Check the parallax to make sure it's still correct by fixing

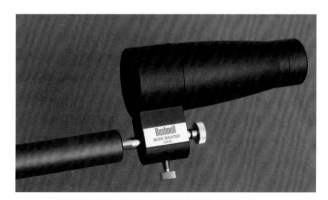

▲ The Bushnell Boresighter allows you to check if the scope adjustments are working correctly and tracking properly.

the gun in something to hold it with the crosshairs on a 100-yard target. If the parallax is adjustable, set it for 100 yards. Look through the scope without touching the rifle and move your eye back and forth and up and down. The crosshairs should remain fixed on one position on the target. A little movement is usually to be expected, but if they are moving more than an inch or so on the target, the scope has some parallax problems that may be the source of the accuracy issues.

Use a boresighter. The kind with a grid, not a laser. Fix it on the gun and run the scope adjustments up and down and back and forth to make sure they are tracking correctly.

▲ Check to see that the adjustments track correctly.

With any doubt, install another scope. Most of us have a scope or two hanging around that we can use temporarily to eliminate the original scope as a potential problem.

CHECK THE BEDDING

It's very unusual for this to be the problem when a good gun suddenly goes bad, unless somebody has been messing with the bedding, but it's not uncommon for the screws to be loose or the stock to be cracked.

▲ Check for cracks in the stock.

Make sure the action screws are tight. Pull the stock off the gun and check for cracks or splits. Check the bedding for flaws.

Reinstall the stock and check the bedding by holding your fingers on the line where the action and the stock meet. Alternately loosen and tighten each of the action screws. If you can feel any movement of the action in the stock, the bedding is incorrect and putting stress on the action. With your fingers on the junction you can feel movement that often you cannot see.

If the bedding is the problem, it can usually be repaired by glass bedding the action. There are detailed instructions in my first book, *Gunsmithing Made Easy*, so I have not repeated them here.

Check to see that the barrel is floated. A dollar bill is still the best way to check this. Wrap the dollar around the barrel and pull the ends up. If it can pass through between the barrel and the stock for the full length without binding, the barrel is floated with enough clearance.

With wood stocks, this is often the source of problems when the wood warps and contacts the barrel. Any wood stock that has been subjected to a lot of moisture can cause problems. Remember, humidity is moisture. If

a stock absorbs a lot of water and the wood swells, it can trash accuracy very quickly.

Be aware that some stock designs have contact with the barrel. For example, many Remington Model 700 rifles use a pad at the tip of the stock to put pressure on the barrel. If a stock with tip pressure has warped it can really mess with the gun's accuracy. If you suspect that has happened, remove the pad and float the barrel.

If you have another stock around that you can install temporarily on the gun, you can eliminate the bedding and/or stock as the problem. Don't hesitate to rob a stock off another gun long enough to test if the issue is the stock or bedding. Glass bedded stocks do not swap rifle to rifle well, but any factory stock, chassis or stock with a bedding block should work to eliminate another check mark off the list.

On the rifle that was brought in by my competition shooting buddy, he had glass bedded the action trying to fix the problem. It was his first time and with no experience he had followed a YouTube video. He actually did a good job, but there were a few small issues that the internet expert didn't mention.

Perhaps the most important is that the bedding material had flowed into the bedding pillars. That meant that the action screws were taking some of the recoil stresses. I drilled out the material so the screws were floating. Also, the recoil lug was in full contact.

▲ Any wood stock can swell, shift, or crack due to moisture.

▲ When glass bedding a rifle tape off all but the bearing surface of the recoil lug to create an air gap.

It's probably not an issue, but it's always best if the recoil lug only makes contact on the rear, load bearing surface. I removed some bedding material from all surfaces except the rear contact surface so that the only point of contact with the recoil lug was the flat, rear bearing surface.

RE-CROWN

A bad crown is probably the second most common reason guns go bad, right behind a fouled bore, so while I was at it, I re-crowned the muzzle on my friend's rifle. There are detailed instructions on how to do that in chapter 7.

The cumulative effect of repairing all of these things brought my friend's rifle back to shooting as well or even better than it had before.

If the rifle is still not shooting well, use a bore scope to make sure the barrel is not shot out. If it is, it will need to be replaced. There are instructions on how to do that, at least for a Remington Model 700, elsewhere in this book.

If none of this solves the problems, either trade the rifle or contact a priest for an exorcism.

▲ This is what your targets should look like after correction or exorcism.

▲ This .243 Winchester rifle's crown had some damage. By using the lapping method, it was restored. Note how the crown goes all the way from the top of the lands to the bottom of the grooves.

Chapter 3

BUILDING YOUR OWN .308 WINCHESTER TACTICAL RIFLE WITHOUT A LATHE

How I built my "Snake Gun" using only hand tools.

Some knucklehead asked me a few years ago, "Don't you have enough guns?"

Once I recovered from the shock of such a ridiculous question, I went to look, just to be sure.

Of course, I did not.

While inventorying the current deficits at the time, I found that I desperately needed a bolt action tactical rifle in .308 Winchester, but I wanted one that was a little different from all the others. As a hobby gunsmith, it was never in doubt that I would build one rather than buy somebody else's idea of what I needed.

▲ The first group ever shot with the .308 Winchester tactical rifle built by the author. The five-shot group is .6 inch center to center.

The mandate for the project was that it could be done with hand tools by anybody with a working knowledge of hobby gunsmithing and at least eight or nine working fingers. While I have a lathe and other power tools, I wanted to see if it was possible to buy the parts, assemble them on the bench without using anything more than hand tools and end up with a rifle that not only looks good, but shoots well enough to make me happy.

WHAT YOU NEED

The first stop was the action. I know Remington actions best and have had good luck with them, so I ordered a Remington Model 700 short action from Brownells. Also from Brownells, I ordered a 1:10 twist rate 26-inch Shilen barrel. This medium-heavy barrel is in the Remington "Varmint" contour, and as a "short chambered" barrel it comes with all the lathe work done, which means it's already threaded and chambered. The chamber is left about .010 inch "short" so the gunsmith can fit the barrel to the action and then use a chambering reamer to carefully finish to exactly the headspacing required. This allows a hobby gunsmith to very easily create the "minimum spec" chamber favored by a lot of custom gun makers.

I ordered an H. S. Precision Series 2000 tactical stock. This stock comes with an adjustable cheek piece, which is important if you are going to use tactical style rings and rail to mount a scope. The scope will be a bit too high for a standard stock, so the adjustable comb allows you to put your eye exactly behind the center of the scope while maintaining the correct cheek contact with the stock. The stock is also adjustable for length of pull. The vertical grip positions the hand comfortably for shooting either prone or off the bench.

The stock has a molded in, machined aluminum bedding block. The barrel channel is large, which allows a lot of air to circulate around the floating barrel to aid in cooling. I also ordered the H. S. Precision Detachable Magazine bottom metal. This comes with a four-round magazine and I added a couple additional 10-round magazines.

I already had most of the tools in my shop from previous projects and any I did not, I ordered from Brownells as needed.

GETTING STARTED

The first step was to lap the bolt lugs to the action. For the best accuracy in any rifle, the bolt's locking lugs must seat evenly and completely in the receiver and of course lapping also smooths up the feel of the action.

Lapping the bolt lugs is covered in detail in chapter 14.

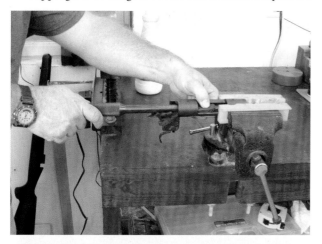

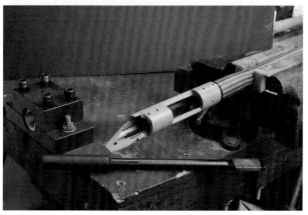

▲ The action raceways should be smoothed before the spray-on coating is applied and again after the coating is dry.

▲ Using the Receiver Way Polisher.

After lapping the bolt lugs, I smoothed the bolt raceways. Any trace of grease or oil should be removed. Then coat the surfaces to be polished with Dykem or color them with a felt-tipped marker.

The tool for this job is called the Receiver Way Polisher. It holds a replaceable piece of 220 or 330 grit abrasive paper. The tool is inserted in the rear of the action and rides on the bolt raceways and with a small amount of stoning oil and plenty of elbow grease it will polish the surfaces.

There is no point in polishing the raceways and then running a rough bolt over them. Polish the bottom of the lugs, the surfaces that ride on the action raceways. This can be done with a fine stone or by using a handheld Dremel grinder with a small polishing wheel and buffing compound. Be very careful not to touch the back of the lugs or any other surface or edge other than the bottom of the lugs where they ride on the raceway and polish them only sparingly.

▲ Polishing the feed ramp.

Finally, use a Cratex polishing bit in a Dremel tool to polish the feed ramp on the action and then finish with a felt polishing tip with red compound.

BIGGER SCREWS

Tactical optics tend to be big and heavy and I wanted this gun to be as "bulletproof" as possible, so I decided

▲ Changing the scope mounting screws to 8-40.

to replace the smaller 6-48 scope mounting screws with the larger, stronger 8-40 screws. This is easy enough to do by simply drilling out the holes and re-tapping them in the receiver. At the same time, I took the opportunity to realign any possible off-center factory drilled holes. I used the Forster Universal Sight Mounting Fixture which ensures that in re-drilling the holes they are perfectly aligned with the center of the action and bore. I used the Brownells Tactical Scope Base Conversion Kit, which comes with all the drills, taps, counterbores, and screws to do the action and the rail mount.

The rifle building section in this book in chapter 14 gives detailed instructions on exactly how to do this simple job.

RECOIL LUG

On Remington Model 700 actions, the recoil lug is fitted like a washer between the barrel and the action. The thickness of the recoil lug will control how far the barrel screws into the rifle's action and there are several different thicknesses available. The barrel must not hit the front of the

▲ With a pre-fitted, short chambered barrel the thickness of the recoil lug is critical.

bolt lugs, but it must not have an excessive gap between them either.

You can check this by laying the recoil lug on the action and measuring with a depth micrometer from the face of the bolt lugs to the top of the recoil lug. Then measure the length of the threaded shank on the barrel. The barrel shank should be .005 inch to .015 inch shorter than the measurement to the bolt lugs. If it's off, you can make some adjustments with a recoil lug that is thicker or thinner as needed. That change, though, will have an effect on the chamber as well. The short chambered barrels are designed to work with a specific recoil lug thickness, so check with Brownells when ordering to make sure you have the correct thickness.

Put a little anti-seize lubrication on the barrel threads. Use a bench mounted barrel vise and an action wrench for the 700, both available from Brownells, to screw the action and barrel together and snug up very tightly. Make sure the recoil lug is lined up properly, using the recessed lug cut in the front of the action wrench. Torque to 80–100 foot-pounds.

There is a detailed sidebar in the section on building rifles that covers several other options for indexing the recoil lug as the barrel and action are tightened.

FINISHING THE CHAMBER

Put the barrel in a padded bench vise to hold things while you work on chambering.

It's best if you strip the bolt and remove the extractor, ejector and firing pin. Place a no-go headspace gauge in the bolt, clipping it behind the extractor if you could not remove

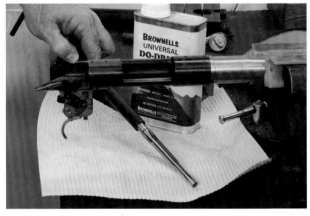

it from the bolt. (Some headspace gauges will have a cutout for the ejector, which eliminates the need to remove it as well.) Close the bolt gently. It should not close on the no-go gauge. If it does, you have excessive headspace. This can be adjusted by using a slightly thinner recoil lug or in excessive cases by setting the barrel back using a lathe. However, usually with a short chambered barrel and the correct thickness recoil lug you cannot close the bolt on a no-go gauge.

Now install a go gauge and try to close the bolt. It also should not close. If the bolt will close on a go gauge and will not close on a no-go gauge, the chamber is in spec; however, with a short chambered barrel this should not happen and the bolt should not close on either gauge.

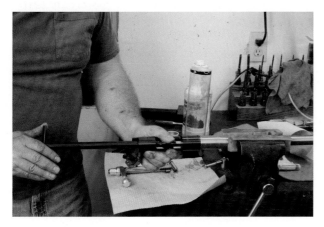

▲ Cutting the chamber to final depth.

Remove the bolt. Fit a piloted .308 Winchester chambering finish reamer with an extension and T-handle and coat it with a lot of cutting oil. Also squirt some oil into the chamber; you cannot use too much cutting oil. Carefully cut the chamber a few rotations with the reamer, using light pressure. Remember, always turn clockwise. *Never* reverse a reamer, as that can ruin it instantly. Take very little metal as we have just a few thousandths of an inch to deal with here and if you go too far, things get very complicated and expensive. So go slowly, cut a little and check often.

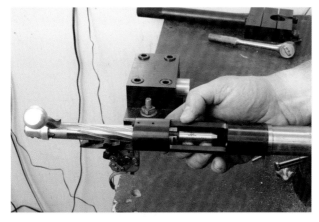

▲ Installing a headspace gauge to check to see if the chamber is cut correctly.

Clean out all the chips and oil from the chamber. Blowing it out with shop air works well, but use a rag to catch the chips and oil as they exit the muzzle. Then wipe out the chamber with a long cotton swab.

Install the headspacing go gauge and try to close the bolt. If the bolt still will not close (and it should not) clean the chips from the reamer, re-oil everything and take another small cut. Usually you will need to repeat this several times until you can feel the bolt close with just a little resistance on the go gauge. Once you are at that point, make one more *very* light cut, clean up the chips and check again. When the bolt just closes all the way without feeling the gauge, you will have a "min-spec" chamber. This is the trickiest part of building this rifle, so go slowly and get it right.

Now check with the no-go gauge to be sure the bolt will not close. If you did this correctly, the handle on the bolt will still be high when it stops against the gauge. This means you have a chamber that is close to the minimum specification, which is best for accuracy.

APPLYING MAKEUP

At this point, you could put the gun together and shoot it. It will be ugly and prone to rusting, but it will work. A big part of any custom gun is the finish, so let's look at that next.

▲ Coating the action.

Use a center punch to make two corresponding index marks on the bottom of the barrel and action, so you can line them up to exactly the same place. Remove the barrel from the action and degrease both completely. The best way is to soak them in a degreasing agent that dries without residue. I used DuraCoat TruStrip for this rifle and it worked great, but acetone works well, too. I simply fill a bluing tank and soak the parts.

Another alternative is to buy Brakleen designed for automotive use and available in gallon containers.

All this is nasty stuff, so use lots of ventilation and observe all the appropriate safety protocols. Always use goggles or a face shield, gloves, and long sleeves.

After degreasing, use clean gloves to handle the parts. Fill the critical areas that you do not want coated with clay or tape them off with masking tape. Then sandblast both the barrel and the action with aluminum oxide, using #80 to #100 grit, with 80 psi of pressure. You want a uniform, slightly rough finish over the entire part.

▲ This is the tube made from a laundry bag that was used to create the pattern.

As I said, I wanted something a bit different on this rifle, something distinctive and unique. I coated the barrel and action with Magpul Flat Dark Earth color. Then, I had my wife sew up a piece of mesh laundry bag into a tube to fit the barrel. I am not promoting sexist stereotypes here. Like Clint said, "A man's got to know his limitations," and mine peaked trying to do this. I simply do not have the ability to make anything in a straight line. So my wife Robin came to my rescue and made the tube for me.

COATING THE BARREL

Once the first application of DuraCoat was dry, Robin also helped me to fit this tube to the barrel, seam down and

▲ An inexpensive blasting gun will work for prepping the metal.

You can buy an inexpensive handheld blasting gun and consider the blasting sand to be a consumable. If you blast into a cut off plastic drum as I do, you can recover much of the medium for reuse. Make sure you have a respirator, eye protection and leather gloves.

If you plan to do a lot of gun finish work, invest in a blasting cabinet. I have one I bought at a local chain store and it's proved to be one of the best investments I've ever made.

After blasting use shop air to blow off all the dust. I usually degrease again at this point, although Steve Lauer, the owner of DuraCoat, tells me it's not necessary or recommended. I never did listen well. I hang the parts and spray degreaser, letting it flow off.

The next step is to apply the metal finish. I coated the barrel and action with DuraCoat spray-on finish. The beauty of DuraCoat gun finish for a hobby gunsmith is that it can air dry and you do not need a curing oven.

▲ Spraying part two of the pattern.

with pattern lines straight. Then I sprayed the barrel again using DuraCoat Flat Black. After that dried I removed the mesh bag, which left a "snakeskin" pattern on the barrel that gives this gun a unique look.

I taped off the last quarter-inch of the barrel and covered it with Flat Black to add a "cap" at the muzzle. Then I touched up a few thin spots on the action and let them both dry long enough to allow using the barrel vise and action wrench to reassemble them without damage. A week is usually long enough, but I went off on an extended shooting and hunting trip in Texas, so they dried for about two weeks, which is more than enough. I carefully wrapped both the action and the barrel with brown wrapping paper and installed them in the barrel vise and action wrench. I again applied some anti-seize lubrication on the threads and tightened until the two witness marks I had made with the center punch on the bottom were aligned. I checked the headspacing again, which was perfect, as expected. Finally, I used the raceway tool to clean off any coating that got on the bolt raceways and the Dremel tool to clean up the feed ramp.

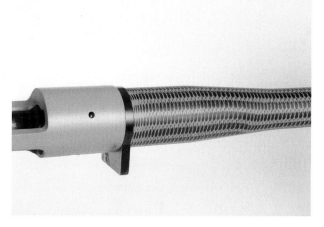

▲ The "snake" pattern.

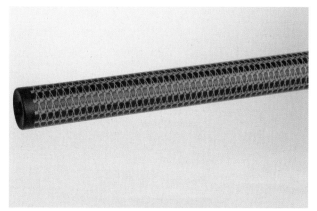

▲ I added this end cap to give the gun a finished look.

I installed a Timney 1.5-pound pull weight trigger (again, look for an extensive piece on how to do that in chapter 7 in this book). I installed the stock and a Swarovski Z6 5-30X50P scope using Brownells Tactical Rings.

BREAK-IN

If you want to start a fight on the internet, bring up the issue of barrel break-in, then stand back and protect your face.

I broke in this barrel by shooting two shots and cleaning the bore, two more shots, clean the bore and repeat *ad nauseum*. I quit after 10 cycles. It's tedious work, but it does seem to help make a good barrel even better. This barrel not only shoots well, but it hardly fouls. I find very little metal fouling in the bore, even after a lot of shooting, and it cleans up easily.

The question of breaking in a barrel comes up often. My answer is simple. It never hurts. It won't make a bad barrel shoot well, but it might make a good barrel shoot better.

I don't typically do it with factory guns because far too many of them come through here for me to have the time to do that to every gun. But, with a custom gun that has a high-dollar barrel installed, I do break in the barrel. Every time I have gone through the process the gun turns out to be a good shooter. So I hate to vary from the recipe. On the other hand, I only break in guns with high-end barrels, so is it the dog or the tail that's doing all the wagging? I don't know for sure, but it's never a mistake to break in any new barrel. It's tedious, tiresome and a complete pain in the butt, but never a mistake.

FEEDING ISSUES

The H. S. Precision box magazines needed to be tweaked a little in order to feed properly. This is done with a tool sold by Brownells that allows you to slightly bend the feed lips one way or the other until the cartridges feed properly from the magazine.

▲ Adjusting the feed lips on the magazine.

▲ Nathan Towsley shooting the "Snake" gun.

TEST RUN

At the 100-yard range, I fired the first five-shot group and was pleasantly surprised to see the holes were all grouped up like pigs on a cold night. Rather than a fluke, this proved to be rather common for this rifle.

Like all rifles, this one has its ammo preferences, but I didn't try any ammo it didn't like. With ammo it prefers, Black Hills 175-grain Match and Federal 168-grain Match, it can shoot amazingly small groups.

Over the years I have worked up some very good hand-loads. My favorite, using Sierra 168-grain MatchKing bullets and Hodgdon's Varget powder will consistently shoot at half-MOA for five-shot groups. That's pretty good, considering that the action was never blueprinted or trued and that the barrel is not custom fitted. No, check that; it's not "pretty good," it's *outstanding*.

I am delighted with the performance of this rifle as well as the unique looks. I still don't have "enough" guns and hope I never do, but I have filled one small gap in my line-up in a most satisfying way. Every time I shoot this gun and look at the snug little groups on the target, I think, *I made this* and I smile.

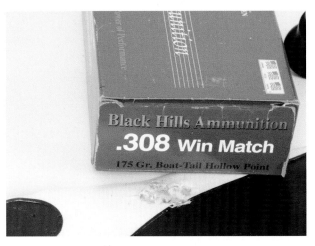

▲ This rifle loves Black Hills Match ammo. This is a five-shot group.

MORE SNAKESKIN

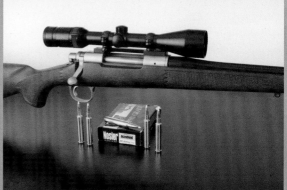

This is the author's Remington 700 custom rifle in .280 Ackley Improved. Note the "snakeskin" look to the barrel.

I used that same laundry bag technique again when building my .280 Ackley Improved. First I sprayed the barrel with DuraCoat Flat Black. Once it dried, I put a laundry bag tube, again one my wife made, over the barrel. I mixed DuraCoat Flat Black with Olive Green, two parts green to one part black. I sprayed that over the laundry bag "stencil" for a subtle snakeskin look.

Some people at first glance think it's a carbon fiber barrel, but when I tell them to look closer. the response without fail is "Oh *wow!*"

This unique hunting rifle has been good luck for me, accounting for a lot of game over the years. It's always a topic of conversation in any hunting camp.

This Mississippi whitetail fell to the author's .280 AI "snake" gun.

The Remington 700 action came with a Remington bolt. My original plan was to modify that bolt by installing a tactical bolt knob and a Sako type extractor, but then I discovered that I could order a complete bolt from Pacific Tool and Gauge.

PTG offers lots of options for Remington bolts, even including a 3-position safety on the Remington 700 bolt like on a Winchester Model 70. I ordered a spiral fluted bolt with an M-16 extractor and an oversized tactical bolt knob. The only thing I had to add was the ejector, ejector spring and the pin, which I got from Brownells. Most gun guys agree that the extractor is the weak point on a Remington bolt. The addition of this larger, stronger M-16 extractor eliminates that problem.

The bolt handle is not welded to the bolt, as it should be fitted to the action when welded in place. I thought about brazing it on myself using a jig sold by Brownells, but in the end sent the bolt and action to Nathan Dagly at Straight Shot Gunsmithing to be welded. He did a great job and his TIG welds are much stronger than any braze I can do with a torch. On a tactical rifle, I think the strongest weld available makes a lot of sense.

The PTG bolt came with an M-16 extractor installed.

I had to open the recess in the barrel that the bolt head fits in, as the slightly larger diameter bolt head was hitting the barrel and the M-16 extractor needs a bit more room to pivot. In this case, I chucked the barrel in the lathe in a 4-jaw chuck and, using a boring bar, opened the bolt counterbore recess to allow clearance for the M-16 extractor. I know that violates the "no major machine tools" concept of this project, but let me point out that if you use the factory bolt that comes with the action, or a Sako extractor, this operation is unnecessary. My bolt is an "add on" and it's exempt from the "no lathe" clause. If you don't have a lathe, most gunsmiths will be happy to do the job for you. Other than that, the only fitting was to lap the bolt lugs to the action. This bolt adds a touch of class and a much higher level of performance to this rifle. There are detailed instructions in the rifle building section in chapter 14 of this book on how to install both a Sako and an M-16 extractor in a Model 700 bolt and how to install an oversized tactical bolt handle.

The PTG bolt came with an oversized handle installed.

The M-16 extractor requires that the bolt counterbore recess be opened to a larger diameter.

CHAPTER 4
THE GREEN GOBLIN

▲ This rifle really likes Hornady .358 Winchester ammo.

This is another rifle that I built before I had access to a lathe or other major power tools. It follows the same process as the .308 Snake gun, but with a few different twists and turns. I adapted this chapter from a magazine piece I wrote for NRA's Shooting Illustrated Magazine. *It's been rewritten and edited to fit the book better. I have also added a bunch of notes, which appear throughout this chapter in italics for easier identification.*

The .358 Winchester was introduced to the world the same year I was, 1955. It's really nothing more than a .308 Winchester necked up to take a 35-caliber bullet and it pushes a 200-grain round nose bullet out the muzzle at 2,490 ft/s.

At one time there were many options when buying a .358 Winchester rifle, but the American public began demanding anorexic bullets approaching Mach III, which is not a description of the .358 Winchester's performance. The magnum mania that started in the '60s and continues today doomed the .358 Winchester to a hard and harsh life. It is still popular with a lot of knowledgeable gun guys, but the masses ignore it and for the most part so do the gun companies.

I woke up one morning and decided I had been far too long without a .358 Winchester. The configuration I wanted was a compact, reasonably light, bolt action rifle. Because no gun company wanted to offer one, I took matters into my own hands and made my own rifle.

At first glance, it's a little intimidating for a hobby gunsmith to build a rifle, but when you look at it in a step by step context your heartrate slows a little and you begin to see the possibilities.

When I built this rifle actions were difficult to find. As of this writing, twelve years later, Brownells has a good supply of Remington actions for considerably less than the cost of a new rifle.

GETTIN' SOME ACTION

The first stop is the action. In years past you could easily buy a barreled action or even just the action, but for the most part those days are past. (At least they were in 2006.) There are a few actions on the market, but most are priced way too high for a hobby guy, so, I simply bought a new Remington Model 700 SPS rifle in .308 Winchester. This inexpensive, blue/synthetic rifle is moderately priced, but it's a 700 through and through. The cost cutting comes mostly from the injection molded stock and the less than fancy metal finish. Neither is important here, as they are being replaced, so the money saved by Remington makes this a very viable option for any rifle build.

For the parts and tools I turned to Brownells. I ordered a Shilen barrel in #2 contour, short-chambered for .358 Winchester and with a 1:14 twist rate. This barrel came with the lathe work already done. I also ordered a Bell &

▲ The donor rifle, a Remington Model 700 SPS in .308 Winchester.

Carlson synthetic stock and a new magazine follower and spring. The follower in the 700 SPS would have worked, but it's a cheap, stamped thing that I didn't like, so I replaced it. I already had most of the tools and those I did not I ordered from Brownells as needed.

I removed the bolt and the trigger from the action. Then I clamped the action in an action wrench and the barrel in a bench mounted barrel vise, both from Brownells. The threads on this Remington were locked with some sort of sealer and required a long piece of pipe for a cheater on the action wrench handle and a lot of power to break the action loose from the barrel.

Some heat would probably have helped here. A MAPP gas or oxyacetylene torch might have sped up the process. Go easy, though, as you do not want to heat the receiver enough to damage the hardness and temper. Use heat very sparingly on any rifle action.

It finally came free and I removed the barrel, still virgin and never defiled by a bullet fired by me.

This barrel later proved to be a big help as a visual aid when trying to figure out how to thread and fit new barrels on a lathe.

I wanted to do a few things to improve the accuracy and function of the rifle, so the next step was to lap the bolt lugs to the action. For the best accuracy in any rifle, the bolt's locking lugs must seat evenly and completely in the receiver. Lapping will also smooth up the feel of the action.

I deleted a long section on how to lap a bolt and polish the raceways that appeared in the original Shooting Illustrated *article, because both topics are covered in detail in chapter 14 of this book.*

MURPHY COMES TO THE PARTY

Everything was going along fine until I installed the barrel. I did not have a lathe at the time, so I ordered the barrel ready to install, except for the final chamber reaming. That

▲ The recoil lug on a surface grinder. If you cut the chamber a little too deep, thinning the recoil lug slightly can correct the problem.

should have meant the barrel would screw into the action and be in the correct position. But when I threaded this barrel into the action, the bolt would not close. The face of the bolt was hitting the back of the barrel, which meant the barrel threads were too long.

Once my initial panic receded, I did what I always do when I am in trouble on a gunsmithing project: I picked up the phone and called my buddy Mark Bansner. Mark is one of the top custom rifle builders in the country and he always has the answers.

I figured that I would have to send the barrel down to him to be fitted with a lathe and he confirmed that was one option. But then he asked me to take a bunch of measurements using a depth micrometer and the headspace gauge. He did a little math based on my measurements and told me that all I needed was a thicker recoil lug. I discovered later that Brownells usually packages the thicker recoil lug with the Shilen barrels. However, because mine was a .358 Winchester, it was a special order barrel shipped direct from Shilen and the recoil lug kind of fell through the cracks. I was trying to use the thinner, original Remington recoil lug that I took off the rifle. With the correct recoil lug, there is no machining work needed, just bolt it all together and finish the chamber.

On Remington Model 700 actions, the recoil lug is fitted like a big washer between the barrel and the action. The thickness of the recoil lug will control how far the barrel screws into the rifle's action. Because I ended up with a different brand of recoil lug than is normally shipped with that barrel, we had to make a few adjustments. By changing the thickness we were able to correctly position the barrel in the action. I sent the recoil lug to Mark and he used a surface grinder to modify the thickness of the oversize recoil lug until it was exactly correct. He could have fitted it so perfectly that all I would need to do is screw in the barrel, but I chickened out on that approach and had him leave the headspacing .005 inch short so that I could finish-ream the chamber.

One problem with a Remington 700 action is trying to keep the recoil lug lined up properly when screwing the barrel to the action. It must be oriented exactly straight down from the action. The Brownells action wrench has a recessed lug cut in the front to hold the lug in position as the barrel is tightened into place, but it will not fit some of the custom recoil lugs like the one we used. There are other tools to solve that problem, but in this case the recoil lug that Mark machined had an indexing pin, so I cut a groove in the bottom of the receiver to lock it in place as I tightened the barrel to the action.

It's much better to use the Holland jig to drill the receiver to accept the pin as detailed in chapter 14 of this book. In this case, I resorted to "redneck gunsmithing" by cutting an awful looking mess in my receiver that happened to work out perfectly.

CUTTING THE CHAMBER

I finished cutting the chamber by using a .358 Winchester finish reamer with an extension and T-handle. I carefully cut the chamber until the headspacing go gauge would barely allow the bolt to close. This gave me the tight,

▲ Chamber reamer and headspace gauges for the .358 Winchester.

minimum spec chamber that I wanted for better accuracy. With Winchester factory loads (all that was available at the time) I could feel the shoulder of the case hit the front of the chamber as I closed the bolt, so I knew the case was firmly supported and centered in the chamber.

As I intended to shoot primarily handloads and it's easy to control the case dimensions, this is a good approach. If I was going to shoot mostly factory loads and considered reliability more important, I would ream the chamber a bit deeper so that it fell in the middle of the tolerance specifications.

I later learned that this was not the best approach to accuracy. Later, I recut the chamber slightly deeper so that it would just close on the go gauge without contact, as detailed elsewhere in this book. That simple adjustment resulted in a rather substantial improvement in accuracy. When I mention in the section on chambering a rifle barrel that I've discovered I get better accuracy with the chamber cut so it closes on a go gauge without feeling it, this is one of the rifles that taught me the lesson.

SHORTENING THE BARREL

Perhaps the hardest thing to do was taking a hacksaw to that new high-end rifle barrel. A hacksaw? On a brand new, top-quality rifle barrel? Isn't that against the laws of man? Or, at the very least a venial sin? I seriously

considered chickening out, but who on earth would build a .358 Winchester rifle with a 26-inch barrel? It had to be done and this was the only way, so I took a deep breath, closed my eyes, and pushed on the hacksaw to start the cut that reduced this barrel to 21 inches. Actually, I cut it to 21.25 inches to allow squaring the muzzle later.

I have done so many rifle barrels since this one that it's no longer traumatic, I just grab the saw and start hacking.

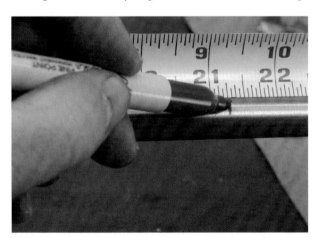

▲ Marking the length.

The key is to try to keep the cut as straight and square as possible, then to use a file to square it up. Don't worry if it's not perfect; trust me, it won't be. Once again, it's Brownells to the rescue. You will need a 90-degree muzzle facing cutter that is larger than the diameter of the barrel's muzzle and a pilot to fit the bore of the rifle.

The cutter comes with a T-handle to turn it and you can certainly use that to do the job, but it's much easier and faster to buy the muzzle facing/crowning cutter drill chuck

▲ The cutoff barrel.

▲ The barrel after cutting with the hacksaw. Note the yellow paint from the new hacksaw blade.

▲ The muzzle after facing it off with a Brownells 90-degree muzzle facing cutter.

adapter. This inexpensive little adapter allows you to chuck the cutting tool in a handheld cordless drill. This makes things go much faster and easier. Simply turn the drill to its lowest RPM setting and remember to use plenty of cutting oil. The cutter will soon have the face of the barrel a perfect 90 degrees to the bore. Just be careful, as this cutter works fast and you can shorten your barrel more than you planned. Also,

▲ The muzzle with a Brownells 90-degree muzzle facing cutter with the anti-chatter stop installed.

always turn the cutter in a clockwise direction. Reversing the cutter will roll the edges of the blades and ruin them.

I crowned the barrel as detailed elsewhere in this book to a recessed 11-degree crown, then added a radius to the outside of the muzzle with a Brownells Muzzle Radius Cutter.

I stamped "358 Win" on the barrel using a punch stamp set with an alignment jig to maintain alignment and spacing.

▲ Brownells Muzzle Radius Cutter.   ▲ The finished muzzle.

The stamps work, but the results are not always pretty. I have since started taking my finished guns to a commercial engraver to put the cartridge name on the barrel. That is much more professional looking.

▲ Tony Kinton's rifle after a commercial engraver marked the cartridge.

BARREL, BEDDING, AND STOCK MATING

Next, I fitted the barreled action to the Bell & Carlson stock and glass-bedded the action and first three inches of the barrel.

Lots of notes here, right? A decade-plus teaches a few

things. *Bedding the first several inches of the barrel is still a good approach for a hunting rifle, but I found that it can have a negative effect on accuracy with rifles that are shot a lot and are used with the barrel hot. For a precision rifle that has to maintain accuracy while hot, this approach may not be the best. The barrel is tapered and as the steel heats and expands that taper starts to act as a cam against the bedding. It introduces stress to the barrel and action and can have an effect on the accuracy. I now float the barrel all the way back to the recoil lug on those rifles. For hunting guns, I usually continue to bed the first few inches of the barrel.*

The rest of the barrel was free-floated using .010-inch bedding tape from Brownells to cover the barrel. The stock is relieved to give more than .010-inch clearance, and then filled with bedding material. The action and barrel are fitted into the stock and the bedding compound is allowed to set up.

Once the compound has finished curing, the barrel and action are removed from the stock. When the tape is removed from the barrel and the barreled action is fitted back into the stock, it leaves a nice clean gap of .010 inch around the barrel. I sanded the bedding flush to the top of the stock and set it aside for refinishing in Flat Black DuraCoat.

I used a center punch to make two corresponding index marks on the bottom of the barrel and action. Then I took

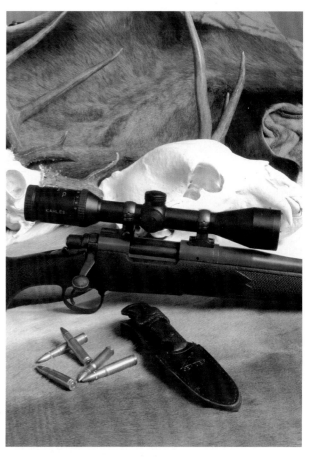

▲ The Green Goblin.

the barrel off the action, filled the critical areas with clay or taped them off and sandblasted both the barrel and the action for a uniform, slightly rough finish. I reassembled the barrel and action, tightening until the two index marks lined up. This ensures the barrel is in the same position and that the headspacing is again correct.

Again, this is all covered in other areas of the book. I no longer do the spray-on coatings with the barrel and action assembled. This is mainly because I like to use anti-seize lubricant on the threads and the surfaces of the action and barrel where they contact the recoil lug. I feel it gives a better installation, but the lube can be detrimental to any spray-on coating. With an oven cure, the heat can make the grease leak out and really cause problems. I now process the barrel, action, and recoil lug separately and assemble them after the coating is cured.

After degreasing, I sprayed the barreled action with DuraCoat finish. The beauty of DuraCoat gun finish for a hobby gunsmith is that it can air dry. I like to experiment, so I tried one of the multitude of colors DuraCoat offers called Sniper Green. This is a good example of why my wife picks my clothes for me. I think it looks good, but I am in the minority as most people don't like the color on this rifle.

This was also one of my early attempts at coating a gun

and I got it on way too thick. It looks painted rather than like a coated firearm.

I had thought about recoating the gun in Flat Black, but on a hunting trip soon after finishing the gun another gun writer, Richard Mann, dubbed the rifle the "Green Goblin" and the name has kind of stuck.

No matter, the important thing is this gun will shoot. I fitted it with a Kahles 3-9X42 scope in a Leupold mount. Almost any handload I tried will average around one inch for three-shot groups at 100 yards. The new Hornady factory load is very accurate too, just under MOA on average.

While I finished the gun too late in that season for much hunting, I did shoot a whitetail doe in West Virginia using a handloaded Hornady 200-grain bullet at a chronographed muzzle velocity of 2,495 ft/s. Complete penetration and an exit wound the size of my fist made this deer into venison very fast. That deer had the distinction of being the first in a long line of whitetails that I expect this rifle will account for in the years ahead, because this rifle is sticking around.

In the years since I first wrote the first article, the Green Goblin has accounted for a bunch of whitetails and wild hogs. The Hornady 200-grain FTX bullet is a grenade in this thing. When it hits the boiler room of a deer, the lights just turn off.

▲ The Green Goblin will shoot.

That bullet is designed for the .35 Remington, so the extra velocity from the .358 Winchester really makes it expand. It's not the bullet I would use on anything much bigger than deer, but it's something to see when it hits a whitetail.

I would also note that after a few magazine articles were published about the rifle, the owner of DuraCoat, Steve Lauer, told me they were getting a lot of calls asking for the "Green Goblin" color.

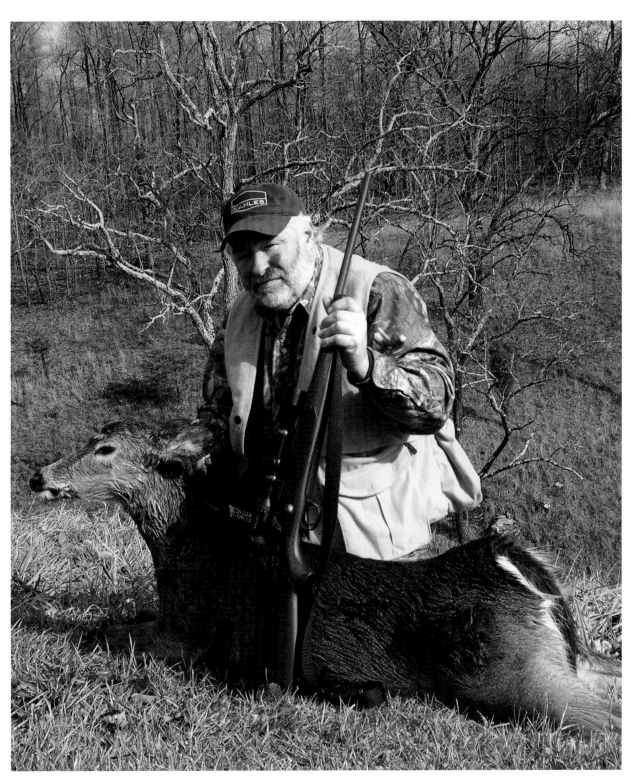

▲ This soggy doe, shot on a rainy day, was the first critter to fall to the Green Goblin.

CHAPTER 5
SPRAY AND PRAY

The modern approach to gun finishing.

I love the look of a traditional bluing job, but for a hobby gunsmith bluing is a bit complicated and requires a lot of chemicals. So, if I want a traditional bluing job I send the gun off to somebody like Viktor's Legacy Custom Gunsmithing. Jim Majoros has a large room dedicated to bluing and has enough pipes, tanks, and heaters that he could probably repurpose them and give SpaceX a run for its money.

I much prefer to finish the metal, and often the stocks, frames and even grips on my guns, with a spray-on coating. Spray coatings are much easier to deal with and have a lot of color and finish options. They protect the metal and right now they are popular with the "in" crowd of gun people. They can be applied to just about any material, which gives you a lot of choices.

There is a wide range of spray-on coatings available. Some require oven curing, while others will air-cure. Air-cure products I have had good luck with include Cerakote C, DuraCoat and Brownells Aluma-Hyde II. The last two are available in several application options, including rattle cans, which are a fast and easy way to finish a gun. They can also be applied with a spray gun or airbrush. Cerakote is spray gun only.

The bake-on products include Cerakote H and Elite, DuraCoat DuraBake and a few from Brownells, Gun-Kote, and Teflon/Moly. The Cerakote and Teflon/Moly are spray gun only, while the others have multiple application choices. There are a lot of other products on the market, but these are what I have some experience using.

I will note that while you can get a pretty good finish with a rattle can, using a spray gun usually produces a better result because you have more control over the volume of spray. In my experience an air brush splits the difference and, while it works quite well, it's not as good as a spray gun. An air brush is, however, a low-cost alternative if you do not have an air compressor and a spray gun.

▲ Some of the custom Cerakote work done by Jamey Majoros of Viktor's Legacy Custom Gunsmithing.

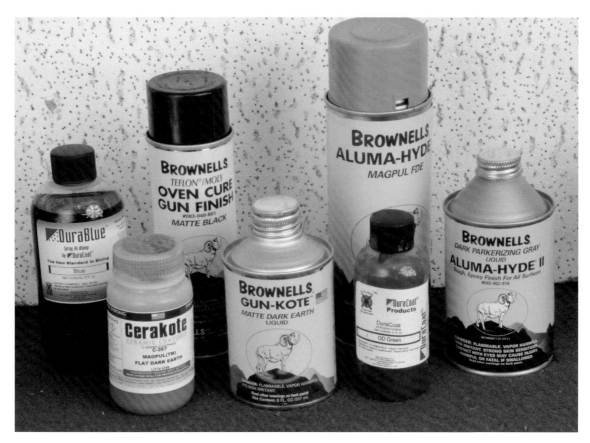

▲ Some of the spray-on coatings I have used.

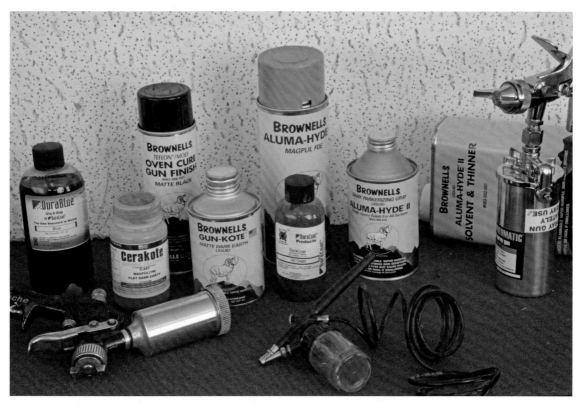

▲ Spray-on coatings can be applied with a rattle can, spray gun, or airbrush.

Some products can be used over old finishes, most cannot. DuraCoat says you can rough up the metal with a Scotch-brite pad and spray over. I have done that with a pretty good result.

Cerakote has a pretty strict preparation protocol, one I think gives the best result with any spray coating. I have reduced it down to the basics here.

I highly suggest that you read the instructions with the coating you are using and follow the recommendations contained in them. There are always some differences in procedure. That said, I think that a degreased and sandblasted surface will give a reliably good result.

Always wear a respirator, not a cheap painting mask, but rather a high-quality respirator when doing any blasting or spraying operations. Safety glasses are a must, as are leather gloves for blasting.

▲ This is the 1911 from chapter 10.

▲ Duracoat suggests Parkerizing the metal before spray coating. This provides a good foundation for the spray-on coating to grip.

HORNADY HOT TUB ULTRASONIC CLEANER

High tech comes to gun cleaning.

I believe that ultrasonic cleaners were first introduced to the shooting world as a way to clean empty brass cartridge cases, but it was soon discovered that they work very well for cleaning gun parts too. Hornady has introduced several models over the years and the most recent is the Hot Tub Ultrasonic Cleaner. I have found it to be a very useful addition to any gunsmithing shop.

It's large enough to put a broken down AR-15 upper or lower in to clean. If you have ever struggled with a filthy AR-15 upper, this makes life easier. The ultrasonic cleaning gets into the

The Hornady Hot Tub

nooks, crannies, and crevices that are hard to access with conventional cleaners.

I have a smaller ultrasonic cleaner dedicated to brass in my reloading area, but I added the Hot Tub to my shop, where I use it for cleaning parts. For example, the Remington 742 shown in the photos was a cruddy mess when I first got it in the shop. It showed years of neglect and was filled with crud, carbon, old grease and what I suspect was desiccated cow manure. I broke the gun down to parts and put everything metal in the Hornady cleaner. I ran two cycles and the parts came out crud-free. No scrubbing, no soaking, just push the button, wait a bit and done. No harsh solvents eating away at your skin, no need for rubber gloves. Simply dry the parts, and spritz them with degreaser to remove any residual soap and oil against rust.

If you hate cleaning guns as much as I do, The Hornady Hot Tub Ultrasonic Cleaner is a must-have tool for your shop.

Mike Brookman removes an AR-15 upper from the Hornady Hot Tub Ultrasonic Cleaner.

GETTING READY

Take the gun apart and clean all the parts. I used to recommend a degreasing tank with solvent and still do for really crudded-up gun parts. Lately, I use a Hornady Ultrasonic cleaner for most parts cleaning (see sidebar).

▲ The Remington 742 after Cerakote.

If your gun is a "seasoned" firearm, you need to make sure all the pits and scratches are removed if possible and any rust is removed.

The photo of the Remington 742 shows a pretty good outcome. What it does not show are the hours of prep work I put into that gun. When my friend called, he said he had a stainless steel Remington semi-automatic. They never made such a critter, so I wasn't surprised to see a gun with no bluing left and lots of deep, rusty pits.

I suspect it spent some time in a barn, as one side was much worse than the other. Here in dairy country it's not uncommon to see that on a rifle or shotgun. The farmer stands the gun in the corner of the barn, ready to grab when varmints show up and need shooting. The side that is exposed takes a beating. Cow manure is pretty abusive and the little bits the bovines flick off their tails as they walk by wind up digging pits in the steel. I have a Remington Model 14 in .32 Remington that is almost pristine on one side, while the other side looks like a typical Vermont dirt road in late March. The lady I bought it from said her dad used it in the barn.

On the 742, I used a sanding block and a draw file to remove as much of the pitting as I could. It's important to

▲ Using a sanding block on the receiver of a Remington 742 rifle.

keep the lines straight, the planes flat and to avoid dishing. If I were to just sand on the pits, the gun would look like the surface of the moon with all the craters. With a sanding block and a draw file, I worked the entire flat side of the receiver rather than spot sanding.

However, when I started to see the serial number and logo fade a bit, I stopped. The law requires that the serial number has to stay and be readable. I could have continued and had an engraver recut them, but that was a much bigger investment than this gun was worth.

▲ Using the shoe-shine motion on a Remington 742 barrel to remove pits while keeping the barrel round.

I worked the top of the action and the barrel with strips of emery paper, using a shoe-shine motion to keep the contour round. In the end, I removed most of the pits from the barrel and the gun looks pretty good. If it had been a bolt action I could have used a spinning frame to sand the surface of the barrel, but the 742 has a lug attached to the barrel that prevents use of that method.

The key is to do the prep work until you have the part looking smooth and even, as machining marks, file tracks, pits, dings, etc., will all show through the finish. Blasting helps smooth out minor imperfections, but will not remove most visible marks. The spray coating will not cover them up either, so do your prep work. Make the part look as pretty as you possibly can, then proceed with the rest of the work.

Of course, if there is any rust it must be completely removed or the coating will not stick properly. Rust remover works pretty well, but will also remove bluing. That's not an issue if you are planning to coat the gun, but I hate even having it on my bench. Sand blasting removes rust as well, but it can contaminate the blasting medium if there is a lot of rust or grease.

Once the parts are clean and prepped, completely degrease using a solvent that dries without residue. Brakleen is good, acetone is better. Use caution on plastic or other non-metal parts and check to make sure the

▲ Mark Bansner using a spinning frame to polish a barrel on a sanding belt.

▲ This is a spray degreaser. Use it last and let it run off the part.

solvent does not eat the plastic. It's probably best to not soak non-metal parts, but to spray and wipe with a clean cloth dampened with degreaser.

Small parts can go in a coffee can (is it still called a can if it's made out of plastic?), or I have a few stainless steel salad bowls I use for cleaning. A bluing tank is perfect for degreasing barrels and actions. There is no need to fill it, just turn it at a 45-degree angle, put in enough solvent to cover all the parts, then agitate.

▲ Acetone and Brakleen are both useful degreasing agents.

DuraCoat recommends submerging a barreled action and letting it soak for a while to remove any grease from the threads. With an air-dry product this works fine. If you are oven-curing, it's far better to take the barrel off the action. The heat can release grease or oil trapped in the threads and spoil the coating. If removing the barrel isn't possible, use the gas-out procedure recommended by Cerakote and explained later in this chapter.

Once the parts are degreased, only handle them while wearing gloves. Powder-free latex gloves are excellent.

Protect sensitive areas with tape. If you are going to heat-cure the part, use a tape that can withstand the heat. Regular masking tape cooks on and can be difficult to remove.

Plug both ends of the bore. I use tapered rubber plugs, because I have some on hand and they seem to work fine for the muzzle end. I have also made tapered plugs from a wooden dowel and lightly tapped them into the bore with a hammer. There are a lot of commercial plugs on the market as well and I recently bought a selection of silicon plugs which are working great.

I have tools I made to fit on a Remington Model 700 action and barrel thread. On other barrel designs, I cover the threads and chamber end with tape.

TOOLS YOU CAN MAKE THAT WILL IMPROVE YOUR QUALITY OF LIFE AND IMPRESS YOUR FRIENDS

When working on rifles, I much prefer to apply any spray-on metal coating to the receiver and barrel separately. Reason number one is that when I assemble the barrel to the receiver I use anti-seize grease on the threads and recoil lug. This can cause a lot of problems with spray coatings as the grease can leak out, particularly under heat, and cause the coating to fail to adhere. I suppose it's possible to soak the barreled action in a bluing tank full of degreaser and/or to "cook" the grease out as the Cerakote instructions suggest. But, in the end, I find it much easier to just consider the barrel and action as two separate parts when spray-coating. It's much easier to degrease them and finish them individually to get a good final result. Besides, when they are assembled they can be pretty long and often do not fit well in my sandblaster or oven.

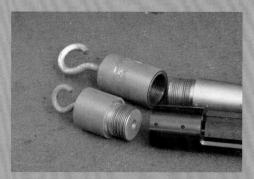

The tools I made to use for spray-on coatings and sandblasting Remington 700 actions and barrels.

The face of the receiver and the shoulder on the barrel are precision machined and how they fit together has an effect on headspacing, so they should be protected from any spray coating and kept as clean metal. Any spray-on coating provides dimension and can impact how the parts fit together. Also, after taking great pains to precisely machine them to a perfect fit, why on earth would you spray something on them that adds thickness and is not perfectly even in that thickness? It's also important to protect these machined edges when sandblasting prior to applying any spray coating.

(continued . . .)

For a long time, my approach was to use tape on both the barrel and the action, but that's time consuming and never seems to work out exactly right. For example, when we were building Tony Kinton's 9.3X62 hunting rifle I wrapped a loop of wire around the threads on the barrel shank and twisted it tight, so I would have something to hang the barrel with. Then I wrapped the threads with masking tape and finished using vinyl electrical tape stretched tight and wrapped to a diameter larger than the barrel shoulder, the idea being that it butted up to the shoulder and protected it from overspray. I spent quite a bit of time making sure the machined shoulder was protected and that there was no overlap, so the barrel would be properly coated.

I did two coats of finish, baking both and doing a careful inspection each time. Still, when I removed the tape, there was a small sliver of the barrel that was not coated, because the tape had slipped up over the edge of the shoulder. I was lucky that time, because when I torqued the barrel into the action the spot was on the bottom and was hidden inside the stock. If it was in a visible location, a third coat of finish would have been needed.

Doing an action is even worse. I would carefully fit tape over the machined face and the tape would always come off. Besides, the tape attracts sand from the sandblaster and after baking in the oven the tape is often difficult to remove. All in all, it was just a poor approach to this problem.

Heat resistant tape and barrel plugs.

A while back, I needed something to hold a Remington 700 action while I worked. I found that I could use a Manson Tooling Block designed for truing the bolt face. This tool will thread into the action and, using a wooden dowel through the center hole, makes a pretty good handle. An unintended benefit was that it fit tight to the machined face of the action and protected it from the spray coating. It is, however, abuse of a very expensive precision-machined tool. Still, it gave me an idea to make a couple of tools for this job, one to fit the barrel threads and protect the shoulder and the other to screw into the action and protect the machined front edge.

These tools also provide a handle to hold when spraying, sandblasting, or transferring the part to the oven. They also have a ring on top to allow hanging the parts for spraying, drying, and/or baking in the oven.

Making the action tool is easy. Pick a piece of round stock larger than the outside diameter of the action you will be using it with. I used steel so that the expansion rates would be similar when heating the parts in the oven.

Tool for a 700 action.

Machine a threaded section just as you would with a barrel you are fitting to an action. Face off a nice clean shoulder, just as you would when fitting a barrel. Make the threads short, so they will fit into a range of actions without bottoming out. It's fine if the threads are a bit undersized or "sloppy," as that will help the machined edges self-align when you tighten everything together.

I drilled and tapped the front end to take a ¼-20 bolt. Then I bought a short ring bolt and screwed it in and locked it with the supplied jam nut. If I ever build another, I might go to a 5/16 ring bolt. The quarter-inch, while more than rugged enough, looks small on the tool. The aesthetics might be better with a bigger ring bolt. Also, I cut out a section of the ring to make it into a hook and the quarter-inch ring bolt is just a little small to easily slip on and off the shepherd's crook I use to hold parts that are being sprayed when working outdoors. (See more on that in the section on spray coatings.) All in all, one size larger on the ring bolt would not be a bad thing.

The tool for the barrel was a bit of a larger problem. I did not have the tooling for cutting an inside thread. (Besides, inside threads in a blind hole are how new machinists get into trouble.) I pondered it for a while, going so far as to start an online order for the tooling. I left the tools in my cart while I checked my shop inventory to see what else I needed to justify the insane shipping charges. Often, ten tools ship for the same price as one, so I try to bundle.

I am sometimes like a little kid with my attention span and while looking through one toolbox to see which indexable cutters needed replacements I noticed my copy of *Machinery's Handbook*, so I decided to check out the specs for a 1 1/6-16 inside thread. Then I started doing some math to adjust for the .010-inch difference needed when using the oversized Dave Manson Receiver Accurizing kit. That led to one of those forehead-slapping moments. I had exactly the correct tap I needed to cut the inside thread in the Dave Manson Receiver Accurizing kit that I use to blueprint receivers.

Tool for the barrel.

Again, I picked a piece of steel stock that was large enough to cover the rifle barrel shoulder. I turned the outside diameter to clean off the crud and rust and to true it up. (Using a 3-jaw chuck is fine for this work.)

I used a center drill to start a pilot hole and then using a series of progressively larger drills, I drilled into the center about 2.25 inches deep. That's more than enough to make sure I've covered all the bases with any barrel. I ended with the largest drill I had, which was one inch. I switched to a boring bar to true up the hole and to hit a final diameter that was just slightly under the +.010-inch Receiver Reamer's recommended 1.012-1.014-inch diameter.

Tools I made for spray-on coatings and sandblasting Remington 700 actions and barrels.

Next, I drilled a half-inch hole the rest of the way through the tool to guide the mandrel of the reamer and tap. I finished by facing off the end of the tool and used a file to put a slight radius on the edges. I removed the tool from the lathe and clamped it in an action wrench, which I in turn clamped into my bench vise.

Just as when using the Receiver Accurizing Kit, I finished the cut with the reamer, using lots of cutting oil. (Remember to put a trash can under your work to catch the oil that runs out.) Looking back, I probably could have just made the final cut with the boring bar and saved this step. After all, this is not as precision as it would be when truing up a rifle action.

Once the inside diameter was correct, I cut the threads using the tap from the accurizing kit. This made the threads perfect for mating up with barrel threads that are .010 inch oversized, as used with a blueprinted action. It works fine with a standard-diameter Remington barrel thread as well.

Making the action tool.

I found that the half-inch hole I had to drill for the mandrel created a small problem. My first thought was to drill and tap it for the next size bolt, but I didn't have a tap large enough or, as noted earlier, any tooling to cut inside threads on my lathe.

I did have some 5/16 ring bolts left over from another job. It was easy to clamp one into the 3-jaw chuck on the lathe and run two nuts on and lock them together. I turned the first one down to .60 inch. Then I used a file to taper the front edge enough so it would start into the hole on the tool. Using a bench vise, I pressed the nut into the quarter-inch hole. It is a

(continued . . .)

very tight, jam fit and works fine to hold the 5/16 ring. I cut the ring bolt to length and put it on with another jam nut. I cut the ring so it's now a hook, easy to clip on my holders in the oven or when spray-coating.

The machined faces fit tight enough to keep out any spray coating. But, if you have any problems with infiltration it would be easy enough to use a fiber washer to seal the junction. Just test it in your oven to make sure it can withstand the heat before using it. I suspect that melted washer does nothing to improve the look of your new finish.

These tools have worked very well now for several rifle builds. By clamping vise grips on the rings, I had full control over the units, even when hot from the oven.

Using a one-inch drill during the process to make the barrel holder.

Cutting the threads using the tap from the Manson kit.

BLAST IT

Sandblast the parts with #100-grit aluminum oxide. Use 80 to 100 psi for the metal and 30 to 40 psi for non-metal parts such as wood, fiberglass, plastic or polymer. Anodized aluminum parts will require only 30 to 40 psi. There is no need to remove the anodizing, but you must resurface it.

After blasting, nothing should be shiny. There should be an even, matte-finish appearance. If there are shiny spots on any part, hit it again.

▲ Jim Majoros at his blasting cabinet.

The idea is to rough up the surface and give it "tooth" to help the spray coating adhere to the part. Do not use any blasting medium that is coarser than #100-grit, as the microscopic valleys on the part's surface will be too deep for the coating to completely fill.

Using a blasting cabinet is the best approach. However, you can get by with an inexpensive gravity-feed sandblasting gun. Before I bought a cabinet, I used my handheld sandblaster over a cut-off 55-gallon plastic drum to capture some of the sand for reuse. Of course, you can consider the abrasive a consumable and just buy more. Either way, do this outdoors, as you don't want the abrasive dust in your shop. Always wear a respirator, safety goggles and heavy gloves. Don't think you can get by without the gloves. Sooner or later you will mess up and blast your hand. Without gloves it hurts like hell. I know this for an absolute fact.

I'll note that I moved my blasting cabinet out of my shop. No matter what I did, it would fill the air with a fine dust. That's a horror show on precision equipment like a lathe or milling machine and it can cause premature wear on the parts. For a long time I kept a plastic drop cloth over the cabinet and myself as I worked, but the dust was still

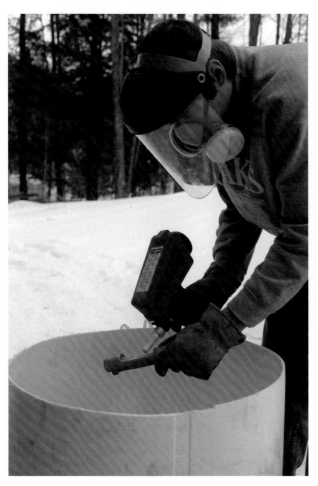

▲ A handheld sandblaster will work.

▲ My larger blasting cabinet.

escaping into the shop, so I moved the blasting cabinet to a small, unheated shed close to my shop.

I'll also note that I buy the cheap, magnetic LED lights that are sold at the checkout of any hardware store and put several in my blasting cabinet. This makes it a lot easier to see what I am doing.

After blasting, blow the dust off all the parts with compressed air. I like to hang the parts, spray them with a degreaser and let it run off. This helps remove any residual dust. It's not a horrible idea to first remove the tape, clean out all the sand and re-tape the parts, then degrease again, letting it run off.

HAVING A BLAST

One of the most useful additions to your gunsmithing shop is a blasting cabinet. This tool allows you to create different finish effects on a firearm's metal as well as being very useful for removing old finishes, rust, and corrosion. It's possible to sandblast with a handheld gun, but that makes for a couple of problems. One is the mess and danger as the work is out in the open; you will need full face/eye protection, a respirator, and tough gloves. The other problem is that you cannot reliably recover all the blasting medium, so it becomes an expensive consumable.

A cabinet allows recovery and reuse of the blasting medium and has the work piece enclosed for safety. Your hands are safely protected by the built-in gloves. Working on long guns will require a cabinet that is large enough to accept the length of the barrel or barreled action. My primary cabinet will accept up to 40 inches, but it was a bit pricey. If you are working on handguns, actions, short barrels, or small parts, you may consider a smaller cabinet. There are also tabletop models available for a much lower cost.

The process is generically called "sandblasting," but that's really not completely accurate. In fact, use of some

(continued . . .)

types of sand can be dangerous, as inhaling the dust can cause serious health problems. It's best to use only commercial medium that is known to be safe.

There are two basic types of commercial blasting medium that a hobby gunsmith will use for most work. Glass beads work well for creating a soft matte finish on the metal. They can be used in preparation for bluing, but glass bead blasting is not recommended as preparation for applying spray-on finishes. The reason is that glass is not abrasive, so the beads sort of beat the metal rather than cutting it. This creates a smoother, softer finish, but one that lacks the "tooth" or gripping edges that are desirable for a good bond with spray-on finishes.

Where bead blasting works well is when the metal will not be finished. For example, I have a muzzleloader in stainless steel that has a very shiny barrel. I like the stainless steel look on the gun, so the answer was to bead blast the finish to a less-reflective matte look.

I also use this softer look on stainless steel parts of the gun that may contrast with a spray-on finish. For example, bead blasting a screw head that will be installed in conjunction with a spray-on finish creates a custom look. I bead blasted the hammer on my 1911 build from chapter 10 for a softer look.

By varying the "grit" or size of the beads, you can control how the finish looks. Bead blasting works best if the piece is polished prior to blasting.

The other commonly used blasting material is aluminum oxide. This is a "sand" of sorts, but a very abrasive one. It can be used for cleaning up old, rusty, and pitted guns. It will remove bluing or old finishes including paint, and will create a foundation for many other finishes like Parkerizing or spray-on coatings. Aluminum oxide can even be used to create a more aggressive looking matte finish on stainless steel.

Aluminum oxide is available in a wide selection of "grits," but the gunsmith will usually use those ranging from #60 to #220. The lower the number, the larger the abrasive and the more aggressively it cuts.

One example of using this medium is when I was reclaiming an old shotgun that had seen a very rough life. It was a barn gun for some farmer, which meant it was stuck in a corner, covered with splatters of cow dung for years, which caused rust and shallow pitting on the metal. I degreased the action and taped off the areas I wanted to protect. Then, with #100 aluminum oxide blasting medium in the blasting cabinet I cleaned the rust from the action, paying attention to the pitted areas. I worked the action with the blasting material until I had removed all the rust and as many of the small pits as possible. Then I worked the entire area until I had a consistent and even finish on the metal.

I completed the job with a spray-on finish, which I cured in a toaster oven. This flat black finish looks good on the action and contrasts well with the gray, air-dry spray-on coating I used on the barrel. The result is a pretty cool looking "truck gun" to carry during hunting season.

With a blasting cabinet, an air compressor, a variety of blasting medium, and a creative mind, a hobby gunsmith is unlimited in the looks created for finished guns.

A tabletop blasting cabinet will handle smaller pieces.

Aluminum oxide on the left and glass beads on the right. Notice the differences in the final finish on this barrel. The glass beads produce a finer, smoother finish.

The soft sheen on this hammer is from blasting with glass beads.

COOK THE GREASE OUT

Cerakote recommends baking metal parts for an hour at 300 degrees to "gas out" any solvent or oil. Non-metal parts should be done at a lower temp, around 150 degrees.

▲ A PID screen showing temperature for "gas out."

If I am working on a gun build and I have all the parts broken down and well degreased, I don't usually do the full gas out. I'll put the parts in for fifteen or twenty minutes to make sure no degreaser is hanging around any nook or crannies, rather than the full hour.

▲ Note the grease bubbling out of the scope-mount hole on this rifle during the gasout process.

On an existing gun (not a build) or if any parts are still assembled the full gas out process makes a lot of sense. When Jamey Majoros did Mike Brookman's shotgun shown in the photos he had some parts that were still assembled and he had to run the gas out process multiple times to get them to stop leaking. I can't remember why he didn't take them apart for more degreasing, but there was a good reason.

RACK THEM UP

Note the sidebar on tools I made for a Remington 700 barrel and action. For any other parts, you will need to get creative with some wire or hooks. The key is to hold the part while you coat it and while it's baking. I have a bunch of wire hooks I have made and if none of them work, I make another. There is usually a hole someplace in the part to put the wire through. Do not depend only on tape to hold the hook in place, as it will fail under heat.

SPRAYING IT DOWN

I have a small shop and do not have a designated spraying area. At least not yet. I have agreed to buy a used spray booth with an evacuation fan. The problem is that it is 500 miles away and I didn't have time to get it before this book's deadline.

▲ Spraying a 1911 slide. Note the painter's drop cloth protecting the work bench.

For now, I cover up with drop cloths designed for painters. These plastic sheets are inexpensive so they work for one-time use for a hobby gunsmith who is not doing this every day. Another approach is to hang the sheets from the ceiling to make a small, isolated paint booth. The trouble with working in the shop without an evacuation fan is that the air becomes filled with the atomized paint.

The folks who make the products hate it if you call it paint, but that's what it is. Specialized paint. The dictionary defines paint as, *A colored substance that is spread over a surface and dries to leave a thin decorative or protective coating.* I think that covers gun coatings pretty well.

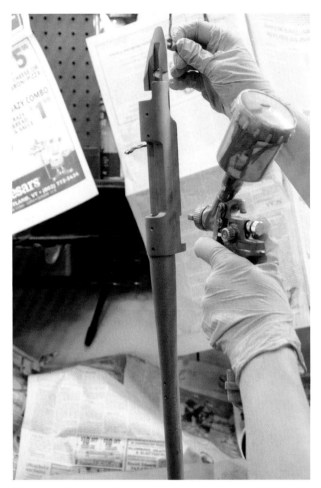

▲ This is DuraCoat, which is an air-dry product. I would just spray, then let the part hang overnight as the air cleared.

In the old days before I had an oven and was just doing air dry, I would time the work for the end of the day. I would just leave it all overnight and the air would clear by morning. Now as I use increasingly more oven-cure

▲ Mike Brookman spraying a rifle action outside on a warm winter day.

products and find I am still working in the shop after spraying, the bad air is a growing problem.

If you can have a designated area to spray away from the work area of the shop, that's best. It's even better if you have a high-volume fan or a paint booth to evacuate the fouled air.

In good weather I often spray outdoors. I have a couple of metal shepherd's crooks sold in lawn and garden departments and used to hold hanging flower pots. I stick them in the ground outside my shop, preferably in the shade, and do the spraying there. I do not let the parts hang outdoors, too many bugs. I bring them inside to flash off or hang dry. This process is less than ideal, but it keeps the mess to a minimum and the air in my shop healthy. Of course, rainy days and wintertime are a problem. If it's not too cold, it works ok if you warm the part a little then step outside to do the spraying and be back inside in just a few minutes. In the photo here, Mike Brookman is spraying a rifle action on a winter day. The total time outside was probably well under five minutes.

Like I keep saying, a hobby gunsmith has to be good at improvising.

▲ Use a respirator, gloves, and eye protection when spraying coatings.

Make a few practice runs on a piece of cardboard with the spray gun or rattle can so you will know how to get the best results. With a spray gun or air brush, adjust to the recommended pressure and spraying distance for the product you are using. It may take a bit of experimenting with the mix of air and paint to get it right. You want a nice, even, thin coating. Use too much liquid and it will look like paint, not a gun finish. It will also be subject to runs, which means you will have to wash it off and start over. If you have too much air and not enough coating, or you are too far from the piece being coated, the atomized paint can partially dry before it coats the metal. This results in a rough, matte finish look that is not durable. So, practice, practice, practice, then spray your gun.

GONE IN A FLASH

Most of the oven-cured products require a little hang time to flash off some of the chemicals before you put the coated piece in the oven. The key is to hang them free from touching anything. One little bump or brush and you will have to do it all over again.

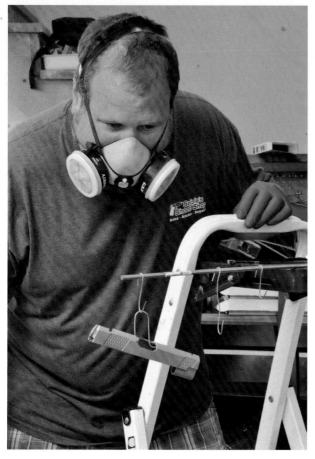

▲ Mike Brookman checks a 1911 slide while it is flashing off. Note the improvised holders.

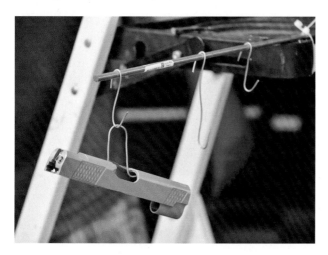

▲ A 1911 frame flashing off.

A word on that. Always keep a bucket with solvent ready for goof-ups. You will have a few, so use the recommended solvent and remove the defective spray coating. Most products recommend that you blast again after washing off with the solvent. I'll confess, I rarely do and I have had fine results. I would never disagree with the people who make the product, I'm just saying I have cut that corner and had a decent result. That choice is up to you. When in doubt, blast again.

COOKING

For small parts, a convection toaster oven works pretty well. I added an oven thermometer so I have better control over the heat. I also have some magnetic hooks that stick to the top and work well for hanging parts. I got the hooks from Robert Lewis Gun Company. If you are going to oven-cure a rifle barrel or similar part, you will need a tall oven. The commercial ovens are horribly expensive, so I built one, which was an adventure. See the sidebar on that project.

▲ These are 1911 parts curing in a convection toaster oven. The rack was later replaced with magnetic hooks.

FINAL

Let the parts cool. With most oven-cures, you can start putting the gun back together as soon as the parts are cool enough to handle. With air-dry, not so much. They need a few days to toughen up. Sometimes they even need a week or more, particularly if you are going to clamp the piece in a barrel vise or action wrench.

Regardless of the type of coating used, before clamping any part in a wrench or vise, protect the coating. I used brown wrapping paper for years with good results. Recently, I read about using the paper tape designed for sheetrock seams. I tried that and it worked very well. It's a bit thicker to protect the finish and just rough enough to minimize slippage.

The key with any wrapping is getting your vise and

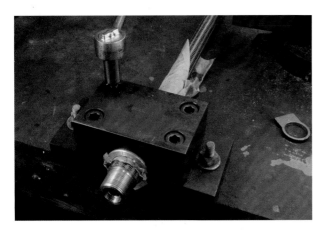

▲ Use brown wrapping paper or drywall tape to protect the finish on the parts when they are clamped in a vise.

wrench tight so there is no slippage. The damage to the finish happens when things slip, so go heavy on clamping the parts. As a reminder, with air-dry products, make sure they are well cured before clamping them tight.

ADVANCED STUFF

As you progress at this, you can add patterns and camo designs.

▲ My custom Glock, which is detailed in chapter 8. Jamey Majoros of Viktor's Legacy Custom Gunsmithing did this one-of-a-kind pattern in Cerakote.

Mike Brookman and Jamey Majoros are both Trekkies. They were holding a conversation that might as well have been in Japanese as far as I was concerned, because I didn't understand a single word. Something about spaceships and cling-ons. I didn't really want to know what that last one was.

The next thing I knew, they had created a stencil in a language they called Klingon with a K, which apparently has nothing to do with what I envisioned a cling-on to be. The message said, "It's a Good Day to Die," which I

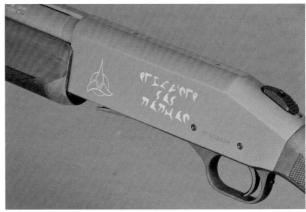

▲ This is Mike Brookman's 3-gun competition shotgun. The Cerakote was done by Jamey Majoros at Viktor's Legacy Gunsmithing. The symbol represents the Klingon Empire. The writing is in the Klingon language and it says, "It's a Good Day to Die."

take is some kind of a Klingon motto. Anyway, they added the Klingon language to the side of Mike's shotgun with Cerakote. As you can see in the photos, it makes Mike's 3-gun competition shotgun pretty unique and interesting, although I have no earthly idea how you pronounce any of the Klingon words. It sounds like a dog choking on a chicken bone to me.

▲ This AR-15 has some interesting pattern work by Jamey Majoros. *Photo by Viktor's Legacy Custom Gunsmithing*

I have done some freehand camo using ferns, leaves, and other products to create patterns. It's the same technique you have seen in every movie ever made about SEAL Team snipers. Also, check out the chapter in this book on building a .308 tactical rifle for a cool idea on creating a snakeskin look.

"The Green Goblin," chapter 4, has information on

▲ This is my snake gun. The pattern is easy to do with a laundry bag and DuraCoat.

spray finishes, although much of it is about what not to do, as that rifle was one of my first spray coating projects.

"Pimp My Pump," chapter 6, is another older project chapter that has a bunch of information on DuraCoat and references some mistakes I made and how to avoid them.

The 1911 build in chapter 10 shows Cerakote on one handgun and DuraBake on the other. The photos illustrate how mixing and matching colors can create a look.

The multiple rifle build sidebars that are scattered through the rifle building section explain the coatings used and have accompanying photos to show how they look.

The chapter on the Savage switch-barrel rifle describes the different coatings I used to color-code the barrels. It has photos to show how each one turned out.

For a peek at an artist at work, check out the chapter on pimping out a Glock pistol for information on how Jamey Majoros created a unique pattern on my pistol. In fact, there are little bits and pieces all through this book about spray-on coatings.

I suppose my point is simple enough, if I can learn to do spray-on gun coatings, anybody can.

One of the great things about spray-on coatings is that the sky is the limit. You artistic types can do some wonderful things with these coatings and a good imagination. It just comes down to how creative you are.

Me?

I am no good with sticky substances and it took me years to learn how to do this right. Painting of any kind is really not my thing. When it's time to paint inside my house, I go fishing while my wife paints. It's just better that way.

A HOT TIME IN THE OLD SHOP TONIGHT
The long strange journey of building an oven for spray-on gun coatings.

Many of the popular spray-on coatings require an oven cure. This can present a daunting problem for most hobby gunsmiths. Handguns, small parts and even rifle receivers can be cooked in an inexpensive toaster oven. Get the

▲ My oven for curing spray-on coatings.

biggest one you can find, but make sure it has a convection feature. That simply means there is a fan to circulate the air while it's baking to prevent hot spots. The temperature controls are not very reliable, at least on mine, so I also bought an oven thermometer to fit inside. I use magnetic hooks that stick on the top of the metal oven to hang my parts. The best thing is these ovens are inexpensive. Just get the biggest one you can find.

Barrels or barreled actions are another issue. They require a tall oven. I started looking at the commercial ovens and the price tags sent me into depression. Even the entry level ovens are thousands of dollars. That's fine if you are doing commercial rifle coating and making a lot of money, but, for a hobby guy, it's out of reach. So, I set out to build my own oven. I learned a lot of things along the way and suffered through a lot of frustration, but, in the end, I have a viable oven that I have used to finish a bunch of guns with outstanding results.

A BOX TO PUT IT IN
The cabinet itself is the first step. I looked at some on-line information about building an oven and some guys were suggesting using an old locker. I looked at a few, but they

were too small for any practical application, which told me that like a lot of people posting on the web, those guys were full of crap. I doubt they ever created anything other than offensive body odor.

A few other guys, the ones who actually posted photos, were using some of the cheap gun safes sold by the discount chain stores. Because it's closest, I went to our local "farm supply" chain store. (The names have been changed here to prevent my being sued.) They had a safe, exactly the one I was looking for. It took me half an hour to locate somebody who worked there to ask them if they would get one out of inventory for me.

"All we got is that floor model, take it or leave it," the person (I still have no idea if it was a man or a woman) who finally showed up told me rudely.

"We can't find the key, so you got to contact the company to send you a new one."

Then I noticed the door was bent and didn't close properly.

"So, no key and the safe is damaged in addition to being the scratched-up floor model? Can you discount the price?"

"Nope," was the answer as the employee turned his or her back and walked to the door while digging a cigarette out of a shirt pocket.

I found another safe, the same brand and model, at a local mart (now closed), marked on sale. As usual, the gun stuff was at the back of the giant store and as I was just looking, I didn't have a cart. I wrestled the heavy beast to the checkout, where a girl with purple hair, no teeth, and enough metal in her face that she looked like an extra from a Mad Max movie rang it up at the retail price.

"That's wrong," I said as politely as I could manage as I stood there dripping sweat on everything. "It's on sale."

"No, it's not."

"Yes. It is. There was a big red tag that said it was on sale."

"No, it's not."

This went on for a while and after ten or fifteen minutes, I concluded that "no, it's not" was her entire vocabulary. So I asked for the manager.

When she finally showed up after another twenty minutes, they must have been sisters, because all she could say were the same three words. So, at my insistence, we left the gun safe in the middle of the aisle, ignored the long line of people waiting to check out at the only register open and we walked all the way to the back of the store. I showed the "manager," who I guess got the position because she still had a few teeth, the big red tag showing the sale price and listing the name and model of the gun safe.

"Oh, that was last week," she said.

"Well, there is no date listed, the tag is still here and by state law you must honor this price."

"No, we don't."

That's when I just turned and walked out of the store.

I figured it was much cheaper in the long run to buy it someplace else than to choke a store manager.

I have no idea who got to carry the safe to the back of the store again. I hope it was the meth-skinny, toothless guy with the facial prison tattoos who followed me to the door trying to look all bad in his "Loss Prevention" shirt.

I like to keep my money in my small, dying community, but this is why people buy online.

An hour later, I found the same safe at another discount sporting goods store for twenty bucks more than the "sale" price, but still lower than the retail price. I bought that one, put it in my truck, and headed home, vowing to never go shopping in public again.

Insulation is the key to making any oven work. I initially lined the inside with some heat-resistant, reflective insulation that the guy at the big-chain home supply store said was "just what I need."

It wasn't.

I could not get the heat high enough inside the oven. By coincidence, I was talking with Vermont gunsmith Dennis Amsden and he told me he had built an oven out of the same gun safe. He lined his with Roxul insulation. I tried to find some locally, but had little luck at any of the building supply stores. I called the Roxul Company and was promised that, if I emailed the little Millennial who said he was their PR director but didn't want to talk on the phone, he would get right back to me. I emailed several times and I am still waiting.

So, I bought a hot water heater blanket and fitted that to the outside of the gun safe with duct tape. It worked, but the oven looked like a week-old gas station burrito. It was not pretty and not photogenic, but it worked—sort of. It still didn't hold heat as well as I liked. I put stove gasket on the door to seal when it's shut. That was like peeing in the Atlantic and expecting a temperature change.

For heat, I had planned to use an old hot plate that my grandmother had given me when I left for my first attempt at college in '73. That was *1973*, smart-ass! I think it was an antique even then. They built them well back in the old days and it still worked, even though it had spent a lot of those years melting lead for bullet casting, rather than cooking meals for a diligent college student. Not quite what Gram had in mind, I am sure.

I cut the plug off the cable to fit it through the hole I drilled in the cabinet. Some fluffy stuff came out of the fabric insulation around the cord. I just fitted the new plug and taped everything back into place, but I was suspicious. I went online and did some research and, yes, it was asbestos. Sorry Gram, it went in the trash.

I bought another hot plate at the local mart, the one without a dental plan. It was the largest single burner I could find, because none of the double-burner models would physically fit in the cabinet. This one is 1,100 watts. It works, but, if I had it to do over I would look for one a little bigger.

Because it's a bad idea to expose the parts to direct heat,

I made off with one of my wife's slotted oven pans. I think it's designed to allow drainage, but the slots work well to allow the heat to pass through. It was a good fit, until later when I installed the Roxul insulation (I am getting to that part); after that it was too big. So, I bent a corner into it and now it fits well. It ain't pretty, but it works and it was cheap. At least until Christmas, when my wife wants to roast a turkey. No telling what it will cost me then.

I set the heater in the bottom of the cabinet and turned it on. I had a thermometer probe inside with an external digital read out. (These are made for grills or meat smokers and are pretty inexpensive.) I could never get the heat up higher than 200 degrees. So, I took the hotplate apart and found it had a safety switch. If the ambient temperature got too high, it shut down. I took that out and hardwired the cord to the heating coil. Now the temperature easily would go to 350 degrees and beyond, but I didn't have any way to control it. So I went back to the big-chain home supply place and bought a dimmer switch that the "expert" working there assured me was just what I needed. I pointed out it was rated for a much lower wattage than my heater, but, he said again, "It's fine." Like a fool, I believed him.

Almost immediately after I plugged it in, the dimmer switch got very hot and started smoking like a teenager hiding behind the bleachers. Then the plastic started to melt and the room filled with odd smelling, eye watering fumes, so I pulled the plug, literally. In the end it saw a total of about 20 seconds of use, so it cost me more than a dollar per second.

I researched a lot of options, including rheostats for power tools that allow you to control the current. Late one night, unable to sleep again, I was surfing the web when I stumbled onto a PID controller. This gizmo uses a thermocouple to measure and manage the temperature. It was relatively inexpensive (less than the 20-second rheostat), so I ordered the PID and the recommended relay.

I went to a local electrical supply store and bought a box to house all the electrical stuff, including an on/off switch. I used my milling machine to make the cuts in the box to house the switch and the PID controller.

The only issue was wiring the damn thing. I tried to understand the instructions for the PID, which clearly were translated from Chinese to Sanskrit to Latin, and finally to English, all by somebody who spoke none of those languages. I was baffled, so I called an electrician buddy who was also baffled. Together we sort of figured out the schematic and wired it as instructed.

It didn't work, of course, and my electrician "buddy" suddenly remembered he had to be someplace else.

I got the bright idea I could program in offsets to compensate for the damn thing not working. That really didn't work and I only wasted forty or fifty hours trying.

It baffled me to the point of obsession. My neighbor is an electrical engineer who works with robotics and I am sure he could make it work, but he didn't answer his phone or door. I figured he was hiding from me, until his wife showed up and told me he was off on vacation for two weeks. Still, I swear I saw him peeking through the drapes. At the rate I was beating my head on the wall, I would need a different shaped hat pretty soon.

Finally, I called my brother-in-law who does some voodoo job that requires him to wear a Tyvek suit with a hood, fancy goggles and enter his work space through air locks. He works with some ultra-high-end electronics, something about making machines that make the machines that make computers. He tried to explain, but I am thinking this is how we end up with Cyberdyne Systems. He lost me for good once he starting talking about flooding coatings that are a millionth of a millionth of an inch thick. Or maybe he was talking about his car, I really don't know. It was very confusing and I stopped listening after a few minutes.

I finally got him to stop long enough to ask him if he had wired a PID.

"You mean today?"

"Well, no, I mean ever."

"Oh yeah, I do them all the time."

"I need some help."

"Okay, so, take a photo of that little paper on the top and send it to me."

I did and about ten minutes later my phone dinged. There was a drawing on how to wire the PID. I followed it and the problem was solved.

Well, almost. It still didn't give me the right temperature. So at my brother-in-law's suggestion, I put the thermocouple in boiling water. Then I used the offset to adjust to 211.5 degrees, which is the boiling point for water at my shop's elevation.

After that, everything worked fine, which scared the hell out of me. Mostly because it was such an unusual situation.

I drilled some holes in each side of the cabinet about two inches from the top, spaced evenly. I fitted three 3/16 threaded rods through, clamping them with fender washers and nuts on the outside of the wall for hanging parts. Later, after I changed the insulation (be patient, I told you I'll get to that part), I drilled them again, two inches lower. That's the trouble with prototype engineering, often the results are less than pretty.

The oven was a poster boy for redneck engineering but it worked. Except I still had trouble hitting the temps I needed and as it aged, it looked more and more like a decaying dumpster diaper.

My faith in shopping locally was restored when I stopped into a local home supply store and was directed to a guy in a back office. He'd never heard of Roxul, but he did a tremendous amount of research and found some for me. I had to order an entire bag, twice what I needed, but it worked out fine. I used the 1.25-inch-thick boards that were 2X4 feet. I installed them with a press fit on all sides except the door, where I glued it on with some high-temperature contact cement.

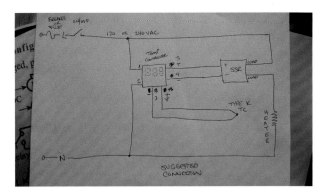

▲ The drawing that my brother-in-law sent me.

With some regret, I removed the hot water heater blanket and trashed it. Like an ugly girlfriend, I just didn't want it to be seen in public. You will note that the photos in this book reflect that.

I removed the locking mechanism from the door so the insulation would fit and replaced it with two four-inch barrel-bolt fasteners, one near the top and one near the bottom. These work much better at keeping the door sealed.

The final issue was the fan. Again, I spent a lot of time online and browsing the local electrical supply stores. About one hundred man-hours into it, a helpful clerk sent me to a refrigeration supply shop I had no idea existed in the small town where I shop.

"It's just around the corner, in this same building," the guy said.

I will note it was 22 below zero that day, with a wind chill that would make an Eskimo beg for mercy and it was a very big building. By the time I found the store, I was having trouble talking in complete sentences.

The kid behind the counter sold me a small fan that he assured me was for high temperature. It was perfect. I mounted it using four quarter-inch threaded rods and wired it to the start switch. It was so quiet that I stuck my hand in front to make sure it was working and the fan hit my thumb, causing a huge and painful blood blister.

I coated a barrel with Brownells Teflon/Moly Gun Finish. This product comes in a rattle can, so it's convenient to use. It bakes at 325 degrees, which is hotter than Cerakote or DuraBake require, so I thought it would be a good test for the oven. (I have since discovered that the rattle can option for this product has been discontinued.)

I went to eat lunch while the oven baked my rifle barrel.

I don't hear all that well, even with my high-dollar hearing aids. Too many years of shooting and loud machines I guess, but I could hear my oven before I even opened the door to the shop. My quiet little fan was getting pretty belligerent and the entire shop was filled with an ear-splitting howl that anybody who has been around machines recognizes as a failing bearing. The oven was vibrating as the fan squealed out its death cry.

I called the company who made the "high-temperature"

fan. The very nice lady on the phone asked me a lot of questions. When I got to the 325-degree temperature she stopped me and said, "Oh my, that's way too hot, it will burn the grease out of the bearings on that fan."

No kidding lady, I figured that one out all on my own.

Apparently "high temperature" means 200 degrees or less. So, it's okay for a sauna, but not much use in an oven.

It was back to the drawing board. After a lot of frustrating research, I concluded that nobody made a fan that would take the heat of being mounted inside the oven. Clearly, the answer was to use a fan inside and powered by a motor mounted on the outside of the oven where it's a bit cooler.

On Jim Majoros' advice, I ordered a 1/100 horsepower 110V motor and a three-inch metal fan from an online supplier called Zoro. Installing them was another adventure, as it required drilling more holes and removing and replacing a section of insulation. The shaft was too short, so I used my lathe to make a coupler and an extension. It took some innovative engineering, but, in the end, it's working. The motor is mounted outside the oven and I left an air gap so it will stay cool. The fan is not shielded, but kind of hangs out in space. As I am the only one using the oven, it's staying that way. If I had other people to worry about, I would probably build a cage to protect it.

(The first time I used the oven a hanger failed and a freshly coated barrel fell on the fan, damaging both. Clearly I should have made a cage.)

After that long, strange trip, I finally have a working oven for spray-on, oven-cure coatings. It's even "convection," with the fan circulating the air to prevent hot spots.

In the end, I have more time into this oven than any other project in this book.

Crazy, right?

▲ This is the fan motor mounted on the outside of the oven.

So here in a nutshell is a recap on how to do it without all the aggravation.

Buy the cabinet. The "gun safe" I bought has these dimensions: External height 55 inches. External width 21

▲ Making a coupler to extend the fan shaft for the oven.

▲ Inside the oven, showing the insulation and the fan.

▲ I modified this electrical box to hold the PID controller, switch and all the wiring.

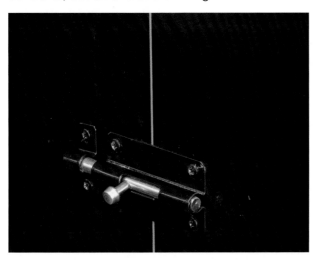

▲ These bolts work well to keep the door closed on the oven. One on top, another on the bottom.

inches. External depth 16 inches. I would never trust it to safeguard my firearms but it makes a decent cabinet for this oven build.

Insulate it with Roxul insulation, preferably the foil lined type. That will protect the insulation and prevent loose fibers from floating around. I did not use the foil lined and I wish I had.

Change the door locks to something that will lock tightly closed top and bottom. The four-inch barrel-bolt fasteners I used worked fine.

A 1,200 watt hot plate will make a good heat source, but you must remove the safety that shuts it off when ambient temperature is too high. I have also heard about using one or two electric charcoal lighters. Shield the heating unit somehow so the parts are not exposed to direct heat.

Get a PID controller with the relay and thermocouple. Look for one with a good wiring diagram. Wiring one is actually simple, so when they start making it complicated and adding jumper wires, stop. Back up and find the simple route.

I used a heavy duty extension cord and cut it in half for the outside wiring. Make sure you have an on/off switch. I used a basic metal electrical box to house the controls and wiring. I made the cuts I needed on my milling machine, but you could do them with a Dremel with a cutting wheel.

Install a fan to keep the air circulating. Make sure you mount the motor outside so it doesn't cook the bearings and cost you a bunch of money to find out about yet another thing that doesn't work.

That's it, pretty simple.

Unless you do it my way.

Then it sucks.

Chapter 6
PIMP MY PUMP

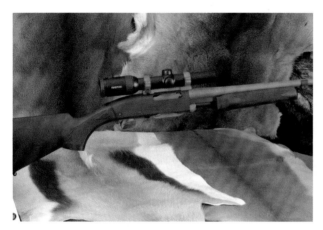

▲ The "Pimped Pump."

▲ Thad Stevens with a Utah mountain lion shot with the pimped .30-30.

One of the first things I did after graduating high school and starting work fulltime was to begin saving for a new deer rifle. I thought I was in hog heaven that summer, twisting wrenches for a car and motorcycle dealer for the big money of two dollars an hour. It took most of the summer to scratch up enough, but before I headed to college in the fall, I bought a new Remington Model 760 pump action rifle in .30-06. As I recall, it was on sale at K-Mart for $124.95, or about two weeks' worth of take-home pay!

It was my first dedicated, straight-up deer rifle and for years it remained my favorite. That rifle and I had some adventures over the decades, including a few I won't tell you about . . . ever!

When I was writing my book *Gunsmithing Made Easy* some years ago, I planned to use that 760 as my "donor

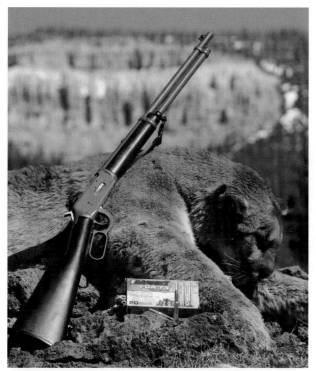

rifle" for the chapter called "Pimp My Rifle." I got as far as taking it out to the shop, but I couldn't do it. Every scratch, every ding, every worn spot had a memory. This rifle might look like a road kill, but it comes by that patina honestly. I couldn't rob my own memories by turning it into something it wasn't meant to be, so I put it back in the vault and went shopping for another Remington pump action rifle to use.

Normally they are easy to find here in Vermont, but a good economy is bad for the used-gun market. Every gun shop I visited told the same story: "Nobody is getting rid of guns this year. Usually we see a bunch just before Christmas and again at tax time, but I guess people don't need the money right now." (This was during the Bush 43 years.)

My problem was that I had a deadline, so in the end I bought a pathetic, abused Model 94 Winchester for the project. The result is a very cool .30-30 rifle that has been on a few adventures of its own, including taking two large mountain lions in Utah. One was mine and the other was my buddy Thad Stevens's, who at the time was the ballistics guru for Barnes bullets.

FIND A DONOR AND STRIP IT DOWN

Still, the Remington pump action is my favorite Northeastern deer rifle and the idea of a project gun stayed in my mind. One day when I wasn't really looking,

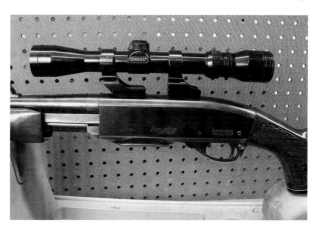

▲ The donor rifle.

I found my rifle. I stopped at Dattilio's Gun Shop in South Burlington, Vermont, and Jimmy Dattilio had a beat-up, sad-looking Model 760 cowering on the shelf and softly whimpering my name.

It was a gun only a gunsmith could love. The stock was cracked, the metal rusty and the scope cloudy. But the bore looked good and the price was reasonable, so that rifle got to ride home in my truck that day. I put it in the vault, got busy and forgot it for nearly a year, until the constant nagging every time I entered the vault became too much

▲ The author's lion.

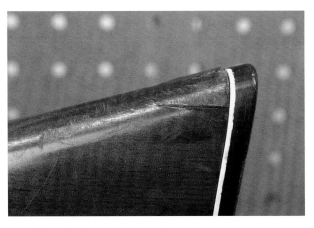

▲ The stock was cracked

▲ Rusted!

to take. Each time I spotted it on the rack it started in on me: "Hey, what about me? You promised a makeover!" So, I finally took it out to the shop and here's what happened.

The first thing was to remove the scope and the goofy see-through mount. I cleaned about two decade's worth of grime and grease from the scope lenses, which made them considerably less opaque. I put it on a shelf with a mental note to give it to some kid with a new rifle and no money.

I took the gun completely apart, which caused all kinds of problems. Everything with threads was rusty. I had a

▲ All the parts and pieces ready to go back together.

heck of a time getting the buttstock off, but after soaking the bolt with penetrating oil for several days, I finally succeeded. The forend was rusted to the metal action bar assembly and I had to use a hammer to pound them apart.

THE RIGHT TOOL MAKES A DIFFERENCE

I had similar luck with the action tube that serves to hold the barrel to the receiver. There are four holes on this part, two opposing two, which are designed to accept a punch

▲ Showing the Menck tool in use.

▲ The Menck tool.

or rod to turn the action tube. Or at least that's how it's normally done. I bent or broke several of each before giving up on that idea. The other problem is that this method will damage the holes if the tube is really stuck and this one was. You can file the burrs and get the tube back into service, but the holes will be oblong and look terrible.

As always, the key is to have the right tool for the job. Several calls to my "I am in trouble" gunsmithing posse turned up a phone number for a guy named Tom Menck who made a wrench to remove the tube and a phone call had one on the way. This forked-shaped tool fits over the action tube, then a pin is inserted through it and through two of the holes in the action tube. The wrench is much stronger than any punch and I could put some muscle behind it. In minutes I had the gun apart.

The problem is that Menck recently retired and this tool is no longer available. If you can find one used, you better grab it up. It's one of those tools you don't use all that often, but when you need it you need it badly.

I have included a photo of the tool for those of you who want to make one.

Clearly, I was not the first guy to try to take this gun apart. Like most of these older rifles I encounter, the holes were already elongated and the edges raised. I filed the burrs in all of the holes flush and polished the action tube smooth. The holes were still slightly egg-shaped, but that couldn't be helped.

CLEAN AND MODIFY

I removed the sights, took the trigger assembly apart and reduced everything to the smallest parts I could. All the metal went into the degreasing tank to soak for a few days. (This was well before I discovered using an ultrasonic cleaner.)

I wanted to cut off the barrel for two reasons. First was accuracy. Almost any of the older Remington pumps I have seen have some crown damage, either from cleaning rods or carrying the gun muzzle down in a collection of

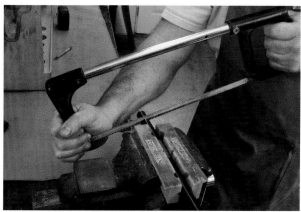

▲ Cutting off the barrel.

mud and gravel on the truck floor. The second reason was to have something unique. Like most 760 rifles, this one had a 22-inch barrel. The Carbine model has an 18.5-inch barrel and I wanted something in between. So, I marked it just past 20 inches with a felt-tipped marker, clamped the barrel in a soft-jawed vise and started hacking with a hacksaw.

I squared the face with a file and finished with a piloted 90-degree facing tool. I followed with an 11-degree crown cutting tool. See more on this in the section on crowning in chapter 7, "This and That."

I had no plans to have sights on this rifle, so I filled in the holes from the sight screws. Check out the sidebar on the options for doing that.

FILLING SCREW HOLES

With the almost universal use of optical sights on hunting rifles today, it seems a bit silly to include open sights on a rifle. I can't recall the last time I saw an experienced hunter in the woods with a rifle using the factory installed open sights. I'll admit that a front sight is handy for keeping a rifle from slipping when leaning it against a tree, but other than that, the factory installed sights are pretty much a waste of money. When making over a hunting rifle, I almost always remove them.

Use blue Loctite with screws if you plan to remove them at a later date.

The problem is that the threaded screw holes remain. There are a few ways to deal with them. The simplest is to put in a plug screw; fill the gaps with bedding compound and sand them smooth. Although they will show with many finishes, if you match the texture with the surrounding metal, most spray-on finishes will cover them up reasonably well.

If you simply must have metal in the void, a welder who knows his stuff can fill the holes. There are TIG welders that can accomplish good results without heating the barrel too hot. If you are not an accomplished welder or are not sure the other guy is, use caution. Years ago I was working in a machine shop and a guy claiming to be a gunsmith asked me to fill a front sight screw hole with weld. I told him I didn't have the right equipment, but he insisted that I do it anyway. I used an acetylene torch to do the job, but, in heating the barrel, it raised scale inside the bore (just as I told him it would). I was sure it ruined the gun, but he said the customer was happy.

I refused to do the next one he brought in. There just are not that many dumb customers and I didn't want to tempt the odds too much. If you decide to use this approach, at the very least coat the bore with an anti-scaling compound before starting. This will prevent scaling, pitting and decarb loss, all of which can cause dimension changes and are bad for a rifle bore.

Using a cut-off wheel on a Dremel to cut filler screws.

Peening the screws.

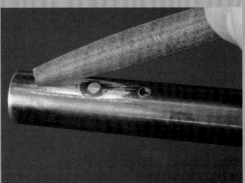

Filing the screws.

I do not recommend using a torch. A good TIG welder can fill the hole without adding a lot of unnecessary heat. However, any welding adds heat and is not really the best idea for a rifle barrel.

Jim Majoros at Viktor's Legacy Gunsmithing says, "I hate to weld on a barrel for the simple reason that it induces stress into the barrel and depending on how many spots you weld, it could warp the barrel as well. The best way is to just put in plug screws and clock them so the slots are running the same way. Use a dab of blue Loctite so you can take them back out if you want to remount the sight in the future."

If not peened, the screws will show.

Another traditional way is to peen a screw to fill the hole. Start by beveling the screw hole at the top. The easiest way to do this is to just kiss the holes with a drill bit sized slightly larger than the outside diameter of the threads. Make sure to do this with a drill press or mill and set the stop so that the drill barely kisses the metal and can go no further. If you attempt to do it by hand, you risk the drill catching and going too deep.

Use an annealed screw. These can be purchased or made by heating the screws red hot and letting them cool. Clean the threads in the rifle and on the screws with degreaser, coat the screws with thread-locking red Loctite #271 and turn them in tight.

Cut the screws off close to the barrel. I use a cutting wheel on a Dremel tool for this, rather than a hacksaw. That's because the cutting wheel is thinner and easier to get close to the barrel without hitting and marring the surface. A hacksaw will do the job as well, it just might leave a longer stub.

File the screws down close to the barrel, leaving about .030 inch. Use a small ballpeen hammer to carefully peen the screw with light taps to flatten it and meld the metal into the bevel at the top of the screw hole. Be extremely careful not to hit the barrel, as it will leave a permanent mark on the metal.

When filled with DuraFil and covered with a spray-on coating, they are not very noticeable.

Make sure that the bevel is completely and tightly filled. File the excess until it's as close to the barrel surface as possible. Sand first with a rubber block and then with a strip, using a shoe-shine motion to follow the contour of the barrel. If you did it right, the screw holes should disappear. This type of repair should not show with a spray-on finish, but if you elect to blue the gun, the difference in the steel of the barrel or action and the screws might show up as a different hue in the bluing.

Because I use primarily spray-on finishes, I use another approach that I find much easier and that has less potential for dinging the metal on the gun with a stray hammer blow. Degrease everything, Loctite the screws and snug them tight. Then cut them off. Next, file and sand until the screw stubs are flush and the same contour as the surface. There will be a ring around the screw where the threads show. Fill that with DuraFil surface filler made by Lauer Custom Weaponry, the makers of DuraCoat spray-on gun finish. This product fills in any dents, dings, scratches, and other imperfections on a metal surface.

DuraFil is easy to use. Simply mix it according to instructions and spray it on. An airbrush is the easiest, but any paint sprayer will work fine. Once it dries, in about four hours, sand it off. The filled areas will take on a lighter color as you sand, which tells you that the void is filled. If the DuraFil fails to change color, you are not hitting it with the sandpaper because it is below the surface of the metal. Spray another coat and sand again. It will probably take at least two applications to fill the screw threads.

DuraFil works only if you are going to use a spray-on finish rather than bluing and even then it may show a little if you look very closely.

COLOR COORDINATE

I degreased all the metal parts that I planned to refinish with a solvent that will flash off without leaving any residue. Then I sandblasted the parts using #100-grit aluminum oxide blasting material at 80 psi for a deep, rough, matte finish to the metal.

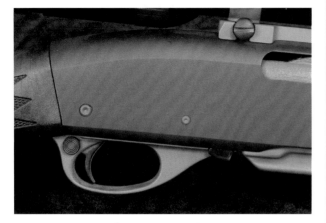

▲ Note the contrasting colors.

Rather than my first plan of doing the rifle all in Flat Black, I decided to add a little class with a two-tone color scheme. I used DuraCoat, which is easy to apply with a spray gun or air brush and comes in a wide selection of colors. The best part for a hobby gunsmith is that DuraCoat will air dry. Bake-on finishes are fine, if you have a big enough oven. At the time, my shop had only a large toaster oven for rifle actions or handguns, but it wasn't big enough to hold a barrel, so I liked the air-dry aspect of DuraCoat.

▲ The Remington Model 760 receiver after sandblasting.

◀ Using two contrasting colors gave this gun a unique look while still being subdued enough to use for hunting without drawing the game's attention.

There is a lot of territorial bickering on the internet and in gun guy circles about which coating is the best, the strongest and the longest lasting. To be honest, some of the bake-on coatings do seem to stand up to wear a little better than DuraCoat. That said, DuraCoat has worked fine for me on a lot of guns and the idea of air drying is a pretty big deal for a hobby gunsmith lacking an oven large enough for a rifle barrel. Are there tougher coatings? Probably, including, I suspect, their own DuraBake, but DuraCoat is a very good option for a hobby gunsmith.

I covered the action, the action tube, and the action bars all in Flat Black. I also did the windage adjustment screws for the scope mount, the Williams front swivel band and the safety in Flat Black. I did the barrel, which includes the barrel lug visible in front of the action, in a flat gray called Wolf Gray. I also did the scope mount rings and base, the ejection port cover, the magazine, the trigger housing, and the cross pins that hold the trigger group in the action all in gray. The contrasting colors look great, but are still muted and non-reflective flat because, after all, this is a serious hunting rifle.

DURACOAT MISTAKES

Let's talk a little here about applying DuraCoat from the perspective of more than a decade down the road from this project.

As I often state, I am not good with sticky substances and this was one of my early attempts at using any spray-on finish. At that time, I had done a few other rifles with DuraCoat and as I am inclined to do, I put it on way too thick. That resulted in runs and a painted look to the rifle. I was trying to avoid that with this gun and went too far the other way.

Give me a break, it's a learning process!

I turned the paint way down on the spray gun and I ended up with a very flat-looking finish. When talking with Steve Lauer, the owner of DuraCoat, he told me that because

The new sling swivel attachment, blasted and ready for coating, next to an old attachment.

I had the paint too low and the air too high it was actually drying a bit before it hit the surface to be coated. He told me that's why I'd gotten that flat look. He also told me that it would probably not be as durable as if I had done the application correctly. Now, several years later, I can see he was right.

This has become a favorite rifle for hunting deer here in the Northeast. I love to track deer in the snow and I have carried this rifle a lot of miles. That shows, as I have worn the finish off on all the edges. Of course, any finish will wear if you carry a gun enough but, just as Steve predicted, this happened a little faster than expected. So, the gun will be refinished again soon and, yes, I will be using DuraCoat again. The upside is that I have learned from my mistakes and have done many guns with DuraCoat in the years since. This time I'll get it right.

The moral of the story is two-fold. There is a right way and a wrong way to do most things. Always strive to learn that right way, but understand that it's a learning process and you will make mistakes. That's how you learn. This gun has survived more than a decade of hunting seasons and still looks pretty good. I think the only one bothered by the wear is me. Certainly no deer I have ever shot complained.

In the end, I'll just recoat the rifle, not because it really needs it, but because mistakes are meant to be fixed.

Check out chapter 5 in this book on spray coatings for firearms. It goes into much greater detail about the preparation and application of spray finishes.

SHAKE RATTLE AND ROLL

One complaint I hear often about the Remington pump rifles is that they rattle. That's true, but it's because they have a problem. There is a rubber O-ring that fits in a groove on the end of the action tube. This keeps the action bar assembly centered on the action tube and also keeps things tight. That O-ring is missing on many of the older guns and that's why they rattle. This gun was no exception, so I repaired it with a new O-ring ordered from Remington.

▲ A new O-ring shown with the parts. Note the groove for the O-ring.

It is simple enough, once the gun is disassembled, to install the O-ring on the action tube. Make sure that the inside of the action tube is smooth, clean, and free of burrs or defects. If it's not, it should be replaced.

▲ Polishing the outside of the action tube on a Remington 760.

I cleaned and polished the inside of the tube. I started with a 12 gauge bronze brush with plenty of CLP. Then I finished with steel wool and CLP on the end of a muzzle-loader cleaning rod to smooth it up a bit. Make sure to use some silicon grease for lubrication on the O-ring,

as running it dry will cause it to fail again. Many petroleum-based lubricants can also damage the rubber, so make sure you use a safe, long-lasting lubricant.

STOCKS AND OPTICS

I looked at several options for the stock. I really like the looks of the Ram-Line Synthetic stock. It has a low comb that works very well with iron sights and acceptably well with a scope, making it a great all-around compromise stock. In fact, it's the stock on my custom 7600 .338-06. That gun has a custom modified quick-release scope mount with a flip-up peep sight. The gun can be used with the scope or quickly switched to the peep sight for nasty weather hunting.

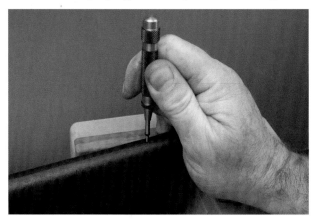

▲ Marking the stock to drill a hole for installing a sling swivel stud.

If I were going to go the route that a lot of hunters in the Northeast do and use a peep sight, I would pick the Ram-Line stock, but this gun was going to be used only with a scope and I wanted a higher comb to help align my eye with the optic. I experimented with several stocks before settling on the Remington synthetic replacement stock, which works great.

▲ This Swarovski scope was expensive, but I believe it's helped more than once when hunting whitetail deer.

I selected the Swarovski Z6 1–6X24 scope for its wide power range, as well as the extremely large field of view. The scope fits in the Leupold low 30mm rings with just enough clearance to move the power ring. This is a woods rifle and this may well be the ultimate scope for fast shooting at running deer when it's set on 1X. With a 6X upper end, the scope can handle precise bullet placement when taking a long shot across a clear-cut. I have used this same scope in 3-gun competition and have hit targets out to 920 yards, which I think ends any argument about 6X being enough magnification for hunting deer in the Northeast, or any other area for that matter.

I have made a few shots with this rifle that have astounded me. The first deer I shot with it gave me a two-second chance at a small part of his neck through a lot of brush. So much brush that, when I stood beside the dead deer, I could barely see the red backpack that I had left back at my stand.

I stood in that spot again a few days before writing this, as I have done every year since and I wonder how I ever pulled it off. Part of it was because I was deep into 3-gun competition then and I was shooting rifles as well as I ever had in my life. Perhaps the bigger reason is that scope. High-quality optics do earn their keep now and then and I honestly think I owe that deer wearing my tag in its ear to the Swarovski.

TRIGGER IMPROVEMENTS

I tuned up the trigger by polishing the engagement surfaces and fine-tuned the return spring tension. These pump rifles can be very accurate, but the triggers often need attention to bring out that accuracy. Mine still has a bit of creep, but it is clean and crisp when it breaks at less than four pounds.

Trigger work is tricky and anytime you start polishing sears, particularly without a proper jig, you risk disaster. Perhaps a much better option would be to install a Timney trigger kit. The trigger group in the 760 and 7600 rifles is similar to the one used in the Remington Model 870 shotgun. Timney's 870 trigger kit will fit in the Remington pump-action rifles.

This rifle has undergone an amazing transformation. From an ugly, misused, and abused rifle, it has become what might well be the ultimate woods rifle. It's fast, accurate, and dependable. With Federal Premium 165-grain Trophy Bonded Tip ammo it shoots groups on demand that measure less than 1 MOA. It's nearly weatherproof and it looks very cool. It still speaks to me when I enter my gun vault and see it on the rack but, rather than nagging, it's bragging.

I can hear it say, "Look at me, I am the ultimate whitetail rifle."

I am proud to think I made that happen.

▲ The Timney Triggers kit for a Remington pump-action shown with trigger group.

▲ The author with a Vermont whitetail taken with the "Pimped Pump."

Chapter 7
THIS AND THAT

A collection of projects and techniques that didn't fit in anyplace else.

#1—CUTTING A NEW CROWN ON A RIFLE BARREL

The last physical influence the rifle has on the bullet occurs at the crown and it can have a huge effect on accuracy. A perfect, concentric crown is imperative to your rifle shooting to its potential.

A poor crown or a damaged crown is often the reason for rifle accuracy problems. This can even happen with a new rifle. I have seen some factory guns with horrible crowns. One .45-70 sent to me to test for a magazine article had a huge dent in the crown that had pushed a big wedge of metal into the bore. It would gouge the side of the exiting bullet and send it off to who knows where. Accuracy was not even minute of house. Once I repaired the crown, the rifle shot so well I bought it for my personal collection rather than send it back to the manufacturer.

One big culprit for crown damage is carrying a hunting rifle muzzle down in a truck. The crown grinds in the dirt and gravel on the floor and accuracy deteriorates. Another is cleaning rod damage resulting from improper cleaning technique and poor tools.

Look at the crown for visual damage. Use magnification and a good light to see that it is even and free of defects and that it goes all the way to the bottom of each land. Wipe around it with a Q-Tip to see if any sharp edges catch the cotton fibers.

If there is no visual damage and the gun was shooting well before it took the dark path, usually the crown is not the issue. However, when in doubt, repair the crown. It's easy and fast to do with a brass lap and some compound.

LAPPING
You can remove the barrel from the action and recut the crown in a lathe as detailed in the gun-building section of

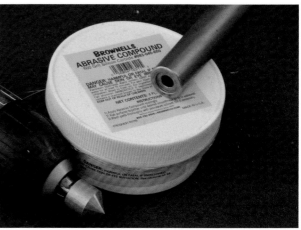

▲ Brownells muzzle lap with compound.

this book. Or you can simply do a fast, down-and-dirty repair with an inexpensive lapping tool from Brownells. It's not only an easy process, it also works great. I sometimes use this method as a final touch to finish a crown that I have cut on the lathe.

I have watched a gunsmith at Jarrett Rifles, a company with a reputation for accuracy, finish a lathe-cut crown with a brass lap. Don't think for a minute this is a compromise. Done correctly, it results in an accurate crown.

▲ Using the Brownells Muzzle Crowning Lap. The compound is wiped off on one side of the lapping tool for clarity.

The Brownells Brass Muzzle Crowning Lap is a tapered "cone" of brass with a stem to allow it to be inserted into a handheld drill. It is used to lap the final edge of the bore. The idea is to get it completely concentric and at a perfect 90-degree angle to the bore. The crown should also be smooth and free from any imperfections.

Before starting, plug the bore with a tight-fitting cloth patch and leave it a few inches down from the muzzle. Put the lapping tool in a variable-speed drill, coat it well with 600-grit lapping compound and insert it into the bore until it contacts the muzzle. It's best to cover the scope with a rag to prevent any compound from getting on the lens.

The tapered brass lapping tool is self-centering. By slightly wobbling the tool as it turns and by reversing the direction of rotation often, any minor imbalances or imperfections are compensated for and the crown will be true to the axis of the bore.

Start the drill and rotate the lapping tool at a slow to moderate speed while slightly wobbling the drill. After 10 seconds or so, reverse the direction of rotation and continue to wobble the drill. It's better to work slowly and check the results often.

After 10 seconds of rotation in each direction, stop. Wipe the compound off the muzzle and check your progress. There will be a bright ring on the muzzle from the lapping compound wearing away the metal.

The best way to inspect your work is with a magnifying glass or a magnifying headset like those used by jewelers. If the ring is still not complete, apply more lapping compound to the tool and continue. Keep working until you have a clearly defined ring all around the muzzle. It must

go all the way to the inside edge and all the way to bottom of each of the rifling lands. The ring must be even all the way around and fully formed on the lands and the grooves.

Once the crown is complete, push the plug out of the barrel from rear to front. Then wipe the bore with a few solvent-soaked patches to remove the residual lapping compound. When possible, always work from the breech or action end of the gun and push the patches out of the muzzle so that the gunk is not pushed into the action. This stuff is very abrasive and, of course, must be kept out of any moving parts of the firearm. If you are working on a rifle where you can't do this and can't remove the barrel from the action, be very careful to capture the crud and always clean the action thoroughly after you finish.

Use a dry patch to remove any solvent. Then run a few patches soaked with a CLP like Clenzoil. Finish with one dry patch. This wipes out most of the oil but leaves a thin protective coating.

Remember that the fresh metal will be exposed after cutting. On a stainless steel barrel, it will be barely visible. For a blued rifle, you can leave it like that or re-blue with cold blue. Either way, the metal must be protected from rust with oil, even if it's stainless steel, which can and will rust if not protected.

CUTTERS

If you wish to change the type of crown or the look of the muzzle, consider using a cutter like the Brownells Muzzle Crowning Cutter with the appropriate pilot.

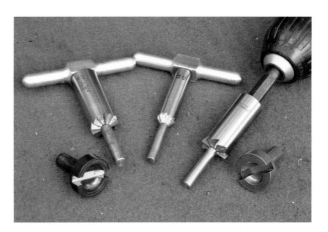

▲ Brownells muzzle cutting tools. Left to right: Muzzle Radius Cutter .815 inch; 79-degree Crowning Cutter with T-handle; 45-degree Crowning Cutter with T-handle; 90-degree Muzzle Crowning Cutter with Drill Adapter; and Muzzle Radius Cutter .615 inch.

Before starting, plug the bore of the rifle with a tight-fitting cloth patch and leave it about three or four inches down from the muzzle.

▲ Brownells 45-degree Crowning Cutter with T-handle and pilot before re-cutting crown. Note the pilots in the background.

Brownells also offers a cutter to square up the muzzle called the Muzzle Facing Tool, which squares the muzzle to the bore. Use the muzzle facing cutter first, remembering to use plenty of cutting oil as with any cutter.

Insert the pilot in the bore and turn the cutter until you have achieved the desired result. The cutter can be turned by hand or with a handheld drill with a Brownells Muzzle Facing/Crowning Cutter Drill Chuck Adapter. Next, put the pilot on either the 11-degree or 45-degree crown cutter, as you prefer, and finish contouring the muzzle.

▲ Brownells 45-degree crowning cutter with T-handle. Note the pilots in the background.

I often like to finish a cut crown with a brass lapping tool. Some gunsmiths don't believe you should lap after cutting, but I have had good results with both approaches.

When you are done, push the plug out of the barrel from rear to front. Then wipe the bore with a few solvent-soaked patches to clean out the residual lapping compound. Always work from the rear or action end of the gun and push the patches out of the muzzle so that the gunk is not pushed into the action. Finish with a dry patch.

The metal will be raw, so you must re-blue, finish it with a coating, or just put some oil on that newly exposed surface to protect from rust.

▲ The Brownells 11-degree cutter, used with a cordless drill, will provide a good crown.

▲ The Brownells 11-degree cutter with a cordless drill after use.

CHITTER-CHATTER

One problem with doing this job without a lathe is that the cutter has a tendency to chatter. Once that starts it becomes all but impossible to correct while using the cutter either by hand or in the drill. The answer is the Brownells Muzzle Facing/Chamfering Tool Stop Collar System. This is a stop designed to control the depth the cutter can travel, so any high spots will be cut down while the low valleys are not, until the entire surface is even.

This tool can be a real life saver.

EDGING INTO DONE

Finally, a radius on the outside edge of the muzzle gives the barrel a finished look and removes the sharp edge. For that I use a Brownells Muzzle Radius Cutter, designed to put the finishing touch on the barrel crowning job. This tool removes the sharp outside edge that remains after shortening a barrel. Chuck the cutter in the hand drill, make a few turns on the end of the barrel until the desired effect is achieved and you are done.

AR rifles were born to be used, not to languish in a dusty gun safe. They inspire no giggles or glee if you don't shoot them. Training, competition or just busting caps, these rifles are at their best when burning through high-capacity magazines and making lots of empty brass.

Just remember though, they are machines and like any machine they require maintenance. Of course you have to clean them, but you also need to replace a few parts now and then. The gas rings on the bolt are among those parts.

▲ Worn rings are hard to spot. The top rings are new, the bottom is worn out.

▲ The Brownells Muzzle Radius Cutter makes a nice finish to the crown.

#2—REPLACING THE GAS RINGS IN AN AR-15

The gas rings in your rifle should be changed periodically. Parts wear out if you shoot a lot and it's a good idea to change them on a schedule to head off any trouble.

Like the piston rings in a car's engine, the job of an AR's gas rings is to seal against the high-pressure gasses during firing so that the bolt can move and operate the action. If they are worn or broken the gun will not run at peak efficiency. Even if the rifle is not currently giving you problems, it's best to head any issues off at the pass. Also, gas blowing by worn rings can potentially cause damage to the rifle. Continuing to use the rifle with broken or damaged rings is just inviting trouble. Replacements are only a few bucks and it only takes a moment to change the rings, so it's a good idea to stay ahead of any problems.

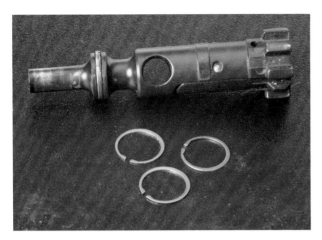

▲ Replacement rings are inexpensive.

Broken rings are pretty apparent if you look closely. Of course, any broken ring means the entire group of three rings must be replaced. Worn rings are less apparent. It's hard to see the difference as it's often a matter of losing tension as much as wear, so when in doubt, replace them.

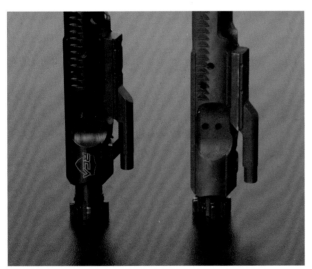

▲ The bolt on the right has worn rings, the one on the left is new. See how the worn gas rings will not support the weight of the carrier?

The most common test for worn rings is to extend the bolt and then stand the bolt carrier group on the bolt face. If the bolt collapses into the carrier, the rings are worn and not providing enough tension. They must be replaced. Also, as with oil changes in your vehicle, it's a good idea to replace the rings on a schedule regardless of any visual indicators or test. Replacing them every twenty-five hundred rounds will keep your rifle running at peak performance.

All you need is a few simple tools and a new set of three gas rings. Brownells has them, of course.

Remove the rear pin and let the upper swing open on the front hinge pin. Remove the bolt carrier group and charging handle.

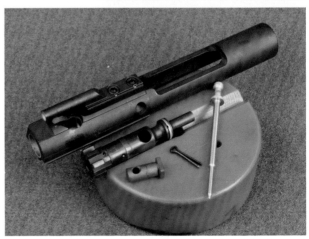

▲ Taking the bolt carrier group apart is simple.

From the bolt carrier group, remove the firing pin retaining pin. Remove the firing pin. Remove the cam pin and then pull the bolt free from the bolt carrier.

It's a lot less messy if you clean everything before doing the work. An ultrasonic cleaner is fast and easy. If you don't have one, good old-fashioned scrubbing with solvent still works.

▲ This tool cleans the carbon from hard to reach places.

There are several tools designed to clean the hole in the carrier that houses the bolt, but the Mark Brown Custom AR-15/M16/AR-Carrier Carbon Scraper from Brownells works as well as any I have tried.

▲ Getting the gas ring started out of the bolt groove.

Using a sharp pointed tool like a small knife blade, dental pick, or sharpened paper clip, work one end of the rear-most ring out of the slot and then grasp the ring to roll it out of the slot completely. Repeat this with the next two rings.

▲ After removing the old rings, clean the slot in the bolt.

Make sure the slot is clean and free from any carbon build up. Clean it with a brush if necessary. Use gun degreaser, or CRC Brakleen, which is pretty much the same thing, but a lot less expensive. Make sure you have

▲ Installing the new gas ring.

▲ Starting the new ring into the groove. Old rings on the bench.

gloves and a face shield. You do not want any splash-back getting in your eyes.

Slide the new ring over the tail of the bolt and start the leading edge into the slot, reversing the removal process. Now roll the new ring into the slot. Repeat with the remaining two rings. Stagger the openings in the rings so they do not line up with each other.

▲ Use a light to check the bolt carrier for damage.

▲ Run a cotton swab inside the bolt carrier. If it's damaged, it may catch fibers.

Check the bolt carrier to make sure there is no damage inside. Make a visual check with a strong light. Then rub a Q-Tip around inside to make sure there are no burrs to snag the fibers. This is particularly important if one or more of the gas rings have been damaged. If there is any damage inside, you should replace the bolt carrier.

▲ Installing the bolt, with the new gas rings, into the bolt carrier.

Reassemble the bolt carrier group. The bolt should be a tight fit in the carrier due to the tension from the new rings.

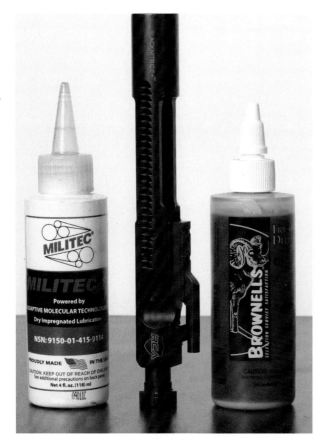

▲ Lubrication is very important with any moving parts.

Make sure to apply some lubricant. You wouldn't think of running your car engine without oil, would you? An AR-15 rifle is a machine and machines need lubrication. I slobber it on and then blow off the excess with shop air (outside) or wipe it off with a rag. It's better to over-lube than to under-lube.

The shooter's saying is that if the lube is spraying all over your glasses when you shoot, it's just about right!

This is a good time to clean the rest of the rifle, then reassemble the gun and run a function check. If everything appears to be working correctly, check the gun by shooting half a dozen live rounds. If it functions correctly, and it most likely will, you are done.

▲ This rifle is ready for a lot more use after replacing the worn out gas rings.

#3—REPLACING A SHOTGUN MAGAZINE SPRING

Like many security-conscious gun owners, I keep a few tactical shotguns for home-defense. Because I can safely do so, I choose to keep the magazines loaded.

The trouble with this approach is that the magazine spring can lose strength from being compressed and over time it will "take a set" and no longer reliably feed the ammo in the magazine. Even the springs in guns that are not kept loaded will lose strength over time, so a

▲ Replacing the magazine spring on a tactical shotgun is an easy DIY project.

hunting gun that spends most of its days empty and safely ensconced in the gun safe is not immune.

No matter how you store your shotgun, loaded or unloaded, it's a good idea to replace the magazine spring on a regular basis, just like rotating the tires on your car. In a defensive gun, reliability is everything and a new spring is cheap insurance. It makes sense to replace the magazine spring once a year if you keep the magazine loaded and every five years if you do not.

▲ This Wolff XP spring from Brownells is very inexpensive.

The Wolff XP spring, available from Brownells, provides up to 20 percent more power than a factory spring and is relatively inexpensive. The Wolff spring is 40 inches long and must be cut to fit the specific shotgun tube, which is an easy project.

The first step is to remove the old spring and follower from the shotgun. With many shotguns, that's just a matter of unscrewing the top cap on the magazine and dumping out the spring and follower. Others will have a magazine spring retainer inside to hold the spring so it doesn't fly out and hit you in the face every time you unscrew the cap. A common design is split in the center part way through and fitted inside the magazine with a little spring pressure by compressing at the split. It's usually pretty easy to pry this cap out of the magazine tube with a screwdriver, which of course results in the spring flying out and hitting you in the face. So, always wear safety glasses.

Other retainer styles require that you push them down with a screwdriver and turn until a detent in the magazine tube lines up with a groove in the retainer. This releases the retainer, so the spring can fly out and hit you in the face. There are probably several other types of spring retainers, but it is pretty easy to figure out how to remove all of them.

For this project, I changed the spring on a pistol grip Mossberg Model 500 shotgun that I have owned since the early 1980s. That last point is important, because of the difficulty I encountered. I might also add that to my shame

it still had the original spring, which was no longer working at all.

With the Model 500, the entire magazine tube unscrews from the receiver to remove the spring and follower. This shotgun has been on a lot of adventures with me and for years it rode in a case under the seat in my boat, just in case we were ever attacked by pirates.

I kept a close lookout for the Jolly Roger, but never saw it or any buccaneers pillaging on Vermont lakes or ponds.

I have always taken care of the gun, but, like a lot of Mossbergs of this age, the magazine tube was stubbornly stuck in the receiver.

▲ The tape allows gripping the magazine tube without damage.

After removing the barrel and discovering the magazine tube was stuck, I clamped the receiver in a soft jaw vise. Then I wrapped the magazine tube in two locations with several layers of friction tape. I then covered that tape with several wraps of vinyl electrician's tape, stretching it to half-width as I wrapped. The friction tape provides some bulk and protection while the vinyl tape adds tension

▲ The magazine tube on this Mossberg Model 500 shotgun screws into the receiver. It has become stuck over time. Heating the receiver allows the magazine tube to become free and unscrew.

to help it grip. Using water pump pliers on one section of tape and my other hand on the other, I attempted to unscrew the magazine tube, but it was stuck fast.

There is probably a commercial wrench for this job, but I didn't have one, so I improvised, because that's what gunsmiths do.

The receiver on this shotgun is aluminum, while the magazine tube is steel. That's part of the problem, the dissimilar metals can experience galvanic corrosion, also called bimetallic corrosion. This is an electrochemical process in which one metal corrodes preferentially when in contact with another and in the presence of an electrolyte, like water. It can cause these tubes to really stick.

The upside is that the two metals expand at much different rates when heated, so I used a heat gun to rapidly heat the aluminum receiver where the magazine tube attaches. This can also be done with a propane torch, but be very careful not to overheat the part. The heat causes the aluminum to expand faster than the steel and will break the seal that time created between the two. Once I heated the receiver, I could easily break the magazine tube free and unscrew it from the receiver. FYI: I have heard that some of the new shotguns have the tubes glued in with Loctite and heat is the answer for that as well.

▲ The old magazine spring in this shotgun is so weak that it is now only as long as the magazine tube. It will no longer function reliably. The new magazine spring should be 12 to 18 inches longer than the magazine tube.

When I got the spring out of my gun I found it was so weak and compressed that it was about the same length as the magazine tube, which is why it no longer worked.

Inspect the magazine tube and the follower to make sure they are not damaged or rusty. If they are, replace them.

The next step is to clean inside the magazine tube. If it's really dirty and caked with gunk, try a 10-gauge bronze brush and bore solvent. Otherwise, a shotgun cleaning rod with a jag works well. As the tube is larger than a shotgun

bore, you might have to stack up several patches to get the proper fit. After it's clean, rinse well with acetone to remove the solvent. An oversized bore swab or even one of those fuzzy stick shotgun cleaners works pretty well to lightly lubricate the inside of the tube with Clenzoil or a similar CLP, or you can use patches on the jag again. This is also a good time to clean and polish the follower or replace it with a new one.

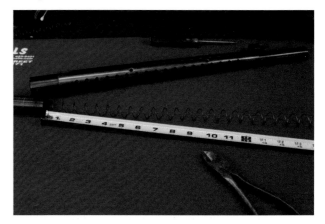

▲ As a starting point it's best to cut the new magazine spring to be 12 to 18 inches longer than the magazine tube.

When installing a new spring, experts like Mark Roth, owner of RCI (The X-Rail company) and Kenny Andersen, formerly with Nordic Components, suggest that the spring must be 12 to 18 inches longer than the magazine tube to start. These guys are the shotgun magazine experts, so pay attention. Both companies make replacement magazine tubes and both these guys have a lot of experience fitting magazine springs.

The length of the spring depends on the length of the tube. A long tube like those used in a 3-gun competition shotgun needs to have more additional spring length than a three-shot tube on a hunting gun. Most tactical shotguns have longer tubes, so err on the long side with the spring.

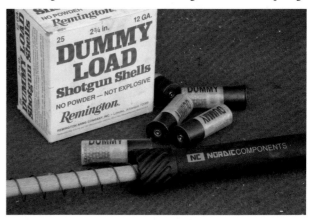

▲ Using a wooden dowel to help install a shotgun magazine spring.

It's always easier to cut off some of the spring than to buy another, which is what you will need to do if you cut it too short. I cut this spring 12 inches longer than the tube and it was acceptable, but borderline. I should have listened to the experts and made it longer. The right approach is to make it long, try the fit, then trim and try again until it's correct. I thought I could shortcut the process and I almost got into trouble.

When reinstalling the magazine spring most first-timers are going to try to work the spring into the magazine tube with their fingers. This approach works, but never on the first try. It's a law, written down someplace, that when you get close to finished you will lose control of the spring and it will fly out of the magazine tube and hit you in the face. There is no set number of times for this to happen, but it will be several before you find success, that much I can promise.

It's much easier if you use a half-inch wooden dowel and slide the spring over the dowel, then fit it into the shotgun. Slide the dowel into the magazine tube. Compress the spring along the dowel until you can capture it with your fingers and hold it inside the tube. Then remove the dowel and screw on the end cap and replace the magazine spring retainer or screw the tube into the receiver, depending on the design. It's pretty certain that you will still lose control of the spring a few times even with this method, but in the end using the dowel will be easier and faster.

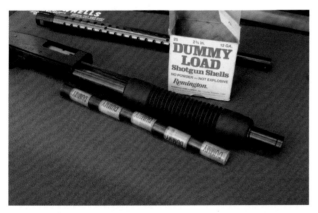

▲ The goal is for the magazine to hold the correct number of shells and feed them with 100 percent reliability.

The goal for the final spring length is to be able to load the number of shells the gun is designed to hold and then insert one more shell about a third of the way before hitting a hard stop. With the Mossberg the shell went almost halfway, so I could have left a bit more spring length.

For safety, it's always best to use dummy ammo when working on the gun and checking function. These are available, of course, from Brownells.

It may take a few attempts to get the spring length right, but be patient. It's better to go slow and get it correct. It's like a guy I worked with on a construction project back in the '70s would say to me over and over until I wanted to strangle him: "If you ain't got time to do it right, where in the hell are you gonna find time to do it over?"

He was about six and a half feet tall, three hundred plus pounds and had spent time in prison for bar brawling, so I decided not to try that strangle thing.

Besides, he did have a point.

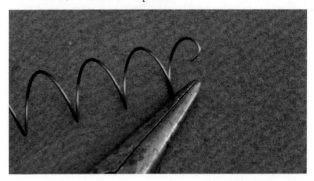

▲ After cutting the magazine spring to the correct length, bend the end in and down so that it will not bind or catch.

Once you have the spring length correct, bend the last quarter inch of the spring on the end where you cut it, in and down. This is so it will not catch inside the magazine tube or block the rest of the spring as it compresses. It also hides the sharp edge, so when the spring hits you in the face it won't cut you.

Put the gun back together with the end you bent at the top of the magazine tube, not at the follower.

▲ To function test, stand the gun up with the muzzle down so that the spring is pushing against gravity. Cycle the gun through at least two full magazines of dummy rounds. All shells should feed with 100 percent reliability.

Load the magazine using dummy ammo rounds that are fully weighted. Position the gun with the muzzle pointed down so that the spring is pushing against gravity. Cycle the gun through at least two full magazines. All shells should feed with 100 percent reliability.

▲ The gun after repairs.

▲ Always finish by testing at the range with live ammo.

It's important to also function test with the different types of live ammo you will be using. For example, slugs are often longer than birdshot or buckshot shells, so make sure that they fit into the magazine and function correctly.

It goes without saying, or at least it should, that you must be careful when working with live ammo. If you have a bullet trap in your shop then you can safely do the function checks using that in the case of an unintended discharge. If you lack a bullet trap, it's always best to do the function checks at the range. At the very least, do them outside with the gun pointed in a safe direction, as in at the ground. With luck, after your neighbors call the cops, you can claim the giant divot in your lawn and the loud noise was really fireworks. Just remember fireworks are illegal in most places, so blame it on the neighbor's kid. They were jerks for calling the cops in the first place.

Finally, test fire the gun at the range with a variety of live rounds to insure complete reliability and function.

#4—REPAIR A BROKEN STOCK

It happened in the blink of an eye. My buddy Steve Shaw caught his foot on an old piece of barbed wire hidden under the brush and fell head first. He was fine, but the stock on his muzzleloader shotgun was split lengthwise. It ended our hunt that day, but it was not the end for that gun.

While this is a muzzleloader shotgun, the techniques I used to repair it are the same for any wooden stock. The idea is to pin the broken area as you glue it by using brass

▲ The split stock.

stock repair pins to provide structural strength along the damaged area.

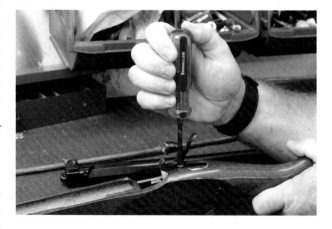

The first step is to take the gun apart so the stock is free and clear from the rest of the gun. Make sure you use screwdrivers that correctly fit in the screw slots and that have parallel or hollow ground sides. Never use a hardware store screwdriver on a gun. Those screwdrivers have tapered sides which do not play well with gun screws. The end result is often the screwdriver slipping from the slot and doing some new and unwanted engraving on your gun.

This is probably the most important sentence in this book: buy a set of gunsmithing screwdrivers and use only them on your guns.

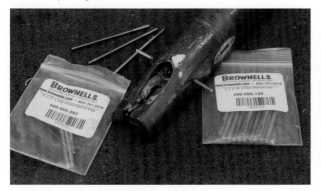

▲ Brownells stock repair pins.

Simply gluing the stock back together will not produce a strong enough repair. Using brass stock repair pins from Brownells will reinforce the stock and prevent it from splitting again. Two or more will be used for a long split. They are placed in sections of the stock that are solid and have plenty of material to accept them. On this stock I used four pins. Two repaired the split and two more reinforced other weak areas to head off future problems.

▲ Measuring to the center of the stock.

With a muzzleloader stock it's a little tricky to make sure the pin is centered through the small web of material between the barrel channel and the ramrod hole. Use a machinist's ruler to find the center of the web and then mark where the hole will be located.

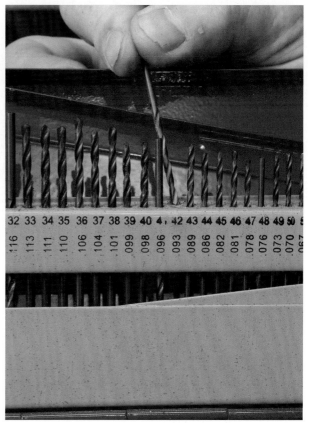

▲ Select a drill that is slightly smaller than the reinforcing pin.

Pick a drill that is just a few thousandths of an inch smaller than the pin. The pin should be a snug fit, but not too snug. If the hole is too small it will be difficult to drive the brass pin into place without bending or damaging it.

▲ Using levels to ensure the drill is running true.

Drill the holes for the pins. Care should be taken to make sure the drill runs true and is lined up correctly so it exits in the desired location on the back side of the stock. Here I am using two levels 90 degrees to each other to make sure that the stock is held level and square to the drill.

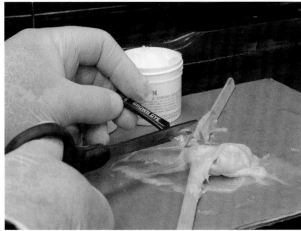

After drilling the holes, mix up some Acraglas Gel stock bedding compound and dye it to match the color of the stock finish. This is an epoxy gel that forms a very strong bond and is a good choice for a glue.

Pry the split open carefully. You do not want to make the split bigger. Fill the split with Acraglas Gel, forcing it into any cracks you can't open up enough to reach into. Too much is better than not enough, as you want all the broken surfaces to be well coated.

Note that the stock repair pins have grooves in them. This will hold the bedding compound and help form a tight bond with the stock. Coat the stock repair pins with Acraglas Gel and carefully tap them into place. Make sure the stock is held tightly together as the pin is inserted and that there is no gap between the pieces.

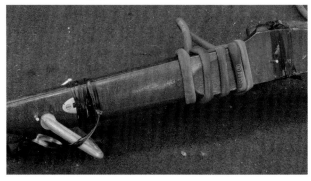

▲ Clamping the stock often requires some ingenuity.

Clamp the broken pieces together. This often requires some ingenuity. Several wraps with electrician's tape works well. Stretch the tape to about half its width with each pass to build tension. Surgical tubing also works well for clamping uneven surfaces. Stretch it tight as you wrap it around the stock to put plenty of tension on the piece. Mechanical clamps such as a vise or C-clamp provide power to make sure the parts are tightly bound together. Be aware of what you are doing, as mechanical clamps can damage the stock.

▲ Filing the pin flush with the stock.

Clean up all the excess Acraglas Gel and let it set overnight or longer.

Clip the ends of the stock repair pins off close to the stock. Use a file to bring them down flush with the stock surface. Also, use a file to remove any excess glue. When you get close to the stock surface, switch to sandpaper in a sanding block for the final finish. In places like the mortised areas it might be necessary to use a rotary grinder such as a Dremel tool with a small cutter to work the excess Acraglas Gel flush with the wood surface.

▲ Final fit of the pins will often require the stock be refinished.

With a small repair, you can often work carefully and avoid damaging the finish on the stock. But for a very large and extensive repair like this one, it is better to sand down to the bare wood. This gives the best fit with the stock repair pins and the least noticeable repair with the glued areas.

▲ For best results, remove all the old finish and refinish the stock.

You can try to match the stain and stock finish. Or simply strip and refinish the entire stock. Complete refinishing will provide the best result. That's what I did here and the result was outstanding. This gun is better looking now than it ever was in its factory finish.

I stained the stock to the color I wanted using stain I bought at the local home supply store. Once that was dry, I applied several coats of Pro-Custom Oil Finish from Brownells. The dry wood on this stock soaked up multiple coats, so it penetrated deep into the wood. Between coats, I smoothed the finish with a #00 steel wool. After the final coat, I lightly smoothed the finish with #000 steel wool.

▲ After staining, I used this gun stock finish from Brownells. The dry wood in the stock soaked up several coats and it penetrated deep into the wood.

The gun looks better than ever and is back out hunting rabbits in the Vermont winters.

▲ After repair.

#5—REPLACING THE TRIGGER ON A NEW HAVEN MODEL 70

Some years ago long-range, precision rifle shooting was exploding. Interest was up and there were matches springing up all over the country. Out of the box, ready-to-go

▲ A Model 70 Laredo.

rifles at that time were extremely expensive and I was looking for a way to jump into the game without spending the winter's heating money. I started looking around the dusty corners of my gun vault and came up with an idea.

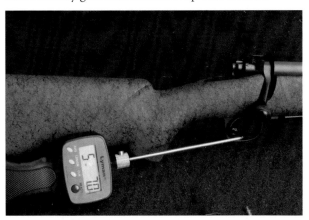

I had an old Winchester Model 70 Laredo rifle in .300 Winchester that had been collecting dust for a while. It's a good shooter and with a new scope it would make a decent rifle to get started in long-range shooting. I ordered a rail mount and a Leupold VX-6 4-24 with a TMOA reticle.

The trigger was never all that great on this rifle, so while I was waiting for the scope, I decided to install a Timney trigger with a 1.5-pound pull weight.

Timney makes triggers for a wide range of rifles and just about any rifle will benefit from installing one. In fact, when I finished this project I installed another Timney in a different Model 70. That one was a hunting rifle so I ordered the trigger with a three-pound pull weight.

▲ Use a proper screwdriver designed for gun work to remove the screws.

Remove the bolt from the gun and make sure the gun is empty of all ammo. Now remove the stock from the gun using a screwdriver that fits the slot correctly.

Remove the magazine box from the action. Using a punch the correct size for the pins, remove the front and rear trigger retaining pins. Note that they are removed in opposite directions.

▲ The old trigger parts shown with the Timney replacement.

Remove the old trigger, including all the springs. Remove the bolt stop and the bolt stop spring.

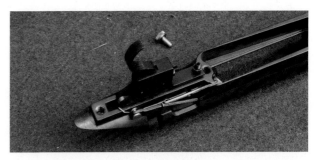

▲ Installing the Timney trigger.

Replace the bolt stop and bolt stop spring, but only push the pin in far enough to hold them and not block inserting the trigger. Slide the trigger into place, pushing back on the bolt stop spring and stretching it enough that the trigger can be inserted and the rear pin pushed into place to hold it.

▲ Gently tap the pin into place.

The bolt stop spring is under tension, so be careful not to lose it. I lost one once when working on a friend's rifle. He is a brown bear guide in Alaska and had the ugliest rifle I have ever seen. This thing looked worse than a roadkill. I figured out why when he was packing my bear's head and hide down a steep mountain.

He was crossing a tricky, deep-sided ravine that drained the mountain. It was boulder strewn, very steep and filled with leg-breaking traps. He dropped his rifle and it clattered from boulder to boulder while it flipped and flew down one hundred feet of this rocky riverbed. I retrieved it and when I handed it back on the other side of this mess he shrugged and said, "It's not like that was the first time."

Anyway, I told him I would make his rifle pretty and I did. But, as I was putting it all back together, I dropped that damn spring.

I looked for days for that spring. He needed the rifle as he was heading into the bush to guide hunters, so I finally gave up and robbed one from one of my personal rifles and I ordered a new spring to put into my rifle.

About a year later I found the spring deeply embedded into the rubber anti-fatigue mat in front of my bench. The moral of the story? Don't lose the spring. If you do, buy kneepads.

Back out the screw on top of the front of the trigger. Now, push the front of the trigger into place and insert the front retaining pin. Tap the front retaining pin into place with a brass punch.

Tighten the front screw on the trigger until it's snug. This screw is designed to place tension on the locking pins and to remove any movement in the trigger.

▲ Tighten the screw to hold the trigger in place.

▲ A drop of thread locker helps make sure nothing comes loose.

Put a bit of thread locker on the front screw.

▲ Tighten the retaining nut.

Then install and tighten the retaining nut.

▲ Make sure the new trigger will clear the stock.

Make sure there is clearance in the stock for all the screws and other parts of the trigger. In this case the retaining screw was hitting the aluminum bedding block on the stock and preventing the action from seating properly.

▲ Note the towel used to pad the vise jaws and prevent damage to the stock.

I used a milling machine to remove some metal and provide clearance for the trigger screw. Drilling it out with a drill press or even using a Dremel tool to remove the metal would also have worked.

▲ Checking the safety function.

Reassemble the rifle, including installing the bolt and checking the function of the trigger and the safety. Make sure the safety will go on and off and that it is working in both the on and center positions. Once in a while the safety will not work, which will require the bolt be disassembled and a bit of clearance cut with a file. Timney can provide instructions on how to do this in the unlikely event it is necessary.

Check to make sure the trigger releases properly. The trigger function should also be checked by cocking the gun and, with the safety off, thumping the butt hard on the floor to make sure the trigger will not jar enough to release. I trust that nobody is stupid enough that I need to remind them to make sure the gun is not loaded.

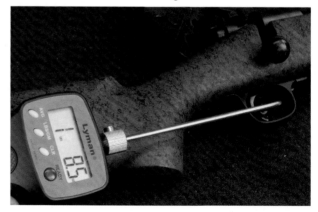

▲ This new trigger breaks cleanly at 1.5 pounds, which is excellent for precision long-range shooting.

Please note: This article deals with Model 70 rifles made in New Haven, CT, before 2006. If you have one of the newer Model 70 rifles made in South Carolina (and now Portugal) it will require a different trigger from Timney, so make sure you specify this when you order.

#6—REPLACING THE REMINGTON 700 TRIGGER

This is for a trigger replacement. If you are building a rifle on the Model 700 then you will have already removed all the old trigger parts as well as the bolt stop and spring. So you can skip this next part.

▲ Make sure the rifle is unloaded. Check both visually and by putting your finger into the chamber.

▲ Remove the stock. Remove the barreled action from the stock by removing the two action screws and separating the two. If they are stuck due to a tight bedding job, hold the stock and alternate pulling up on the barrel and the open bolt.

▲ The old Remington trigger parts that were removed.

Remove the bolt from the action. Move the safety lever to the safe position. Use a correctly sized punch and a small hammer to tap the rear pin out of the action. This also frees the bolt stop and spring. Once the bolt stop is removed it's easy to remove the front pin and all the trigger parts should now be free.

▲ Inserting the new trigger.

Insert the new trigger and tap the front pin into place, but not so far that it contacts the bolt stop. The bolt stop must move freely in the slot and not touch the front pin.

▲ The rear pin is inserted far enough to retain the bolt stop and the bolt stop spring.

Put the bolt stop in place and slide the ring on the spring in behind it. The short arm of the spring hooks into the trigger recess in the action and the long arm pushes on the bottom of the bolt stop.

Start the rear pin in from the bolt stop side of the action and push it through enough to hold the bolt stop. Then compress the spring by pushing on the top of the ring with a punch or screwdriver until the pin will push through enough to hold the spring in place. Put the trigger in place, making sure the sear is down inside the trigger housing. Insert the rear pin fully. You may need to tap it gently with a punch and small hammer.

Adjust the bolt release so it moves the bolt stop without any binding. Do this by very slightly bending the tip with needle nose pliers so it perfectly engages the notch in the bolt stop. Bend and test. This may take several tries before you get it right.

Timney Triggers are slightly wider than Remington factory triggers, so you may need to enlarge the opening on the trigger guard where the trigger protrudes from the stock. A milling machine does the most precise job. Lacking that, a good old fashioned "hand mill" (a file) will also work well.

▲ Installing the rear pin.

▲ This shows proper installation of the rear pin.

▲ Adjusting the bolt stop release.

Sometimes other adjustments must be made to ensure the trigger clears the stock and that the safety operates unimpeded. Use small carving tools, files or a Dremel tool as required to make the necessary adjustments. The key is to make sure the trigger hangs off the receiver without contacting the stock or trigger guard in any way.

The screw on the rear of the trigger adjusts sear engagement. This screw is pre-set and should not be adjusted. The bottom front screw adjusts pull weight. Turning this screw in increases pull weight. Turning it out decreases pull weight. Do not reduce pull weight below 1.5 pounds (or ½-pound for the Calvin Elite Series triggers). A dab of fingernail polish on the lock nut helps ensure everything stays where it should be. (For best results, don't mess with any of the adjustments. Timney ships triggers with a specific pull weight. They do a good job of hitting that number, so order what you want, install the trigger, and don't mess with it.)

Test the trigger by putting the safety on and pulling the trigger firmly. Then push the safety off and make sure the sear does not release when you move the safety. Next, pull the trigger to make sure it will release properly. Do these checks several times.

Cock the rifle and with the safety off, slam the butt-stock against the floor forcefully to make sure the trigger

▲ This is what you are looking for in a trigger pull for a long-range rifle.

does not release. Do this several times. Make sure there is a pad or carpet on the floor so the buttplate is not damaged.

#7—INSTALLING A CONTRASTING COLOR FRONT SIGHT ON A REVOLVER

Black on black handgun sights are fine for shooting bull-seye competition, but not for much else. With everything the same color they can be very hard to see, particularly in poor light and/or with a dark target.

I once waded into a roaring fight between a large and angry black bear and a bunch of Walker hounds. There was not a lot of light deep in that swamp and when I tried to shoot the black bear with a handgun with black on black sights I couldn't tell where the sights left off and the bear began. All I could see was a dark blob and I had no idea where the front sight fit into the matrix of black.

▲ This shows the common black, serrated ramp-style front sight.

I learned a lesson not only about hunting guns, but also about fighting guns. I will not risk trying to protect my life

▲ Contrasting color inserts in a front sight make aiming the handgun much easier than with a black on black sight.

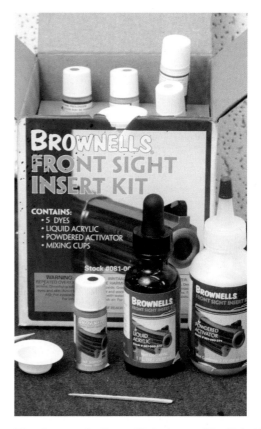

▲ The Brownells Front Sight Insert Kit. This kit contains all you need to modify several handgun sights. There are five color options included.

or my family's life with black on black sights. Bad things usually seem to happen in poor lighting and if the bad guy is dressed in dark clothing, it's going to be hard to tell which "black thing" is the front sight. With a contrasting color front sight that problem goes away.

This is an easy DIY project using the Brownells Front Sight Insert Kit. This kit contains all you need to modify several handgun sights. There are five color options included.

▲ This shows the two files needed for this job, a safeside pillar file for the initial cut and a safeside dovetail triangle file for the dovetail cuts.

Clamp the barrel in a soft-jawed vise so that the sight is parallel with the bench. Using a pillar file (Brownells #360-312-121), make a cut as wide as the file, which is 17/64 inch wide and about 1/8 inch deep. The file is 1/8 inch thick, so use that as a guide.

▲ Making the primary cut in the sight.

This file is "safe" on the edges, which means there are no cutting teeth on the edges, so you can control the width of the cut easily. Make sure that the bottom of the cut is square and 90 degrees to the edges of the sight.

▲ This shows the dovetail cuts partially completed. They need to be a little bit deeper.

The top edge of the cut should be just below the top serration on the front sight. You want the insert as close to the top of the sight as possible, but the dovetails will extend further, so you must leave enough room for that.

▲ This illustrates using a safeside dovetail file to make the dovetails deeper in the cut.

Switch to a sight base file (#080-648-165). This is a parallel sided (no taper) triangle file with two sides safe, or non-cutting. It's designed for making or enlarging dovetail

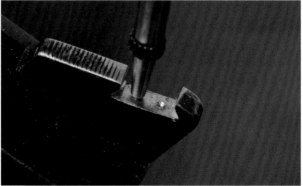

▲ Using a center punch to make a mark for the drill to follow.

cuts. You will use it to add a dovetail to each end of the cut, to help hold the insert in place. Make sure the dovetail cuts are nice and square to the edge of the sight and that each end is of equal depth.

Use a center punch to make two marks on the bottom of the cut. These will guide the drill when you make the insert anchor holes.

▲ Drilling the anchor holes in the front sight.

Using a #51 (.067-inch) or smaller drill bit, drill each of the holes about 1/8 inch deep. These will fill with the insert material and form two pegs off the bottom of the insert to help hold it in place against any lateral movement.

▲ Using an aerosol degreaser.

Degrease the sight with a solvent that dries without leaving any residue. Brownells TCE is a good choice.

Cut a couple small pieces from a soda can, about .375 inch by .75 inch, sized to fit on the sides of the sight to form a dam. You might have to trim them a little for the best fit. Leave them slightly higher than the sight and clamp them to the sight. Brownells recommends parallel jaw pliers. I didn't have any so I used a small parallel clamp.

▲ Using a parallel clamp to hold the two metal dams made from a soda can.

Make sure the gun is oriented so the blade of the sight is level. Mix up the acrylic powder, dye, and activator according to the instructions supplied. You must work fast from now on as it hardens quickly. Pick up a drop with a toothpick and leave it in the cut you made on the sight.

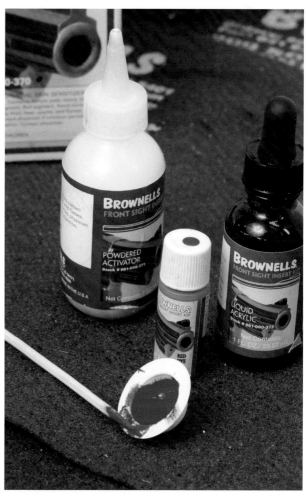

▲ Mix up the filler.

▲ When applying the mix to the sight, it's better to have too much rather than not enough. However, this is a bit excessive. (I have never been good with sticky substances.)

Repeat until the slot you cut is filled. Make sure to work the mix into the anchor holes and the dovetails. Fill the cut to slightly above the top of the sight. Overfill a little bit as it's better to have too much than not enough.

Let the mixture set up. Thirty minutes is enough, but an hour is better.

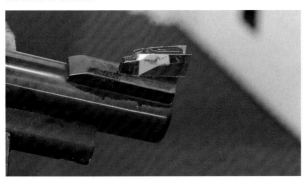

▲ After removing the clamp. This shows the metal dams made from a soda can.

Remove the clamp and peel off the metal dams. The insert should fill the slot completely, be flush with the sides and higher than the top of the sight.

▲ This shows the insert after removing the dams. It's a bit excessive, but it's better to have too much than not enough.

File the top of the insert down with a flat mill or pillar file until it is flush with the top of the sight. Work very carefully as you do not want to mar the metal on the sight. Be very careful with the final cuts as that's when accidents happen! Once gone, metal can't be replaced, so watch where your file is contacting at all times.

▲ This shows the insert after filing it to shape. Note that the metal will need to be re-blued; however, this sight was badly abused before the project was started.

For a finer finish, use 400-grit wet or dry sandpaper with a drop of oil to polish the top of the insert. Wrap the paper around a flat stick so that you keep the edges of the insert sharp. Using just your finger will round the edges. Clean up any overflow on the sides with the file or sandpaper.

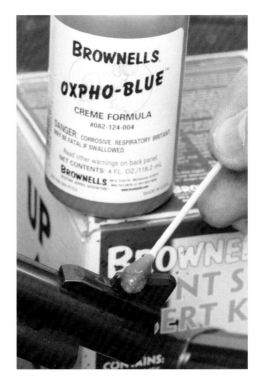

▲ Applying cold blue to the metal. Keep it on the clean metal until the colors match and blend.

Note that the sight shown in the photos was abused previously and that part of the serrations were filed away before even starting this project. To repair this type of damage, use a needle file to carefully re-cut the serrations.

If you scratched the sight or hit the top with the file you may need to do some repairs.

Degrease the metal and apply some cold blue with a Q-Tip. Once the color is correct, wipe off the sight and apply a few drops of oil to stop the bluing process and protect the metal.

Your gun is now ready to shoot.

▲ The finished product. This previously abused front sight was salvaged and is now a viable and useful sight.

#8 — CHOKING UP

I am a gun collector.

Not the kind of collector who has museum-quality pieces kept in climate-controlled boxes and handled only while wearing white cotton gloves. In fact, I am kind of at the other end of the spectrum; I love the misfits, the clunkers and the disenfranchised in the gun world. I collect

▲ This homeless, decrepit shotgun was perfect for a project gun. Part of that was cutting off the barrel and installing threaded chokes.

▲ This is the shotgun after completing the makeover.

them for project guns, but I am a collector nonetheless. At least I am if the definition of a "collector" is that I love to add more guns to my "collection."

As a result, I spend an unhealthy amount of time prowling around gun shops looking for bargains. With a gun writer's meager income, my interests are divergent from those of most collectors and I tend to buy the stuff nobody else wants. One big reason is that I can afford these guns. (Well, at least some of them!) Another is that they are often the best project guns for hobby gunsmithing. If the mechanics and the bore look good I don't worry about the outside, because I am going to refinish it anyway. As a result, I often buy what most condescending collectors define with a specific and technical term: "junk."

A lot of these guns are shotguns and many of the older guns have fixed chokes. I am old enough to remember when shotguns didn't have screw-in chokes and shotshells used fiber wads rather than plastic shot cups. A lot of the

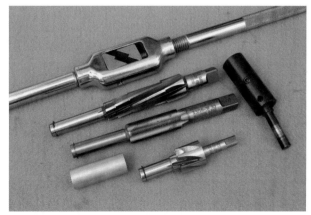

▲ The primary tools needed for modifying a shotgun barrel to accept screw-in chokes. Top to bottom: Tap handle, reamer, tap, pilot bushing and muzzle facing cutter. On the right is a floating drive adapter used to turn the reamer with an electric drill.

guns from that era are choked up tighter than Hillary Clinton at an NRA meeting and are difficult to shoot well with today's tighter patterning ammo. (Besides, when it comes to hitting moving targets with a shotgun, I need all the pattern spread I can get.) Part of my "shotgun renewal" program for these guns is to modify them to take screw-in chokes. Here's how a hobby guy without a lathe can do the project. (Although, doing it on a lathe will be easier.)

You will need a reamer and a tap for the type of choke system you will be installing. I like the Rem Choke system because that's what I have the most choke tubes for. You will need other tools as well, which I'll describe as they come into play. Brownells offers several different makes of reamers and taps. Mine are made by Dave Manson Precision Reamers, a company I have come to trust for quality. I have several Manson chamber reamers, including two made for my wildcat rifle cartridges as well as a wide range of other tools, reamers, and cutters from them. The quality is always outstanding and customer service is excellent. Dave Manson has also been a great resource for information when writing this book.

MEASURE TWICE

The first step is to make sure you have enough barrel thickness to allow for a screw-in choke. Brownells sells a wall

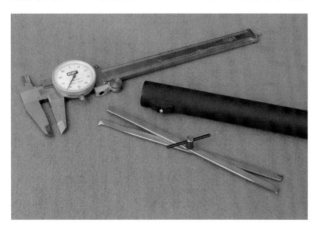

▲ Measuring the inside of a shotgun barrel will illustrate where the fixed choke is positioned. This is the Brownells barrel caliper shown with a dial caliper to measure it with.

thickness gauge, but you can do the job with a caliper or micrometer and a few math skills.

Remove the barrel from the shotgun. Measure the outside diameter of the barrel where you will install the choke. Then measure the outside diameter of the threading tap. Subtract the OD of the tap from the OD of the barrel and divide by two. This will give you the thickness of the barrel walls after installation.

◀ Measuring the inside of a shotgun barrel will illustrate where the fixed choke is positioned. This is a shotgun bore micrometer.

▲ To determine if there is enough metal in the barrel for a screw-in choke tube, first measure the outside diameter of the barrel where you will be installing the choke.

Brownells does not recommend installations where the resulting barrel thickness is less than .015 inch. That's providing that the inside diameter of the barrel is concentric with the OD, which it usually is not, so a little "wiggle room" on that number is a good idea. Also, the inside diameter must not be too large. For example, on a 12-gauge it cannot exceed .735 inch. If it does, the choke will form a lip inside the barrel which can cause all kinds of problems. So, back-bored or jug-choked barrels are not candidates for this process. Neither are chrome-lined barrels.

With most old fixed choke, single-barrel shotguns none of this is a factor. They used thick-wall barrels and are almost never back-bored, but you still must check. Also note that there are several choke tube systems with different diameters, including the Briley Thin Wall chokes designed for use on thin barrels like those on double-barrel shotguns, so there is almost always a system that will work for your gun.

OUT WITH THE OLD

The old choke must be removed. If it is not you can't get the proper size pilot bushing in the barrel. If the bushing fits the choke, as it moves down the barrel and past the choke portion it will become sloppy, allowing the reamer to wiggle and ruin the job.

▲ Clamp the shotgun barrel in a soft-jawed vise and mark the barrel where it will be cut off.

The easiest way to remove the choke is to cut off the barrel. Most of these old guns are too long anyway. Remember that federal law requires that a shotgun barrel must be at least 18 inches, so don't go too short. On a hunting gun 24 to 28 inches is more appropriate anyway.

My project gun seen in the photos had a 30-inch barrel which I cut to 27 inches. I picked this number for three reasons. One, it removed the entire old choke. Two, it's unique and different. Three (and most important!), it left me the option of cutting off more barrel and starting over if I made a mistake and screwed up the project.

Measure the inside of the bore to determine where the choke ends. This is easy with a professional-quality shotgun bore micrometer, but they are a bit pricey. It can also be accomplished with a much less expensive barrel caliper sold by Brownells. This tool has two very precise

▲ Use a fine-toothed hacksaw to cut off the barrel.

metal arms joined exactly in the middle with a pivot to form an "X." If you insert one end in the barrel and open it to barrel diameter, the other end can be measured with a micrometer or a caliper to give you the inside diameter of the shotgun bore.

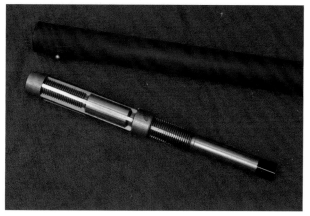

▲ Brownells Angle Blade Expanding Reamer, used to remove the existing choke in a fixed-choke shotgun barrel.

If you do not want to cut the choked portion off the barrel, the choke can be removed by reaming it with an Angle Blade Expanding Reamer, which is designed for this job and offered by Brownells. Once you have a straight cylinder in the bore you are ready for the next step.

If you are cutting off the barrel, simply clamp it in a soft-jawed vise, mark your spot and use a hacksaw to cut off the barrel. You must true the end, which you can do with a file and a square. But it's much easier to use something like a Clymer Shotgun Barrel Facer. This is a cutter that uses a bronze pilot bushing to keep it square with the bore and will face off the muzzle quickly and accurately. Make sure you first remove any burrs left inside the bore from cutting with the hacksaw, as they will prevent the proper bushing from fitting in the bore.

▲ Clymer Shotgun Barrel Facer.

▲ After cutting off the shotgun barrel, remove the burr left inside the bore. If not removed this burr will prevent the proper sized pilot bushing from entering the bore.

If this is your first project and money is an issue, you may not wish to invest in this cutter, so square up the muzzle the best you can with a file. The choke tube reamer will finish the job later.

▲ Brownell's Muzzle Radius Cutter is used to finish the muzzle's outside radius.

It's a good idea after finishing, either with the barrel facer or with the choke tube reamer, to put a slight radius on the outside of the muzzle using Brownell's Muzzle Radius Cutter. This gives a nice professional look to the end product. It also eliminates any sharp edges on the muzzle of the shotgun. The best way to do this project is, of course, with a lathe. But, it can also be done without a lathe and that's the process I am covering here.

IN WITH THE NEW

Remove any burrs inside the barrel and find the tightest fitting bronze pilot bushing you can get in the gun. Usually it will be .001 inch smaller than the bore diameter, so if you are ordering only one bushing, measure carefully and order that size. It should fit without wobble, but also move freely to pass though the bore.

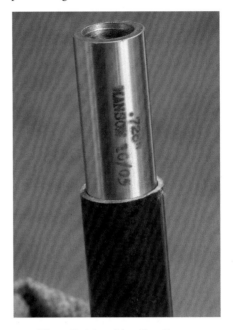

▲ The pilot bushing for the reamer and tap must be a snug fit, but still be able to move. Usually the best fit will be about .001 inch smaller than the bore diameter.

▲ Using a tap wrench to turn the reamer will work, but will take a long time.

Clamp the barrel vertically in a soft-jawed vise. Fit the bushing to the reamer and insert it carefully into the barrel. It's possible to use a wrench to turn the reamer by hand to do this job, but, if you elect to go that route pack a lunch, because it's going to take a while.

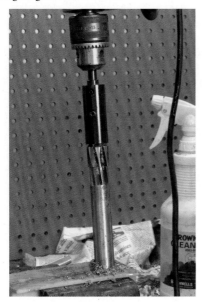

▲ Using a floating drive adapter and an electric drill to turn the reamer used for modifying a shotgun barrel for removable chokes.

A far better approach is to buy a floating drive adapter to allow the use of an electric drill. These adapters will allow for misalignment between the drill and the reamer, so that even if you are not holding the drill perfectly true to the bore, the reamer runs true. Run the drill at the slowest speed you can and not more than 75 RPM maximum.

▲ Spraying cutting oil while using a floating drive adapter and an electric drill to turn the reamer.

As with any cutter or reamer you must keep lots and lots of cutting oil on the blades, so flood the work area often. Work slowly and clear out the chips frequently. You are cutting deep into the bore (about 2.5 inches for the Rem Choke) and it's going to take a while. Don't rush it. Keep lots of cutting oil flowing and keep clearing the chips.

If the reamer chatters, stop. Remove the drill and use a tap handle to turn the cutter by hand. By using enough pressure you will feel when the chatter marks are removed and it's safe to return to the power drill.

▲ Reamer for screw-in chokes in a 12-gauge shotgun. Note the buildup of chips. Use lots of cutting oil and clear the chips often.

When the cutter is deep enough that it faces off the muzzle you are done with this step. Clean out all the chips before starting the tap.

▲ Mark the tap so that it will only cut deep enough to allow the choke to be installed.

Measure the length of the choke tube against the tap and mark the tap to prevent going too deep. Install the pilot bushing on the tap and place the tap in a handle. Insert the tap into the bore, flood with plenty of cutting oil and, using a firm and even downward pressure, start the tap to begin threading the inside of the barrel.

▲ Don't reverse the tap until the job is complete.

The instructions with my Manson tap recommend that it not be reversed to break the chips, as is a common practice with many threading processes. Rather, keep turning it clockwise until the job is complete. Be careful not to go too deep and bump into the shoulder at the bottom, as this can damage the barrel. Thread only deep enough to accept the choke tube. Once the tapping process is complete, unscrew the tap. Clean the bore with degreaser, paying careful attention to the threads. If there are chips lodged in the threads,

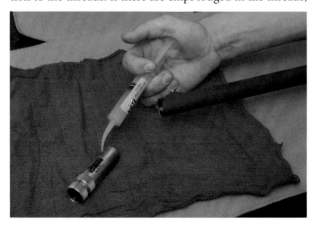

▲ Always lubricate the threads on a choke tube before installing.

insert a bronze bristle brush and clean them out. Blowing with compressed air will aid in removing any stubborn chips.

If the shotgun is not getting any further finishing treatment you will probably want to touch up the muzzle with some cold blue at this point. Degrease the metal first. Be careful to put the solution only on the raw metal portions of the barrel. If it bleeds over on to existing bluing it can etch it and change the color. Once the bluing is complete, coat it with oil to stop the process.

After cleaning and degreasing are complete, lubricate and protect the bore and threads with a good oil or synthetic spray. Lubricate the choke tube threads and screw the choke tube into the shotgun barrel. Unless you did something wrong it should be a perfect fit.

▲ Installing a choke on the finished product.

Look down the bore from the muzzle and point the chamber at a light source. You should see a dark ring around the end of the choke tube, indicating that the I.D. of the choke tube is smaller than the I.D. of the barrel. To double-check this, use a wire probe with the end bent at 90 degrees to feel the ridge. If everything checks out okay, you are done. Put the barrel back on the shotgun and go shooting.

Of course, all this is much faster and easier to do with a lathe. It's pretty much the same process. Dial the barrel into a 4-jaw chuck and hold it with a spider on the other end. Use the reamer in a floating reamer holder. Run the lathe at its slowest speed and feed the reamer with the tailstock quill. Do the tapping with the lathe turned off and turning the chuck by hand.

FRONT BEAD

If you cut off the barrel you will need to replace the front bead. If the barrel has a rib, there is no problem, simply drill and tap in the center of the rib and install the bead. However, on a plain barrel shotgun this can pose a dilemma.

If the metal is thick enough, the simplest way is to drill and tap a hole and then screw in a new bead. But, after

▲ The finished product with a choke tube installed. Note also that I refinished the badly pitted metal. This style bead can be glued or soldered on. Solder is better.

reaming for chokes, the thickness of the metal left near the muzzle is often not enough to allow threading for a bead. One of the most common sizes is a 6-48 thread. That will require at least .020-inch thickness of material to get one complete thread.

One solution is to move back on the barrel behind the choke. This will work, but looks a little ridiculous. A better idea is to use a sight that is designed to be glued or silver soldered on the barrel. There are lots of them on the market. Most will result in a higher sight than just a bead. If this is a tactical shotgun, a higher sight used in conjunction with a rear ghost ring works well. The two sight system works well with the concept of gluing or soldering on the front sight because the front sight can be higher. That allows using a base to attach to the barrel.

Some sights come with a barrel band that clamps on.

If you are using the gun for wing shooting, you will want something mounted low to the barrel. There are lots of options, so look around before you jump in. There is something that will work for you.

I will say I have had a lot better luck keeping the sight on the gun with silver solder than I have with any kind of glue. Others I talk with report good results with glue, but that's not my experience. Sometimes, however, you don't have an option. For example, some night sights should not be heated. In that case, glue it is, but if there is an option, I prefer solder.

On a round barrel, the trick is to find the top dead center. There are several different methods. One is to clamp the gun in your milling machine, level the receiver and use an edge finder on the barrel. Then, go over exactly half the diameter of the barrel and the mill will be top dead center.

If you don't have a milling machine, Brownells has an ingenious tool made by Gauge-Rite Products called the Top Dead Center Indicator. To use it, first level the barrel by using a flat surface on the gun. If the gun is assembled, the side of the receiver will work with an L-shaped level. There is a "rear sight" groove milled in the back of the barrel on my gun and the two sides of this provide a flat surface that is centered on the barrel. I leveled the barrel to that and clamped it in a soft-jawed vise.

Then I placed the Top Dead Center indicator on the muzzle and leveled it with the internal level. There is a punch that fits in a machined hole in this tool and when it was leveled and centered I gently tapped the punch with a hammer. That left a dimple in the barrel that was top dead center. I then made the dimple slightly larger with a spring-loaded Starrett Automatic Center Punch.

▲ Using the Top Dead Center indicator to mark the barrel before installing the front bead ramp.

Now drill and tap for a bead, or use this as a visual indicator to center a front sight base that is being soldered or glued.

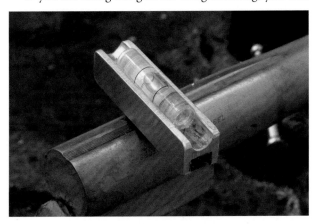

▲ Using a level on the flat portion at the rear of the shotgun barrel.

▲ This illustrates how the level and the Top Dead Center indicator work together.

#9—ALL TORQUED UP

The word "torque" is defined as a rotating force. When the term is applied to a threaded bolt or screw it is a measure of how much force is used to tighten that bolt or screw. Depending on the size and application, torque is measured in either inch-pounds or foot-pounds of torque.

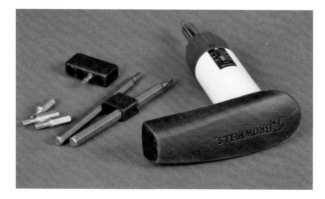

▲ The Brownells Magna-Tip Adjustable Torque Wrench will accept any Magna-Tip bit.

▲ Magna-Tip screwdrivers and bits on Jim Majoros' bench.

The official definition of torque I found online says:

"The moment of a force; the measure of a force's tendency to produce torsion and rotation about an axis, equal to the vector product of the radius vector from the axis of rotation to the point of application of the force and the force vector."

Anybody who can understand that scares the heck out of me.

In simpler terms, torque is a measurement of twisting force.

There are two ways to measure it: make a wild guess or use a torque wrench. Obviously, the second option will bring a far better end result, but it's a rather uncommon tool on most gun guys' workbenches.

I learned the importance of using a torque wrench to measure how tight a screw or bolt is turned back in the prehistoric '70s when I was in my "motor head" phase and spent a lot of time elbow-deep in car, motorcycle, and snowmobile engines. I started with the school of thought that you tightened everything until just before it broke. That, of course, took some "trial and error" and led to other issues.

Over-torqued bolts can cause all kinds of problems, like broken bolts, stripped threads, and distorted parts. The scale is smaller on a rifle and a scope ring screw is not the same as a cylinder head bolt on a 340 cubic-inch car engine, but the principles of correct torque are basically the same.

Under-tightened gun screws can loosen and let things that are not supposed to move, move. Over-tightened screws or multiple screws that are unevenly tightened can lead to even bigger problems. Twisting scope ring screws too tightly or unevenly when mounting a scope can damage the scope. It can result in stressed, bent, or dented scope tubes and misaligned internal parts. The scope adjustments may not work correctly, making it impossible to sight in the gun or in some cases, retain zero. Or it can cause the scope to break at a later date, as recently happened to me at the shooting range. One of the internal lenses shattered, possibly from a misaligned scope ring. (For the record, I did not install the scope.)

Rifle action screws that are under-torqued can work loose, causing accuracy problems and even damage to the gun. If they are over-torqued, they can damage the stock, bolts and even the receiver. Unevenly or improperly torqued action screws can result in poor accuracy. It's a fine line between getting any important screw tight enough and turning it so tight that things break or distort.

There is a school of thought that says you do not absolutely need a torque wrench to mount scopes on guns or to mate the action to the stock. Thousands of each are accomplished every year by people who have never heard of a torque wrench. But for the very best job and for an eye-opening look at how much torque is correct, a torque wrench is the only answer. It might also lead to better accuracy from your rifle. A good torque wrench is not horribly expensive and probably should be on your workbench.

When I first used a torque wrench it shocked me by just how much I have been over-tightening most gun-related screws all these years. This tool will really open your eyes to the mistakes you have been making and it will ensure that you don't continue to make them in the future.

Leupold recommends that 6-48 screws in a ring or base be tightened to 18 inch-pounds and 8-40 screws to 28 inch-pounds. Windage screws on the back ring of the scope mount should be tightened to 40 to 45 inch-pounds.

Other sources recommend that base screws be tightened to 30 inch-pounds. Ring screws in aluminum rings should be torqued to 10 to 15 inch-pounds and in steel rings to 15 to 20 inch-pounds. The windage screws on the rear rings of Leupold and other mounts should be torqued to 30 to 40 inch-pounds.

Without a torque wrench, how can you know? Chapman Manufacturing says that with their screwdriver's relatively small handle and full hand pressure, most men will achieve 17 to 50 inch-pounds, which is a pretty wide margin of error. With the thumb and first two fingers, they say most will apply 10 to 17 inch-pounds, but that is subjective at best. I can apply a lot more torque with this method than somebody smaller. The bottom line is, the only way to know is with a torque wrench and what I learned when

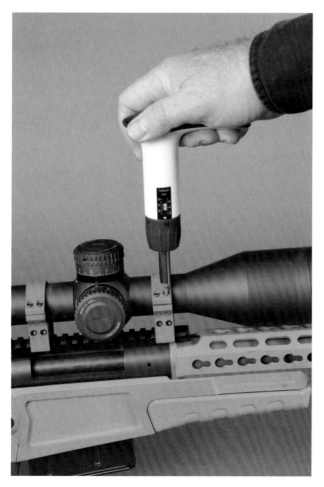

▲ Scope mounting screws should not be over-tightened.

▲ For best accuracy the action screws should be tightened to a specific torque.

I first got one was that I have been screwing up for years. (Pun is intended.)

Action screws are another torque-sensitive application that can affect accuracy and prevent damage to the rifle. Sources recommend that wood, fiberglass, or synthetic stocks be torqued to 40 inch-pounds. If the stock has pillars, go to 65 inch-pounds.

I took a survey of several rifle manufacturers a few years back to see what they recommend on their action screws. Browning recommends 30 inch-pounds on their A-Bolt rifle action screws. Remington recommends 15 to 25 inch-pounds on their wood, synthetic or laminate stocks. On the synthetic stocks with integral aluminum bedding blocks they recommend 45 inch-pounds of torque on the action screws. Ruger provided more detail, including sequence.

"First, tighten the front bolt to 90 inch-pounds. Second, tighten the back screw to 50 inch-pounds. Third, tighten the middle screw to 50 inch-pounds."

For years I just "cranked the hell" out of the screws with a big screwdriver. This new approach of actually measuring the torque has improved the accuracy of some of my rifles.

Doing it right actually works.

Who knew?

#10—REPLACING THE AR-15 A-2 FRONT SIGHT/GAS BLOCK WITH A 4-RAIL GAS BLOCK

The modern AR-15 style rifle sometimes has a problem in trying to evolve away from its military roots. Many continue to be shipped with the A-2 style front sight integral with the gas block. That made sense when most AR-15 rifles had fixed carry handles and were always going to be used with iron sights, but one manufacturer told me several years ago that in the civilian market flat-top rifles are 90 percent of their sales. I would bet that number is even higher now. Yet the A-2 sight persists. Even on a lot of flat top rifles.

▲ The G2 front sight is visible in this low-power optic.

▲ The G2 style front sight and gas block.

The reason we choose a flat-top is almost universally for mounting optical sights. When using a low-power optic like a red dot, a holographic sight, or a low-power scope, the A-2 front sight is visible through the optic and can be a huge distraction to the shooter.

Still, a lot of owners want backup iron sights, particularly on tactical rifles. A solution is to replace the A-2 sight/gas block with a lower profile gas block with a Picatinny rail on top. It's easy enough to add a flip-up front sight that will fold down out of the way when not in use. This sight can be popped up quickly if your optic goes down and you need to revert to your backup iron sights.

Replacing the gas block is a simple project for the hobby gunsmith. Make sure the gun is unloaded. Remove any optics from the gun. Separate the upper from the lower and remove the bolt carrier and charging handle.

The best way to support the upper while working on it is with an upper receiver vise. This hinged plastic vise clamps around the outside of the upper receiver and an insert goes inside the receiver to prevent distortion or damage. Then the block is clamped in your bench vise. You can do this job without it, but the receiver vise makes life easier. This is also a very handy tool for working on or cleaning your AR rifles.

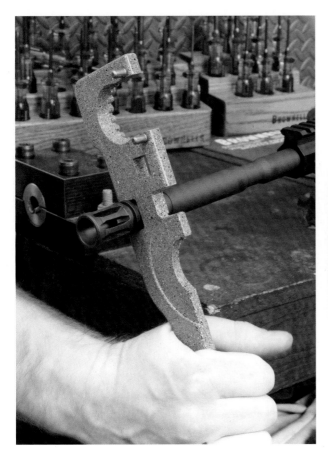

▲ Using a DPMS wrench.

Note the orientation on the flash hider or muzzle brake so you can replace it in exactly the same location. One way is to use a straight edge and a felt marker to draw a line along the barrel and the brake. This works as a witness mark so that you can torque the brake back to the same orientation when it comes time to reinstall it. A little acetone on a cleaning patch will remove the line after you are done. Using the correct size wrench to fit the flats on the sides of the muzzle appendage, unscrew and remove it.

▲ If you use the Brownells front sight pin block you can't go wrong.

Remove the two pins holding the sight/gas block on the rifle barrel. The pins are tapered and must be driven from left to right. The left is the left side of the rifle when it's held in the shooting position. Brownells has a front sight bench block that makes this foolproof. It is machined to accept the sight on a mil-spec rifle and is clearly marked "pins in" or "pins out" depending on which side of the block is used.

▲ I modified my bench block so it would fit with a floating handguard.

Because this block is for mil-spec guns it is designed to be used with the handguard removed. Many of today's civilian model rifles use a floating style handguard which cannot be removed with the sight/gas block in place. The handguard will often contact the Brownells front sight pin block and not allow the sight to seat properly in the block. The solution is to modify the block. I clamped my block in my milling machine and modified it to allow clearance for the four-rail handguard. It might have been easier to simply use a hacksaw to cut the end off the block and then clean it up on a disk sander, but I like playing with my machines.

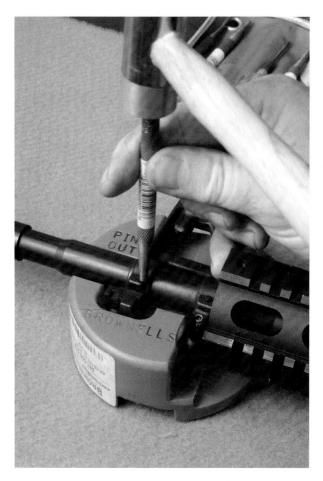

If you do not have a bench block, support the barrel and sight with wooden blocks, making sure there is clearance for the pins to come out. Support it very well, because sometimes the pins are tight and require quite a bit of force to remove.

Use a tapered starter punch to break the pins free, making sure there is enough pin protruding from the frame to allow this. Then switch to a straight pin punch to push the pins out of the block. Make sure the pin punch is small enough to pass through the holes without damaging the metal.

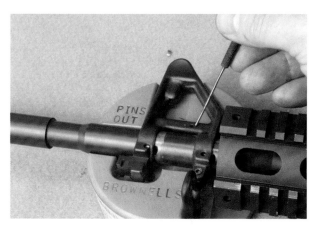

Now use a 5/64-inch roll pin punch and carefully punch out the roll pin holding the gas tube in place. Be careful, as these tiny punches will bend very easily. Note that the bench block has a hole to receive the pin.

▲ This shows the gas block, gas tube, and muzzle brake off the gun.

Twist the gas block very slightly to break it free from any carbon build up, but be very careful not to damage the gas tube. Carefully slide the gas block and gas tube together off the front of the barrel. Now, remove the gas tube from the gas block. Or better yet, leave it on and install a new gas tube on the new block.

There are a lot of options for replacement gas blocks. One good choice is the JP adjustable gas block, which allows you to adjust the gas pressure and tune your rifle to the ammo you are using.

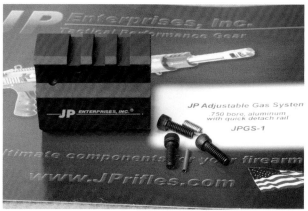

▲ This JP adjustable gas block fits a .750 barrel diameter.

Make sure you order a gas block that correctly fits the diameter of your barrel. When in doubt, remove the old block and measure the barrel with a dial caliper or micrometer. Most rifles with a standard barrel use a .750-inch inside diameter gas block. The bull barrel guns will most likely be .936 inch. There are some other diameters used, .850 and .940 are a couple, but the first two will cover most common barrels.

The most important feature for this project is to have a top rail for mounting the new front sight. While the market is flooded with gas blocks that have that feature, one I like is the Brownells Modular Gas Block, in part because it's relatively inexpensive and it gives you lots of options. It comes with a top rail and the option to add more rails on the sides and bottom. You can even add a bayonet lug. The additional rails can be purchased and added on at any time, or you can buy the block and three extra rails as a package deal.

The extra rails increase your options for mounting other accessories such as a laser or flashlight. If you have a handguard that has no rails on it, this can be important. On the DPMS rifle I used to photograph much of this project, I already have a four-rail handguard, but I think the gas block with all the rails mounted carries the lines of the forend out well and looks great, so I installed them all.

▲ The proper size drill can work as a slave pin.

The first step is to install the gas tube into the new gas block. It's a little tough to line up the hole inside the tube with the hole in the block. I used the shank of a #47 drill as a slave pin to hold the tube in alignment while I tapped in the roll pin. Make sure you have the large hole

in the gas tube facing down. If you don't, your rifle will be single shot!

▲ Note the position of the gas port on the barrel.

Clean and inspect the barrel where the gas block will mount and make sure the gas hole is clean and not badly worn. Slide the gas block over the barrel, being careful to fit the gas tube through the hole in the barrel nut and into the receiver. The Brownells Modular Gas Block is held in place with three set screws on the bottom and each should receive a drop of #242 Loctite before installing. Be sure to degrease the threads in the block and on the screws before adding the Loctite.

Place a level on the rail on the receiver and level the upper assembly in the vise. Then place the level on the gas block rail and turn the block until it is level and in perfect alignment with the rail on the receiver. Tighten the screws on the gas block.

If you want a more secure lockdown of the gas block, line it up correctly, then remove the set screws one at a time and drill a shallow dimple in the barrel for the screws to lock into. I don't think that step is necessary unless you are going to be mounting some heavy accessories on the

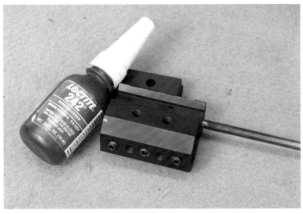

▲ A little bit of thread locker makes sure the gas block stays put.

rails of the gas block. If you do it, be careful to use a drill press or milling machine with a stop so you do not drill too deep and ruin the barrel. Do one screw at a time, replacing each one before removing the next so that alignment is maintained.

Replace the flash hider or muzzle brake.

It's important to make sure you order a new crush washer when you order the gas block. If the installation uses a crush washer, install a new one and do not reuse the old washer.

Remove the vise block and insert and replace the charging handle and bolt assembly. Check to see that the bolt is functioning correctly and is in alignment with the gas tube. Make sure that the bolt is not binding or hitting the gas tube. Reassemble the rifle and test fire.

▲ This shows the level on the block, which should match with the level on the receiver rail.

▲ Now is a good time to consider changing to a muzzle brake.

◀ Note the flip-up front sight on the gas block rail. This can be folded down out of the field of view when not in use.

CHAPTER 8
SILK PURSE GLOCK

You can't make a silk purse of a sow's ear
—Old Proverb

Wanna Bet?

The Glock is probably the most popular handgun in America today. Love them or hate them, it's undeniable that they are prolific. They are also one of the easiest handguns for do-it-yourself types to modify.

I was looking around for a project gun for this chapter and, as always, my timing sucked. I wanted a Glock 19 in 9mm, mostly because I didn't have one. The evidence said it should have been easy to find one. To be honest, for months, or perhaps even years (I wasn't paying much attention) you could find used Glocks cheap. At least that's what everybody kept telling me. "Heck, they are everywhere, mostly used cop guns so they haven't been shot much."

Then, in a fit of foolishness, the FBI decided that they wanted to go back to the 9mm. Never mind the agency had had a disaster in Miami in 1986 that led to abandoning the 9mm, ultimately in favor of the .40 S&W. In fact, that debacle was why the .40 S&W was created after the FBI decided the 9mm simply was not enough cartridge for serious work.

Now it is.

Go figure.

They say it's "new bullet technology," most of which has been around for years, that has made this formerly inadequate defensive cartridge a dragon slayer. Having read all the supporting documents, I have little doubt that the decision was based much more on social pressure than ballistic performance. The bottom line is, all the "me too" law enforcement departments soon followed suit and for a while the supply of used Glock 9mm pistols evaporated.

Of course, true to my usual luck, that's when I decided to look for a project gun for this chapter.

I visited a lot of gun shops and put a lot of miles on my truck and my Harley checking them out. (I really didn't mind the excuse to go ride the bike.) I made a bunch of phone calls, but it was always the same thing. "Man, we had a bunch of them a month or two ago, but right now we got nothing."

So, I put it out on social media that I was looking for a project gun. That's when I heard from an old high school buddy who is a Glock guy.

"I have a Glock 22 in .40 S&W I might be convinced to part with," he said. Further inquiry got this response, "It's been shot a little bit, but it's still pretty functional."

▲ These pictures do the gun more justice than it deserved. It had been run hard and put away wet.

▲ Note this handgun has been stippled front and rear but not the sides. This is a carry gun often carried inside the waistband and harsh stippling against the shirt or skin can wear holes in both.

He is a hard core shooter, so I should have used a bit of caution. His idea of a "little bit" means something different than for a normal human. The gun was a trade in from law enforcement, no doubt as they switched to the 9mm for no reason other than "me too" and to waste tax dollars. My buddy had owned it for a while and had done his best to wear it out, but it's a Glock and they don't give up easily. He was getting into long-range rifle shooting, so we worked out a trade for a tactical scope I wasn't using.

He might have oversold it just a bit. The gun was a nasty old G22, beat up, worn out and looking like an abandoned orphan that had been living rough.

My intention was to breathe new life into it and turn it into an "Oh, Wow!" gun. You know, the kind of gun that gets that reaction when you pull it out of the box at the range.

I think I achieved that goal.

Here's how.

GET A GRIP: HOW TO RESHAPE AND STIPPLE THE GRIP ON A POLYMER HANDGUN

The first step in the process and one of the easiest for a DIY person to do is to modify and stipple the grip. This not only changes the look and feel of the gun; the stippling provides a very aggressive gripping surface for your hand.

My buddy Mike Brookman had been reworking and stippling the grips on a bunch of handguns for members of our informal shooting group and I was impressed with his work. I asked him to do my Glock while I shot photographs.

When the Glock hit the market in the mid-'80s it was unprecedented for its use of polymer (a fancy name for plastic) in the frame. Just about every other handgun maker followed Glock's lead and now polymer frame handguns are the most popular style on the market.

The use of plastic made the manufacturing process much faster and easier. It also opened the door for a lot of modifications by the gun owner. In the past, if you wanted to modify a metal frame handgun it meant using expensive and complicated equipment such as a milling machine, or a file and a lot of courage. The polymer frame of the Glock (and all its imitators) simplifies the process. You still need a bit of courage, but the tools and techniques are much simpler.

These techniques will work with any polymer frame handgun as indicated by the Glock, FNH X-45 and the Springfield XD shown in the photos. Just keep in mind that they do not all use the same polymer. What works on one in terms of temperature and technique may not on another, so approach each new project with caution and maybe a bit of practice.

▲ FNH, Springfield Amory and Glock. All use polymer frames. Be careful, as the plastic might be different from gun to gun.

▲ This AR-15 magazine made a good practice piece.

The place to learn is on practice pieces, not the handgun. It's a good idea to practice with all of the tools you will be using on something you don't mind trashing. It's not hard to find plastic in today's throw-away society. I use the plastic trays that come with pistol ammo to work out the basic technique. They are a bit harder and a slightly different consistency than the Glock plastic, but it still helps you get the general feel for the tools and techniques. The ammo boxes are destined for the trash can anyway so I feel no remorse when I mess up or if a new technique I am trying doesn't work out.

Practice until you have it down. Then try something less expensive to start with other than a serial numbered handgun frame. Many suggest using the extra backstraps from the Gen4 Glock handguns if you have them.

The polymer in some AR-15 magazines is similar to that used in handgun frames. Try stippling a few of them before you start on your pistol. A $20 magazine is a far better practice piece than a $500 handgun.

Now that I have sufficiently scared you into practicing,

let's start on the pistol. The first step is to take the gun apart and then strip the frame of its parts. You can probably do the work by simply "field stripping" the gun, but it makes life easier to remove all the parts from the frame, if for no other reason than it prevents damage to them. If they are in a box on your bench, you can't slip and mess them up.

It's always a good idea to shoot some photos of how it all goes back together before you take the gun apart; this will aid in getting the parts back in place. I also like to have an exploded view of the gun to aid in putting it back together.

Remember that you will be working with plastic and it can melt very quickly. When you are modifying the grip with a sanding disk or other abrasive tool you are generating heat, so turn down the RPMs and work slowly and carefully. If you go too fast or push too hard the plastic can melt and flow ahead of the tool. The result is not pretty and can be very hard or even impossible to repair. Never forget that you are making modifications.

▲ We reshaped and reduced the finger grooves and removed the factory texturing in preparation for stippling.

That means you are removing material, which is easy, but almost impossible to replace if you take off too much. Also be aware when you begin stippling that you will be using a hot metal tip that can easily melt through the frame of a handgun. It all requires a light touch. Work slowly, be careful.

The first step is to use a sanding drum on a Dremel tool to modify the grip to your liking. Many shooters like to remove the finger grooves as they find the spacing less than ideal for their hand size. I elected to simply make them smaller and less prominent on this gun. I also chose to remove all the texturing on the grip between the finger grooves and to stipple the entire area.

▲ Using a sanding disk to reshape the trigger guard and provide a little relief for the middle finger.

A common complaint about Glocks is that the middle finger of the shooting hand hits the trigger guard, often making that finger sore after an extended shooting session. An easy modification is to cut a crescent into the trigger guard to allow clearance for the finger to ride a bit higher.

You may also want to put a radius on the edges of the

▲ Smoothing the sharp edge on the trigger guard.

trigger guard. This is smoother on your fingers and gives the gun a "softer," less industrial look. Some shooters like to round out the front of the trigger guard so it looks more like a conventional pistol. I chose to leave mine alone. I think doing that removes a lot of the Glock look and identity. Also, it might make finding a holster that fits correctly a bit more difficult.

▲ Remove only to the bottom of the existing "terrain." Leave enough material for stippling.

As we planned to stipple the entire grip, we smoothed up the back and sides, including removing the textured surface. This makes the grip a bit smaller, which is a good thing for most people. Mike is about the size of an average Wookie, so no handgun is too big for his massive hands; but my "normal" size hands like a smaller grip than is traditional on the Glock. So if it ends up a bit smaller, that's a good thing from my perspective.

Be very careful not to go past the bottom of the existing "terrain" on the grip. You must leave enough plastic for the stippling. If you burn a hole through the grip, it may be ruined. You also need to leave enough material for the grip to maintain its integrity and strength after stippling.

▲ We dished around the magazine release for more positive access to the button. The final polish is done with sandpaper.

I am a lefty and don't like the long, extended magazine releases found on the G34, G35 and other competition handguns as they hit my trigger finger. But, with the factory Glock magazine release it's often difficult to push it in far enough to work correctly with my index finger. I know, it's a "thumb" activated release, but that's how we lefties do it. So we sculptured out around the magazine release to give it a little relief, so that I could push it without hitting the frame. I suspect that most right-handed "commoners" will appreciate this modification too.

Once you have the frame smoothed and shaped to your liking, smooth out the modified areas using sandpaper and working by hand. Wrapping the sandpaper around a mandrel helps in maintaining the correct curves and contours.

▲ Smoothing the worked area with sandpaper wrapped on a mandrel.

I had a practice piece left over from machining a mandrel for blueprinting the action during my .223 Ackley Improved rifle build. It had a round mandrel and a larger threaded section that made a good handle. I made a few

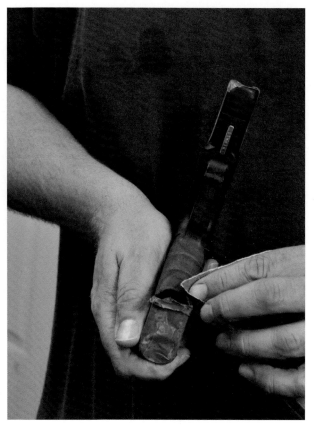

▲ Smoothing the worked area with sandpaper.

small modifications to remove the sharp edges and it became a permanent tool for this work.

For the flat surfaces, wrap the sandpaper around a piece of wood or use a small commercial sanding block to help maintain shape. Use progressively finer grit until you have the finish the way you want it.

Remember, this will be your final finish on the areas you are not going to stipple. You might also buff it with a cloth buffing tool on your Dremel with a bit of abrasive compound for a smoother finish. Or, if you have

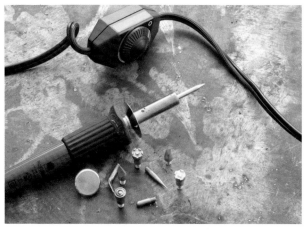

▲ The kit. Note the heat control.

a bench mounted buffing wheel, you can use that with some rouge compound. Isopropyl alcohol works well to clean the worked areas and remove any buffing compound wax.

The stippling tool can be a wood burner or a soldering iron. It's important that you can control the heat. If it's too cool it will not properly melt the plastic. Too hot and you risk burning through or having strings of plastic follow the tip out when you remove it from the grip. Mike uses an inexpensive wood burning kit with a built-in rheostat to control the temperature. I bought the same model on line for about $25.

▲ It's important to have control over the amount of heat.

If you look into what others have done with Glocks, you will see some very elaborate stippling patterns, but for your first time it may be best not to get too ambitious. A simple stippling over the grip area and perhaps a few other selected sections for aesthetic balance is a good way to start. On my pistol we kept it simple. The entire grip area was stippled for a better grip as well as the "look." Mike added a small stippled section on the front of the trigger guard. For those who like to shoot with their off-hand finger on the front of the trigger guard, this provides some purchase. While I do not shoot this way, I was surprised to find this "old school" method is still used quite a bit, even by some of the top shooters.

We did not stipple the bottom of the tang where it hits the web of the hand. Instead, we kept that smooth so it's not gouging a hole in my skin every time the gun recoils.

You can plan the pattern to fit your needs and likes. This gun will be used mostly with a belt holster, so we did the entire grip. For a gun carried in an inside the waistband holster a rough texture against your skin or even a T-Shirt can wear holes in both. On his personal carry gun, Mike stippled the grip in the rear and front for a secure grip and left the side panels alone. He also stippled the sides of the trigger guard to provide an interesting look.

▲ Laying out the pattern.

Lay out the pattern you are planning to stipple on the grip using a pencil. Once you have it in place, you can use masking tape to lay it out and give you lines to follow with the stippling tool. You can cut the tape to give you any curved lines to follow.

▲ Do the borders of the pattern first.

When you start stippling, follow the tape edges with your stippling tool and create the border first. Then fill it in. It's as simple as that. There is no way around the "filling

▲ Mike Brookman advises to use patience. Work slowly and be careful when modifying a polymer grip.

it in" part and it is tedious work. If you enjoy mowing the lawn, you might like doing this. Me? I put the mower in high gear, slam the throttle wide open and try to finish that hateful chore as fast as I can. So, if you are like me, force yourself to slow down when stippling. Do not try to rush it, simply work slowly and methodically. If you get tired, stop and rest. If that's not enough, stop. Put it away and come back another day. If you try to do it all in one session, the odds of making a mistake rise dramatically as fatigue sets in.

I am a type A person and I know this from painful experience. Fight the urge to "get it done" and instead devote the time needed for a good job. (Or get an easy going guy like Mike to do it for you!)

▲ Brookman, "mowing the lawn."

For this simple pattern we picked the pointed tip for the wood burning tool and adjusted the heat using a practice piece. To stipple, touch the tip to the grip and allow it to melt into the plastic very slightly. It doesn't take much, just a small fraction of a little part of an inch. (For the record, yes, that is an accepted unit of measurement.) This raises an edge around the point. Pull it out, move over a little and do it again, keeping the penetration the same each time, as well as the spacing.

▲ Filling inside the borders.

Repeat while keeping the tight pattern so that you wind up with a rough surface with holes or "stipples" that are even and closely spaced. Make sure you keep the tip clean as you work. Mike keeps a small block of wood on the bench to rub the tip on to keep it clean.

▲ Stippling a Glock frame.

Of course, you can experiment with different tips and patterns, but the standard pointed tip is a good way to start. It provides a rough texture for gripping the handgun and looks good. I found that some of the other tips are a bit

▲ Note the different tips that come with the kit.

▲ The finished pistol. Note the stippling and the changes in the grip and trigger guard.

more difficult to use and require a finer touch. It's better to leave those for after you have done a few guns and are comfortable with the techniques.

Once you are done, you can simply leave it like that and have a very nice looking and very practical handgun. Or, if you want a unique look, you can finish the gun with a spray-on coating as detailed elsewhere in this chapter. I have also seen some patterns on which the gun is finished with a spray-on coating, but the stippled area is not coated. It's left raw to contrast with the new finish on the gun and they look fantastic. On my gun we elected to put a camo-type pattern on the entire gun, including the stippled area.

Mike and I traveled to Fairport Harbor, Ohio, to spend some time with the good folks at Viktor's Legacy Gunsmithing. Jim and Jamey Majoros taught me several new gunsmithing techniques for pistols, rifles and shotguns and were a great help in this book. In fact, they kind of took over this Glock project from here.

Jim showed me how to do the lightening cuts in the slide. Jamey installed a Lone Wolf trigger kit and a Lone Wolf replacement barrel to convert the gun to .357 Sig. Then he painted it up "real pretty."

Jamey is a master with gun coatings and likes to use Cerakote, which is a bake-on gun finish with a reputation for durability. It can be applied in a wide range of colors and patterns. We discussed at length what to do with this gun and I finally said, "Surprise me." He did the camo pattern you see on my gun in its finished form and I could not be happier. He coated the barrel to match the same black used in the pattern and then added the red highlights in the flutes.

Trijicon HD sights finished off the package.

It's a very "Oh, Wow" gun now and it all started with reshaping and stippling the grip. Like I said, you can end there with the stippling, or go on to any number of custom applications limited only by your imagination and budget.

Read on to learn how we did the rest of it.

I wanted to do some lightening cuts in the slide, mostly because I like the way they look on a custom handgun. There is some thought that it increases the slide speed and cycle time, which I suppose it does. But I can't outrun a Glock when shooting; at least not and still hit anything, so that's a moot point for me and for the vast majority of shooters. There is also a theory that the lighter slide reduces the weight of the parts that are moving, changing the felt recoil. Less weight slamming back and forth means it's easier to control the gun.

I am sure it's all true, but the cuts just look badass, particularly with the highlights on the barrel flutes. So, while it may be shallow and a bit foolish, aesthetics rather than practicality drove my personal motivation.

In theory I could do this. I have a milling machine and a decent knowledge of how to run it. But after I put out on Facebook that I was doing this project and looking for ideas, Jim contacted me and suggested I travel to his shop in Ohio. That way I could not only learn the techniques from an experienced professional, it would free me up to shoot photographs at the same time. So it came to pass that Mike and I, along with a bunch of guns, were stuffed in his wife's little car (better gas mileage than our trucks), and heading west.

They make movies about this sort of thing, two buddies on a road trip and to be honest we did have a few "moments" that would have made good cinema, but let's keep this focused on gunsmithing.

With luck his wife will never find out about most of it.

MAKING THE CUT

This part of the project is a bit more advanced, as it requires the use of a milling machine. I know that violates the mandate of this section, so I will point out it's not mandatory.

I am assuming that if you own a milling machine, you have learned at least the basics of how to operate it. So, before you start cutting on your gun, you should have an understanding of how to pick up the edge and find center, how many RPMs the machine should be set for with each size and style end mill and other basic machining techniques. Buy some books, watch the videos, enroll in night classes, but learn machining before you start cutting on your expensive guns. Practice on scrap metal, make some tools, whatever it takes to learn the skills. It's really a lot of fun to learn and in the end you can do awesome things with your guns.

You don't have to be a master machinist before you work on your gun, just have a basic understanding of the processes. If you are smart (and of course you are, you bought this book didn't you?), you can pick up the basics in just a few weeks and be ready to make good guns even better.

▲ Jim Majoros buffing the slide on the author's Glock.

The first step was to make the cuts in the slide. The key is to do all the layout work in advance. Jim sandblasted the stripped slide and then coated the area to be machined with Dykem layout blue. It's important to figure out what the cuts are going to look like and where they are going to be located. He worked it out on paper and marked the locations on the slide using a dial caliper, machinist's square, and a scribe.

▲ Marking the limits for the cut.

▲ Jim Majoros starting the layout process for the slide cuts.

▲ The limits are scribed.

Before starting, ensure that the mill table is trammed to the spindle and that the vise is square to the spindle. Then clamp the slide in the vise and true it in place. The slide must be aligned perfectly for the side cuts so that the mill can plunge through both sides and keep them in alignment. The hole on the bottom must be exactly opposite of the top hole.

▲ Coating the slide with Dykem to lay out the cuts.

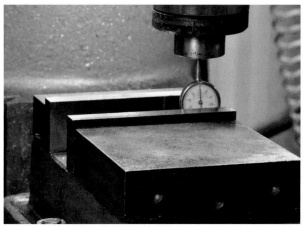

▲ Making sure the mill vise is trammed to the spindle.

Jim clamped the milling machine vise snug on the slide, but not tight. Then he used a machinist's parallel and a plastic hammer to tap the slide down until it was exactly flush with the top of the vise before tightening it in place.

▲ Fitting the slide into the milling machine vise.

Jim has a nice, new Kurt vise, so that approach is an option for him. I am a poor hobby gunsmith and a new Kurt will trash a grand with little change, so I use my old Bridgeport vise I bought used for considerably less money. It's older than I am, so it is lot more "seasoned" and a bit more beat up than Jim's. It works fine, but the jaws are not perfectly level and do not precisely match on the top edge, so I can't use Jim's technique.

I tried to machine them, but they are hardened steel and I just ended up with a damaged end mill. So, late one night I took the vise off the mill and wrestled the heavy thing up on to my old surface grinder. This would have made the jaws perfect on top again, except the surface grinder ran about 30 seconds and quit. It did this once before some years back and a few taps with a hammer on the controls fixed it. This time it ignored my efforts until sometime around midnight I gave up and went to the house looking for an aged bourbon to ease my frustration. (A good gunsmith always knows when it's time to back off and call it a day. He also knows when it's time to call in an electrician.)

(Follow up note, two weeks later. Forget getting an electrician. I could not even get one to return a call. After wasting far too much time looking for help, I decided to fix the surface grinder myself. I found a corroded contact that was the problem. Once it was running again, I ground the top of my vise jaw inserts square and parallel.)

The point to this (and I do have one) is that before I fixed my vise, I had to use a different approach for leveling any work piece. I supported it with parallels or with precision gage blocks underneath. I made sure it was square to the spindle with an indicator, then I locked it in place.

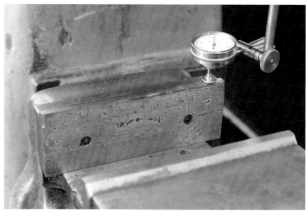

▲ Truing my milling machine vise after using a surface grinder on the top of the vise jaws.

To check that it's true in the vise, install the indicator in the spindle and check both ends of the slide by moving the table back and forth. Adjust until they are exactly the same height and square to the spindle.

It's important with this approach to make sure there is clearance for the end mill to plunge through without hitting any of the support structure, including the vise or any parallels or gage blocks. If that's not possible, once the slide is locked firmly in place the supports can be removed.

▲ Using a flat stock piece to make sure the slide is flush with the top of the vise.

Jim's approach is much faster, but I spend money at this gunsmithing thing, not make money, so I often need to find a way to work with what I have. That's my point. Be creative, be inventive and find a way to work with the tools you have or make the tools you need. There is no wrong way to do any of this if the results are the same.

We planned to do the top coffin cut first, which is one big long cut. On my gun it ended up half an inch wide and 1.65 inches long, although this is not a critical dimension. You can make the cut any length or size you like, as long as you leave enough metal to protect the integrity of the slide.

▲ Starting the fireworks show.

▲ Things are heating up.

Jim and I have become friends since then, but it's important to understand, at that point we had just met and we were still in that "trying to impress the other guy stage." He started his mill, lowered the big .5-inch end mill to the slide, applied some oil, and started the plunge cut.

Glock slides have a case hardening that can be tough to get through. That's why it's important to use an end mill with sharp cutting edges. Except the end mill Jim had was rather "experienced" and let's say it wasn't the sharpest tool in the box. Normally that's not a problem, except that the slide on this Glock was particularly hard and the case hardening was extra thick. It must have been made on a Monday or something.

The mill started to spark a bit.

"Is that normal?" I asked.

"It's okay," Jim said, thinking it would break through any second.

But it didn't, and the pyrotechnics just increased.

The oil got hot and started to billow smoke, as the fire and sparks really started to fly off the cutter.

Jim was in a bit of a dilemma and I knew it, but, of course I didn't let on. He had to make a choice, stop and regroup, admitting to these guys he'd just met that he (at least in his mind) had made a mistake, or keep going and pretend this was just business as usual. He is very experienced and knew exactly what was happening and if the damned cutter would just break through the case hardening all this would go away.

He played the odds, kept going and lost the hand.

I, of course, just played dumb.

I knew exactly what was happening and wanted to see how it played out. You can learn a lot about a guy by how he handles something like this, plus it was starting to become funny as hell.

The bottom line is that an end mill, like any cutting tool, has a life span. This one was getting old and near the end of its useful life, but it should have had a few more jobs left in it before it hit the trash can. Except we combined it with a particularly tough slide and it became the perfect storm.

About the time the room was full of white smoke and glowing from the fire off the cutter, it broke through. It was impossible to see the slide to continue, so Jim turned off the machine to let the smoke clear.

There was an awkward silence that lasted just a little too long and then Jim started to laugh. I knew then I would like this guy.

"I guess should have ordered a new end mill," he said. "I think it might have made a better first impression."

I like a guy who can laugh at himself. It tells me he has confidence in what he does. I am proud to call him a friend now. He is also a hell of a gunsmith and has been a tremendous help on this book. A book, I might note, that I promised to write without ever mentioning this incident.

I guess I just can't be trusted.

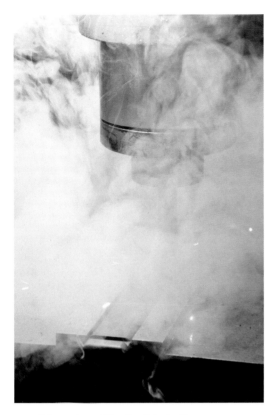

▲ There is a Glock slide in there someplace!

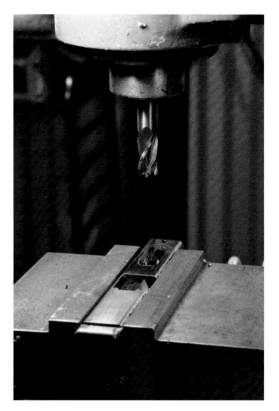

▲ The completed cut.

Once the smoke cleared it was easy to finish the coffin cut on the top of the slide and then flip the slide 90 degrees for the series of cuts on the sides. Jim laid out a pattern on the side. It's important to keep the cuts back far enough to avoid the thicker section in the front that supports the barrel.

▲ Making the top coffin cut.

▲ Using an edge finder to locate the top of the slide.

The first cut is a quarter-inch circle. Next is a longer cut measuring .420 inch. This repeats with another circle, another long cut and ends with a circle for five cuts total, three round and two elongated. The pattern starts a half inch in front of the ejection port and ends a half inch from the front of the slide. They are spaced evenly between.

The center of each cut was marked with a scribe line that is 90 degrees to the length of the slide. Once the slide is in the milling machine, the center line can be found. Measure the width of the slide. Then find the edge with an edge finder. You can locate the edge of the vise jaw if the slide is deep in the vise. Do the math and move the cutter to dead center. Then it's easy enough to move the quill along the axis of the slide to pick up the first etched line for the first cut.

For each successive cut, use the milling machine to advance the correct distance, keeping track with the dial on the handle or digital readout. Each cut should line up perfectly with a scribed line. If it does not, stop and figure out why. Once you cut, the metal is gone, so remember the old adage, "measure twice and cut once."

▲ Jim Majoros measuring the Glock slide to locate the cuts.

▲ After measuring the slide and using the edge finder to locate the edge, the math is simple to move to the center with the end mill.

This time the end mill was new and sharp and it cut without issue, or setting the place on fire. Once it has plunged through the top of slide, run the mill to the

▲ Note how the end mill has cut through the top and is about to plunge through the bottom so the holes align. Also note how this is done outside of the vise so the mill has clearance to plunge through the bottom.

bottom side, ensure it's in the correct location and plunge through for the cut on the bottom. The end mill must be long enough to reach through the bottom, of course. This Glock slide is 1.020 inches wide, so the mill has to be long enough to reach through and do the cut on the bottom. The smooth shaft on this end mill is the same diameter as the cutting flutes, so it can be used as a bump stop when milling the elongated holes on the bottom. That way they are exact mirror images.

Once a hole is finished on both sides, raise the quill to remove the end mill and advance the correct distance to the next cut. Make sure the end mill is aligned correctly, add some cutting oil, and plunge through again using moderate pressure. As Jim pointed out, "You don't want to hang on the handle like King Kong, instead use some finesse when running the quill." You can go by "feel" as to how much pressure is needed to keep the cutter running correctly. Once the cut is through both sides, advance to the next location and repeat until all the planned cuts are completed, both on the top and the bottom sides of the slide.

▲ Milling is messy work, but it's important to use a lot of cutting oil.

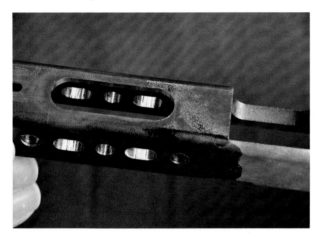

▲ The slide after milling.

Remove the slide from the vise and clean up any burrs with a file or by carefully using a Dremel with a Cratex polishing tool.

▲ Cleaning up the cuts.

I would point out here that the *Machinery's Handbook* has information on spindle speed and feed rates that help when setting up the mill for these cuts.

APPLYING THE LIPSTICK

We turned the gun over to Jamey for the next phase of the "Oh Wow" quest. I work with spray coatings on guns all the time and I have even done a few projects beyond a simple overcoat, but I bow to the master. Jamey is a maestro with this stuff.

▲ Jamey Majoros is a master at Cerakote. Here he is applying the pattern to my pistol.

Again, preparation is the key. Both the slide and the frame were stripped and degreased in acetone. Jamey is so fond of this stuff that he buys it by the barrel and the rumor is he makes his girlfriend wear it as perfume. I swear I saw him slip a few drops into his soda at lunch. For a "flavor enhancer," he said.

Jamey convinced me and I have started using acetone. I get mine a gallon at a time and am not a fan of the taste. My wife flat out refuses to wear it as perfume, but it does work great as a degreasing solvent.

Both the slide and the frame were hit with the sandblaster. The metal slide is blasted at 80 psi with 100-grit aluminum oxide blasting medium. Because the slide was sandblasted before, it just got a light going over and a little attention to any areas that had smoothed out when clamped in the vise. The goal is a smooth, even sheen on the surface.

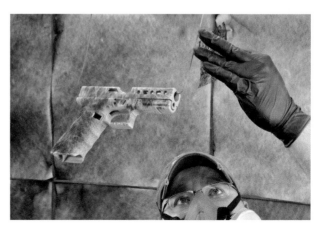

When sandblasting plastic, turn down the pressure by half to 40 psi and/or extend the distance from the blasting gun to the part. The idea here is just to rough up the surface enough to give it some "tooth" to accept the coating and help it adhere, but without removing any material. Even the stippled areas get the sand blast treatment.

The parts are never handled with bare hands again, gloves only. The oil from fingerprints can wreck a spray coating.

Everything is hit with high-pressure shop air to remove any dust and then degreased again with acetone sprayed on and allowed to run off. The parts are then put in the baking oven to gas out. Of course, the temperature must be kept lower for the plastic parts; Cerakote recommends 150 to 180 degrees Fahrenheit. The idea here is the heat will bring out any hidden solvents, grease, or oil, making it run and be noticed. It also dries any residual degreaser.

▲ Jamey Majoros carefully mixes the Cerakote in preparation for spraying the Glock.

If there is no sign of any oil, the Cerakote can be applied. To achieve the effect we decided on, Jamey used three colors: Crushed Silver, Burnt Bronze and Graphite Black. He first applied a base of Crushed Silver and did a "flash" cure for about ten minutes at 150 degrees.

▲ Laying down the base coat and spraying inside the mag well.

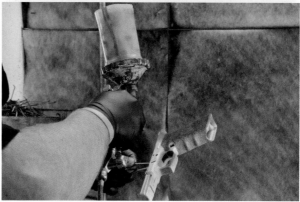

▲ Doing the base coat.

Abaca fabric has a unique, random pattern to the fibers that makes it a good choice to use as a spray-through screen for creating a pattern. Jamey used a small piece of it to spray through with the Burnt Bronze and black colors. He worked the pattern slowly and methodically, sometimes switching colors back and forth, even going back to the silver for a bit. He watched the finish as it developed and added to it as needed until he achieved the look he wanted. Then the parts were put into the oven for a full cure. Again, the plastic must be kept at a low temperature, 180 degrees or less to prevent risk melting. Metal can bake at 250 or even 300 degrees for curing.

▲ Spraying through abaca fabric creates a pattern.

▲ Spraying through abaca fabric to create a pattern.

We added a Lone Wolf drop-in replacement barrel in .357 Sig. That cartridge was created by necking the .40 Smith & Wesson down to take a .355 diameter bullet. So, the breech face and the magazines designed for .40 S&W work fine with .357 Sig ammo. I wanted something different and I had never owned a gun in this cartridge. This is a very easy conversion. Just swap out the barrel and it's done. Besides, I have a large box of empty .357 Sig brass I had sorted out from brass picked up at the Sig Sauer Academy during classes I attended there, so of course I needed a gun, right? Lone Wolf has a good reputation for replacement barrels and this one was a perfect drop-in fit. It turned out to be a good shooter, too.

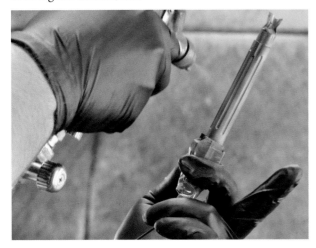

▲ To get the red flutes, first paint the entire barrel red.

Jamey coated the barrel Crimson Red Cerakote, then filled the flutes with clay and sprayed the barrel with Graphite Black so it matched the color in the pattern on the frame. When the clay was removed, the colored flutes provided a striking contrast.

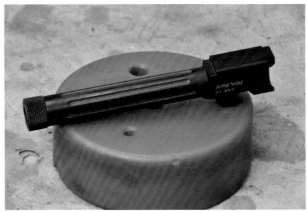

▲ My sole contribution to the color was to paint the thread protector black.

I had ordered a threaded barrel if for no reason other than it gives the gun a "tactical" look. It also gives me the option of adding a break or suppressor if I wish. I mention this because we forgot to do the thread protector cap. When I discovered that after returning home, I used Brownells Flat Black Aluma-Hyde II to coat the cap. It was my sole contribution to the "look" of the pistol.

▲ The side cuts. ▲ The top cut.

SIGHTS

The original plan was to cut the slide to take a Trijicon RMA red-dot sight, but I liked the look of the gun so much I changed my mind and installed Trijicon, HD night sights. These are my current favorite sights for any carry gun. They have tritium vials front and rear, while the front sight also has a large yellow or orange photo-luminescent dot that is easy to find in almost any lighting condition.

One problem with night sights that use three vials all the same color is telling which one is the front sight when you are in a hurry. You have three dots that all look the same and it can get confusing. If there is any ambient light at all, this front sight does not have that problem.

The front sight is tall and the rear sight uses a U-shaped notch wide enough to provide plenty of daylight on each side of the front sight so you can pick it up fast in most lighting conditions. The rear sight is cut on the front to provide an edge that can be hooked on a belt or boot for one-hand operation.

Night sights should only be installed with a sight pusher. The tritium-filled glass vials that give the sights that glow in the dark quality can break if you try installing them with a hammer and punch.

Jim has the B&J Machine P500 Pro Universal Sight Tool. I had an older version of this tool, but, after seeing Jim's, I upgraded to the P500 Pro, ordering it from Brownells, of course. If you are doing much work replacing sights, this is a great tool.

▲ This is the drop-in trigger package.

We added a Lone Wolf drop-in trigger package. The silver colored trigger looks great on the gun. It also resulted in a clean and crisp four-pound trigger pull weight.

▲ The gun now has a nice, clean four-pound trigger pull.

The trigger is short, crisp, and much better than most striker fired trigger pulls. I am from the school of thought that says if you are trying to feel the reset, you are not shooting fast enough. (I might add that I learned this from some of the fastest and best pistol shooters in the world.) However, I recognize that some shooters are focused on the reset. With this trigger, the reset is very short and very tactile.

The first Glock I ever bought was a G22 so I have a good selection of holsters and magazines that all fit this new gun. I also have the old barrel we took out, so I can change it back to a .40 S&W in a minute or two. (Assuming I can find it in my shop when that time comes. It could go either way.)

The gun is a great shooter, very accurate and very dependable. I might add that when I show the gun to anybody, the response is almost universally "Oh, wow!"

Mission accomplished.

This book is designed to teach you hobby gunsmithing, but sometimes you need to send stuff out. Perhaps you want a gun hot blued, or maybe you want your Glock slide machined and you don't have a milling machine (yet). No matter; for any gunsmithing need, I highly recommend these guys.

Jim & Jamey Majoros
Viktor's Legacy Custom Gunsmithing
1180 High St
Fairport Harbor, Ohio 44077
(440) 352-4867
www.viktorslegacy.com

▲ All these rifles were built from parts.

CHAPTER 9
BUILDING AN AR-15
ROLLING YOUR OWN FROM PARTS

The AR-15 has become the most popular rifle in America. It's also the ultimate kit gun, with unlimited numbers of accessories and parts available.

While I suppose the purist might argue that it's not really "gunsmithing" to do so, building your own AR-15 from parts is a wonderful DIY project. Besides, I say it is gunsmithing and this is my book, so they can kiss my back cover.

THE LOWER

One tool that is very helpful for this project is a Brownells AR-15/M16 Lower Receiver Vise Block. This inserts into the magazine well and allows you to clamp the bottom end in a bench vise to hold the lower while you work on it.

▲ The lower receiver.

Or, for a different approach, consider the Present Arms Gunner's Mount which provides support for a bunch of operations with an AR-15.

The key to any good project is the foundation and the foundation of any AR-15 rifle is the lower. Think of it like a house. You can build the most incredible house (the upper) imaginable, but it will never be all it could be if the foundation (the lower) is not good enough to support it properly.

The lower starts with a receiver. There are a lot of receivers on the market today. Shop not only for price, but quality as well. This part will need to be shipped to an FFL and is treated as a firearm. It contains the serial number and to buy it you must complete ATF Form 4473 and pass a background check.

You will need a lower parts kit that contains all the smaller parts needed to assemble the lower. The kit typically comes with a mil-spec trigger, which will never make you happy. Toss those parts in a drawer and order an aftermarket trigger if you can afford one.

You will also need a buttstock and related parts. Again, lots of good choices here, so shop around. I don't think you can go wrong with Luth AR buttstocks.

PUTTING IT ALL TOGETHER

What follows here assumes that you are going to use the trigger parts that shipped with the kit. If you are going with a self-contained aftermarket trigger, check out the sidebar covering that installation.

My grandfather told me years ago, while teaching me

▲ The parts needed to build an AR-15 lower.

to repair auto engines, that the best strategy is to do the toughest job first. He was a part-time gunsmith and noted that philosophy applied to anything mechanical, including guns. So, with that in mind, tackle the trigger assembly first.

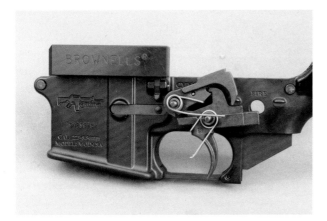

▲ This shows the trigger configuration in the cocked position. When installed inside the receiver, the two legs of the trigger spring would be resting on the bottom of the receiver.

DPMS founder Randy Luth pointed out there is another good reason to start there.

"The alignment of the trigger or fire control pins is critical to how well that receiver is going to work. If they are off, even a little bit, you have a problem. So, install the trigger assembly first to be certain the holes are located properly on the action. Better to find out first thing than to do all that work on the other parts, only to tear them down if the action is not true."

INSTALLING THE TRIGGER GROUP

Parts needed:
Hammer
Hammer and trigger pins (2)

Hammer spring (the larger of the two similar springs in the kit)
Disconnector
Trigger
Trigger spring (the smaller of the two similar springs)
Disconnector spring (similar to the bolt catch spring, but is identifiable by its one end being wider than the other)
5/32-inch roll pin punch (optional)

▲ This view shows a conventional JP AR-15 type trigger.

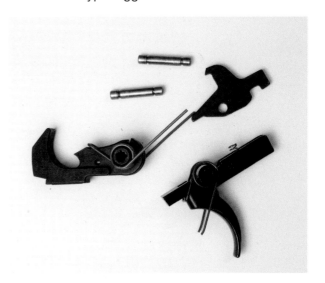

▲ Trigger parts.

Install the trigger spring on the trigger. The top square loop will hook under the front of the trigger and the legs will point forward with the bent tips pointing up. The legs will push on the bottom of the receiver when the trigger is in place.

Install the disconnector spring in the hole at the top-rear of the trigger. The larger end goes in the trigger. Push it in until it locks.

The disconnector goes into the trigger, with a single pin to hold both in place. Insert the trigger assembly into the receiver and align the hole with the rear-most of the two pin holes in the receiver. You will have to push on the trigger and/or disconnector assembly to load the springs and help align the holes for the trigger pin. It helps to use a straight-sided 5/32-inch pin punch as a slave pin to keep everything in alignment before you install the trigger pin. The trigger pin has two grooves in it, but it doesn't matter which way it is inserted.

Install the hammer spring on the hammer. The legs of the spring should point down and the square looped portion of the spring will be on the rear side of the hammer. Install the hammer in the receiver with the spring feet pointing back and resting on the trigger pin. When the spring is loaded, the legs will point to the back of the gun and one leg will fit in the groove on the trigger pin. Use a slave pin punch to align the hammer as you compress the spring. Then install the hammer pin, pushing the slave pin out as you do.

FUNCTION TESTING

Cock the hammer. Pull the trigger and make sure it releases the hammer. Do not let the hammer hit the receiver. The Brownells AR-15 Hammer Drop Block is a

▲ The trigger assembly installed and held with slave pins. The trigger pins are started. Note the block to catch the hammer when dry firing.

great tool for dry firing, as it stops the hammer before it hits the receiver.

Keep holding the trigger back. Push the hammer back and the disconnector should catch and hold the hammer. Releasing the trigger should cause the disconnector to release the hammer, which should then catch on the trigger sear in the cocked position. Repeat this test several times to ensure the trigger, hammer and disconnector are all working properly.

TRIGGER UPGRADE

Replacing an AR-style rifle trigger with a self-contained drop in trigger system.

The trigger is one of the most critical components of any rifle. Without a good trigger, it is impossible to extract all the potential in the rifle.

Yet, a lot of AR-style rifles are shipped with military style triggers. The hard, gritty, battle triggers are a poor choice for precision shooting. A standard trigger in an AR rifle can be complicated and difficult to adjust or tune. So the best solution is to replace with a self-contained trigger.

There are several good triggers on the market, but three I have had very good luck with are the AR Gold, Velocity Triggers and Timney Triggers.

(Make sure you buy a trigger model that fits your rifle brand. For instance, many replacement triggers will not fit some Colt rifles.)

Installation

The installation presented here is for the Timney or Velocity triggers.

The Timney AR-15 Competition Trigger. A standard curved design is on the right, the skeletonized on the left.

(continued . . .)

BUILDING AN AR-15   129

The AR Gold is slightly different and has a different series of safety checks. AR Gold has a very good instructional video on its website.

Remove the upper from the lower. Remove the grip. Go through the bottom with a screwdriver or correctly fitting wrench and unscrew the bolt visible through the bottom of the grip. It should be easy to see the type of head to determine the correct tool. Be very careful not to lose the spring and safety detent, as they are held in place by the grip.

An AR Gold trigger.

Note the spring in the top of the grip in the photo.

It's much easier to perform this work if the gun is held solidly in place, so place a Brownells lower receiver vise block into the magazine well and clamp it in your bench vise.

Using a straight punch, push out the two pins holding the trigger parts in place. Remove all the trigger parts and the safety lever, which is sometimes called the fire control selector. Clean the receiver with a degreasing spray to remove all dirt and debris.

Insert the new trigger into the receiver and place the rear pin through the holes. It sometimes helps to use a slave pin to hold everything in alignment while starting the pin. Insert the safety and then insert the front pin. Replace the grip, making sure to put the detent and spring into the hole in the receiver. This step is easier if you turn the receiver upside down.

You must now tighten the two small set screws in the trigger assembly body. Hold the hammer as you pull the trigger to release it. Then move the spring arms out of the way so you can access the screws that are underneath. Tighten each screw against the bottom of the receiver, alternating back and forth a couple times to make sure they are tight. Now install the two locking screws, one on each side, in the same holes. I also like to add a drop of blue Loctite to the threads on each one.

Function Test

Velocity Trigger.

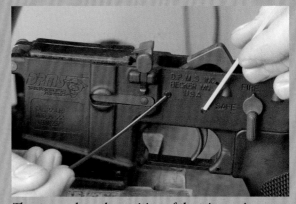
The straws show the position of the trigger pins.

With the lower only, check that the trigger is functioning properly by cocking it and pulling the trigger several times. I like to use a Brownells Hammer Drop Block for dry firing. This is a handy tool if you are doing a lot of this work. If this is a onetime deal, you can get by without it by catching the hammer on your finger.

Check that the disconnect is working. Pull the trigger and hold it back. Cock the hammer and then slowly release the trigger and you should hear and see the disconnector release. There should be a "click," and the hammer will move forward slightly. If that checks out, test the safety. Cock the hammer, put the safety in the "on" position and pull the trigger several times. Don't be afraid to pull it firmly. If nothing happens, push the

Tightening the locking screws in a Timney trigger.

The Brownells Hammer Drop Block allows you to function-test the trigger without the upper receiver installed.

safety off, making sure the sear does not release as you do, then pull the trigger to make sure it releases correctly.

Assemble the upper and lower. Cock the hammer and put the safety in the "off" position. Thump the buttstock on the ground soundly several times. The hammer should remain cocked.

At the range or other safe location load the magazine with two rounds. Then fire the first round to make sure it does not double. Doubling is rare, but it can happen. Test this from several shooting positions. I find doubling happens more often when shooting from a benchrest or prone, so try multiple shooting positions. Always load only two cartridges at a time in the magazine. If the rifle does double, remove the trigger immediately and contact the trigger

A decent trigger is the best upgrade you can do to any AR-15.

manufacturer. Trigger failure is a dangerous and potentially illegal situation, so always remove the trigger from the gun right away.

The new trigger should have a much lower pull weight and a much cleaner feel than the original. I believe that there is nothing you can do to an AR-15 rifle that will improve its performance more than a new trigger. Once you shoot the gun, I think you will agree with that statement.

INSTALLING THE SAFETY AND GRIP

Parts needed:
Safety (called the "fire control selector" in AR jargon)
Fire control selector detent
Fire control selector spring (This is similar to the pivot/takedown detent springs, except there are two of them and only one fire control selector spring. Look them over carefully and you can see the difference.)
Pistol grip
Pistol grip lock washer
Pistol grip screw

Tools needed:
A screwdriver or Allen wrench to match the grip screw.

▲ Installing the safety. (Fire control selector in AR-15 speak.)

Insert the safety from the left side. Check to see that the safety turns freely and that it locks the trigger so the hammer will not release when in the safe position.

Turn the receiver upside down. Insert the detent into the small hole at the rear of the trigger guard on the left side of the upside-down receiver. Insert the spring in the hole in the pistol grip and install the grip, aligning the spring with the detent and the hole in the receiver. Make sure the safety is in the off position. Carefully push the grip in place while compressing the spring and secure the grip in place with the screw and washer. Most are slotted for a screwdriver, but some require an Allen wrench. I like to put a drop of #242 blue Loctite on the screw.

FUNCTION TEST

Turn the safety to make sure it rotates to both safe and fire positions and that it locks into those positions. Note that the hammer must be cocked for the safety to move to the "on" position. Check again to ensure the safety is preventing the trigger from releasing the hammer by putting the safety on and pulling the trigger forcefully, multiple times. Push off the safety and verify that the hammer stays cocked. Verify that the trigger will release the hammer when the lever is in the fire position.

INSTALLING THE MAGAZINE RELEASE

Parts needed:
Magazine catch
Magazine release button
Magazine release button spring (largest spring in the parts kit)

▲ The parts needed for installing the magazine release.

Tools needed:
A punch or dowel

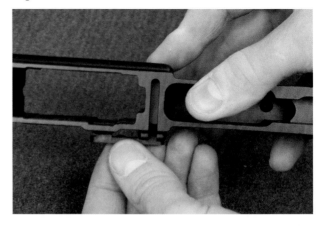

▲ Installing the magazine release. Be very careful to not scratch the receiver.

Slide the shaft of the magazine catch through from the left side of the receiver. Put the spring over the shaft and then put the button on the end and push, letting the magazine catch slide back until the button is captured in the hole on the right side of the receiver. Keep finger pressure on the button, push on the mag catch and turn to start the threaded end of the shaft into the threaded hole on the button. Using a punch or dowel, push the mag button deeper into the receiver. Screw the mag catch holder until the end of the threaded shaft is flush with the top of the release button. Be very careful not to hit the receiver with the mag catch, as that can damage the finish.

▲ After installing the magazine release, the threaded shaft should be flush with the mag release button.

FUNCTION TEST

Push the button down flush with the receiver. Make sure the mag catch is still captured in the receiver. If it comes out of the receiver enough so that it can turn, you must make another revolution of the threads. Make sure that the mag catch will go past flush on the inside to ensure it releases the magazine.

Insert an empty magazine and make sure it is captured tightly. Push the mag button. The magazine should release cleanly and easily.

INSTALLING THE BOLT CATCH

Parts needed:
Bolt catch
Bolt catch pin (the smaller of the two roll pins in the kit)
Bolt catch plunger
Bolt catch spring (easily confused with the disconnector spring, the disconnector spring is wider on one end)

Tools needed:
Small hammer, plastic- and brass-tipped preferred
3S pin holding punch (optional)
3/32-inch roll pin punch
Brownells Bolt Catch Pin Punch (Optional)

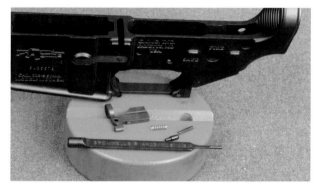

▲ The parts needed for installing the bolt catch. Shown with the inserted Brownells Bolt Catch Pin Punch. This tool helps prevent scratching the receiver as the hole for the roll pin is lower than the receiver on the left side.

Insert the roll pin into the pin holding punch, or hold it with needle nose pliers as you start it into the rear side of the pin hole, tapping lightly with the hammer to start it in the hole. Place the spring in the hole centered under the bolt catch and follow with the plunger. Install and push down on the bolt catch to compress the spring and insert the Brownells Bolt Catch Pin Punch from the left to act as a slave pin. This tool is machined to allow using it from the left side as a slave pin or to remove an installed bolt catch pin by driving the pin out to the rear. Without it, you risk scratching the finish on the receiver. Trust me, I speak from experience and have gotten very good at touching up the marks. Still, they will always show, so not scratching the finish is a much better option.

Using the 3/32-inch roll pin punch and hammer, drive the roll pin into place, using it to push out the slave pin. Insert the pin deep enough so that it is of equal depth on each side.

FUNCTION TEST

For now, make sure the bolt catch operates smoothly and does not hang up or bind. You will test it further once the upper is installed.

TRIGGER GUARD INSTALLATION

Parts needed:
Trigger guard
Trigger guard roll pin

Tools needed:
Small hammer (plastic or brass-tipped preferred)
4S pin holding starter punch (optional)
⅛-inch roll pin punch
⅛-inch pin punch (optional)
Bench block

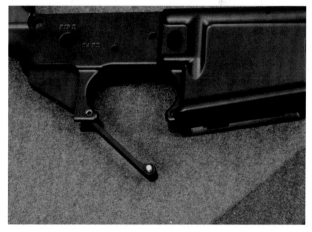

▲ The trigger guard with the pin installed.

The front of the trigger guard should have a spring loaded detent already installed. Compress this and insert the trigger guard into the front, making sure the detent is on the same side as the hole.

Put the receiver on a bench block to support it. A block of wood will work. This is one of the functions of the Present Arms Gunner's Mount. Use the roll pin holding starter punch to start the roll pin, or hold it with needle nose pliers as you start it. It's usually a tight fit and it's easy to damage the end of the roll pin. It is easier to use a slave pin as you gently start the pin through the receiver and into the trigger guard. Carefully use the roll pin punch and hammer to drive the roll pin into the receiver. Check to see it is of equal depth on both sides.

▲ Shows using a slave pin to align the trigger guard to start the roll pin.

▲ Using a roll pin punch to install the roll pin on the trigger guard.

FUNCTION TEST

Depress the detent on the trigger guard and make sure the trigger guard will pivot open.

INSTALLING THE BUTTSTOCK

Parts needed:
Stock
Buffer tube
Takedown pin
Takedown pin spring
Takedown pin detent
Buffer tube retainer
Buffer tube retainer spring
Carbine style buffer
Carbine length buffer spring
Receiver lock plate
Lock nut

Tools needed:
Wrench for locking nut (I suggest the DPMS Multi-Tool.)

▲ A selection of collapsible buttstocks.

Insert the buffer retainer spring and buffer retainer into the hole in the threaded section to the rear of the lower. Thread the locking nut onto the buffer tube and spin it all the way to the rear.

Place the receiver lock plate over the buffer tube and thread the buffer tube into the receiver while compressing the buffer retainer. The buffer tube must go in enough to capture the buffer retainer, but not enough to bind it.

▲ The takedown pin detent and spring ready for installation. Note the buffer tube has captured the buffer retainer.

Place the takedown pin (rear) in the receiver. Insert the detent and spring in the hole in the rear of the receiver. Push the receiver lock plate into place to align the buffer tube while compressing the detent spring.

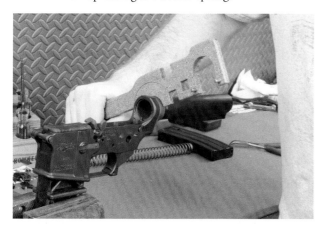

▲ Tightening the lock nut against the receiver lock plate with the DPMS Multi-Tool.

Now tighten the lock nut. There are several wrenches to do this, but the DPMS Multi-Tool will also do many other functions on the AR-15 rifle and it represents an excellent value. There are pre-cut locations for staking the nut to the receiver lock plate if you wish. Most, including myself, don't bother unless the rifle is going to war.

Cock the hammer, depress the buffer tube retainer, and

▲ Installing the buffer spring and buffer.

▲ The buffer spring and buffer after installation.

insert the buffer spring, followed by the buffer. Push them in past the retainer and allow the retainer to pop up to hold them in place.

INSTALLING THE FRONT PIVOT PIN

Remember I said we would do the toughest job first?

I lied.

Installing the front pivot pin is simple on the surface and aggravating in reality. If you are going to attempt this without the correct installation tool, make sure there are no children present, because this job will make even the Pope cuss like a drunken sailor.

Parts needed:

Pivot pin
Pivot pin detent
Pivot pin detent spring

Tools needed:

Pivot pin installation tool
3/32-inch pin punch
Big jar of swear words

▲ The parts and tool used for installing the pivot pin. Shown with the pivot pin. This is the less expensive tool that works with some practice. However, I recommend you buy the other tool.

This can be done with just the pin punch, but it's not pretty. You must compress the detent and spring and then insert the pivot pin. Sounds easy, but it's not. The detent and spring will fly out and you will be spending a lot of time on your knees looking for them.

Brownells sells two tools for this job. One, called the AR-15 Front Pivot Pin Assembly/Disassembly Kit, is simply a bent shaft with a hole drilled in it, shown in the photo above. It works well in theory, but proper execution requires that you can chew gum, walk, talk, text and dance all at the same time. I apparently cannot.

▲ This is the pivot pin installation tool from Brownells, stock number 100-003-308, that works best. Note the block to catch the hammer when dryfiring.

Trust me, you want the two piece set called AR-15/M16 Pivot Pin Installation Tool, stock number 100-003-308. It costs more, but it works a lot better.

Install the jig on the front of the receiver to align over

the right side. Insert the tool pin from the left and rotate until the hole is lined up with the hole in the receiver. Insert the spring and detent. Push them into the receiver using the 3/32-inch pin punch until you can rotate the tool pin to capture the detent. Now insert the pivot pin in the tool guide with the slot toward the detent and push until you hear the detent click into the slot. Remove the installation tool and you are done building this lower.

Unless you used this tool, say three Hail Marys as penance for your foul language and then start thinking about your upper, because this thing is a wrap.

THE UPPER

In building any AR-15 rifle, the upper is where the magic happens. The lower lays the foundation, but the upper has all the parts that shoot. First among them is the barrel and this is one place where I could exercise some options that are harder to find in a low price, off the shelf rifle.

▲ The upper receiver.

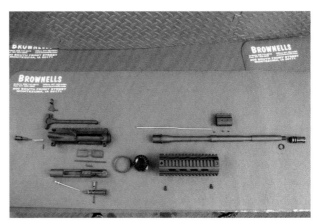

▲ The parts needed to build an AR-15 upper.

The barrel options are almost limitless, so do some homework and pick a barrel design and rifling twist rate that fits your needs. I have builds with everything from ultralight, pencil thin barrels to one rifle with a Hi-Power match barrel that will shoot ½-MOA out to 500 yards.

Many barrels are threaded on the end with a ½-28 thread for a flash hider or muzzle brake. I ordered a DPMS A2 flash hider and a crush washer for this build.

Consider a muzzle brake, depending on your intended use. Although muzzle brakes are a bit noisier, replacing the flash hider with a muzzle brake will aid in controlling the rifle for fast follow-up shots.

There are a huge number of upper receivers on the market. I have built rifles using half a dozen or more different receiver brands and have never had a problem. But, as always, if you stick with a known brand name it usually means fewer problems.

The upper receiver shown in the build photos is from DPMS. I have several of their rifles and have used DPMS receivers, both upper and lower, on multiple builds, so I trust them. I ordered a DPMS Lo-Pro flat-top model with an integral rail from Brownells. The flattop receiver provides the widest range of options, as I can still mount a carry handle with sights if I wish to emulate the classic AR-15 look, or mount an infinite number of optical, iron, or electronic sights.

I also ordered a DPMS bolt and bolt carrier complete assembly. This is a bit less expensive than ordering the individual parts and it eliminates some assembly headaches with the ejector, gas rings and other parts.

When using a scope, it's sometimes hard to reach the charging handle. I added a Badger Ordnance extended "tactical" charging handle latch for easier operation.

Another area where building your own rifle gives you more options is in the front gas block. Most M4 style carbines are going to be shipped with the familiar triangle-shaped A2 front sight/gas block. When using low power optical sights this high front sight is visible in your sight picture and is a distraction, so I elected to install a Brownells Modular Gas Block. This low profile, low cost gas block has a rail on the top to allow mounting a front sight, including a flip-up sight. It also has the option of adding rails to the other three sides. I added a carbine length gas tube with a retaining roll pin to complete the gas operating system.

Once again, most low priced M4 style rifles are going to have an A2 style handguard that attaches front and rear. I prefer a floating barrel and a floating handguard because they usually provide better accuracy. On this build, I ordered a Yankee Hill Machine Company four-rail floating forend. This comes with the barrel nut.

Other parts include a dust cover with spring, pin and retaining clip, as well as the forward assist with spring and pin.

After checking the parts list to ensure I had everything I needed, I started with the forward assist assembly.

INSTALLING THE FORWARD ASSIST

Parts needed:
Forward assist retainer pin
Forward assist spring
Forward assist assembly

Tools needed:
3/32-inch roll pin punch
Hammer, plastic or brass

▲ Inserting the forward assist.

▲ Installing the forward assist retainer pin.

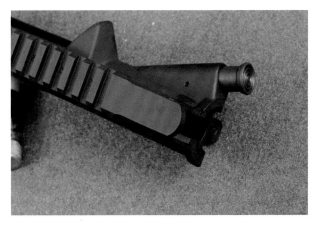

▲ The completed forward assist.

The forward assist comes assembled and ready to install. The first step is to start the roll pin that holds this part in place into the receiver. After starting the pin, simply place the spring over the forward assist, orient the part and insert it into the upper receiver. Hold it against the spring, while tapping the pin into place. Use a 3/32-inch roll pin punch to drive the pin past flush.

FUNCTION TEST

Push the plunger to make sure the pawl moves forward and returns back under spring pressure.

INSTALLING THE EJECTION PORT COVER

Parts needed:
Cover hinge pin
Cover hinge pin snap ring
Cover Spring
Ejection port cover

Tools needed:
Needle nose pliers
Plastic hammer

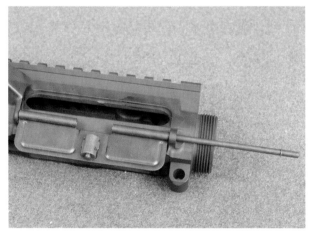

▲ The ejection port cover pin is back to allow for insertion of the spring.

▲ The ejection port cover spring can be difficult to install.

▲ The completed ejection port cover.

   Install the small snap ring on the cover hinge pin using the pliers. Tap it in place with the hammer to ensure it is seated. Place the cover on the receiver and start the pin from the front. Make sure the snap ring is at the far end. Do not push the pin all the way through.
   The spring must be pre-loaded by turning the long arm one-half turn. Then you need to hold the spring in place, maintaining the tension as the pin is inserted all the way through. This is one of those "multi-curse" projects for me, as with my abused, arthritic hands I find it difficult to hold the spring pressure while installing the pin. Brendan Burns was doing the work while I shot photos and I cautioned him it would take several attempts. The show-off got it together on the first try.

FUNCTION TEST

Make sure the cover will close. Then reach in through the front of the receiver with your finger and push the locking pin down to open the cover.

INSTALLING THE BOLT, BOLT CARRIER, AND CHARGING HANDLE

Parts needed:
Charging handle
Charging handle latch
Charging handle spring
Charging handle latch pin
Bolt carrier and bolt assembly
Cam pin
Firing pin
Firing pin retaining pin

Tools needed:
1/16-inch roll pin punch
1/16-inch roll pin holder punch
Hammer, brass or plastic
Bench block

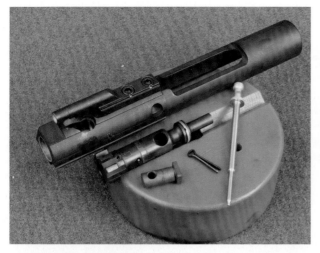

▲ The parts needed.

▲ Insert the cam pin.

▲ Insert the bolt into the carrier.

▲ Insert the firing pin retaining pin.

▲ Insert the firing pin.

Push the bolt into the bolt carrier, making sure the extractor is oriented to the right side. Drop the bolt cam pin through the hole in the bolt carrier, rotate it a quarter-turn and slide the firing pin into the bolt. Insert the firing pin retaining pin through the bolt carrier, with the head of the pin matching with the large recess on the left side of bolt carrier so that the head of the pin is below flush when installed.

▲ The parts needed.

▲ Fitting the retaining pin. Note the oversized latch beside the bench block. This is an option when building the gun.

The charging handle is easy to assemble. Start the retaining pin in the charging handle. This is easier if you use a 1/16-inch roll pin holding punch. Place the spring in the hole, insert the latch and hold it under spring pressure so the holes are lined up, then tap the pin home using a 1/16-inch roll pin punch. You can use a 1/16-inch punch as a slave pin if you have trouble lining up the holes. Install the charging handle into the receiver. Pull the bolt forward in the carrier and then install the bolt assembly so the bolt carrier key rides in the trough on the underside of the charging handle. Make sure they can move in the receiver without any problems, then take them both out and set them aside.

INSTALLING THE BARREL

Parts needed:
Barrel
Barrel nut

Tools needed:
DPMS Multi-Tool or other barrel wrench
Brownells upper receiver action block with insert.
½-inch drive torque wrench
Bench mounted vise

▲ Torqueing the barrel nut.

▲ The action held in the action blocks, shown with insert.

This instruction is for installing the barrel using the Yankee Hill forend and barrel nut and is typical for floating forends. However, the process may vary a bit with other forends.

Slide the action block insert inside the action to support it and prevent distorting under pressure as you install the barrel. Then clamp the action in the action block tool and clamp the action block in a bench mounted vise.

Clean the threads on the receiver with a small brush and coat them with an anti-seize compound or high-quality grease. Insert the barrel. Thread the barrel nut with the wide threaded portion to the rear of the receiver end. Tighten the barrel nut using the DPMS Multi-Tool wrench designed for this job. The wrench is designed to be used with a half-inch drive torque wrench. The Mil-Spec technique is as follows:

▲ The Yankee Hill barrel nut is installed. Shown with the gas tube in place.

"Torque to 35 foot-pounds. Loosen. Torque again to 35 foot-pounds. Loosen again. Torque past 35 foot-pounds, until the next gas tube hole in the nut is in alignment, but do not exceed 80 foot-pounds."

INSTALLING THE HANDGUARD

Again, this is for the Yankee Hill handguard. Others may be different, so use the directions supplied with the one you are installing. I have installed a lot of handguards and for the most part each one is a little bit different.

Parts needed:
Yankee Hill Machine handguard
Jam nut
Anti-rotation screws (2)

Tools needed:
Yankee Hill Machine Forend Wrench
Level
Brownells Upper Receiver Action Block with Insert
Bench mounted vise
Screwdriver

▲ Put some grease on the threads before installing the handguard.

▲ Installing the handguard.

Screw the jam nut onto the barrel nut until it is flush with the end closest to the upper receiver. Then unscrew it one and one-half turns. A little grease on the threads will make it easier. Install the handguard, turning it in until it contacts the jam nut. Make sure the sling swivel holes are to the front. Align the anti-rotation screws at three and nine o'clock.

With the receiver clamped in the vise, place a level on the rail on the receiver and level the upper assembly in the vise. Then place the level on the handguard top rail, and turn the handguard until it is level and in perfect alignment with the rail on the receiver. Tighten the jam nut using the YHM forend wrench. Put some #242 Loctite on the anti-rotation screws and install them in the forend with the screwdriver.

INSTALLING THE GAS BLOCK AND GAS TUBE

Parts needed:
Gas block
Gas tube
Gas tube pin

Tools needed:
1/8-inch Allen wrench
5/64-inch roll pin punch
#47 drill bit

▲ Using a drill as a slave pin to locate the gas tube hole.

Put the pre-shaped gas tube in place, with the solid end through the hole in the barrel nut. Slide the gas block down the barrel, being careful not to mar the finish. Put a drop of blue #242 Loctite on the set screws and install them, but do not tighten.

With the receiver clamped in the vise, place a level on the rail on the receiver and level the upper assembly in the vise. Then place the level on the gas block rail and turn the block until it is level and in perfect alignment with the rail on the receiver. Tighten the screws on the gas block.

If you want a more secure lockdown of the gas block, after lining it up correctly, remove the set screws one at a

▲ Use levels to make sure all the top, flat surfaces match.

time and drill a shallow dimple in the barrel for the screws to lock into. I don't think that step is necessary unless you are going to be mounting some heavy accessories on the rails of the gas block. If you do it, be careful to use a drill press or milling machine with a stop so you do not drill too deep and ruin the barrel. Do one screw at a time, replacing each one before removing the next so that alignment is maintained.

Insert the gas tube into the gas block. Make sure the end of the gas tube with the three holes is at the gas block.

Start the gas tube pin in the gas block using a 5/64-inch roll pin holder punch. It's a little tough to line up the hole inside the tube with the hole in the block unless you use a slave pin. The shank of a #47 drill is the right size for this job. After aligning the holes, carefully drive in the roll pin using the 5/64-inch roll pin punch until it is equal depth on each side.

INSTALLING THE FLASH HIDER OR MUZZLE BRAKE

Parts needed:
Flash hider or muzzle brake
Crush washer

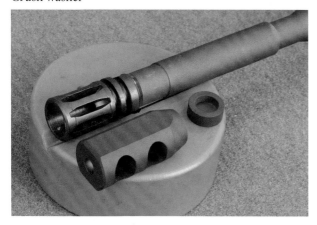

▲ This rifle has a flash hider installed. The brake beside it is another option.

Tools needed:
DPMS Multi-Tool or other barrel wrench
Brownells Upper Receiver Action Block with Insert
Bench mounted vise

Slide the crush washer on the threaded end of the barrel with the narrow end to the barrel. Put a bit of #242 Loctite on the cleaned threads and install the flash hider or muzzle brake. For a more permanent and heat-proof installation use Rocksett on the threads. (To remove Rocksett, soak in hot water.)

▲ A little Loctite helps.

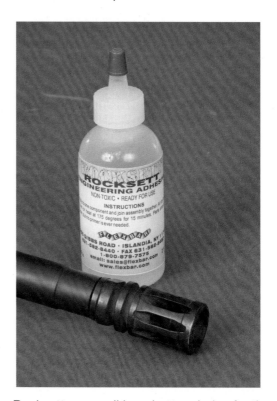

▲ Rocksett may well be a better choice for the flash hider or muzzle brake, because it does not lose adhesion with heat.

▲ Tightening and orienting the flash hider.

Use the DPMS Multi-Tool wrench to tighten until it is properly oriented. The flash hider should have the solid section facing down. The muzzle brake will be level with the ports to the side, or slightly cocked to counteract twisting under recoil, as the shooter prefers.

CHECKING HEADSPACE

Tools needed:
Headspace go and no-go gauges for 5.56X45 or .223, depending on the chambering of the barrel.

Other cartridges will of course require the correct headspace gauges.

The barrel is shipped with the barrel extension in place and in theory everything is machined so that the headspacing will be correct when the bolt is closed, but it's a very good idea to double-check.

If your gauge has a notch in the rim, align so the ejector fits into the notch and clip the extractor over the rim on the go gauge. If there is no notch, you will need to either remove the ejector or compress it with the gauge.

With the gauge held in place on the bolt face, install the bolt carrier assembly and charging handle in the rifle. Push the bolt forward, inserting the gauge into the chamber like a cartridge. The bolt should fully close and the bolt head should rotate into battery. Now install the no-go gauge and repeat. This time the bolt should not close. If the bolt closes on the go gauge and does not close on the no-go gauge, you are done.

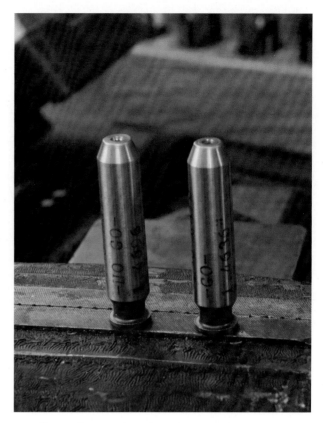

▲ Go and no-go headspace gauges.

▲ This shows the gauge captured by the bolt and started into the chamber.

I have encountered headspacing issues a few times, particularly with chrome lined barrels. If the headspacing is not correct, it will require a gunsmith with a lathe and other tools to correct. A chrome lined barrel with a short chamber can't be corrected. The best approach with any barrel is to just return it to the maker and ask for another.

Install the bolt carrier and charging handle and then mate the upper to the lower, attaching them by the front pivot pin and rear locking pin.

▲ The completed rifle waiting for optics and ammo.

FUNCTION TEST

Run through a few dry cycles to make sure the bolt cycles. Shut the bolt and close the dust cover. Now, pull back on the charging handle. The dust cover should open as the bolt is pulled back. Make sure the forward assist is working and will push against the bolt and release cleanly. Insert an empty magazine and make sure the bolt locks back and will release with the bolt release.

Clean the barrel, install some sights, lubricate the moving parts, and go with pride to the range to shoot your new rifle.

This five-pound AR-15 was made from parts. ▶

CHAPTER 10

BUILDING A 1911 HANDGUN FROM PARTS

▲ The author's 1911.

▲ Reynolds' 1911.

If there is one lesson I could make readers of this book understand it's this: *Listen to the people who do things for a living.*

You know the old saying, "do as I say, not as I do"? I kinda wish I could have made myself listen to the expert on this project.

When I was ordering the parts for this build I thought the idea of a titanium frame sounded pretty high-tech. It would be lighter to carry and much cooler to talk about with fellow gun guys.

"I don't recommend it," said Gary Smith, the sales manager at Caspian Arms. Caspian is the leading manufacturer of frames and slides for 1911 builds and their parts are probably used by more custom builders than all others combined.

We were at Caspian's Vermont headquarters to order the parts for this build and Gary was explaining what we needed. He continued, "The titanium frames are much more difficult to fit and they just lead to a lot of problems unless you are very experienced in working with them."

While I had never built a 1911 at that time, or worked with titanium for that matter, I was pretty cocky about my abilities in the shop. I figured, what could really be that different?

I can tell you that I damn sure found out.

Building a 1911 with a traditional frame in stainless or carbon steel compared to the problems of fitting the parts into a titanium frame would equate to putting together a child's model car kit versus building a functioning space shuttle. Or at least it seemed that way before I was done. Nothing fit right, not one damn part. Even after I made them fit, they didn't like running against titanium.

2422		8/6/2012	UPS		Net 10		8/16/2012
QTY	ITEM CODE	DESCRIPTION				EACH	AMOUNT
1	RECEOFFT	Officers Model Receiver, Commercially Pure Titanium. MSRP $441.13				352.90	352.90T
1	45	.45 Feed Ramp On Receiver				0.00	0.00

▲ When Caspian's Gary Smith said "Don't order titanium," I should have listened. This section of the invoice is evidence that I did not.

Making everything fit was mind altering, as most of what I thought I knew about fitting parts didn't seem to apply. On top of that, titanium has a reputation for being very bitchy about being worked or machined. In my never humble opinion, that reputation is far too kind. It's not any one thing I can point to as the issue, but a multitude of little things. I have built and will build more 1911 handguns, but it would take several strong men with big clubs to convince me to attempt another titanium frame. At least until the pain of this one fades away and there is no telling how long that's going to take.

In the time since, Gary has retired and Caspian has stopped offering single-stack titanium frames. I suspect I had a little to do with both. Not directly, mind you, but the little voodoo doll I made up to look like a 1911 titanium frame has a lot of pins stuck in it and I guess somebody finally noticed.

Eric Reynolds bought stainless steel parts at the same time and we built the guns together. That made a perfect "real-time" comparison of building two different guns and opened my eyes to one simple truth: Don't assume you know it all. Instead, listen to the people who truly do know what they are talking about.

Eric's gun was a pleasure to build and caused very few problems or temper tantrums. Mine? Let's just say it was something different and all walk away before somebody gets hurt.

That said, it worked out in the end and I have a very interesting and unique handgun that weighs in at slightly less than two pounds with an empty magazine inserted. I used the Commander size slide with a 4.25-inch barrel. The frame is the smaller Officer size. This allows easier concealed carry. The shorter Officer size magazine holds seven rounds and the gun will accept full-size eight-round magazines, they just stick out the bottom a little bit. The mid-size Commander upper eliminates the function and feeding problems often associated with the smaller Officer size handgun.

Eric went with the straight Commander size in stainless steel, but with a Race Ready Recon frame that has a flared magazine well built into the grip frame. In addition to being a custom carry gun, he uses his pistol in competition for USPSA, IDPA, and other shooting events.

▲ A Series 80 1911 will have this trigger-activated link that contacts the firing pin block shown below in the slide. This design has many moving parts that must be activated by the trigger, but have nothing to do with the true function of the trigger.

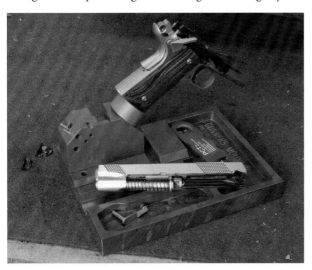

▲ This gun has a stainless steel slide and a titanium frame. While the end result was excellent, the path to that result was not.

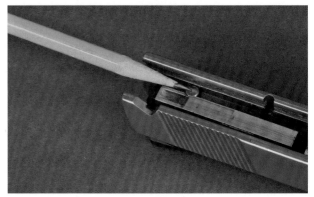

I should note that not all 1911 pistols are created equal. That is to say, not all brands and designs are made the same and parts are not necessarily interchangeable. For example, the Series 80 and its copycats use a block on the firing pin that requires the trigger to be pulled before the gun can fire. The idea is that this prevents the gun from firing if dropped on its muzzle.

For the record, I am not a fan.

I know all the literature says that it is just as easy to get a clean, crisp, light trigger pull with a Series 80 pistol, but I don't find that to be true.

I am the first to admit that, compared to a lot of other people, my 1911 experience is limited, but I have been fooling with these pistols for a couple of decades and have worked on a bunch of them. Besides, it's simple logic. When the trigger is required to move several parts that are not part of the function of firing the gun, it introduces more drag, adds spring tension, and increases the trigger pull weight. That is simple physics. I suppose that the Series 80 is safer, but, like most lawyer designs, it is not better, at least in terms of trigger pull.

I have seen multiple "experts" who seem to have chips on their shoulders, claiming the Series 80 is capable of producing just as good a trigger pull as other 1911 handguns.

▲ This S&W 1911 is a Series 80. I used it for IDPA competition after adjusting the trigger pull. It's a nice clean three pounds now, so clearly you can get a decent trigger in a Series 80 pistol.

It simply cannot be true. While a Series 80 trigger can be made to have a decent trigger pull, to say that it is equal to a standard trigger simply ignores the laws of physics.

In a 1911 without the Series 80 firing pin block, the firing pin spring keeps the gun from firing when inertia acts on the floating firing pin if the gun is

dropped. If the spring is of the proper tension and length, it does this job nicely. Just to be safe, some gunsmiths like to install a lighter-weight titanium firing pin to reduce the inertia if the gun is dropped, something to consider when ordering your parts.

Studies have shown that some 1911 handguns can fire when dropped, so if you are worried, pick a Series 80 design. However, this chapter does not deal with making all those parts function, so you will need to find that info elsewhere. In fact, I urge you to check out multiple sources for any build. This book is a guide and I like to think it's a good one, but I am a big believer that there is no such thing as too much information, so I urge you to explore what's out there.

Let me make a confession. Building these pistols was a challenge and often I had my mind so deep into solving the problems and fitting the parts that I forgot to take photographs. We finally got deep enough into the process that I made the decision to deviate from my usual routine of shooting photos as a build progresses. My new plan was to later tear down the handguns and recreate the photos. Before I knew it we finished both guns, including spray-on coatings. Then Eric moved to Kentucky with his gun. As a result, many of the illustrative photos shown here are after the fact, or may even be of another gun. No matter. They illustrate a point or process, which is their main job.

▲ A Remington 1911 R1 Enhanced.

Some of the photos here, particularly in the trigger sidebar, are of a Remington R1 Enhanced 1911, which is a Series 80 design. I can't begin to tell you how many hours I spent working on the trigger on my early production R1 pistol. I could never get it to a satisfactory trigger pull until I got a kit from Brownells to remove the Series 80 parts and effectively turn the gun back into a conventional design, at least in terms of the trigger. This is often erroneously called a Series 70 handgun. It still has the Series 80 hammer with the half-cock ledge, which I have no problem with. Once I eliminated the Series 80 firing pin block and all the linkage, I was able to achieve a fine trigger pull.

I might also note that I wound up buying a new hammer during that process, but we need not go into why. Let's just say that every part plays a critical role in the function of the gun. If you remove too much metal from the wrong places, it might stop working correctly. Like I keep saying, once metal is gone, it's all but impossible to replace. So always be thoughtful, deliberate, and methodical about anything you do that modifies a part.

Okay, I changed my mind. I'll confess. No secrets here, right? I recut the hammer hooks one too many times in attempting to figure out this trigger. That changed the geometry so the trigger never worked right and as a result, I had to buy a new hammer. Lesson learned.

That said, my friend Dean Weatherby bought the same model Remington R1 a few years later and his came from the factory with a fine trigger pull that really needed no attention at all.

So, clearly, Series 80 handguns can have a good trigger pull, but the extra parts can make achieving one much more difficult. For the builds here, our pistols are more of the conventional design without the Series 80 firing pin blocking parts. Just like John Moses intended.

Caspian is the choice for frames and slides for a large number of 1911 builders, as there are a lot of features to select from. Both of our guns have very aggressive checkering, as Caspian offers a wide range of checkering options to choose from.

They also allow custom serial numbers. Mine is 8 28 82 BRT. That is my wedding date and the letters are our initials, Bryce and Robin Towsley. I picked this because I started this project just before August 28, 2012, which was our thirtieth wedding anniversary. I might note that we celebrated early on the twenty-seventh, eating a frozen pizza while we packed for a hunting trip I was leaving for early the next morning.

Who says romance is dead?

▲ With a serial number like "Pretty Boy 1," it should be pink.

Eric's serial number is Pretty Boy 1. I think it has something do to with one of the girls at Caspian calling him a pretty boy. Aside from the clear evidence that she needs glasses, there might have been some of his shooting posse making a dare to pick that as a serial number.

There are entire books written on how to build a 1911 from parts. There are also a multitude of hands-on schools, some lasting as long as a week. This is a complicated subject and I don't pretend that one chapter in this general gunsmithing book is going to be comprehensive enough to cover all the aspects of building a 1911 from parts. However, this does cover how we built our 1911 handguns and wound up with a couple of pretty good pistols. It's a good guide for anybody starting their first build.

As first-time builders, Eric and I took a few shortcuts. Nothing to compromise the outcome, but things that kept us away from the most complicated aspects of building custom 1911 handguns. Some of them, such as using a drop-in barrel, might have some big-name custom gun builders rolling their eyes, but it makes a lot of sense for a hobby gunsmith on his first build. Fitting the barrel is one of the most critical and difficult aspects of building a 1911 pistol. It requires a deep knowledge of the subject and often some specialized tools. The drop-in barrels worked just fine for our first builds with minimal tweaking. Mine took a little bit of fitting of course, but it did not require a full-blown fitting process. Our barrels also came with bushings that were already fitted and the link installed.

▲ Most drop-in barrels come with the bushing fitted.

The drop-in barrel should fit without interference and lock up at or near full engagement of the top locking lugs. Often you will need to tweak the top lugs a little for them to fit. Brownells has a special file made just for this job with two sides safe so the cut is not made any wider. The hood should enter the slide without interference and should not make contact when the gun is in battery. The lower lugs should be riding on the slide release pin to push the barrel into battery and the link should not be influencing the barrel when in battery. The fit in the bushing should be snug with little or no play. The only thing I had to do to my barrel was tweak the top lug cuts just a little bit to make the barrel lock up correctly. On Eric's pistol, the drop-in barrel fit without any tweaking.

If you find you enjoy building 1911 handguns, your

first build will likely be far from your last. With each build you will explore new territory and learn new skills, at some point including how to install a gunsmith-fit 1911 barrel. But, for your first attempt, I think following our lead makes more sense.

Just don't use the titanium lower!

That thing will give you nightmares.

▲ Ed Brown has some easy to install drop-in 1911 barrels. They come with a fitted bushing.

Another concession to being first-time 1911 builders is that we took advantage of the service offered by Caspian to fit the slide to the frame. This is a critical part of building a 1911 and one that is filled with myths, traps, and potholes for first-time builders. For a reasonable fee, the experts at Caspian will do this critical step for you.

One more word of advice, if you decide to do it yourself: I once had a custom 2011 handgun built as part of a series of articles I was writing for NRA's *American Rifleman* magazine. I watched in horror as the builder coated the slide and frame with valve grinding compound and then used a giant soft-blow hammer to pound them together and back apart.

"It's how all the top builders fit their frames," he told me when I asked.

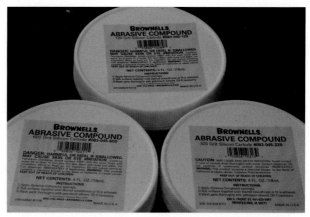

▲ Various lapping compounds from Brownells.

I doubted that, so I checked with a few of those builders. Apparently some of them do use this method, while other "name" guys are violently opposed to the practice.

Personally, I am seriously opposed to fitting any moving part that is critical to operating the firearm with lapping compound. Doing a final lap with ultra-fine compound, yes, that makes sense. That is polishing and should be done sparingly. There are some non-critical parts that can be fitted using lapping compound, but using lapping compound as a shortcut to fit most moving parts is, in my never humble opinion, a horrible idea. You have no control over the metal that is removed. Lapping compound will always go for the high spots, corners, and the edges first. That will reshape the contours of the metal in ways that are not good. I have seen several rifle and handgun actions ruined by somebody putting lapping compound on moving parts in an attempt to smooth them up or make them fit.

There are better methods to fitting anything, including a 1911 slide to the frame. These are time-honored, skill-driven techniques. With lapping compound, you are not in charge or in control of anything.

Before you ask, I have tried fitting frames with both

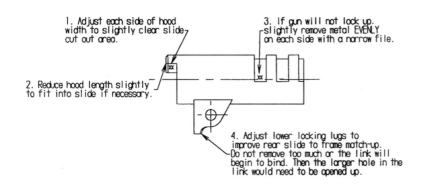

1. Adjust each side of hood width to slightly clear slide, cut out area.

2. Reduce hood length slightly to fit into slide if necessary.

3. If gun will not lock up, slightly remove metal EVENLY on each side with a narrow file.

4. Adjust lower locking lugs to improve rear slide to frame match-up. Do not remove too much or the link will begin to bind. Then the larger hole in the link would need to be opened up.

◀ Drawing of the barrel showing points that may need adjusting.

Ed Brown Products, Inc.
573-565-3261 • www.edbrown.com

techniques. I like to know my opinions are right before I express them. So, at least for now, I am firmly in the "don't do it" camp. You may choose to ignore me, but I warned you, so my conscience is clear.

GETTING STARTED

First of all, this assumes you have at least a working knowledge of the 1911 handgun. You should understand the parts of the gun, how they go together and how they function. If you are not capable of stripping a 1911 to its parts and putting it back together, it's not the time to try building one. It is best to get a basic education on the handgun and its workings before attempting this project.

Any fit or function procedure that requires ammo should be done with dummy rounds. They are available from Brownells and it's also easy for any handloader to make them. Mark handloaded dummy rounds clearly so that you can easily identify them and there is no chance of mixing them up with live ammo.

▲ Make sure you have all the parts needed before starting the build.

Gather up all the parts and do an inventory to make sure you have everything you will need. Most of our parts came from Caspian Arms. Everything else came from

Brownells. Both these companies can assist you when you are ordering to make sure you have all the parts you need and that they are all compatible.

As you work, take a little time to polish all the contact surfaces on any and all moving parts. Also, check the slide and frame to make sure all the holes are clean and polished and free of burrs. Chase out the holes with a correctly fitted drill bit, turned by hand, to remove any burrs.

Look at how all the parts go together and take a moment to polish the contact surfaces of any place they rub on each other, not only the internal parts, but also the frame or slide.

Do not remove any metal or change the contours, simply polish. Depending on the part, you can do this with a hard Arkansas or fine ceramic stone. For some parts, a felt wheel on a Dremel tool is also very handy, as is a bench-mounted buffing wheel. I use fine rouge compound on both the Dremel and the bench-mounted buffing wheel, which produces a nice polish. Chuck the pins in a drill press and run the Dremel polishing tool or bench mounted buffing wheel against them as they spin. It's worth a few extra hours making sure all the moving parts are smooth and polished. This helps the gun run well, and also gives it that slick "custom" feel when you run the slide or pull the trigger.

▲ If the slide and frame fit needs work, this file may be useful. It's designed specifically for fitting a 1911 slide to the frame.

Double-check to make sure the slide-to-frame fit is correct. They should slide together smoothly and without any sticky spots. It's said that one good way to check is to put them together and hold them vertically over a soft pad. Hold just the grip on the frame and the slide should come off the frame with its own weight. Make sure it has a soft landing zone, not a concrete floor.

There should be very little wobble or wiggle in the slide-to-frame fit. If you are building a defensive pistol where reliability is the primary concern, a little bit of clearance might be acceptable—but damn little. A good fit should feel like it's on bearings.

▲ Polishing all the contact surfaces of any moving parts helps make things run smoothly.

Gently polish the feed ramp on the frame and barrel. Don't remove any metal, just slick it up. Make sure there is a slight flat section between the frame feed ramp and the barrel.

Much of building a custom 1911 is aesthetics. If you spend a little time fitting the parts closely together, you will get a nicer looking firearm.

THE GUNNER'S MOUNT 1911 WORK STATION

When working on a 1911 it's always handy to have at least three hands. Since that's not possible for most of us, there is always the Gunner's Mount from Present Arms, Inc. The guys at Present Arms are engineers, gun guys and machinists. They recently visited my shop and explained their products and the genesis of how they came about. After three decades in this business and with everybody with an idea wanting me to buy in, I am a bit jaded. I was skeptical, but these guys impressed me. Not only are their products well thought out, they are always improving, changing, and looking for new opportunities. They asked questions and actually listened to my answers—pretty unique in my experience with people with new products.

This Gunner's Mount is like having a third hand.

Present Arms makes several tools to hold firearms while working on them, but for this project, the M1911 Special Package is hard to beat. I am not sure how I ever did 1911 work without it. It has a post that inserts into the magazine well to hold the gun while you are working on it and it is adjustable so that you can get just about any angle you need. When putting the fire control parts back in the frame it acts as that third hand. Since getting this tool my language while working in my shop is much improved.

There are several other functions with the work station, including locations on the armorer's plate for mainspring housing pin removal and barrel link pin removal. There is also a fixture block for critical repairs and inspections. This allows you to install the fire control system on the block to see how the parts interact and to inspect them to make sure all the parts are in harmony. There is also a location to hold the safety while you file it to fit. This is just scratching the surface of what this kit can do.

Present Arms' barrel bushing wrench.

The system also includes one of the company's patented barrel bushing wrenches. Finally, a wrench designed by somebody who actually works on guns! The designers turned the angle of the cut 90 degrees so that the wrench captures the recoil plug. If you have ever had one go airborne, you'll appreciate that. Most of us who have worked on 1911 handguns have a few scars from flying spring plugs. I even had one take out my shop lights one time.

Present Arms has also added some kits and tools for working on AR-15 rifles that have a lot of innovative features that I have found helpful.

FITTING THE GRIP SAFETY

The first step we tackled was to fit the grip safety to the frame. First I polished the surfaces inside the frame with a fine India stone and finished with a hard Arkansas stone. I didn't remove any metal, just polished the contact areas and removed any burrs or rough spots.

The grip safety was still a very tight fit and I found that I had to modify it slightly to make it fit inside the frame. As always, the best approach when you need to remove metal is to cut on the cheapest part. In this case it was the grip safety, so I used a file and stones to work the sides until it fit the frame easily. Then I polished the surfaces until the fit was free from any sticking.

▲ This is the tang jig used for fitting the grip safety. I wish I had bought it before I did my first build.

▲ This shows the jig installed for illustration. This is a frame from a factory 1911 that is completed. The jig is shown installed to illustrate placement, but is clearly not intended to be used on this frame.

The tangs on the Caspian frame are oversized and must be fitted to the grip safety. Brownells sells several different jigs to accomplish this task while maintaining the correct angles and contours. I took the redneck gunsmithing approach of, "we don't need no stinking jigs" and did it freehand. This works, but let me give you a bit of advice . . . buy the jig. It's a lot less work and ensures a better outcome. They are not all that expensive. I will admit, while my gun looks good and functions well, one area I am not 100 percent satisfied with is the fitting I am about to describe. I could have done a better job if I had just ordered the jig.

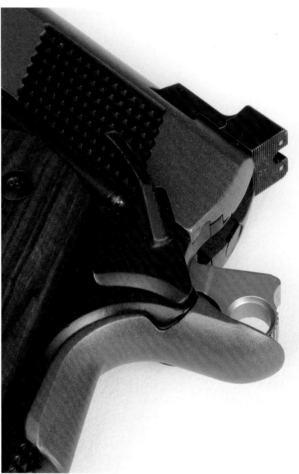

▲ The fit between the frame and the grip safety is not too bad, but it could have been better if I had used the jig instead of doing it freehand.

Before starting, make sure the thumb safety stud will fit through the grip and through the hole in the grip safety without interference. Measure the diameter of the stud on the thumb safety.

I have an inexpensive set of drills I bought some time back on sale from one of the machine tool mail-order places. One function they serve other than as drills, is as slave pins for a lot of different processes. There is a wide range of drills in this kit and the shanks work well for this job. They are much cheaper than precision gage pins and in this case precision is not critical. So, find the drill that matches the diameter of the thumb safety pin. Set it aside along with a few smaller drills. You will use them later when final fitting the grip safety.

The key is to fit the tangs on the frame to the grip safety so that the thumb safety shank can fit through the hole in the grip safety without any tension or drag. At the same time, the tangs on the grip should fit the grip safety closely and without any unsightly gaps, yet allow the grip safety to move freely.

I fitted mine by hand, using files and a Dremel tool. I put Dykem on the tangs, then fit the grip safety to the tangs and moved it back and forth. Then I gently removed metal off the high spots on the tangs as indicated by the Dykem being rubbed off. Once the grip safety was fitted well enough that the holes were almost lined up, I used the size drill that fit snug through the holes to put a little pressure on the grip safety and hold it in place.

Before inserting the grip safety and the drill to hold it, I inked them with Dykem and applied #320-grit lapping compound on the tangs. *Yes, lapping compound does have useful properties.* I lapped the two by rocking the tang safety until I could fit the next larger drill through the hole. I continued this until I could finish with the drill that is the same diameter as the pin on the thumb safety. To finish I switched to the finer #600-grit compound.

After cleaning up the lapping compound the thumb safety should fit through to hold the grip safety in place. The grip safety should move without sticking and should have a nice looking fit to the frame.

At some point the tab on the grip safety will need to be fitted to the trigger bow to ensure it works properly. Of course, to do this requires waiting until after completing the trigger installation. Even so, I'll explain the process here.

The grip safety should block the trigger when the grip safety is not compressed and allow the trigger to move without interference when the grip safety is compressed. The release point should be when the grip safety is compressed to about 50 percent of its travel. To adjust for this,

▲ The shiny spot on this grip safety shows where to file to adjust the release point.

the leg contacting the trigger should be thinned by removing a bit of metal from the bottom. This moves the trailing edge up so it releases from the trigger bow sooner in its travel.

Take just a little metal and try the grip safety. Repeat until completed. I like to keep the release at no deeper than 50 percent of the grip safety travel. If you have the release point too deep, say 75 percent into the grip safety travel, it may fail to release if you have a poor grip. On a defensive pistol, this can be a problem, as you may not have time to readjust the grip and if the pistol won't function, you could be in big trouble.

I have also seen texts that suggest filing on the bow of the trigger rather than the grip safety. It's the "cut on the cheapest part" school of thought. Grip safeties are more expensive than triggers and you will have spent a lot of time fitting the grip safety. If you mess it up and cut too much off the grip safety's trigger block, you not only have to buy another grip safety, you will also need to spend all that time fitting it again.

Personally, I still prefer to fit the safety. I am sure

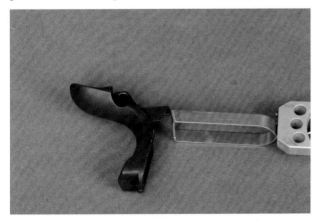

▲ This shows how the grip safety blocks the trigger bow to prevent the gun from firing.

cutting the trigger bow is fine, but I am not comfortable weakening that part. If it breaks, the gun could be out of commission. The grip safety, on the other hand, is less critical. If it happens to break, which is very unlikely, the gun will still fire.

▲ Peening can sometimes save a grip safety that has too much metal filed off.

I'll note that if you go too far on the grip safety you can sometimes peen the metal and stretch it back. I recently was doing a trigger job on another 1911 when I found the grip safety would not prevent it from firing. This was the factory grip safety and it had not been modified. I gently peened the leg that blocks the trigger by working both sides to make it slightly longer and the grip safety worked fine. This saved the price of buying a new grip safety.

For a really professional looking job, you can contour the top of the grip safety to the frame. To do this you will need to make sure the grip safety is in the "on" position by using something to hold it in place to simulate the spring pressure that will position it later. There are commercial tools, but a clever gunsmith can figure something out. Use a half round file to do the contouring and finish with emery paper for a smooth finish. Make sure the emery paper is backed by something such as the file, so that you have nice straight lines and no dishing.

You can also blend the backstrap to the grip safety. This is typically done with the grip safety fully into the frame as it would be in the "off" or shooting position.

Of course, any time you file and blend any part, you need to move to progressively finer abrasives until the final product is polished and free of any file or tooling marks. All this is tedious work and it is easy to start rushing and make a mistake. Remember, once the metal is removed, it's hard to put it back. Go slowly, work thoughtfully, and stop when you get tired or distracted. Come back another day when you are fresh.

With Eric's stainless steel gun, all of this took about a quarter of the time it took to do all the fitting with my titanium grip safety and frame.

FITTING THE FIRING PIN STOP

The firing pin stop is usually oversized. However, it's easy enough to fit using a file, if you go carefully and remove the same amount of material from each side. It's critical that the hole for the firing pin be centered. That's easy to check by installing the firing pin and spring and the firing pin stop. If you get it right, the firing pin will protrude from the hole in the firing pin stop and will slide in and out with no drag or interference. If you don't keep the sides

▲ The firing pin stop is in black here in the center of the photograph and has the round firing pin sticking out through it. Its fit is important, as it does several jobs.

even as you fit the firing pin stop, the firing pin will drag or perhaps not even enter the hole.

This fitting is fairly critical as the firing pin stop also holds the extractor in place. It needs to be a correct fit so the extractor can't rotate or wobble, which can lead to problems.

They make gauges to measure the slot that the firing pin stop slides into. Lacking those tools, you should be able to get a measurement using a dial caliper to measure the slot width and then cut the firing pin stop until it is close. Then use the cut and try process until you have a perfect fit.

The radius on the bottom of the firing pin stop is what contacts the hammer and pushes it into the cocked position when the gun cycles. A few minutes on a buffing wheel helps make that work more smoothly. Don't remove metal, just polish the radius with a fine rouge compound.

This is a good place to note that Caspian slides are designed to be used with a 9mm/.38 Super firing pin, not a .45 firing pin, so make sure you order correctly.

THE EXTRACTOR

Our guns use the internal extractor style of course. It was good enough for Mr. Browning and it's good enough for me. I also think it's stronger than an external extractor. The 1911 is a controlled round feed design where the extractor captures the cartridge as it exits the magazine and maintains control as it feeds into the chamber.

▲ This shows the extractor properly fitted. The hook is not touching the rim of the cartridge, but the extractor is providing spring pressure to hold the cartridge in place.

▲ This shows the slide for my pistol with its JMB-approved internal extractor next to a 1911 with an external extractor.

A properly fitted extractor should contact the rim of the cartridge to hold it in place. However, the extractor hook should not make contact with the front of the rim. There should be a gap between the hook and the cartridge rim when the cartridge head is flat against the slide.

The extractor should have a bevel or radius on the bottom to help guide the cartridge into place. If it does not, use a file to add one. It's also a good idea to polish the surfaces of the extractor and the breech face of the slide. My gun would not function reliably when I first got it together. I

▲ That black dot on the right side of the slide is the end of the internal extractor. It's held in place with the firing pin stop and is its own spring.

polished all the surfaces mentioned and removed a very slight bit of tension off the extractor and now it functions just fine.

The internal style extractor is its own spring and the amount of tension is important to function. You may need to add or subtract a bit of spring pressure to find the sweet spot for it to function correctly. It's easy enough to pull it out of the slide, then reverse it and start it back into the hole in the slide. The frame acts as a vise for holding the extractor while you bend it one way or the other to adjust the spring pressure.

So how do you know when the extractor spring tension is correct? Obviously the pistol should function. If the extractor is too tight it might impede the cartridge from feeding into place. Too light and it may not pull the empty cartridges out of the chamber.

Of course, this is all done later after the pistol is completed and you are function testing. If the gun is running well with no jams, check to make sure the extractor tension is not too loose. Remember this is a controlled round feed, so it needs to hold the cartridge securely. The way to test that is to remove the barrel from the slide and insert a dummy cartridge from the bottom just as it would feed up from the magazine. Now shake the slide. The old rule of thumb is to shake it somewhere between a hearty handshake and shaking down a mercury thermometer.

Of course, a lot of you are probably too young to remember mercury thermometers and how hard your mom had to shake them before taking your temperature when you were sick. (I might also add that those thermometers were used a couple of ways, under your tongue or inserted into the orifice on your backside. It was never a good idea to confuse the two. Just be glad you were born in the digital age.)

If you don't know about the thermometer, just shake the slide moderately vigorously. If the cartridge stays in place, you are fine. They make expensive, elaborate tools to measure extractor tension, but this method has been around as long as the 1911 and it works just fine.

Once you have the firing pin, spring and the extractor all in place and locked in with the firing pin stop, the slide is done for now. It still needs sights and coating if you are going to paint, but the assembly is completed.

FITTING THE EJECTOR

There are two legs on the ejector that fit into two holes in the top of the frame. The holes and the legs are different diameter so the ejector fits only one way. Once the ejector is in place, hold it down tight and insert a magazine to make sure the magazine is not hitting the ejector. If it is, you must file clearance into the ejector.

There is a small hole through the frame inside the groove for the slide. This is for the ejector pin. If you look through the hole with a strong light behind, you can see that the leg

▲ A small drill slid in and out will mark the Dykem and show where the groove must be added.

of the ejector protrudes into the pin hole. That metal must be removed from the leg on the ejector so the pin will pass through and hold the ejector in place.

I have no idea why they don't cut the groove during manufacturing. With today's tolerances and CNC

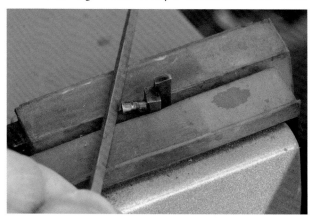

▲ Using a triangle file to get the line started straight on the ejector leg.

machines it would be fine, better than a hand-filed groove in most cases. I suppose it is tradition or maybe stubbornness, but they don't. So, you must file a groove in the leg of the ejector to allow the pin to pass. It must be tight enough so the pin locks the ejector in place.

Coat the ejector legs with Dykem. With the ejector inserted and held tight to the frame, use a small drill that will just pass snuggly through the hole and scratch a mark at the location on the ejector leg for the groove.

I started the cut with a three-corner file to help get a straight line. Then I switched to a rat tail needle file, using the small end to try to match the diameter of the pin as closely as possible. Be careful to take only enough material as is needed to insert the pin. Make it a bit tight on the bottom to help hold the ejector in place.

▲ This shows the ejector and the ejector pin properly installed on the 1911 frame.

▲ Using a rattail needle file to finish cutting the groove in the extractor leg.

I used a drill that was two-thousandths smaller than the pin, measured with a micrometer. I cut until I had a snug fit with the drill but could insert it with my fingers. That will give me a tight interference fit with the ejector pin. I chucked the pin in my drill press and filed a small radius on the leading edge. A roll pin starter punch works well to support the pin while starting it past the leg of the ejector. If the fit is too tight you can damage or bend the pin, so there is a fine line here. You may need to file a bit more on the pin and it may take a few tries. I actually started the pin several times, only to drive it out using a very small punch from the back side. Then I would take another pass on the ejector leg with the file and try again.

Once the pin starts past the ejector leg with mild persuasion, switch to a brass punch to get it flush with the frame, then finish carefully with a small punch to match the pin diameter until the pin is just past flush with the frame. Be careful, as these small punches bend very easily. I confirmed the pin was deep enough by coating the slot in the frame, including the head of the pin, with Dykem and carefully running a hard Arkansas stone along the

groove. The Dykem was removed on the slide, but not the pin, confirming it was below the frame.

This is the traditional way to fit the pin. Jim Majoros told me he just runs a 1/16 end mill in the hole with the ejector in place. Sounds easier to me.

FRAME AND SLIDE FIT

If the barrel is fitted to the slide and is functioning properly, you can fit the slide and frame together and insert the slide stop, making sure it captures the barrel link. Make sure the ejector is installed on the frame and the extractor in the slide.

When the gun is in battery, the slide might be protruding a bit past the frame. If the barrel fit is final, you can blend them together using a file and then polishing the surfaces. The extractor can also be fitted to be exactly flush with the frame at this time.

Finish by polishing out all the tool marks using emery cloth and honing oil until you have a nicely fitted and

▲ Note how the frame, slide and grip safety are blended together. The gun still needs some final polish and a finish. The frame can be blended to the extractor a bit better.

smooth surface. Be careful about keeping the correct contours and to keep the back of the slide and the frame square, 90 degrees to the sides and even.

MAGAZINE CATCH

Before fitting the magazine catch, check to see that a magazine can be easily inserted into the magazine well on the frame. It must also exit easily by its own weight. There should be no drag or sticking. If there is, you must relieve the high spots on the frame until the magazine will go in and out without any interference.

The magazine catch has three parts: the magazine release, the catch, and the spring. Once the magazine release is fitted to the frame and will move freely, the spring and catch are inserted. Then the catch is pushed in with a screwdriver against the spring and turned to lock the tab into the slot on the magazine release.

The magazine catch must easily allow inserting the magazine into the magazine well and hold it firmly. It must then release the magazine to remove it easily. Finally, it acts as a stop for the trigger overtravel screw to hit against.

In Eric's gun, it was a drop-in fit. Mine was anything but. In fact, I think I spent more time trying to get the magazine release to fit the frame than I did on any other single step in this build.

It's all part of the titanium curse.

You must fit the magazine release until it slides smoothly in the frame. Use Dykem on both parts and run them together. The high points that are causing any sticking will show with the Dykem worn off. Cautiously file or stone these spots, being very careful to keep things round. When the fit is very close, a little light lapping with very fine #800 lapping compound cut with oil can help with the final finish.

Once the magazine catch fits in the frame, assemble it in the frame. Push on the magazine release while you push on the slotted catch and turn the screwdriver clockwise to install (counter-clockwise to remove). Move them back and forth as you keep twisting force on the screwdriver until the catch lines up with the slot in the frame. Turn the catch into the slot and release all pressure. To remove it, reverse the process.

Look inside the frame with a flashlight and see that the magazine catch protrudes well into the magazine well. Depress the magazine release button and the catch should recede entirely back into the frame so that the magazine will drop free without rubbing on the catch. This is important so the empty magazines will drop free with their own weight. If the release doesn't move deep enough into the frame for total clearance, you must remove the catch and modify it to allow further travel. There is a curved portion in front of the button that can be moved to make the straight section longer. This allows the release to be pushed further into the frame. Use a round file to lengthen the flat

so that you will be able to push the button further into the frame. Go slowly and try it often until the magazine catch will move completely out of the way.

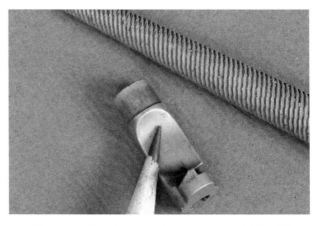

▲ The pencil points to where you would file. The concept is to make this long flat a little longer and provide relief so the magazine release can move further into the frame.

It's a good idea to polish all the surfaces, particularly the catch where it contacts the magazine as this is the surface that will cam the catch against the spring and move it out of the way to allow the magazine to enter the firearm. When the magazine catch is properly installed it should allow the magazine to enter easily. It should also hold the magazine against any attempt to pull it out of the frame and it should release the magazine without drag so that it will fall out of the magazine well under its own weight.

MAINSPRING HOUSING

Assemble the mainspring housing by inserting the spring, end cap and plunger. Compress them and lock them in place with the mainspring cap pin.

▲ Using a bench vise and the slide release to compress the mainspring for assembly.

One good way to compress them is with a bench vise. You can make a tool or use the slide release to compress the plunger.

Make sure the mainspring housing fits easily into the frame. You may need to tweak the fit a little to make it slide in and out easily. When it is in place and pinned, the mainspring housing must not hit the grip safety and prevent it from operating. If that happens, relieve the mainspring housing until the fit is correct.

Always use a full-power 28-pound mainspring. You gain nothing with a weaker spring but the possibility of misfires.

TRIGGER

It's a good idea to do the trigger work as detailed in the sidebar at this time, fitting, adjusting, and polishing all the parts to achieve a smooth, safe trigger pull.

The sidebar deals with installing a trigger on an existing 1911, but all the steps also apply to fitting a new trigger during a build.

I will note that I used an STI brand, short trigger, for this gun. As detailed in the section on triggers, this fits my hands better. In addition to having wide hands and short fingers, I suffered a pretty severe injury to my thumb when I was a kid, which was compounded by an incompetent surgeon trying to fix it. One result is the pad of my

▲ Note the short trigger from STI.

left hand under the thumb is very thick from the muscle being over-developed to compensate for the messed-up thumb. This places my hand further away from the pistol and makes it harder to reach the trigger.

The great thing about the 1911 is that I can install a shorter trigger that is a much better fit for my personal handguns. If you have small hands, this option will help a great deal in improving your shooting. On the other end of the spectrum, those with large hands or long fingers may wish to install a long trigger.

It's good to have options.

1911 TRIGGER TIME
Tuning the trigger on Browning's masterpiece handgun.

Note: This sidebar is about installing a new trigger in an existing 1911 handgun. However, the techniques will apply to fitting the trigger during a build as well.

The thing is, I was never meant to play the piano. Nobody who was sober has ever described my hands as "elegant." They are wide "working-class" paws with short, stubby fingers. So, when anybody asks, "Why would you change the trigger on a 1911?" I just raise my hand.

I have trouble reaching a standard trigger on my favorite handgun. I tend to push on the side of a long trigger and, as a lefty that means my shots go low-right.

I have started working my way through my 1911 handguns, installing a shorter reach trigger in them, although I believe at the rate I acquire new guns, it may be like Sisyphus and his rock, a never-ending quest. For the record, that's a good thing.

You may have other reasons for wanting to change the trigger in your 1911. Perhaps you like the length just fine, but the trigger pull has you unhappy. Maybe you are building a gun from parts and have come to the section where the trigger is installed.

Well, here is how you deal with all that.

Most writers pause here to tell you to unload the gun. If I have to tell you that, you are not smart enough to pull this project off, so please go catch up with the Kardashians and have a gunsmith work on your gun. But if you understand without needing instructions that the first step is to make sure your gun is unloaded, carry on.

Start by taking the gun apart. As I stated in the main section on building a 1911, this project assumes you have a working knowledge of the 1911 and know how to take it apart and put it back together. If you don't,

(continued . . .)

there is a lot of information out there in books and videos. Or you can take the approach I usually do and just start removing the screws and pins and see what falls out. It's always an adventure to get it back together, but once you do, you'll probably remember how to do it the next time.

Separate the upper and lower and set the upper aside. Then remove the grips from the lower, cock the hammer and pull out the safety. Don't let the safety lock plunger fly away under spring power. I have spent a lot of hours looking for those parts after they ran away from home. Most are never seen again. I suspect there is an entire colony of them, homeless and living under a bridge in southern California. If any of them see this, please come home, I miss you.

Remove the grip safety. Remove the pin at the bottom of the mainspring housing and remove the mainspring housing. Remove the sear spring.

Once you reach this point, I recommend that you have a schematic or exploded view drawing of the gun so you can figure out how to put it back together later. If you don't have one in the owner's manual, there are many books containing them or simply Google it. Also, Brownells offers a Schematic Section on their website that includes most of the popular models. The reason you need this schematic is that once you push out the sear and trigger pins, all kinds of parts fall out and it can be a little confusing as to how they go back in if you are not familiar with the 1911. I know I said that this chapter assumes you are familiar with the 1911, but I also recognize that you have to learn sometime and this might well be that sometime. So, have a little insurance around to help get it all back together correctly.

Smoothing and polishing the frame slots for the trigger to run smoothly.

After you have the hammer and fire control parts out, remove the magazine catch by pushing on it while compressing and turning the screw counter-clockwise with a screwdriver. When everything lines up, you can turn the screw and remove the magazine catch. That frees the trigger to be removed.

A new trigger must be fitted to the frame. It's a good idea to smooth the frame slots for the trigger bow using a stone. Brownells makes a stone just for that job called the "1911 Auto Trigger Track Stone." Now try the trigger bow in the track. It's easy, just reverse the trigger, but keep it right side up. If it slides in easily and out smoothly, you are good. If not, more polishing is needed and, perhaps, the bow will need a little modification.

Polishing the trigger shoe after fitting.

The trigger shoe is the part attached to the bow that you put your finger on when you pull the trigger. It is usually a bit oversized and will need to be fitted. Use Dykem or a felt-tipped marker to ink all sides of the trigger shoe. Try the trigger in the frame, forcing it just a little bit. The ink will rub off the high spots and that is where you carefully stone or file the material away. Remove just a little at a time, then re-ink and try again. This is a slow, meticulous process, and it is critical you do it right. Ink, fit, stone the high spots, and repeat until suddenly the trigger runs nice and smooth in the

Brendan Burns inspects the sized and polished hammer hooks to make sure the work is correct.

track with little wobble. Then polish all the contact points on the trigger and break the sharp edges with a stone. Install the trigger and replace the magazine release. (Note: Some triggers have one or two tabs in the front of the bow that can be bent out to remove some of the travel in the trigger.)

The hammer must have the right geometry and the contact surface with the sear must be polished. Forget doing this freehand—you need a jig. I use the Bob Marvel 1911 Auto Sear & Hammer Jig from Brownells. There are detailed instructions for the process included with the jig.

Install the hammer in the jig according to the instructions. The first step is to square the hammer hooks so they are at perfect 90 degrees. This can be done with a square stone if it is new and not worn. Brownells also has a 1911 Auto Hammer Squaring File that is safe on two sides and will not wear like a stone, so it stays square and flat. If you are planning to do multiple trigger jobs, this is a good investment. Remove only enough metal to square up the hooks. Use Dykem on the hooks and stop when it's all removed from the front surface. If you take too much off, the hammer will be ruined. Feel free to ask me how I know that.

Not only will it be ruined, but it might take you a while to figure out the problem. I cut too much off a hammer and installed it without knowing my mistake. The trigger just didn't work right. Sometimes it didn't work at all. It was as if it had developed a mind of its own; the mind of a stubborn, sullen teenager. Finally, in desperation I ordered a new hammer. This time I removed just enough metal to square the hooks and the pistol worked like it was supposed to work. The only damage, other than to my checkbook, was my ego. I had spent hours and hours trying to figure out the problem. The difference was just a few thousandths of an inch.

Once the hooks are square, their height must be adjusted to .018 inch to .020 inch high. Use a hardened shim or a feeler gauge set against the hooks to act as a spacer. Then stone to the height of the shim. Double-check that the hammer is still in the correct position in the jig, then use the stoning guide and a hard Arkansas stone or a fine ceramic to polish the contact surfaces on the hammer hooks. They should be glass smooth and with no visible tooling marks.

Make sure you get all these steps exactly right on the hammer. If they are not done correctly, it will be impossible to ever get a light, smooth, reliable trigger pull.

Following the instructions with the jig, install the hammer and sear to find the correct angle for the sear. Then move it to the stoning slot and carefully cut and polish the primary angle. Next, move the sear holder to the angled slot and cut and polish the secondary angle. These are critical and must be done correctly. They must be finished with a smooth polished surface. Polish the sides of the sear on a hard Arkansas bench stone.

Polish the contact surfaces on the disconnector, including the flat "paddle" surface on the bottom. Do *not* remove metal. Just polish the surface with a hard Arkansas stone or the equivalent ceramic stone, or use a buffing wheel with

This shows the relationship of the hammer and sear.

The feeler gauge is used to set the height of the hammer hooks.

Using the guide and a hard Arkansas stone to polish the hammer hooks.

This is how to use the jig with the hammer to properly set the sear angle for polishing.

(continued . . .)

rouge compound. With this approach and a quality spring the gun will usually have a good trigger pull in the three to four pound range.

I rarely mess with the springs, but if you want the trigger pull lighter, a little tweaking of the spring pressure will make some final adjustment.

The spring tension can be adjusted for the sear and disconnector springs. The "Learn" section at the Brownells website is a wealth of information for DIY gunsmiths and there are very concise and detailed instructions on how to adjust the spring tension there in the article titled "2½ Pound Trigger Pull."

Bear in mind that a 2½-pound trigger pull is very light. For guns intended for uses other than competition, I much prefer a three to four pound trigger. If it is clean and smooth, it will work well for all uses and feel lighter than the pull weight indicates.

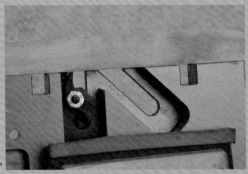
Polishing the primary angle on the sear.

I also believe that messing with the spring on a gun that might be used for defense is a bad idea. Competition shooters often run their guns right on the ragged edge to enhance the performance. In years of shooting competition I have noticed that the shooters who like to do that and push the envelope are the same shooters who have a lot of gun problems. Not too big a deal in a match, it just makes you lose, but it's a very big deal in a defensive situation where it makes you die. So, on 1911 handguns other than those dedicated to competition, I like to find a spring that works well and not mess with it.

Stoning the secondary angle on the sear on a 1911 trigger.

There are differences in the various brands of springs and with a little experimenting you should be able to find one that works without any modification.

Once you have the spring inserted and the tension adjusted if needed, oil the moving parts. I like to slop a light oil on everything and then blow it out with high-pressure compressed air. This leaves a thin film of lubricant on all the parts. Do it outside, because it makes a mess.

Put a little grease on the slide and frame. Reassemble the pistol, cycle, and dry fire the gun several times to make sure everything is working correctly. Be sure the slide and barrel have lubrication. Moving metal parts are never meant to be run dry. They need lubrication. Wipe up the excess with a cloth.

If your trigger has an overtravel screw, adjust that now. Or don't. One school of thought is they cause more trouble than they are worth. The more I learn, the more I am inclined to agree that they are probably better not used.

If a spring is not giving me what I want, I usually replace rather than modify it.

Polishing all the moving trigger parts helps insure a smooth trigger pull. Here the sear and the disconnector have been polished with a hard Arkansas stone.

This is a good trigger pull weight for a general-use 1911 handgun.

If you decide to adjust it, put a little blue #242 Loctite on the screw. Cock the hammer and turn in the overtravel screw until the gun will not dry fire. Back the screw off a quarter-turn at a time until the sear releases the hammer. (Don't forget to compress the grip safety each time you pull the trigger.) Do not let the hammer fall. Once the sear releases the hammer, back the screw off another quarter to half of a turn.

Before you let the hammer fall completely and to prevent damage to the sear, the trigger overtravel screw should be adjusted to ensure that the sear is not hitting the half-cock ledge as the hammer falls. Cock the hammer. Hold the trigger back while gently lowering the hammer to the full forward position. You will be able to feel if there is contact when the half-cock ledge passes the sear. If there is, back out the overtravel screw another quarter to half of a turn. Repeat until the hammer travels without contacting the half-cock ledge, then another quarter to half of a turn for insurance. Once the hammer can fall without contacting the sear, it's safe to dry fire.

Moving metal parts are never meant to be run dry. They need lubrication.

It's time to check the trigger pull using a trigger pull scale. There are several on the market, but my favorite by far is the Lyman Electronic Digital Trigger Pull Gauge. If you are going to do trigger work, this will become one of the most important tools on your bench.

Test the trigger with the gun assembled. The pull weight goal for most 1911 pistols is three to four pounds, but the quality of the trigger is just as important as the pull weight. The trigger should break clean and crisp without hitches or creep.

The slide and frame need a light grease for lubrication. Jim Majoros says he has the best luck on 1911 handguns with this STOS lube available from Ponsness Warren.

Finally, test your work at the range. The first couple times, only load two cartridges in the magazine. That way, if something is wrong and the gun "follows" or doubles, you are shooting just the two, rather than a full magazine. Years ago I watched a buddy test his 1911 after an ill-advised kitchen table trigger job. He got something wrong because it went full auto, dumping all eight rounds, with the last two going through the roof of the covered shooting range. So load two and test. You should not have any trouble, but it's better to be safe.

Once you have a few magazines of ammo through the gun without any problems, you can call this trigger project done.

Adjusting the trigger overtravel screw can cause more problems than it solves.

My goal for this 1911 was a three-pound trigger pull. This is close enough.

SAFETIES

I am getting on the soapbox here. If you want to skip ahead, feel free.

▲ An ambidextrous safety. This is the one thing that John Moses Browning got wrong with the 1911. Note the scratch on the safety, the first battle scar after shooting this gun a lot.

I first started shooting handguns back before Nixon resigned and dinosaurs still roamed the back country. Colt pretty well owned the 1911 market then. Their guns all came with a right-hand safety and there were a lot fewer options for changing to an ambidextrous safety than we have today. I was shooting bullseye competition and wanted a Gold Cup 1911, but to make it compatible with my left-handedness I would have had to pay a gunsmith a bunch of money that I didn't have to install an ambi safety. I saw that as an unfair and discriminatory tax on left-handed shooters. I figured if Colt wanted to discriminate against the left-handed population by ignoring us, I didn't need their products. So, for a very long time I refused to buy a 1911, probably cutting off my nose to spite my face, but I didn't care. I had a point and I was damn sure going to make it.

Just a few years ago, I was at a writer's event with some people who worked for a famous 1911 maker that I won't name for reasons that will soon become apparent. While we were shooting on the range, I had been lobbying one of the executives to install ambi safeties on their guns. That night he showed up at dinner drunk and shouted across the room at me so everybody could hear, "FU** you left-handed guys. As long as I am in charge we will never put ambi safeties on our 1911 handguns."

He then proceeded to make some hugely sexist and insulting remarks to a very nice woman sitting at the table. She was also his boss and he became unemployed soon after. They also didn't change their attitude on the ambi safeties (or several other things) and now that company is not much of a player in the 1911 world.

There are still a lot of 1911 makers who do not put ambi safeties on all of their guns. I find that foolish. First of all, why ignore 15 percent of your potential customers? That's just stupid. (Reports on the percentage of lefties vary. One thing that is not disputed is that left-handed people tend to be much smarter, so they really should listen to us.) On top of that, I think any defensive handgun should be made so it can be used with either hand. If your strong hand is busy or disabled, you need to be able to stay in the fight. That's why we train with both hands.

So why not put an ambi safety on all 1911s? I see no reason not to. Some say they break, but I have never seen one break unless it was abused. Maybe they did break early on, but the brand name safeties today are not going to break any more often than any other part. Guns are machines and of course parts can break or fail. However, I think a well-engineered ambi safety is as reliable as any other part in your firearm.

It's your gun of course, so install any safety you want on your build. But, I think it makes sense to install an ambi thumb safety. Why limit your options? Why limit the resale value?

Ok, rant over.

Installing a Thumb Safety.

Ambidextrous of Course!

Most thumb safeties are made oversized and must be fitted to the handgun. Start with no other parts in the frame. Make sure the thumb safety (referred to as the safety from now on) will fit through the holes in the frame and turn without drag. Check the hole through the grip safety as well.

▲ This thumb safety is held in a jig on the Present Arms, Inc., Gunner's Mount while it is filed to custom fit the 1911 handgun.

Install all the fire control parts, including the spring and the mainspring housing, but leave out the grip safety. If you slide the thumb safety into position it will most likely be blocked from going all the way by the sear. You will need to file the thumb safety lug until it just clears the sear, allowing it to clear the sear leg and enter into the frame all the way. Be careful, work slowly and try the fit often. The idea is to just clear the sear without contact. A jig is helpful here, but, if you are careful, you can do the work using a vise.

Try the safety to see if it will go on and off. If not, you may need to add a bit more clearance for the sear leg. Polish the contact surface so the safety will run smoothly.

The safety should have an adequate dimple for the detent to work correctly when the detent spring and plunger are installed. If not, deepen the detent a little bit with a Dremel or with a ball mill in the milling machine. That will make for a more solid lock up when the safety is off. Check the alignment before making this cut as sometimes the existing detent is not aligned correctly with the plunger. If that's the case, this is the time to correct the alignment.

▲ ▼ Note the relief carved into the wood grip for the ambi safety.

If the safety is ambidextrous, the grip panel on the right side of the handgun may require a relief be cut into it to allow for the leg on the safety that rides behind the grip to move unimpeded. This helps keep the right side of the safety in place. It is easy to do with wood carving tools.

I recently installed an ambi safety on a Remington R1 1911. Everything worked fine for the first few shots, then the safety refused to go to the "on" position. It drove me crazy until I finally noticed that the sear pin was slightly too long. It projected past the frame and blocked the ambi safety arm on the right side of the gun. I filed a little off the end and the gun works great now.

SLIDE STOP

The slide stop must fit correctly to work with the magazine to engage the slide stop on the last shot. The follower in the magazine will have a tab that contacts the slide stop as the follower moves up to the magazine-empty position. This should push the slide stop up to lock the slide open. The slide lock must not intrude deep enough to contact any ammo in a loaded magazine.

Make sure the contact points are all polished and free from burrs. Test the slide lock with at least a couple different magazines. If the nose is too long, it must be adjusted by filing off a little at a time. If it's too short, it must be replaced.

Some builders like to add a bevel on the slide stop to aid in getting it past the detent plunger when inserting it into the firearm. This helps eliminate the "idiot scratches" on the gun's finish caused by trying to insert a balky slide lock.

GRIPS

Install the grip screw bushings. Be careful, as it's easy to get them cross-threaded. Use plenty of Loctite. In fact, using the red #262 high-strength Loctite is probably a good idea here, to make sure they stay in place.

▲ Be careful tightening the grip screws.

FINAL

Assemble the handgun, including the grips. Check for the obvious functions, for example, if the slide will run back and forth without any problems. It's not unheard of for the hammer spur to hit the grip safety and lock up the slide or at least make it difficult to move.

▲ This gun is finished except for coating and sights. Now is the time to do all the function and safety checks.

▲ This is one of the best barrel bushing wrenches I have tried. It captures the parts under spring tension and holds them while you turn the bushing into place.

Cock the hammer and release the slide release. The hammer should never follow the slide, but should remain in the cocked position.

Cock the hammer again and with the safety on, pull the trigger firmly several times. The hammer should stay in the cocked position. Now release the thumb safety and the hammer should still not move. Compress the grip safety and pull the trigger and the hammer should then fall.

Cock the hammer and with the thumb safety off pull the trigger without compressing the grip safety. The hammer should not move. Now compress the grip safety and pull the trigger and the hammer should fall.

Cock the hammer and with the thumb safety on, pull the trigger. Now, put the gun close to your ear. If you are as deaf as I am, find somebody with good hearing and use their ear. Pull back on the hammer and listen for a click. There should not be one. If there is, the safety is fitted incorrectly and should be replaced.

Cock the hammer and put the thumb safety in the off position. Without engaging the grip safety, pull the trigger. The hammer should remain cocked. Put the gun close to your ear, pull back on the hammer and listen for a click. There should not be a click. If there is, the grip safety is incorrectly installed and should be replaced.

What you are checking is to see if the two safeties prevent the trigger from partially moving the sear against the hammer hooks. There should be no movement. If there is, it will be reset when you pull back on the hammer and should be audible. Remember, the hooks are only .018 inch to .020 inch high, so there is very little room for error here.

Cock the hammer and put the thumb safety in the off position. Hold the gun as if you were going to shoot it. Put the muzzle against the bench or a wall and push forward on the grip to compress the slide and barrel backward until they stop. Holding that position, pull the trigger. The hammer should not move. Hold the trigger back and remove the gun from the bench or wall so the slide and barrel move back into battery. Now, slowly release the trigger and listen for the audible click of the disconnector resetting. This time there should be a click. If not, you have a problem with the disconnector. Replace it or at least correct the problem.

Remove the magazine, safety off. Pull the trigger and hold. Rack the slide and listen as you release the trigger. You should hear the disconnector release. If not, correct the problem.

Load the magazine with dummy rounds and cycle them through the action to make sure they feed and eject correctly. If they do, it's a good time for your happy dance. If they do not, mutter some bad words, figure out what is wrong and correct it.

Insert a new, unsharpened pencil with an eraser into the muzzle, with the eraser against the face of the slide. Cock the hammer with both safeties off, point the gun up and pull the trigger. The pencil should be launched out of the barrel by the force of the firing pin striking the eraser. If it is not, the firing pin is not coming through the slide enough to fire a cartridge. Figure out why and fix it.

When all the above exercises produce satisfactory results, it's time for live-fire testing.

At the range or other safe place to shoot, load two cartridges in the magazine. Remember, the 1911 is a controlled round feed gun, so the cartridges should always feed from the magazine. Dropping a cartridge into the barrel and slamming the slide shut can break or damage the extractor.

Fire the first cartridge and hope the second does not follow before you are ready. Repeat this a few times, always loading only two rounds at a time.

If that test is a success, load a full magazine. Chamber a round and remove the magazine. Fire the round. Repeat this with the remaining rounds in the magazine. Chamber, remove the magazine and fire the gun.

Load the magazine and fire until empty with both hands. Repeat the full magazine test with your strong hand, weak hand and with a limp wrist. Load a full magazine and fire it into the berm as fast as you can.

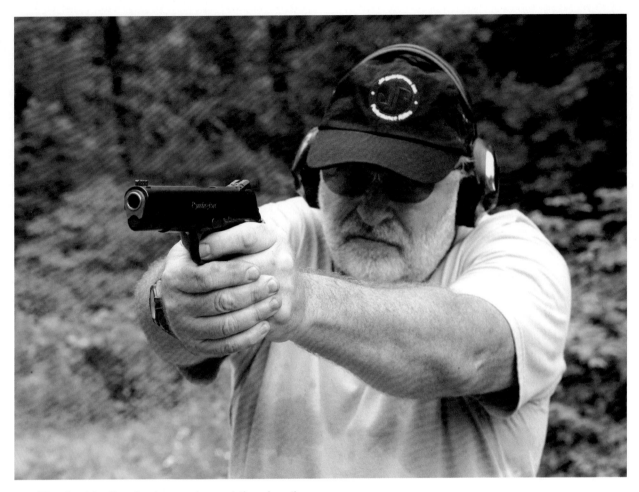

▲ The final testing is always done at the shooting range.

GOING OFF HALF-COCKED

Many thanks to 1911 gunsmith Dennis Amsden for suggesting this.

Test the half-cock by holding the hammer while pulling the trigger to release it. After the hammer is allowed to move a short distance, release the trigger, and see if the half-cock will stop the hammer from falling all the way.

"I like to educate owners about the half-cock," Amsden said. "It is *not* actually a half-cock, even though it is often used as one. It is a passive safety in the event that the hammer/sear engagement fails or the hammer is accidentally dropped when lowering by hand, which really should never be done with a loaded pistol. The half-cock shouldn't be used as a carry or storage option.

"Using the half-cock can actually damage the sear engagement surfaces, especially when owners reef on the trigger when they have the gun in half-cock," he explained. "For this reason, I tend to machine the outer edges of the half-cock ledge so that it only makes contact with the center of the sear, avoiding the part of the sear that engages the hammer hooks. That's not necessary for every gun, but even some of the better component makers are now shipping hammers that way."

If the gun passes all the tests, you are ready to move on to final finish.

FINISH

Because our Caspian frames and slides are stainless steel and titanium we could just as well have left them in the raw, or we could have bead blasted the parts with glass beads for a satin finish. We elected to coat our handguns.

▲ This is my finished 1911.

▲ This is Eric Reynold's finished 1911. Note that I filled in the "Pretty Boy 1" serial number with pink crayon as a joke.

Before you decide on a final finish, take a moment to look over your handgun and try to figure out how you want the color scheme to look. For example, I did the frame,

▲ These parts are ready for Cerakote Graphite Black coating.

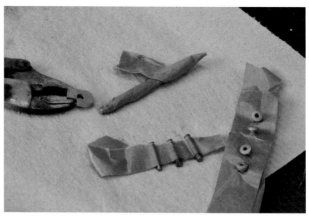

▲ Small parts racked and coated with Burnt Bronze Cerakote. Note the visegrip holding the firing pin stop. With a gentle hand, this works well to handle small parts. The tool is dedicated to finish work and goes right in the oven with the part.

thumb safety, magazine release, exposed barrel in the ejection port, mainspring housing, back of the extractor, and the slide lock all in Cerakote Graphite Black. The slide and grip safety I did in Cerakote Burnt Bronze. Then I taped off the serrations on the slide, front and back, and coated them with Graphite Black.

I polished and then bead blasted the hammer using glass beads for a satin finish. I had planned to jewel the hammer, but my jeweling tool broke and I was too impatient to wait for the new one to arrive. In the end, I like this satin finish look and I think it goes better with the pistol than jeweling would have.

We finished Eric's 1911 with DuraCoat DuraBake. The thumb safety, grip safety, magazine release and slide lock were all in Matte Black. Everything else is Flat Dark Earth.

▲ The great thing about bake-on finishes and handguns like the 1911 is that you can cure them in an inexpensive convection-style toaster oven.

Both of these finishes require oven cure. With a handgun it's easy to find an oven. Just go to your local mart and buy the largest convection toaster oven you can find. You will also need a thermometer as the temperature regulator that comes with it, at least on mine, is not perfect.

The process for doing spray finishes is detailed elsewhere in the book, so I won't cover it again here.

SIGHTS

The final step after completing the finish is to install sights. When ordering the slides from Caspian, we optioned to have dovetails milled front and back with Novak cuts.

We both elected to use Trijicon HD Night Sights. I think this is the best sight system out there for defensive handguns. It also works just fine for competition or target shooting.

See the sidebar on how to install these and other handgun sights. I will remind you again that you must use a sight pusher to install night sights. The tritium that makes them glow in the dark is inside tiny glass vials. Trying to fit the sights with a hammer and punch can cause those vials to break and render your expensive sights useless.

That's it, you are done. Now go the range with your new custom 1911 handgun, kick ass and take names.

Then start thinking about your next build.

▲ Trijicon HD Night Sights. I fitted the sights to the gun so I could shoot it at the range to function check before the final finish and coating with Cerakote.

CHANGING OR INSTALLING HANDGUN SIGHTS

Changing sights may look like an easy do-it-yourself project and for many years it usually was, but often now it is not. The trend today with handgun makers is to use rear sights with "crush-pads" on the dovetail. This may make the manufacturing process a bit easier, but it often causes problems for the end user as the sights can stick very tightly in the dovetail.

Removing most sights installed with crush pads will require a very high-quality sight pusher. I know, because I have bent the frame on lesser tools to the point they were unusable. Attempting to drive the sights out with a hammer and punch will cause damage to the gun, the sight, the punch, and your psyche.

Also, anytime you are working with night sights you must use a sight pusher. The glass vials that contain the glow-in-the-dark tritium are subject to breakage if you use a hammer and punch to move the sight.

I know that we have all heard some loudmouth at the gun club spouting, "That's just bull@#&$, I have installed hundreds of night sights with a hammer and punch." First of all, no; he has not. Second, these sights are very expensive and it's not worth the risk. The people who make them recommend using a sight pusher. That alone should be enough to convince you.

There are a lot of sight pushers on the market. Some of them are considered universal, while many others are dedicated to a single model handgun. They are all expensive.

If you are like me, you work on a wide range of handguns, so the dedicated-to-one-gun tools make little sense. You could go broke just buying the tool boxes you need to store them all. A universal unit is the best option. It may not work on every gun, but it will cover most of them. The best I have found is the B&J Machine P500 Pro Universal Sight Tool. This sight pusher is designed to work with a wide range of handguns and I have yet to encounter one I could not make it work with.

The sight pusher in use.

I had B&J's P500 tool, which is the lower-priced model. It served me well for decades, until the gun companies started using crush-fit sights. I bent the frame trying to remove the sights from an S&W Shield .45 ACP. That's when I called Brownells and upgraded to the P500 Pro, which is basically the P500 with all the optional kits, tools and accessories included.

This model has much more structural integrity. It also uses a different approach to keeping things aligned and supported. The hold-down clamp attached to the tool solves a lot of problems, as it helps keep the pistol slide in position and prevents it from twisting or torqueing as pressure is applied to the slide. The end plate adds strength to help prevent the frame from bending as my old one did and it doubles as a slide stop, which is handy if you are doing a lot of similar handguns.

Installing the front sight on my 1911 using the P500 Pro tool.

The newly designed hardened steel pusher tips are guided by the cross member so they track true as they push the sights in the dovetail. Also, the cross member supports the pusher so it can't ride up and bend the pushing screw or cause the pusher to ride up over the sight, damaging it.

One of the tips is squared on the end for standard sights. The other is made with an angle to fit against a tapered sight, as on a Glock.

To use this sight pusher, lock the slide in place and align the pusher with the edge of the sight. Make sure the pusher will clear the dovetail on the frame. Then, slowly apply pressure by tightening the screw on the pusher until the sight is either removed or is installed correctly in the center.

You can also use this tool to adjust the sights for windage. Those handguns using crush-fit rear sights claim to be drift-adjustable, but doing it in the field is impossible on many of them. The traditional way is to gently tap the sight using a brass punch, but I have encountered several new handguns from multiple manufacturers on which this is impossible. I think you could beat the sights on some of them with a carpenter's framing hammer and a crowbar and they

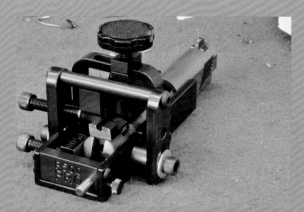

Installing the rear sight on my 1911 using the P500 Pro tool.

would not move. It takes a bit longer, but it's much better to use the sight pusher to make the adjustments. It's much more precise and it can move these new-generation sights when nothing else will.

When fitting new sights to a dovetail, I like to break the sharp leading edges on the sight and the dovetail with a fine India stone. This will remove the finish though, so be careful on the slide. I only do enough to remove the sharp edge, like dulling a knife blade. This allows the sight to start and press into the dovetail without shaving material.

Install it from right to left. The sight should start into the dovetail easily. If the fit is absolutely too tight, you can use a dovetail file that is safe on the bottom, so only the dovetail is cut. Then open up the dovetail *very* slightly. Then, if you elect to cut on the handgun, cut so that the dovetail will have a very slight taper to aid the sight into place. Remove very slightly more metal on the right side of the slide than the left, perhaps something like .001 inch. Be careful, because these sights rely on a tight, press fit. If you remove too much metal, the fit might become loose or sloppy. Take very light cutting strokes with the file.

I much prefer the concept of cutting on the cheapest part, so I usually will modify the male dovetail on the sight, rather than female on the handgun. In this case, use the file to reduce the width of the sight's dovetail very slightly. Add a very slight taper and break the leading edge. Take very light cuts and try the sight in the dovetail. If it starts in under finger pressure, it should be fine to install. Again and I can't say this enough, be very careful and use light cuts, as you can't easily replace the metal.

One old gunsmith's trick for a loose dovetail sight is to take a prick punch and stipple the bottom of the dovetail. This raises the metal around the stippling and will tighten up the fit. I have used this trick on old rifles where the dovetail was worn and on a few newer handguns where somebody got overzealous with a file. For the record, that somebody has not been me . . . not yet anyway.

The rear sight on a handgun needs to be a bit easier to move than the front sight. This is because with fixed sights, the rear sight will be drifted in the dovetail to adjust point of impact for windage. If the sight is easier to move, it can be done with a punch in the field, where the shooter probably will not have a sight pusher available. If the rear sight is not a granite tight fit, a plastic or brass punch with gentle hammer taps will move the sight.

Most of the new sights I have installed come with a small set screw to lock the rear sight in place once the adjustment is made, so keep that in mind when fitting a rear sight. Also remember that the set screw is tiny and will strip rather easily, so be firm, but gentle, when tightening it. Use a little blue #242 Loctite on the screw.

You can also make the sight a tight fit in the dovetail and use the sight pusher to adjust point of impact. This takes longer, but once it is set, odds favor it never moving.

One more note, changing the front sight on a Glock requires a little wrench to remove the screw that holds the sight onto the frame. There really is no viable substitute. They are not expensive, so take a little unsolicited advice. Next time you place an order, get the wrench. There is nothing worse than being in a stalemate for a week while you wait for a wrench to be shipped. If you spend a few bucks now and have it in your toolbox well in advance, people will think you are a genius.

▲ The completed rifle with the two extra barrels.

CHAPTER 11

SAVAGE SWITCH-BARREL HUNTING RIFLE

The Savage Model 110 design makes the perfect project gun for a switch-barrel hunting rifle.

The Savage Model 110 and its offspring are, or at least were, unique rifles.

I believe that they were the first production rifles to use a chambered and threaded barrel that screws into the action until the headspacing is correct. Then, a nut is used to lock the barrel in place. This makes the manufacturing process much simpler and is said to be a big factor in improving accuracy.

This screw-in barrel also makes the rifle a bit of a kit gun, as the owner can swap out barrels relatively easily and without needing a lathe. I thought that a 110 would make an interesting DIY project for the hobby gunsmith. Why not create a "do it all" hunting rifle in multiple cartridges?

So I ordered a new Model 116 FCSS, which is the stainless steel, long action version of the 110.

REDUCING IT TO PIECES

One big complaint over the years has been the appearance of these guns, which has been anything but sleek. In an effort to streamline the look of the rifle, Savage made the barrel nut much smaller and smoother. They also eliminated the notches in the nut for a spanner wrench to grip, so the first thing you will need for this project is a barrel nut wrench to fit this newer nut. There are several on the market, but my friends at Savage suggested I use the one from Sharp Shooter Supply.

This big wrench works for both notched and smooth barrel nuts and is an indispensable tool for this project.

To unscrew the nut, the action or the barrel must be held tight. If you have a bench mounted barrel vise, you are good to go. If not, one option is to drill a hole slightly

▲ The Savage rifle shown with an extra barrel and stock, as well as a trigger, headspace gauges and the barrel nut wrench.

smaller than the barrel diameter in a 4X4X2-inch block of hardwood. Then cut the block in half through the center of the hole. Coat the half circles in the blocks with powdered rosin, insert the barrel and clamp the blocks in a large bench vise.

I also discovered that the Holland's Action Wrench for Remington 700 fits well in the Savage action, which might be a much easier way to go. To insert the wrench, you will need to compress the bolt release. Once the wrench is inserted into the action you can clamp the 7/8-inch hex end in a bench vise and rest the barrel on a support. Then use the Sharp Shooter Supply wrench to loosen the barrel nut. Once it's loose, the nut and barrel should turn off with hand pressure.

▲ I had the best control when holding the barrel in an improvised barrel vise and the action with the Holland Remington 700 Action Wrench.

▲ This improvised barrel vise worked with this moderate sized bench vise, but a larger vise would be better.

I ran into trouble right out of the gate when taking the barrel off my factory gun. The nut was filled with blasting compound that was fine enough to get into the threads and gum up the works, apparently a fairly common occurrence

with new Savages. I spoke with one of the company's representatives and he told me they do a final blasting pass after the rifles are assembled, at least on the stainless steel guns. This allows the medium to enter the barrel nut. He said, "We don't intend for the customer to take our rifles apart, so we don't see this as a problem."

No matter your thoughts about quality control on a final product, it's something you will need to deal with when taking the gun apart.

If you encounter blasting medium in the threads, do not force anything. Use compressed air and a small nylon brush such as a toothbrush to clear the path so, once loosened, the nut will spin off freely. Do not try to force the nut. If it jams, back it off, clear out the debris and repeat until everything is clear. It might help to use a lubricant like Kroil. Unscrew the barrel and take the nut off the

▲ Coating the front of the receiver so I can tell when the ridge is removed.

▲ The receiver after stoning to remove the burr.

barrel. Now clean everything to get rid of all the blasting compound.

I found that the front edge of the receiver on my rifle had a slight burr around the outside radius. I carefully removed that with a fine bench stone. This is a precision machined part so it's important not to change it, other than to remove the burr. Carefully stone off the burr by applying light pressure and rotating the stone a bit as you move it back and forth. Use a very light hand.

MY CARTRIDGE CHOICES

For my project, I ordered the rifle in .25-06 Remington. This is a great crossover cartridge that works well for predators as well as deer and antelope size game. It's capable of very-long-range work as well. I ordered a second barrel from E. R. Shaw in .338-06 Ackley Improved. E. R. Shaw makes barrels in just about any cartridge you can think of, so I decided to take the road less traveled with the Ackley Improved cartridge. The .338-06 AI is capable of taking any North American big game and it's excellent for deer, elk, moose, or bears. I have been an avid handloader for years and have several other rifles in AI cartridges, so I am

very familiar with loading them. Included in that is the .223 AI that I detailed building in another chapter.

If you like a little adventure, consider the Ackley Improved version of your favorite cartridge. It usually picks up about 150 feet per second and, in my never humble opinion, is always a much cooler cartridge. It does require its own headspace gauge from Manson, which added a few bucks to the cost of the project, but more than pays for itself in wow factor.

While I was working on this project, a Facebook buddy posted that he had a Savage .270 Winchester barrel for sale. The price was reasonable, so I sent him a check. The .270 Winchester uses the same headspace gauge as the .25-06 Remington, so it was an easy add-on to the project. Now my two-barrel gun is a three-way.

Who knows, I may add more as time progresses. As long as I stick with the .30-06 parent case, the bolt and magazine are fine for any of these cartridges. The headspace gauge will work for any cartridge in the .30-06-based family except the .280 Remington. That holds true for the AI cartridges in the .30-06 family as well. The AI headspace gauge works for all except the .280 AI.

FITTING THE BARREL

Usually headspace gauges are bought in pairs of one each, go and no-go. In this situation, the go gauge is all that is really needed, so I bought only that gauge for this project.

▲ If I had not elected to have one barrel chambered for an Ackley Improved cartridge, I could have gotten by with one headspace gauge.

The way it works with the Savage Model 110 is that you install the barrel, leaving the nut loose and the barrel backed off a bit. Then insert the headspacing go gauge and close the bolt. Screw the barrel into the receiver until it gently contacts the go gauge and then lock it down with the barrel nut. This gives you min-spec headspace, which is usually a positive factor in good accuracy. You do not need a no-go gauge using this method. However, if you wish to use one just to confirm, I see no harm. By ordering both,

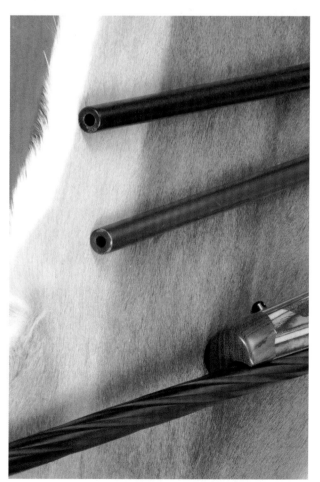

▲ My switch barrel became a three-way.

you also have them for any future barrel change projects with other rifles.

In the interest of full disclosure, I wound up buying the .30-06 no-go gauge later when I needed it for a repair job on another rifle. It would have saved shipping costs to get them both the first time.

▲ When doing the final barrel fit, it's good to control both the barrel and the action as you tighten the barrel nut.

If you don't have a no-go gauge and wish to double-check, one trick is to put two pieces of cellophane tape on the back of the go gauge and trim them to fit. Each piece adds about .0023 inch to the gauge for a total of about .0046 inch, effectively turning it into a no-go gauge. If the bolt closes on the go gauge, but will not close on the go gauge with the tape on the back, the headspacing is correct. Just remember that the tape is soft and easily damaged if you force the bolt. Clean all the tape and adhesive off the gauge before putting it back in your toolbox to prevent problems the next time you use it.

P. O. Ackley developed the headspacing concept for the AI chambers so that they could use the parent cartridge as well as the fire-formed AI cartridges. As a result, headspace gauges for AI cartridges are a little shorter. This not only allows the parent cartridge to be fire-formed to create AI brass, it also allows the rifle to be used with the parent cartridges if AI cartridges are not available.

There is a very detailed explanation on the process for headspacing AI cartridges in P. O. Ackley's Handbook for Shooters and Reloaders. The same information can also be found on the Dave Manson Precision Reamers web site.

ABOUT THE BOLT

It's more work, but the best result is found by removing the ejector and extractor from the bolt before fitting the barrel. This allows the headspace gauge to fit against the bolt face without interference. The extractor slides off from the slot

▲ The most accurate reading from any headspace gauge is with the bolt stripped.

▲ Removing the ejector pin.

in the bolt lug. Be careful to capture the small steel ball and spring underneath. To replace it, compress the ball and spring and slide the extractor in until the ball enters the detent on the back side of the extractor, holding it in place.

The plunger style ejector is similar to the Remington 700. I used my Sinclair International Remington Ejector

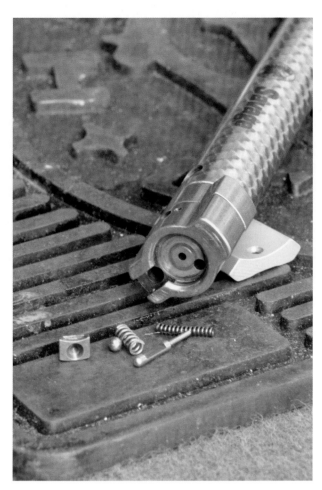

▲ The extractor and ejector removed from the bolt.

Spring Tool to compress the ejector for removal. I had to extend the plunger out a bit farther than for a Remington, but once I did that it worked great. There is a small pin that holds the ejector in place. Once the ejector is captured by the Sinclair tool, use a proper size pin punch to gently remove the pin. Be sure to capture the ejector and spring as you remove the Sinclair tool. Reverse the process to replace the ejector.

Stripping the bolt allows the bolt face to be free of foreign influences or encumbrances when installing the barrel. The headspace gauge will fit against the bolt face correctly for a proper fit of the barrel.

It is possible to use the gauge without taking the extractor and ejector out of the bolt. Clip the rim of the gauge under the extractor. If there is a cut-out for the ejector, align that with the ejector pin.

If there is no cut-out in the gauge, it will be necessary to compress the ejector pin with the gauge. First, make sure the ejector will push into the bolt far enough to clear the bolt face. Use a small punch and push it in against the spring. If it goes deep enough to be past the bolt face, you are good. If it does not and protrudes from the bolt face,

you must make a correction. If cleaning it fails to correct the problem, you may need to shorten the spring a coil or two. Or, perhaps, shorten the ejector, but be careful when doing this not to go too far. The best rule of thumb is to always cut on the least expensive part.

You will need to hold the headspace gauge against the spring pressure to align it with the rifle chamber. Once it enters the chamber, you can slowly close the bolt and the gauge should compress the ejector to allow a correct headspacing measurement.

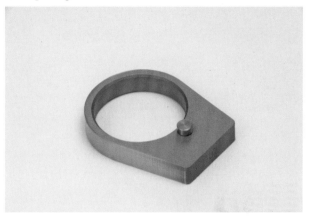

▲ This PTG recoil lug fits a Savage 110. The stud is used to maintain alignment when tightening the barrel nut.

RECOIL LUG

For the best accuracy, it's smart to replace the cheap recoil lug that comes with the Savage rifle. The one on my rifle was also cracked, so it was a no-brainer. Another reason for replacing the recoil lug is to switch to one that maintains alignment. The Savage action has a notch in the front designed to fit a protrusion from the recoil lug that is designed to mate with a notch in the receiver to maintain the correct alignment when tightening the barrel nut. The factory guns once had this protrusion on the recoil lug, but for some reason, probably cost, they no longer have that feature.

A good aftermarket recoil lug will have the protrusion. It will also be precision ground so that the sides are parallel, which keeps the fit of the barrel to the action more precise and aids in allowing better accuracy.

PAINT OPTIONS

My plan was to coat the action and the barrels with some pretty paint. I thought I would use different colors on the barrels, both to code them and to give the rifle a unique look with each barrel.

I coated the .270 barrel first. I did a deep clean of the barrel to remove all the old copper and fouling. This is only necessary with a used barrel and instructions are detailed in another section of this book.

As this was a used barrel and I didn't know its history,

▲ The used .270 Win. barrel got a new crown. I used a lathe, but this Brownells tool is designed to be used by hand or with a hand-held drill as well.

I also decided to recut the crown. This is a simple project that can make a huge difference in accuracy.

I chucked the barrel in the lathe and used a piloted cutter to cut an 11-degree target crown. I then added a small radius to the outside of the muzzle using a file.

This one simple job almost always improves accuracy. If you don't have a lathe, Brownells sells several cutters and laps for use by hand or with a cordless drill to re-crown the muzzle. There is detailed coverage in chapter 7 of this book on how to do this simple project.

After crowning and cleaning, I degreased the barrel in acetone and from then on handled it only with gloves. This is to prevent the oil from my fingerprints causing adhesion problems with the spray-on coating.

The prep work is basic and pretty much the same for all the barrels. Plug the muzzle and tape off the threads. I have tapered rubber or silicon plugs I use to plug the muzzle. I keep several sizes around so there is always one that fits. Put one layer of tape on the threads to protect them before fitting a wire tightly around the threads. Leave enough wire to make a hook to hang the barrel. Then tape some more to help hold it in place.

Sandblast the barrel until it has a uniform appearance. Blow the dust off with compressed air. Degrease again by hanging the barrel, spraying, and letting the degreasing agent run off and dry.

Then apply the coating. For the .270 Win. barrel, I used the Brownells PTFE/Moly Gun Finish. Just spray the prepared metal, let it flash off and bake at 350 degrees for thirty minutes.

I covered the action and the .338-06 AI barrel with Cerakote Graphite Black. I did the third .25-06 Remington barrel in Cerakote Smoke.

To do the rest of the gun is pretty much the same procedure. Strip the action and degrease. Just as with the barrels, the metal should be sandblasted to provide a good adhering surface for the spray-on coating. There are detailed

instructions on this process in chapter 5 about spray-on coatings.

TIMNEY TRIGGER

I have a confession. I was one of the Beta testers for the Savage Accutrigger before it was introduced. I told Savage I thought it had too many moving parts and was too delicate for a hunting gun. I know it's not what they wanted to hear and in the years that have passed since then, I've ended up having to eat those words.

I hate being wrong, but I was wrong about that trigger. It changed the world. It not only caught on with hunters and shooters, but it made the rest of the rifle makers do something about their poor triggers.

For years, gun makers sent out their rifles with horrible triggers. They were terrified of lawsuits and to a man insisted that's the way it had to be, that it was impossible to make a safe trigger with a decent pull weight.

Then along came the Savage Accutrigger and before long every other company found that, "surprise, surprise," they could make safe triggers that didn't bottom out the scale.

The Accutrigger proved to be very reliable and is capable of a decent hunting rifle pull weight, but this was a project gun and no project gun is complete without a trigger upgrade. So, I decided to install a Timney trigger.

INSTALLATION

Please tell me that I do not have to remind you to make sure the gun is empty of all ammo. Do a visual check as well as sticking your finger in the chamber.

▲ Adjusting the trigger pull-weight screw.

To replace the Savage Accutrigger with a Timney Trigger you will need a flat tip screwdriver, a 5/32-inch hex wrench, a 5/64-inch hex wrench and a ¼-inch open end wrench. A small adjustable wrench will also work.

Remove the factory trigger by using the flat tip screwdriver to push the C-clip from the trigger pin. Be careful that when the clip comes free it does not fly off to Mars, never to be found again.

▲ Adjusting the safety screw.

▲ Adjusting the sear engagement screw.

Push out the trigger pin.

Insert the Timney Trigger into the action with the new trigger pull-weight spring lining up the hole in the Timney Trigger with the hole in the trigger assembly on the Savage rifle. Then push in the trigger pin and secure it with the C-clip that you did not lose.

There are three 5/64-inch hex screws. After setting the sear engagement screw, you'll use the other two screws to adjust the pull weight and the safety.

Insert the bolt in the action and slowly tighten the sear engagement screw until the trigger releases. Then, back the screw out about one-sixth of a turn and test the trigger pull weight. For this you will need a trigger pull gauge.

To adjust the pull weight, turn the rear screw. Turn the screw in (clockwise) to increase pull weight and out (counterclockwise) to decrease pull weight. After the pull weight is adjusted, adjust the safety screw until there is no play in the safety.

Put the rifle back together.

Cycle the action and test the safety and trigger. Put the safety on and pull the trigger firmly. Then push the safety off, making sure the sear does not release when you move the safety. Then pull the trigger with the safety off to make sure it will release properly. Do this several times.

Cock the rifle and, with the safety off, forcefully smack the buttstock against a padded floor to make sure the trigger does not release. Do this several times.

The factory installed Accutrigger had a pull weight of four pounds. This of course had a bit of adjustment available, but Accutriggers are a bit mushy when they break; it's just the nature of the beast. The Timney trigger has a pull weight of 2.5 pounds and feels clean and sharp.

▲ The new trigger shown with the parts it replaced.

STOCK OPTIONS

Boyd's Stock

I am not a fan of injection molded synthetic stocks, which is what came with the gun. I wanted to fit a higher quality stock to the rifle, so I ordered a Boyd's laminate wood stock.

This rifle uses a detachable magazine system and I was unable to locate an aftermarket fiberglass stock to fit. However, a laminated wood stock has all the stability of a synthetic stock with, perhaps, a bit more strength. It also gives the rifle a unique and classy look.

I ordered a Boyd's Classic style stock in Coyote color, as it's just a little bit flashy. The stock has a small cheekpiece. I also had Boyd's do a little custom work with a few cosmetic add-ons. There is a small whitetail deer head engraved on the right side. The stock has a bubinga wood angled tip, a bubinga grip cap and a Kick-Eez recoil pad. The gripping areas are stippled and stained darker than the rest of the stock.

I like Boyd's stocks because you can customize them a bit, including the length of pull. I ordered the standard length of pull, as 13.75 inches fits me well. But I have a buddy who is six and a half feet tall with long arms. Standard stocks don't fit him, so I can order a Boyd's with a custom length of pull up to 14.25 inches and even longer on some models.

The stock for this Savage needed a little bit of tweaking to open the barrel channel to fit the .338-06 AI barrel. This was easy enough with a barrel channel scraping tool. It also required a little bit of work to fit the barrel nut. I did this using a wood carving tool set that I have had for years.

Actually, the set belongs to my wife, a gift from her grandfather back when she did custom carving on the grips for single action handguns. She lets me use them. A set like this is another one of those must-have tools for working on guns. They are indispensable for fitting any stock to a rifle, wood or synthetic, and are used often for fitting grips to handguns.

Try the stock and mark the tight spots with a pencil. Then, carefully carve off a sliver of wood and try again. It is tedious work, but you only get one chance to get it right.

It took a little more cutting on the wood to make sure that the barrel and barrel nut were both 100 percent free floated. This is also a very good idea with this switch-barrel concept as the barrel contours might be slightly different and if you bed one, the next one may not fit quite right. However, if the barrel and nut are floated and only the action is bedded, it's all good.

While it was probably not needed, I glass bedded the action and the recoil lug using Brownells Acraglas. I taped off the recoil lug on all sides and the bottom, leaving only the rear, load bearing surface free. This results in an air gap except on the load bearing side, which is the best way to bed a recoil lug.

MOUNTING GLASS

I wanted the ability to switch scopes easily, as I had planned on a dedicated scope for big game and another for varmints and long-range big game. The gun came with a two piece Weaver base for the mount. This is fine, but I

▲ Installing the Talley rail.

wanted to use a Picatinny style rail, because I have scopes mounted in rings and ready to fit. This style rail also works well for swapping scopes and will hold zero relatively well, although I am a firm believer in checking zero every time you change something.

Talley makes some of the best bases and rings on the market, so I installed a Talley rail. I had the option of

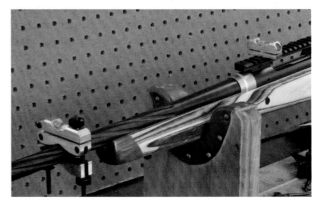

▲ The Wheeler Engineering Professional Reticle Leveling System from Brownells in use. This is a great way to level the scope reticle.

▲ Mounting the scope.

ordering it with 20 MOA of elevation built into the rail. This is a good feature for any long-range gun as it gives you more elevation and lets you do most of the shooting closer to the scope's optical center. I put 20 MOA Talley rails on most of my long-range precision rifles. However, on a hunting gun I didn't think that was necessary, so I went with the straight base.

I mounted a Bushnell Engage 2.5-10X scope in Weaver 6-screw tactical rings. This scope will work well in any big game or predator hunting situation.

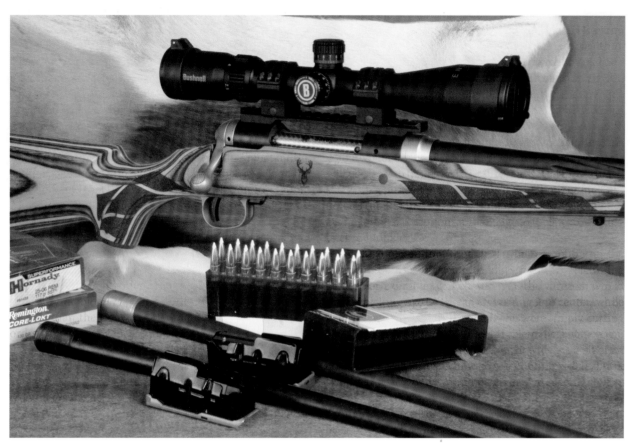

▲ The finished rifle with all the extras.

SECTION TWO
ADVANCED PROJECTS

Maybe it's time to take the leap and buy a lathe and possibly a milling machine. If you love working on guns, this will open a wonderful new world for you and allow you to build and customize firearms at a whole new level.

The lathe should probably be the first purchase. It's not as expensive or as complicated as you might think. The hardest part is working up the courage to pull the trigger and place the order.

You will be amazed at the joy you will have building custom guns. Later, you can go a step beyond even that and get a milling machine. Who knows, you might decide to switch careers and become a paid gunsmith. Or you may just enjoy the satisfaction that comes with a hobby of making good guns even better.

I truly believe that your only regret will be not buying the machines sooner.

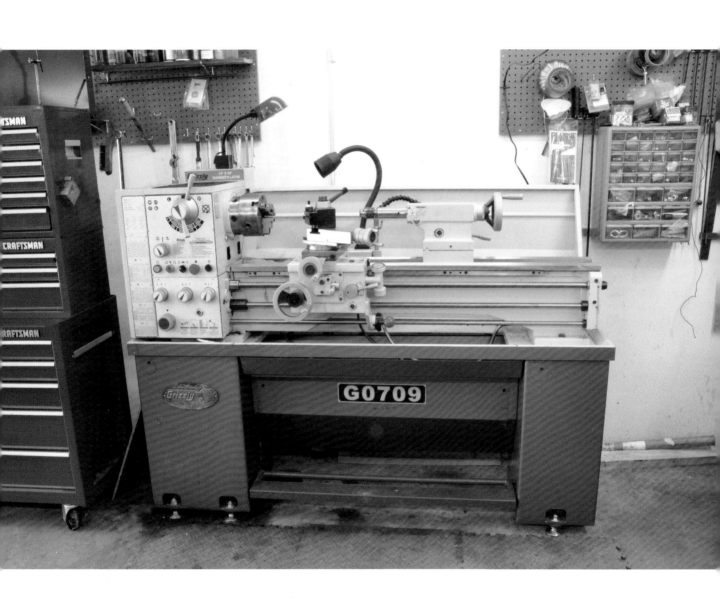

CHAPTER 12
TIME FOR A LATHE?

"Getting a lathe" is the Holy Grail for a lot of hobby gunsmiths. It's that often dreamed of, but seemingly unattainable quest to take your shop to the next level.

▲ A lathe changes everything for the hobby gunsmith.

Just thinking about it is intimidating; lathes are expensive, big, heavy, and full of mystery. The very concept of learning to run a lathe is at first as daunting as mastering theoretical physics. You know in your mind it can be done. Others have done it, but it seems like too much; it's too big, too complicated, too impractical, too intimidating, too overwhelming, too . . . too . . . too . . .

There is always a reason to wait. You say you will get one "soon" but keep finding excuses to justify "not right now."

I would ask the age old question, "If not now, when?"

There has never been a better time.

▲ Nathan Towsley working a rifle barrel on the Grizzly lathe.

If you are reading this then you are at least looking at the idea of jumping to the next level of hobby gunsmithing and perhaps buying a lathe. I have but one regret about doing that myself and that is that I waited so long. I missed out on years of joy and satisfaction because I was intimidated by both the initial cost and the daunting task of learning how to do the work.

If you love to work on guns and you love to learn more about working on guns, which you clearly do if you are reading this book, take the plunge. I promise you will never regret it.

For decades, the only affordable approach for a hobby gunsmith was to buy an old lathe and refurbish it, which is what I did for my first lathe. The trouble is, I didn't know much about what I was doing when I bought it and the lathe is not well suited for the type of gunsmithing I wanted to do. It was old and tired and while I did some excellent work on it, I never felt I was getting the precision I wanted.

▲ ▼ Unpacking a new lathe is a big day in a hobby gunsmith's life.

What I really wanted was a new lathe. The benefit of going new versus used is that you get a brand-new machine with no wear and tear on it and an imported lathe is affordable for a serious hobby gunsmith. A gunsmith will want a lathe with at least a 12-inch swing and a 36-inch bed. At this writing you can get into a decent 12X36 lathe for about half the price you would pay a gunsmith for a custom rifle build.

Grizzly Industrial has developed a line of lathes designed specifically for gunsmithing. They talked with working gunsmiths about what they need and use in a lathe. They used the suggestions to design lathes that are gunsmith friendly.

My lathe is the Grizzly Model G0709. This is a 14X40 Gunsmithing Gearhead Lathe. It runs on a standard 220-volt outlet and does not require a three-phase hookup. This is a big deal, as most hobby guys do not live in industrial areas where three-phase is available, but everybody has 220-volt outlets. It's what your clothes dryer, water pump

and cooking stove use for power. You probably already have an outlet or two in your shop, basement, or garage. Or it's simple enough to have an electrician install one dedicated to the lathe. You might even get him to do it in barter for gunsmithing work.

This model is a step up from the entry level lathes and is about in the middle of the series of Grizzly lathes offered for gunsmithing. The headstock is narrow enough that most rifle barrels can be held in the spider. The hole through the spindle is 1.57 inches (40 mm) so it will pass any reasonable diameter rifle barrel through easily.

▲ Even a short barrel can usually be held in the spider, due to the lathe's narrow headstock.

One benefit of upgrading to a larger lathe is more mass. The bigger, heavier lathes have less vibration than the smaller and lighter weight lathes. That means smoother threads and cuts.

I have been amazed while researching this book at the number of professional gunsmiths I have met who use this exact same 14X40 lathe, gunsmiths with well-earned reputations for building high-quality, extremely accurate

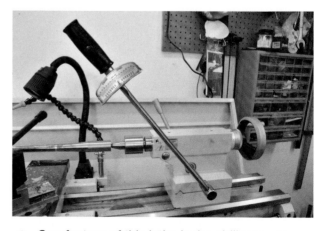

▲ One feature of this lathe is the ability to use a torque wrench to ensure the tailstock is locked down exactly the same each time.

▲ The author working with the Grizzly lathe while chambering Tony Kinton's 9.3X62 rifle.

custom rifles. I think this is a testament to the quality of the Grizzly 14X40 lathe.

The Model G0709 comes with everything you need to get started except tooling. I bought a set of indexable tool holders and a set of boring bars from Grizzly, which allowed me to start building rifles.

I practiced with the lathe so much the first few weeks that my wife mentioned the electric bill had gone up dramatically. In a very short time I was building rifles and discovered that this may well be the best hobby on earth. There is always something new to learn and some new challenge to dive into. The feeling when you are holding the first finished rifle in your hands is one of the most wonderful moments you will experience in your life.

The overwhelming urge to go back to the shop and start another build screams that you are a gunsmith.

SHIRAZ BALOLIA

One company that stands up for hobby gunsmithing is Grizzly Industrial. The owner, Shiraz Balolia, is a shooter and is very supportive of the gun industry. Grizzly Industrial advertises in gun magazines and helps to keep the publishing industry (and, by trickle-down economics, poor gun writers like me) up and running.

"Grizzly has come a long way," Mr. Balolia told me.

That might well be the ultimate understatement. Balolia started by rebuilding old machines and selling them so he could afford a new wood lathe for his hobby. From that beginning, he started Grizzly Industrial in 1983. Today it's a multimillion dollar company. In addition to its Bellingham, Washington, headquarters there are facilities in Pennsylvania and Missouri.

As a serious shooter, Balolia recognized a custom gunsmith's need to have a lathe suited to the type of work that gunsmiths do, so he created a series of gunsmith lathes. Currently, the website features five lathes dedicated to gunsmithing. They range from a 12X36 basic model to the big 16X40 lathe.

"I own two lathe companies, Grizzly and South Bend," Balolia told me. "I can have any lathe I want and I have the 16X40 Grizzly in my shop. It's the lathe used to build the rifles I shoot in F-Class competition."

Canadian National Champion 700, 800, & 900 Meters - 2014, 2015, 2016

The owner of Grizzly Industrial is a hardcore shooter and a true gun guy.

Clearly, the rifles work. Balolia holds too many state, national, and international titles to list here. He is certified as a High Master by the NRA in Long Range, Mid-Range and Fullbore F-Class shooting, the highest classification in those rifle shooting disciplines. He is also the holder of several national records in F-Class competition.

F-Class is a game of long-range accuracy and clearly both the shooter and the rifles built on his Grizzly lathe excel at the sport.

We as hobby gunsmiths owe Balolia a big thank you because he has brought affordable, quality lathes, milling machines and other tools within our reach.

▲ When you have a brand new barrel blank and a lathe, anything is possible.

METRIC MADNESS
Adventures with a .223 Ackley Improved

I am an adventurous kind of person, always willing to jump in feet first and see what happens. That attitude almost killed me in a wild West Virginia whitewater river a few years back, but I still haven't changed.

After getting my new Grizzly lathe, the first rifle build I tackled was with a Zastava Mini Mauser action with a metric thread.

I hit a snag with this one right out of the gate. I had bought the action about fifteen years previously and it had been sitting on a shelf in my shop ever since. In the same spot, on the same shelf, for a decade and a half. But, when I wanted to start the build, it was gone. I looked for days before calling in my wife, who has an amazing talent for finding stuff I have lost.

This is my .223 Ackley Improved rifle I built for hunting coyotes. It was my first rifle build with the new Grizzly lathe, without adult supervision.

Total strikeout for both of us.

This went on for a few weeks and was about driving me crazy. Then, one day I was looking through some old scopes that were in boxes high up on a shelf. One of the boxes looked a bit different. It was, of course, the box with the action in it. It seems that a friend was in the shop a year before while I was working and as a favor decided to tidy up for me. He moved the action without saying anything.

My shop may be chaos, but it's my chaos and when people disturb that it messes with the feng shui of the room. It may look like nothing but clutter, but it's my clutter and I know where stuff is, most of the time.

When I don't, I call my wife.

One reason that action sat around so long was because I couldn't decide what to do with it. I wanted something a little different, so after considering a bunch of different cartridges, I decided to build a .223 Ackley Improved rifle for hunting coyotes. I wanted a lightweight, accurate rifle. Hiking in snow, often on snowshoes, is tough work. The lighter the gun, the happier the hunter.

I ordered a chamber reamer and AI headspace gauges from Dave Manson. Fitting the chamber for an Ackley Improved cartridge is a bit different than the parent case and requires dedicated headspace gauges. The key is to make sure the chamber will fire the parent case as well as the AI fire-formed cases.

There are detailed instructions on the Dave Manson Precision Reamers website and in P. O. Ackley's Handbook for Shooters and Reloaders on the correct way to set the headspace for an AI cartridge.

From Brownells, I ordered a .224 Douglas Double XX, premium-grade barrel in lightweight #1 contour with a 1:9 twist rate. This gives me the option of using heavier bullets if I want.

I cut the barrel to 21 inches. Most barrels are even numbers in length, I like to be a little different, so I usually make mine odd numbers.

I ordered a Timney trigger and a stock from Bell & Carlson, which as far as I know are the only sources for triggers or synthetic stocks to fit this little action.

I made the tools I used for blueprinting the action and bolt, which helped me learn a lot about cutting metric threads before I started on the barrel.

There is a sidebar in the barrel threading section on how to deal with a metric thread. It is a different approach and a bit slower, but has a good outcome.

I coated everything metal and the synthetic stock with Flat Black Aluma-Hyde II, then fitted a Weaver rail and a Bushnell Trophy 2-7 scope in Weaver rings. The entire rig with the scope weighs six pounds, 10 ounces.

With 50-grain Hornady V-Max bullets the muzzle velocity is 3,556 ft/s. The average for three, three-shot groups is .7 inch. This is a perfect illustration of what a good barrel can do for accuracy. It's a tiny, pencil-thin barrel, but it shoots very well.

One reason I did this rifle first is that I had a coyote hunt planned for later in the winter. When I finally got to turn it loose on a big northern Vermont male, that 50-grain Hornady bullet simply turned off all the switches.

I made some of the tools needed to blueprint this Mini Mauser action. That gave me a chance to practice cutting metric threads.

Truing the action on a homemade mandrel.

The .223 Ackley Improved on the right shows the steeper shoulder and reduced case taper characteristic of AI cartridges.

This was the first coyote to fall to the new rifle.   *It was cold that day!*

CHAPTER 13
BARRELS

The long tube that launches the bullet is the only thing the bullet touches once the powder ignites. The influence of the barrel is what determines if the bullet flies with consistency and accuracy or with chaos.

Without a good barrel, you are wasting your time and the gun will never shoot well. That does not mean it has to be an expensive barrel, it just means it has to be a good barrel.

While learning this craft, I built a bunch of rifles. Three of them were with production line, hammer forged barrels that my buddy John Fink from Remington sent me to "practice" with. These are the barrels that go on the factory rifles that compete in a tight marketplace for sales, so the price of the rifle must be held down. As any shooter knows, Remington has a reputation for excellent out of the box accuracy and these barrels kept that intact. All the rifles are outstanding shooters, easily capable of sub-MOA accuracy.

We can and should expect to find great accuracy from expensive aftermarket barrels. Certainly they are a good choice for any new rifle build, particularly when building a rifle where accuracy is the number one goal.

My "Magnum Opus" rifle

▲ This Bartlein barrel is going to be a .300 Winchester. My Magnum Opus.

has a Bartlein barrel. When accuracy is the primary concern, Bartlein is perhaps the best choice you can make. They enjoy a very good reputation with long-range shooters and custom gun makers. This rifle is an outstanding shooter that will group into half-MOA with factory loads and even better with tuned handloads. I also have a custom 6.5mm Creedmoor with a Bartlein barrel that was built by Dave Tooley. That one shoots to ¼-MOA and I think its only limitation is my skill as a shooter. I suspect the rifle is capable of even better accuracy, even if I am not. Both clean up easily and show little fouling which is one indication of a great barrel.

I built a 6mm Creedmoor precision rifle with a Shilen Select Match Barrel I got from Brownells. That gun has produced ¼-MOA groups with regularity and I attribute a lot of that accuracy to the barrel. It simply makes no sense to go cheap on the barrel for a precision rifle build.

Of course, these top-shelf barrels are very expensive. There are other alternatives, depending on your requirements. I built a pair of 9.3X62 hunting rifles that are detailed elsewhere in this book. One was for me and the other for my longtime friend Tony Kinton. We were both on a tight budget and these are big game hunting rifles designed to be used at relatively short range, so I could not see the point in buying high-end, hand-lapped barrels for these guns. The goal was a rifle that can produce MOA accuracy with hunting ammo, which opens the door to less-expensive possibilities.

I have had great luck with E. R. Shaw button rifled barrels. I have several rifles fitted with their barrels and they are all good shooters. Shaw's barrels are priced considerably lower than a high-end, cut rifling, hand-lapped barrel. For these rifles, they were an obvious choice.

I was pleasantly surprised to find that both rifles exceeded our 1 MOA goal. The first time I shot mine was with Norma factory ammo with a 232-grain Oryx bullet. Three three-shot, 100-yard groups averaged .66 inch. The rifle has continued to show this kind of accuracy with several other ammo products. Tony reported .80-inch groups with his rifle first time out with Hornady 286-grain ammo.

My point is that you can match the barrel to the needs of the rifle you are building. If the goal is extreme accuracy for long-range precision work, a Bartlein or similar barrel makes sense. While it's never a good idea to go cheap, you can spend less for a hunting rifle that has less stringent accuracy requirements than a long-range precision rifle. Often you will be pleasantly surprised, as we were with the relatively inexpensive E. R. Shaw barrels.

What you can't do is make a bad barrel act like a good barrel. I know, I have tried. I once had a .280 Remington that was never much of a shooter. This was before I had my own lathe, so I asked Mark Bansner to rechamber it for .280 Ackley Improved. Mark tried to talk me into a new barrel, but I wouldn't listen. I put hours and hours into messing with bedding and handloads and finally got it to be a good shooter; sort of, maybe . . . as long as I didn't set my standards too high. Years later I had Mark install a better barrel, this time while I watched to learn how it was done. Now that rifle is a great shooter. The only difference is the barrel.

More recently I wanted to see about rechambering a 5.56 AR-15 to the new 22 Nosler cartridge. I had an upper in my vault that would never shoot worth a hoot. It was an early production gun from a company that was just getting

into AR-15 rifles and they had some issues with the barrel supplier. I figured it would be a good barrel to practice with for the tricky technique. The rechambering had some problems, but, in the end the new chamber turned out perfect. While I had the barrel out, I also re-crowned it with an 11-degree crown and deep cleaned the bore.

I put it all back together and discovered that accuracy had improved by 100 percent, but it was pretty horrible to start with, so it was still not much in the accuracy department. Just to make sure, I re-crowned using a brass lap. Nothing changed.

When my new Lyman bore scope showed up, this was the first barrel I checked. It was awful, full of machining marks, chatter and in a couple of places some of the rifling lands are missing. It's amazing it shoots as well as it does.

My goal here was to learn the technique for converting to 22 Nosler, so this was a good result. But it again illustrates the point that you cannot make a bad barrel into something it is not. It was a good barrel to use for this experiment because if I messed up I didn't lose much, but that was all the value it offered.

My point here is simple: good barrels come in many different configurations and price ranges. It's a lot of work to fit a barrel, so don't waste your time working with junk, unless it's for practice. If you are doing this for keeps, do a little research on the barrel you are buying.

Accuracy is a simple function of consistency. Some things we can control, some we can't, but if we can keep the things we can control consistent then accuracy follows. One big controllable variable is the barrel. Start with a quality barrel that fits the needs of the rifle you are building. Then thread, chamber, and crown with precision.

The result will rarely disappoint you.

"FATHER AND SON" RIFLES

My son Nathan is an engineer and machinist who lives in Minnesota. He was home in Vermont for Christmas while I was working on this book and my gift to him was the parts to make a rifle. Well, everything except the stock, which he bought on sale from Brownells.

After seeing the finished rifle, I wanted one of my own. So I set out to build another one like his.

We both used Remington Model 700 short actions. The actions were blueprinted using the Manson kit. The barrels are Remington hammer forged with a 1:12 twist rate. These barrels were designed by Remington for a .308 varmint rifle, with the assumption they would be used with light bullets. My favorite load for a .308 is a 168 grain Sierra bullet. Federal and Black Hills both make factory loads with this bullet and it's a standard in a handload with Varget powder. These rifles love that bullet. They also shoot the Sierra 175-grain MatchKing bullet very well too.

Nathan wanted a long barrel and his is 27 inches. Mine is 23 inches. Both are finished with an 11-degree

Nathan's Rifle, "in the Minnesota wildlands."

This is my .308 Winchester "economy precision" rifle.

target style crown. Nathan cut the crown on his rifle using a small boring bar. The key is to start the cut from inside the bore and cut out to the outside edge. This eliminates any burrs from forming inside the bore.

I cut my crown using a piloted 11-degree cutter in a Manson floating reamer holder. The end result is pretty much the same, except mine took about half the time to finish. Nathan cut the bolt counterbore recess on his barrel using a boring bar, while I used a piloted Manson cutter in a floating reamer holder. Again, same result, but I think I did mine at least 10 times faster. Back when we built Nathan's rifle, I didn't have the Mason bolt counterbore recess cutter. Now I won't be without it.

I later added an oversize bolt handle to my .308 precision rifle build.

These barrels are straight off the hammer forge without turning the outside contour, so you can see the spiral imprint of the rifling on the outside contour of the barrel. Nathan liked that look, so we left his barrel unfinished with the factory bluing on the receiver. I have tried to talk him into letting me paint it, but he is pretty set with this look.

I finished my receiver and barrel with Cerakote Elite Earth. A word of caution here. Cerakote makes both

Nathan setting up an indicator during his rifle build.

What do you do when the indicator is on the backside of the lathe? Use a mirror, of course. Problem solving is a gunsmith's domain.

(continued . . .)

oven-cure and air-dry products, often in the same colors. The labels are almost exactly the same and it's hard to tell them apart.

Don't mix them up.

The air-dry does not respond well to mixing in the catalyst for the oven cure and then putting the parts in the oven.

I'm just saying.

I had to blast off all the uncured finish and start over. In the interest of full disclosure, the first time I did this action and barrel I was not happy with the results as I sprayed the Cerakote on too thick. So I dumped it in a bluing tank, washed it off with acetone and started over.

My .308 Rifle after coating the metal multiple times.

Then I used the wrong Cerakote. In the end, I spray coated this project three times. That not only messes with your ego, but using all that Cerakote gets a bit expensive.

The third time I used the correct oven cure product and I have a pretty good looking rifle. The spirals from the hammer forging show through the finish for a unique look. (Though they are hard to see in photos.) In retrospect, maybe Nathan had the right idea in going au natural with his color scheme and at least we got that one right on the first try!

Nathan's rifle has a Timney trigger. Mine has a prototype Model 700 trigger from Velocity Triggers. Both work great.

We used Magpul 700 Hunter stocks with Magpul bottom metal (actually, it's bottom *plastic*) to allow the use of removable Magpul magazines. Mine is black, while Nathan's is grey. This stock is adjustable for length of pull and comb height. While they call it a "hunter stock," it's a very good, low price alternative to use on a long-range precision rifle. They cost a fraction of what a chassis system or most other stocks cost, yet the performance of this stock is excellent.

I call this my economy precision rifle. The cost to build was not horribly high, particularly compared to some other precision rifles using expensive chassis systems, but the guns shoot well enough to run with the big dogs and both rifles will shoot .6-inch five shot groups with factory ammo.

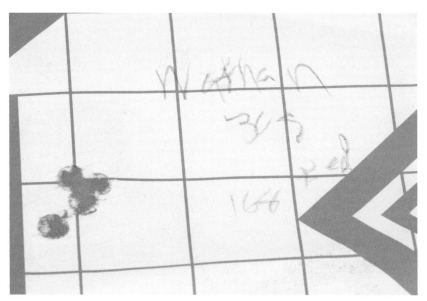

◄ This is the first group out of Nathan's .308 Winchester rifle. The "flier" was the first shot from a clean barrel. Federal Match with 168-Grain Sierra bullets. The 5-shot group measures .6 inch and the last four shots are in .3 inch.

CHAPTER 14
ACTIONABLE GUNSMITHING

You need a good foundation for a good build.

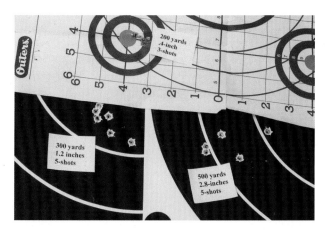

▲ The path to this level of accuracy starts with the action.

▲ The build for this 6mm Creedmoor was as smooth as a lake at sunrise.

The rifle action is the foundation of the entire shooting system. Like any foundation, it is critical to what follows. If a house has a poor foundation, no matter what level of perfection the builder brings to the rest of the build, it will never reach its full potential and it's likely to be plagued with problems. It's the same with rifles. If you do not have the action true and straight, you can never make the rest of the rifle reach its potential. Get it right and things go well. Get it wrong and the rifle will never be right.

How that goes often seems to set the mood for the rest of the build. I don't know why, it makes no sense and follows no logic, but in the rifles I have built, when the action work runs smoothly, the rest of the rifle build seems to be pretty trouble free too.

For example, my 6mm Creedmoor rifle build was as close to glitch free as I have ever encountered. I started with the action and that process ran smooth and trouble free. Everything worked exactly as it should and even little things like lapping the bolt lugs went as fast and easy as I have ever seen. The rest of the build followed suit, just as smooth and trouble free. I think I might have finished that build without using any four letter words, which is a first for me. The rifle is not only an attention getter, but it's a great shooter too.

After that build, I thought I was the King Dude of hobby gunsmiths. I figured I had this thing nailed. Then, along came the next gun to knock me off that pedestal and back down to grovel in the humbling dirt and debris of frustration.

My Magnum Opus rifle started with a curse that seemed to carry the bad juju on to the rest of the build. There is nothing I can really put my finger on, other than to blame it on a cursed action. It looked to be made from steel, but was in reality a matrix of glitches, demons, curses, gremlins, and troubles.

That rifle should have been a smooth build. My skills were tuned up and honed sharp after building several rifles. I used the best of everything in the components and I expected to breeze through it trouble free and end the journey with a super-rifle.

In reality, that rifle fought me every step of the way. Everything that could go wrong went wrong, from little things like hitting a hard spot and breaking a drill while enlarging the scope mount screw holes, to extractor springs flying away to be lost forever, including me messing up and cutting too much metal with both the milling machine and the lathe. It's a vast understatement to say that this gun tried my patience.

Many times I had to fight the urge to accept "good enough" when I knew I wanted perfection. I stayed with it, reworking the mistakes and keeping that concept of perfection in mind. I didn't quite hit it, if it was even achievable, but I got as close as I can. (You should always be your own worst critic, that's how you improve. Perfection should always remain an unreachable goal.) In the end, I fixed the problems, worked through the challenges, and ended up with not just a good rifle, but also a strong urge to quit gunsmithing and develop a drinking problem.

In life, it's the problem child who often has the greatest potential. They are the ones who go on to use their contrary spirit to do great things in life, while the easy going kid lives a life of conformity and boredom. I guess it's the same with rifles, because, in the end, this is a hell of a rifle.

But, if I had it to do over … I would take the action to a priest and request an exorcism before I started.

Bottom line? Blueprinting the action is a very good start to building an accurate rifle. Take your time, get it right. If the gremlins live in the action, like they did with my rifle, stop the build and get rid of them.

Or at least restock the liquor cabinet.

I'LL TAKE THAT ACTION

WHY A CUSTOM ACTION TAKES ALL THE FUN OUT OF BUILDING A RIFLE.

For custom rifle builders, the choice is simple. Time is money. Back in the day, gunsmiths had to work with the rifle actions that were available. Often, that meant a donor rifle that was cannibalized to get the action or at best buying an action, usually a Remington Model 700, Winchester Model 70, or a surplus Mauser. Today, things have changed and there are a lot of very good shovel-ready rifle actions on the market. No need to blueprint them, it's all done.

▲ The Remington Model 700 action is better than a high-dollar custom action. At least for a hobby gunsmith.

There are actions for every use from a precision long-range rifle to an ultralight mountain hunting rifle. They come trued and ready to go. Many will also have custom features like rails that are integral to the action. Often the bolts will have upgraded extractor systems and, for tactical builds, you can get oversized bolt handles.

Skilled gunsmiths at the top of their game and in demand have only so much time available. The only way they can increase their income is to increase the amount of money they are paid per hour worked or to streamline productivity. The best of the best are paid well for their time, so when it comes to a paid custom build, it's actually less expensive for most customers to buy a high-end action than it is to pay the gunsmith's time to blueprint and tune an existing action.

That alone is motivation for most customers to buy a ready to rock, high-end action. Plus there are always the bragging rights of having a big name action as the foundation for your rifle. In some circles this is important and a savvy custom gun builder recognizes that and gives his customers what they demand.

If you can afford a top shelf action and that's the way you wish to go for your rifle build, it's a good decision from the perspective of the end product, but you will miss out on all the fun.

We hobby guys have a little different situation here. Those of us who spend money at this rather than make money are in it for the journey as much as the destination. I enjoy building guns, so if it takes me a bit longer to complete one because I have to blueprint the action, I see that as more time with concrete under my feet and contentment in my heart.

We also need to look at this from the economic side. The Remington Model 700 action is the baseline here. It's what almost all the custom actions mimic, and will often appear in the description of their rifle actions.

For example, this from the website of Defiance Machine:

"Precision bolt action with a standard footprint for ease of stock selection and off-the-shelf custom fit; easily replaces the Remington 700."

From Stiller Actions:

"They are a stainless steel drop in replacement for the Remington 700 series actions . . ."

There are variations of course, but the 700 clones are the most popular for custom builds. One reason is they are easy to work with, as everything is round, which makes life easier when trying to achieve precision.

I picked these two because they were the top two actions used by the top shooters in PRS competition at the time I was writing this. Make no mistake, these are outstanding actions, but they are expensive. I did a quick check on the net and found that the average high-end action costs about 2.8 times as much as a new Remington Model 700 action from Brownells.

Using a Remington action in your build results in a considerable savings if you don't mind doing the work to bring the Remington up to the performance level of the high-end actions. It's often even cheaper to prowl local gun shops to find old beater Model 700 rifles that you can buy for less than the price of a new action. I have a standing order in with a few local gun shops for beater guns I can use for projects. Even if they don't buy the guns, some of them will give my number to the guy trying to sell. It's amazing sometimes how cheaply you can buy a beat up rifle that is the perfect donor of a serviceable action.

TRUE DAT

It's possible to build a rifle using the action as it comes from the factory; after all, that's what the factory produced guns do. But, why would you? The point of a custom build is to create a better rifle. So typically a builder will "blueprint" the action. That means truing the threads, bolt lugs, bolt

▲ I made this tool to lap the bolt lugs in a Mini Mauser action.

face and the receiver face to the center line of the action. Then the bolt lugs will be trued and lapped for a perfect mate to the action lugs.

If you are good with your machines, you can make almost all the tooling you need to blueprint an action. There are instructions and drawings on how to make many of the tools in the book *The Complete Illustrated Guide to Precision Rifle Barrel Fitting,* by John L. Hinnant. This book is available from Brownells and is a wealth of information. Some of the techniques in the book, such as chambering a barrel in a steady rest, are considered outdated by many current gun builders, but there is so much other good information that any shop should have a copy of this book.

I will note that if you are new to machining, making your own tools is a great way to practice the techniques you will use later to build the rifle. It's far less heartbreaking to screw up a piece of practice steel that you bought for a few dollars than to mess up a high-dollar rifle barrel. There is also a lot of satisfaction in making the tools you will use later to build a rifle.

A word of caution, though. Truing an action on the lathe can be tricky if you are still new to this machining game. For example, you should true the threads, which means picking up the thread and truing it to center, while working with an inside thread. If you were simply cutting an outside thread it would be less problematic, but here you must pick up an existing inside thread, which is a bit of an advanced machining technique. It's not impossible, but it requires a very good eye and plenty of patience.

Just remember, one slip up and your action is trash. Truing the action threads on the lathe is a "one-shot" situation. I don't claim to be an expert at this, but I have tried picking up outside threads several times. The technique used for picking up an existing thread is visual, so an outside thread is much easier, as you can see the tool a lot better than you can when you are working inside the receiver. It still took me several tries before I understood how it worked and got it right.

I can tell you with some shame that I have a barrel on a rifle I built that is shorter than I had planned. I tried to pick up the thread I had cut previously for the muzzle brake. I thought I had it perfect, but I did not and the thread was ruined. In that case I just cut the threaded section off the barrel and started over.

That barrel was too damn long anyway.

You do not have that option with receiver threads. There is nothing to cut off and no way to start over. If you have time and the courage of a Viking, truing the action threads on the lathe is an interesting way to go, but my advice is to wait until you have developed your machining skills and have several other projects under your belt.

When I built my .223 Ackley Improved, I needed a way to true the action. In this case, it was a Zastava Mini

Mauser action, which does not have the options of the Model 700 when it comes to available commercial tooling. This was my first build on the new Grizzly lathe and the first complete build without adult supervision. It was also a metric thread, which really complicates things, as the technique to cut the thread is different. I had never cut a metric thread and in fact I had cut very few single-point threads of any kind. (That's me. Jump right in with the most difficult option first. I never claimed to be smart.)

I decided to start by making the tools I would need. By making a mandrel to true the action and a holder for bolt facing and lapping tools, I was able to learn several machining practices, including the different technique used to cut a single-point metric thread on a Grizzly lathe. Without giving a lot of embarrassing details, let me say I was very pleased that I decided to practice on scrap metal first and not expensive gun parts.

For that rifle build, I chose not to attempt to recut the threads in the action. It would have been best, but I realized it was beyond my capabilities at that time. I did however, true the action face to existing threads using a mandrel I made. I also trued the bolt face and bolt lugs, then lapped the lugs. I was rewarded with a very accurate rifle.

The action truing process can be accomplished with a lot of different tools or techniques. You may decide to make your tools or you can use "store bought" tools, but the end result should be the same.

The goal is to true everything to the centerline of the receiver. For best results that should include the threads, the bolt face and lugs, and the front ring of the receiver.

STORE-BOUGHT TOOLS AND THEIR USE

If you decide to buy what you need, there are several tools on the market to help true the action. One of the most popular for working with Remington Model 700 or Winchester Model 70 actions is the Manson Receiver Accurizing System, which you can buy from Brownells. That's the route I decided to go.

▲ The Manson Receiver Accurizing System.

At first glance the price tag for this kit seems a little brutal as it runs about 20 percent more than the cost of a new Remington 700 action. Still, that is considerably less than the difference in price between a Remington action and one of the top of the line custom actions. In other words, you can buy the Manson Receiver Accurizing System and the Remington action and still pay less than you would for a custom action. So, in theory, you are money ahead with the first rifle you build and you still have the tools for future builds. If you are going to do more than one rifle, and of course you are, then this kit more than pays for itself very quickly.

Brownells offers two models of this kit. Dave Manson recommends you get the .010-inch Over Receiver Accurizing Kit, rather than the standard kit. This cuts the threads to .010 inch larger than standard factory threads, which allows plenty of dimension to correct any inconsistencies.

This means that the barrel threads will need to be .010 inch larger than what is standard for Remington 700 barrels. You will custom fit the thread to the action anyway, so this is a moot point.

I have heard some complaints that cutting the oversized threads will mean you can no longer use a pre-threaded replacement barrel on that action, because those barrels are threaded to factory dimensions. I think this is a bit foolish. The reason you are building a custom rifle is so that you can precisely fit every single part of the gun. Why on earth would you want to use a barrel that is threaded to fit a wide range of actions? The tolerances needed for this to work would defeat the purpose of building a custom rifle. So, if you ever did shoot out the barrel and need to replace it, the way to do that properly would be to custom fit the new barrel. At that point, it's not a problem to make the thread .010 inch larger than standard, so that you can maintain the precision of the rifle.

The first step in using the Manson kit is to insert the tapered pilot bushings and that's where I ran into trouble. The directions say:

"Slide the pilot of the reamer first through the bushing in the front receiver ring and then through the bushing in the rear receiver ring—you may have to wiggle the tap slightly to align with the bushing in the rear receiver ring. Once both bushings engage the pilot, seat the bushings into the action's I.D. by pushing them deeper with the brass rod. The reamer's pilot should slide through the guide bushings with minimal resistance."

Fair enough, seems simple. Except that the bushing in the front stuck out too far to allow the reamer to contact the bolt locking lugs. I tried reversing it and it still stuck out too far, so I drove it in deep enough using a brass punch. That squeezed the bushing enough to make the mandrel hard to insert and turn. I ordered bigger bushings, but that didn't fix the problem, they were too big to even fit in the action.

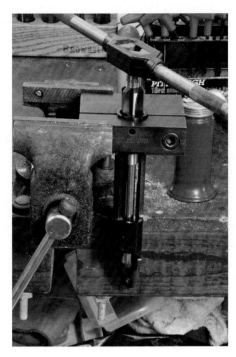

▲ This shows the Remington action locked into an action wrench. Note the bushings are visible.

▲ The reamer from the Manson kit.

Finally, I chucked the bushing in my lathe and cut about a third of the length off it. This was a difficult job, as the bushing is hardened and I had to take tiny cuts. Even at that, I wore out a new carbide cutter and there was a burr when I finished that I had to remove with a stone. In the end, it all worked, but it just didn't seem right.

So I contacted Dave Manson (something I should have done from the start). He explained that the reason the bushing is inserted from the back side of the action is so that the reamer can push it back out of the receiver far enough to allow the reamer cutter to make contact with the bolt locking lug face. He explained that even though the bushing would then be out of contact, the reamer is self-piloting once it has cut at least a quarter inch deep.

Now that I understood the process, I had to order a new bushing to replace the one I had cut shorter. In my own defense, the instructions said nothing about this process, which I pointed out to Dave. I suggested he update the instructions, or better yet, tell all his customers to buy this book so they can read about it here. He liked the idea of people buying this book.

So do I.

Once the bushings are inserted properly according to the instructions, lock the receiver into a receiver vise and put the receiver vise in a bench vise to hold it. The first time I did this I was so focused on the job that I didn't notice much else. After I finished there was a mess on the floor that I discovered after I had stepped in it and tracked the matrix

of oil and metal chips all over the shop. Now I put a trash can under the action to catch the chips and oil drippings.

We learn from our mistakes, right?

The reamer recuts the "bore" of the receiver for the correct diameter for the new threads while centering with the bushings. The idea is to ream until the bottom cutters on the reamer just clean up the bolt locking lug face and

▲ Note how one bolt locking lug recess is trued, but not the other. That means they were not even and you need to cut a little more.

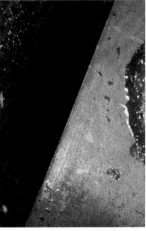

▲ Both bolt locking lug recesses are making contact with the cutter. One more light pass will finish it.

trues them to the center. Go slow, check often, and clean the chips when you do. If you cut too far you can ruin the action, so take your time here.

Once that is finished, clean all the chips and reverse the front bushing per the instructions. Then use the tap in the kit to recut the threads. When you are finished, leave the tap in the action. This is your mandrel to hold the action in the lathe while you true the face. The friction from the tap being tight inside the receiver will hold it in place while you true the front of the receiver. Make sure the top of the tap is below the leading edge of the receiver.

▲ The tap recuts the receiver threads true to the center and .010 inch oversized.

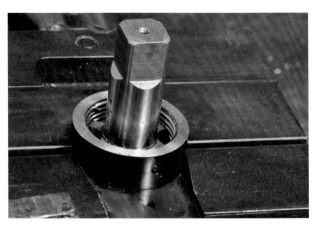

▲ Make sure the tap is well below the leading edge of the receiver.

MACHINERY'S HANDBOOK, 30TH EDITION

Everything you ever wanted to know about machining is found in this giant book that is often referred to as "the bible for machinists." First published in 1914 and updated regularly, the book is filled with information on materials, tooling, threading, feed rates, cutting speeds, dimensions; it's all there. Gunsmiths will find they'll consult this book often to locate machining information such as speed and feed rates as well as info like thread dimensions and much more. This book is one of those things that, once you have it, you will wonder how you ever survived without it in your toolbox.

The book is offered in both the standard Toolbox edition designed to fit in a specific drawer in a Kennedy toolbox and in a large print edition. If you are over 40, get the large print, you will thank me for that. The publishers pack an unbelievable amount of information into a single book and to make it fit the toolbox, the print is a bit small. I got sick of hunting up my magnifying visor to read some of the smaller charts and print, so I ordered the large print edition. This one doesn't remind me quite as often of my faded youth. The book is also available in a digital edition to run on your computer and there's a pocket companion, which is a much smaller condensed version of the book.

The largeprint edition.

Industrial Press has several books on machining, which can be a great help for a new gunsmith learning basic through advanced machining techniques.

GETTING CENTERED

Now you will transfer the action on the mandrel to the lathe. There are several ways to do this next process. The tailstock end will be supported by a live center. The headstock end of the mandrel can be in a collet if you have one. It can also be used in a 4-jaw chuck and trued, but that takes a lot of time. The easiest and best way is to run it on two centers.

▲ When switching chucks on the lathe, always protect the ways with a piece of plywood. If you slip and drop a chuck, it can damage the lathe if the wood is not there for protection.

You will need two 60-degree centers to support the mandrel. A live center in your tailstock handles 50 percent of that requirement. The best way to hold the headstock end will be by making a 60-degree center that is cut to the exact center of the rotation of the lathe. This is easy to do and once you have the tool you can use it again and again. The key is that each time you put it back in the lathe to use, you must recut the angle to a true center. That center is good until you remove the tool from the lathe. Each time it's removed and replaced, you must recut the angled portion to center again.

▲ This center is 60 degrees and is turned on the lathe so it is perfectly true to the axis.

Chuck a piece of round stock in the 3-jaw chuck and cut a smaller diameter shank that is long enough to fit fully into your 3-jaw chuck. Cut this to a square shoulder. You'll probably be using some scrap stock that is hanging around the shop and the initial diameter isn't critical. You just want the shoulder to act as a stop when you insert the shank you are turning into the lathe.

Reverse the work piece and insert it until the shoulder acts as a stop when you put it in the chuck, then lock it down. Now you must cut a 60-degree taper on the front section. You will need to keep the 60-degree tapered nose short so that you can reach the chuck with a small lathe dog.

▲ It is much easier to cut the taper with the cutting tool in the back and the lathe running backwards. This piece turned out to be too long to use with a lathe dog. Moving the shoulder closer to the taper fixed the problem.

When I tried to use the compound to cut a 60-degree taper with the tool set up in the front of the work piece as is conventional, nothing seemed to work. There was never enough clearance and even when I got it set up, the light stand and the coolant tube were in the way of the controls for the compound. So I moved the cutting tool to the back side of the work piece and reversed the rotation of the lathe. Now I can easily cut the taper to 60 degrees using the compound.

Once you finish cutting the taper, do not remove the work piece from the chuck until the job at hand, in this case truing up the receiver, is completed. By cutting this angle, you have trued the taper to the centerline of the work piece and the true centerline of the rotation of the lathe. As mentioned earlier, if you remove the center from the chuck and then replace it, it will lose center and you will need to recut the 60-degree angle to bring it back to a true center.

This tapered center you have made is a tool you will use every time you do this operation on a receiver and each time you use it you will need to cut the 60-degree angle to true up the center. While it has to be short enough to work with a lathe dog, also try to make the piece long enough to sustain that sacrifice of material through several uses.

You don't need to take much off, just enough to true it back to center. Cut until you have a clean cut the entire length of the taper, ending at a sharp point. A few thousandths is usually enough, so the tool should serve you through a bunch of uses. When it gets too short, make another.

TRUING THE RECEIVER

The tap from the Manson Receiver Accurizing System has a 60-degree taper recessed into each end on center to allow you to suspend the mandrel between the live center on your tailstock and the new center you have cut in the chuck. Of course you need a way to turn it, so clamp a lathe dog on the mandrel before you put it in the lathe.

▲ This is the setup with the mandrel reversed.

▲ A lathe dog.

A lathe dog is an angled piece you clamp on the mandrel. It has a 90-degree leg to contact the jaws on the chuck. These are primarily designed to be used with a faceplate on the lathe, but they work fine contacting the protruding jaw on the 3-jaw chuck. Make sure they are in contact before you start the lathe to prevent clunking. Some people use some duct tape to hold them in place. Run the lathe on a very low RPM as there will be an imbalance of weight that can get ugly if you try to spin it fast.

I am indoctrinated into the concept of trying to work as close as possible to the chuck and that is what the instructions with the Manson Receiver Accurizing System suggest.

"This means you'll be working close to the headstock and will need a left-hand parting tool to true the receiver face."

The trouble is there is very little space left to work in after clamping even a small lathe dog on the flats on the mandrel. I did not have a left-hand parting tool, so I experimented with all the tools I did have, even a small boring bar. It is difficult to fit into the small space with any of them.

Then I had one of those *"oh, duh"* moments. I simply reversed the mandrel, put the lathe dog on the other end and found that if I worked on the tailstock end there was all

▲ Truing the receiver face working on the tailstock end.

kinds of room. I use a long nose live center that allows me to get in there to work with even more clearance. To prevent the lathe dog from damaging the mandrel I wrapped the surface with electrician's tape.

Of course, Manson correctly points out in the instructions that any misalignment of the tailstock can cause issues, so before doing this operation I check to see that the tailstock is correctly aligned. It's important that you be able to run a test indicator on the mandrel in front of the receiver and have no runout.

Would it be better to work on the headstock end? Probably. But this is far less aggravating than trying to fit into that tiny work space on the headstock end.

All you are doing here is truing up the front of the receiver, so take the smallest possible cut to clean up the leading edge. A few thousandths is usually all you need. Most carbon steel receivers will be blued, while stainless steel will not. If there is no bluing, coat the front of the receiver with Dykem or a felt marker. Take very light cuts until it just removes all the color from the entire leading surface of the receiver. That's it, you are done, do not cut any deeper.

BROWNELLS LATHE CENTERING BUTTONS

The problem of centering the tailstock to the headstock center of rotation has been the subject of several different solutions.

The conventional way is to turn a long piece of stock suspended on centers and measure the diameter on both ends. If they are not exactly the same, you must adjust the tailstock, make another cut and measure again. Repeat this until they are an exact match. It works well, but takes a long time. Once you have a perfect match, you can keep the bar to use for future adjustments.

Or you can buy a premade bar, except that the one I have is off by .003 inch and nobody can figure out why.

Perhaps the most ingenious tool I have encountered is the set of Brownells Lathe Centering Buttons. These are a matched pair of precision-ground buttons measuring exactly .900 inch. They each have a 60-degree cone so they will fit on a tapered center.

To use them, you will need to have a center in both the headstock and the tailstock. The best and most accurate way to accomplish this for the headstock is to turn a center as is detailed in the text in the section on blueprinting an action. Once you have a center on both ends, place the buttons on the centers and advance the tailstock until the two are mated lightly together. Make sure the tailstock is locked down with the same torque used when working with the lathe.

A micrometer is then placed over the buttons with half the anvils on each button so the seam splits the center of the anvils. If the measurement is anything more than .900 inch, the two buttons are not perfectly aligned and the tailstock must be adjusted until the micrometer reads exactly .900 inch.

Another good feature is that you can use the buttons to measure the alignment side to side as with the conventional methods, and you can measure top to bottom to ensure that the tailstock is correctly aligned up and down as well. Any misalignment can be corrected using the directions provided with the lathe.

These tools allow using the tailstock to do a taper, such as when contouring a rifle barrel. The buttons are used to bring the tailstock back into alignment after the job is completed.

These buttons are the easiest way I have found to do the tedious but necessary chore of aligning the tailstock.

UPDATE

The problem with writing a book is one of time. (Well, that and the blind stupidity of trying to write books for a living when the world no longer wants to read them.) After I wrote this chapter, I continued to build several more rifles. Along the way I discovered another approach. I would be remiss if I did not include it here. I did several rifles with the technique I first wrote about in this chapter and they are all very accurate. Still, it nagged at me that Dave was right: The closer to the headstock, the better the result.

I often had a hard time getting everything trued with the work reversed. It seems like the tailstock end of the mandrel always had some runout, even after I trued and centered the tailstock using the proven methods. It was all very frustrating and time consuming.

I understood that it was at best a compromise due to the tooling I had to work with. So, some months after writing the first part of this chapter, I came up with a better approach. I left the passage in the book because it does work and is a viable alternative if you do not have the

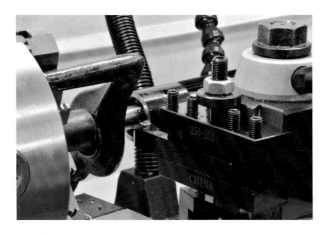

▲ Working on the headstock end is a tight fit.

correct tooling on hand. But, what follows is a technique to turn the receiver face with it on the headstock end, using tools that, as it turns out, I did in fact have on hand. It just took a while to figure out how to make it all work.

By using the headstock end and the center that I just cut to the true center, I had virtually no issues with runout on the mandrel. I could use my best, most accurate test indicator and the needle would not waver. That gives me confidence.

I finally figured out that I could turn a 3/8-inch boring bar upside down and it would fit easily into the space

▲ This shows the boring bar upside down so it will fit in the space available.

between the receiver and a lathe dog attached to the flats on the mandrel.

As with most boring bars, the cutter angles to the left. Using it right side up required turning it at a steep angle that simply would not fit in the space allowed. But by turning it upside down, I can insert it at right angles to the work, the cutter is correctly aligned and it easily fits into the space available.

With the boring bar upside down, the lathe must be run in reverse. I used the power feed on the cross slide to feed the boring bar for a nice smooth cut. In the end, I think this is a better approach.

My boring bar came in a kit from Brownells with a couple of other cutting tools, it's called: *High-Speed Steel Cutting Kits for Lathes–3/8" Turning Kit.* I got the kit to modify Remington Model 700 bolts to take a Sako or M-16 style extractor. This boring bar has proved useful for other work, including cutting an 11-degree target crown on a barrel and for cutting the bolt face counterbore recess on the barrel for a Model 700. Both processes are covered in other sections of this book.

Once you are finished, put the receiver back in the receiver vise and back the tap out. Clean the tools and make sure they are coated with oil to prevent rust before you put them back in the box for storage. I find an easy way to do that is to coat them with oil and then blow off the excess with shop air. Do it outside as it can make a mess.

I should note that Manson sells a receiver face cutter to use with the tap mandrel. Dave told me that he believes the lathe approach is more accurate. Brownells also sells piloted cutters for the receiver face. I do not have any experience with either of these tools and am unable to comment on their effectiveness.

YOU BIG LUG

If you are building a precision rifle, you should use a precision recoil lug. Replace any factory installed, mass produced recoil lugs with an aftermarket product that has both sides precision ground. The recoil lug is the bridge between the front of the receiver and the shoulder on the

▲ The Holland recoil lug.

barrel and it's important that the surfaces on the recoil lug be parallel and precision ground. After carefully machining both the barrel shoulder and the front of the receiver, why risk that precision with a less than perfect recoil lug?

Brownells and Holland's Gunsmithing & Shooters Supply both have recoil lugs designed for the oversized threads that result from using the Manson Receiver Accurizing System. These recoil lugs are also thicker and stronger than the original recoil lug and will provide a more secure fit into the stock or chassis with less chance of flexing under recoil.

That means, of course, that the barrel shank must be longer to compensate for the thicker recoil lug. You should not be working off a fixed blueprint when cutting the barrel thread anyway, as it's a custom fit, but keep that in mind. How to achieve the correct length shank is explained in the section on fitting a barrel.

Darrell Holland's recoil lug is designed to be used with an index pin to fit into a hole drilled in the receiver to maintain correct positioning when tightening the barrel to the action. Holland also sells a jig to correctly drill the hole in the action. This solves a big problem and it allows the use of Holland's Action Wrench. Rather than clamping on the outside of the action, which risks damaging the finish, the Holland wrench is inserted inside the action. The 7/8-inch hex allows the use of a socket and torque wrench. The issue with this approach is keeping the recoil lug indexed properly, a problem the pinned recoil lug from Holland eliminates.

Using a pinned recoil lug makes fitting the barrel to the action much easier. Part of the process of screwing the barrel and action together requires that the recoil lug be oriented correctly. My action wrench has a machined recess that is supposed to fit the lug and keep it oriented correctly. It's designed for a factory recoil lug and of course, the aftermarket precision lugs are often a different shape. Some are smaller and some are too large. I deal with how to adapt for that (at least the smaller ones), in the sidebar here. But I will say here that using Holland's system of pinning the lug is about the easiest approach I have found. He designed it for switch-barrel rifles, so if you are going to be swapping barrels often, then this pinned recoil lug is almost a must. It also allows the use of Holland's Action Wrench, which is an excellent choice as it allows easy use of a torque wrench.

Holland offers recoil lugs with 1.065, 1.075, and 1.085 hole diameters. These are heat-treated, 17-4 stainless steel. He also has a chrome-moly steel version in 1.075 diameter. The 1.075 is the correct size for use with Remington Model 700 receivers that have been blueprinted using the Manson kit.

RECOIL LUG ALIGNMENT

There are several tools designed to keep a Model 700 recoil lug aligned when you tighten the barrel to the receiver. The problem is, there is a wide range of recoil lug shapes and designs. The slots on the Brownells action wrench, or the Kleinendorst Remington F/S Recoil Lug Alignment Tool and similar tools, are fitted to the factory lug or to fit a specific aftermarket recoil lug. Many of the other aftermarket recoil lugs are the incorrect dimension to keep them properly aligned.

If the recoil lug is thinner than the slot, it is easy enough to solve. With the tool or wrench mounted on the action, push the recoil lug to one side of the slot. Using a dial caliper, measure the gap on the other side from the edge of the slot to the edge of the recoil lug. Divide that number by two. The result is the thickness of the filler you will need to keep the recoil lug aligned in the center.

I keep a set of feeler gauges dedicated to this one use. Select the package of feeler gauges that adds up to the thickness you need. When you are tightening the action to the barrel you will notice that the recoil lug tends to twist away from the direction of travel of the wrench. Put the feeler gauges on that side of the lug to fill the gap in the wrench. This will keep the recoil lug centered on the action as you tighten it to the barrel.

Feeler gauges with the Kleinendorst Remington F/S Recoil Lug Alignment Tool.

This set of feeler gauges is dedicated to this job. Here they are used with an action wrench to center a recoil lug that is smaller than the slot in the wrench.

PIN THE PROBLEM

With most of the builds I have done recently, I used a Holland Competition Recoil Lug. This oversized lug is thick and strong and is precision machined with parallel sides. I can order them with a 1.075 hole so they fit perfectly with the oversized threads resulting from blueprinting the action with the Manson Receiver Accurizing System.

These Holland recoil lugs come drilled and with a pin to align them with the receiver. It requires that you drill a hole in the receiver for the pin. Holland sells a jig that helps with this procedure, called the Sine Bar and Recoil Lug Drilling Fixture. It's not an inexpensive tool, but, if you are going to be building a

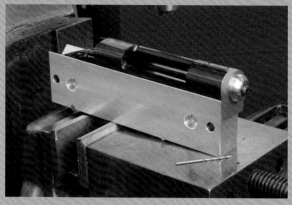

A Remington 700 action in the Holland Sine Bar and Recoil Lug Drilling Fixture.

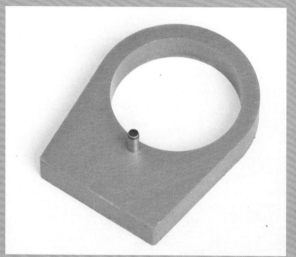

The Holland recoil lug with pin.

Adjusting the quill stop.

lot of guns on Remington Model 700 actions it solves a big problem.

Fit the action to the jig using the supplied screw in the front action screw hole. Place the recoil lug on the front of the action, insert the large alignment nut and snug it up. Align the bottom of the recoil lug with the mark on the fixture to ensure it is square. The hole in the recoil lug is now your guide for drilling the receiver.

Drilling the hole requires that the fixture be true to the drill. On my milling machine the fixture is too long to put in the vise, as I can't lower the table enough to make it fit. So, I simply place the flat end of the fixture on the flat table of my mill. This keeps it square. Measure the length of the pin, then subtract the thickness of the recoil lug and add .010 inch to that as a safety net. Set the quill stop to drill to that depth.

The drill that comes with the kit is 2.4 mm or .094 inch. Drill the hole to the prescribed depth and you are done. Fast and easy.

To install the recoil lug, insert the pin in the recoil lug and slide it over the barrel threads. Start the barrel into the receiver. When the barrel is

Drilling the receiver.

The modified receiver.

The Holland action wrench allows easy use of a torque wrench.

started, push the recoil lug back against the action and insert the pin through the recoil lug and into the action. This keeps the alignment perfect. It works really well if you are using the Holland Remington Action Wrench that fits inside the receiver.

Holland suggests this system for making switch-barrel guns, but it works fine for a single barrel installation. Of course, if you ever want to change the barrel the lug stays aligned.

The recoil lug fits between the front of the receiver that you trued and the shoulder on the barrel that you also trued, so you want it to be perfectly parallel and perfectly square. The mass-produced factory recoil lugs are not necessarily precise.

Dave Manson made a good point about that recently when we were talking gunsmithing. I brought up the concept that most gunsmiths adjust .002 inch to .003 inch when headspacing to allow for "crush."

"If you have blueprinted the action, have precisely fitted barrel threads and use a precision recoil lug you probably don't need to do that," Dave said. "Notice that when you screw it all together it goes 'clunk' and just stops? That's because you have eliminated the crush. Crush is when you have factory-tolerance threads, receiver, and recoil lug. With a precision job, when you have custom fitted everything and used a precise recoil lug there is no crush. Cut to the headspacing you want and it will be right without any allowance for crush."

That's why it's called "precision." Crush sounds so arbitrary.

Let me finish this discussion by saying that while writing the book I have consulted with several top gunsmiths in the country. Most of them still defend the concept of crush, but many prefer to call it "thread stretch." As you will see in the section on chambering a barrel, I take a different route and finish my chambers by hand, so it's all a moot point on my guns. It also means I have not yet been able to personally prove or disprove the crush concept.

That's the great thing about gunsmithing. Everybody has a different approach to how to do things. A lot of them think theirs is the one true way, but I have discovered there is no one single true path. That's a good thing, because deviation from the path is where innovation comes from. If we just accept "that's the way it's always done" as a concept, new ideas would stop flowing and that would be tragic. In the end though, they all seem to work (well, most of them anyway) and get you to the same end result, which is to make a good gun better.

RECOIL LUG REAMER

There is a reamer included in the .010-inch oversized Manson Receiver Accurizing System that is used to open the diameter of the hole in a standard recoil lug to 1.075 inches. This is so the recoil lug will fit the larger thread on the barrel that results from using the kit to blueprint a rifle action.

Dave Manson cautions that some aftermarket recoil lugs are very hard and can damage the reamer, so always check first. If you can cut the metal easily with a file, it's fine for the reamer.

The reamer is self-centering and can be used with a drill press or a milling machine. The recoil lug must be supported perfectly square so that the hole is reamed 90 degrees to the bearing surfaces. There are several ways to do this, including making a jig to hold the recoil lug. However, I think my approach is probably as simple as it gets.

I use a set of thin parallels in my milling machine vise to support the lug front and back. I place the square bottom of the lug against one of the vise jaws, but do not tighten the vise snug, leaving it slightly loose so the recoil lug can float any direction. This allows the recoil lug to self-center on the reamer. The flat bottom of the lug contacts the vise jaw as the lug tries to twist and prevents the recoil lug from turning.

The recoil lug must be able to float enough to allow the reamer to self-center while still being supported by the parallels. Line up the reamer as close to center as possible, making sure the lug can move enough in any direction to self-center. The parallel under the front ring of the recoil lug must be thin enough that the reamer will not contact it when it passes through the recoil lug.

Remove the reamer from contact with the lug before starting the mill. Run the mill or drill press on the slowest setting. Manson recommends 40 to 60 RPM. Flood with lots of cutting oil and feed the reamer through the recoil lug. The reamer will center the recoil lug. Manson recommends that you apply plenty of pressure and ream through the recoil lug relatively quickly.

There will probably be small burrs on both sides after reaming. Remove them with a deburring knife, or use an unworn, square, hard Arkansas stone. Hold the lug flat against the stone and polish until the burrs are gone. It's important that the burrs be removed, as they can interfere with the fit of the recoil lug against the barrel or receiver.

The recoil lug is sitting on the parallels in the vise, but is free to move to center.

After reaming the recoil lug, carefully polish off the burrs with a smooth bench stone like this Hard Arkansas Stone.

SLICK IT UP

You may want to polish the bolt raceways for smoother working of the bolt. The bolt raceways are the "bed" on the action where the bolt's lugs ride. If the surfaces are rough, it will make the action work hard and feel sticky and rough. If they are polished, the bolt will work with that slick feeling that gun guys love.

Once again, my tool for this job is from Brownells. It is called the Receiver Way Polisher. It holds a replaceable piece of 220 or 330 grit abrasive paper. The tool is inserted

in the rear of the action and rides on the bolt raceways. With a small amount stoning oil and plenty of elbow grease, it will polish the surfaces.

I also like to polish the bottom of the bolt lugs, the surfaces that ride on the action raceways. For this I use some abrasive paper wrapped around a flat piece of stock, flat stones, or a combination of the two. Finally, use a Cratex polishing bit in a Dremel tool to polish the feed ramp on the action and then finish with a felt polishing tip with red compound.

Always polish receiver ways before you do any final finish. It's important to smooth up the metal as much as possible before any finish is applied or the metal is sand-blasted prior to final finish. If you are using a spray-on coating, it's a good idea to go back into the action after coating and polish the feed rails again. Many of the coatings will fill in minor imperfections and with a little polishing they become very slick and the bolt will run like it's on oiled bearings.

AVOIDING HEAD INJURIES

How to keep that big, heavy scope on the rifle where it belongs instead of bouncing off your forehead.

The tactical scopes used for long-range work can weigh more than two pounds. When we add in the massive steel rings and bases used to mount them, the weight goes up even higher.

▲ Large scope mount base screws help keep large optics on the gun where they belong.

When a rifle fires, recoil drives it back. If you remember your basic high school physics, a body at rest tends to stay at rest. Well, that massive scope is at rest, until the rifle fires and rapidly accelerates backwards. The scope, which is attached to the rifle, has no choice but to move with the recoil.

Any chain is only as strong as its weakest link and in this case the weak link is the "attachment" to the rifle. The little screws holding the mount to the rifle can shear off and set your expensive scope free to explore its wanderlust by smacking things like rocks, concrete, or your face. The good news is your face will heal. The bad news is those gouges in the scope from the rocks and concrete are forever.

Part of preparing a new action is to take steps to correct this issue. Not just with tactical rifles, but on any hard recoiling rifle.

If you use the proper tooling, this is a good opportunity to correct any misalignment in the screw holes. I don't see it as often on new guns as in the past, but I can remember when it was common for the scope mounting screws

to be out of alignment, even on rifles from the big-name gun makers. CNC machines have corrected much of that problem, but it still can happen.

▲ Using 8-40 screws to fasten the base to the receiver adds strength to the scope mount.

For as long as I can remember, the standard mounting screw size for any scope base to attach to a rifle has been the 6-48. This screw size has worked well for most applications, but the modern tactical world is a tough place to live. Not only are the scopes bigger and heavier, putting more stress on the mounting screws, the environment where the guns are used is often brutal and failure is never an option.

The techniques used here for tactical scope mounts will also apply to any hard recoiling rifle, including dangerous game rifles. The brutal recoil from these big cartridges can make keeping even a lightweight scope mated to a rifle difficult.

For that matter, any hunting rifle can benefit from a stronger mounting system, even your deer rifle. Scopes are getting bigger and heavier and even common cartridges like the .30-06 and its kin can stress the mounting systems on a rifle.

Beefing up the mounts is never a mistake.

By changing the 6-48 base mounting screws to 8-40 you bump the diameter up from .1380 inch to .1640 inch, or .026 inch larger per screw. This is about a 19 percent increase

▲ Always use Loctite on scope mounting screws.

in diameter. But, it creates a 45 percent increase in cross sectional area, shear strength and tensile strength. (Many thanks to my engineer son, Nathan, for that information.)

Two changes are needed for this. First, the holes in the rifle's receiver must be drilled and tapped larger. Then, if your base is designed for the smaller 6-48 screws, it will require that the through holes be larger for the bigger screws and counterbored holes made larger to accommodate the bigger screw heads.

Many bases or base rails are available now with 8-40 screws from the factory. On several recent rifle builds I have used a Talley base rail manufactured to use 8-40 screws. For a precision rifle, I order them with 20 MOA of elevation built into the base for long-range use. With the 8-40 screws no modification to the mount is needed.

On the first .300 Winchester I built, my "Training Rifle," I used a base I had on hand that was made for 6-48 screws, so I had to modify it to take the larger 8-40 screws.

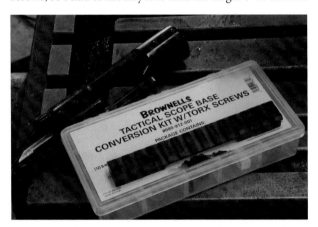

▲ ▼ The Brownells Tactical Scope Base Conversion Kit has everything you need to covert to 8-40 screws.

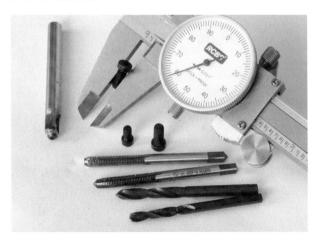

The easiest way to get all tools you need is to buy the Brownells Tactical Scope Base Conversion Kit. This comes with all the drills, taps, and counterbores needed,

as well as a selection of 8-40 Torx head screws and a screw gizzie.

In this chapter we are dealing with tuning an action as part of the build, but I am going to digress a bit here with some relevant information. There may be times when you want to change the mounting screw size on an existing rifle. Remember that on existing rifles with Remington Model 700 actions and many other rifles, the front screw hole will be blind, which means it stops at the barrel threads. The best approach is to remove the rifle's barrel from the action. That way you can drill and tap straight through the front hole just like the others.

If you do remove the barrel, make witness marks on the bottom of the action and on the barrel that line up with each other perfectly. When you reinstall the barrel, tighten until the marks align again and the headspacing will be back exactly where it was before you removed the barrel.

Drilling and tapping the front hole can be done with the barrel in the action by using a bottom tap, but the metal is thin here and you need every bit of thread you can get. Using a bottom tap may prevent full utilization of the available metal, as it may not reach to the true bottom of the receiver. It's much better to remove the barrel and tap through.

DRILLING

Clamp the action in a strong vise with soft jaws and level the action. A milling machine gives you the best control, but a good drill press will also work. Do not try to do this with a handheld drill.

▲ Drilling a Remington action for a larger scope mount screw.

"Here, hold my beer! Get your phone and video me so as we can put it on YouTube to get famous! I'll show them that you don't need none of them fancy tools to be a gunsmith. This drill is fine, 'long as the battery ain't dead."

Not only is it impossible to maintain alignment with a hand drill, but controlling the depth is impossible as well. If you are going to do this operation with the barrel installed, it's imperative you control the depth of the drill.

I have seen more than one gun that was drilled through to the chamber. That not only ruins the gun, it's dangerous if the gun is fired. I have seen scopes that have been penetrated completely by the base screw as the pressure from the ruptured case stripped the threads and spit the screw out of the action like a bullet.

A big part of gunsmithing success is always found in using the right tools and letting them do their jobs. Trust me, a handheld drill is not the right tool here. I don't care what you saw on YouTube.

▲ The barreled action in the jig.

For the best result use a fixture like the Scope Mounting Drill Fixture sold by Brownells, or a Universal Sight Mounting Fixture from Forster Products, also available from Brownells.

If you plan to do a lot of these upgrades the Forster tool is an excellent investment. It will repair any misalignment in the original screw holes. It's also a great tool for any scope mounting job. I have used it on rifles as diverse as the Mosin-Nagant and the Savage Model 99 lever action.

For example, check out the chapter on tricking out a Mosin-Nagant rifle. I struggled with several different approaches to getting the screw holes exactly top dead center over the course of mounting several bases on multiple rifles and having none of them turn out completely satisfactory. Then I used the Forster jig and discovered that it's pretty easy to get it right on the first try. The mistake I made was doing my own rifle first. By the time I did my buddy Eric Reynold's rifle (the one shown in the photos with the Forster jig), I had mounted scopes on a bunch of Mosins and I had this down cold. His turned out much better than mine.

More recently I had a Savage Model 99 brought to me that had been drilled and tapped by persons unknown. It had four holes in the front receiver ring. Three were stripped and the fourth had a screw broken off in it. None of the holes were on center and not one was in alignment with another. (I think this might be that gun

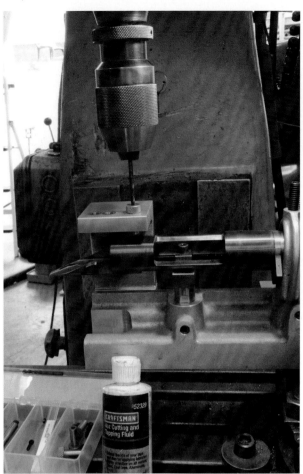

▲ This jig will correct any misalignment in the screw holes.

from YouTube.) With the Forster Jig I was able to correct the problem well enough to mount the front base on the receiver and boresight the scope.

The Forster tool is a bit expensive. It's a great addition to any gunsmithing shop, but I understand all too well how tooling must be collected as the discretionary funds dictate. However, if you do a lot of scope mounting work, this is a tool that is worth the money.

An alternative jig is the Holland Sine Bar and Recoil Lug Drilling Fixture featured earlier. It's used for drilling a locating pin hole in the receiver to hold the recoil lug in place. It also will hold a Remington 700 receiver and when clamped in a mill vise will keep the holes aligned on center.

While one of the fixtures is a far better approach, you can do this job with just a drill press or milling machine if you are careful. Make sure that the receiver is level and that the holes are exactly in alignment with the drill. With the much better quality of today's factory actions the misalignment issue is not the problem it once was. You need the jig to fix misalignment, but if the holes are correctly placed, all you need to do is enlarge them, which is easy with just a drill press or mill.

Using a #28, .1405-inch drill, carefully align with each of the holes in the receiver and drill through. Always use plenty of cutting oil while drilling the holes.

When drilling the front hole with the barrel installed, you must control the depth to prevent drilling though the barrel. Set the stop so the drill only goes as deep as the original hole. You can fine tune the depth as you work, using the pecking technique. It's easy to drill a little more if the hole is not deep enough, but very expensive if you go too far. So, go slowly and sneak up on it.

Or, as I have said repeatedly in this chapter, pull the barrel. It's much easier and produces a far better result in the long run.

TAPPING IT

Once all the holes are drilled, use an 8-40 taper tap to recut the threads. Saying *"I'd tap that!"* to your buddies as you work is funny . . . once. After that, it's just sad.

▲ Tapping a Remington action for 8-40 screws. Note that there is no barrel installed.

Here again, if you use the Forster Universal Sight Mounting Fixture, it will guide the tap so it is perfectly aligned with the hole you are tapping. You can also chuck the tap in the drill press or milling machine to maintain alignment. Keep the power off and hand-turn the chuck to start the threads. If I use this method, once the tap is well started I switch to a T-Handle because it allows much more control. If the tap is several threads into the hole it will self-pilot from there and I live in constant fear of breaking a tap.

Hand holding the tap in a T-Handle to start is the last resort, as it is very difficult to maintain perfect alignment.

If you did not pull the barrel, you may be able to start the front hole with the taper tap, but stop as soon as it bottoms. Then switch to the bottoming tap. Or, if the hole is too shallow, start with the bottom tap. Run it into the hole carefully, stopping when it hits bottom. Trying to continue after the tap hits bottom will result in a broken tap and more aggravation than you thought possible, so be gentle.

Make sure to use plenty of cutting oil when cutting the new threads. Go carefully, and reverse the tap often to break the chips and prevent binding. Use a light touch; this is no time to bully your tools. Instead, use finesse and the delicate touch of a surgeon. These taps are small and very brittle, so be gentle. Be extra careful about hard spots in the metal that can jam up the tap. Work slowly and carefully. If you hit a hard spot, delicately work through it. It's far better to spend a little "careful" time now than to try to remove a broken tap. Broken taps are the reason cuss words were invented.

As I write this I just did the receiver for my Magnum Opus rifle. This is the cursed action mentioned earlier. It was full of hard spots that tried to stick the tap. It was so bad I broke a drill, which is unusual. It hit a hard spot and just snapped. To be honest, I think that is the first time that has ever happened to me when enlarging the scope mounting holes. There were lots of hard spots throughout that action for some reason and they also caused a lot of anguish when I was running the tap to cut the threads.

With the control of hand-turning the tap I was able to work through all the hard spots I encountered in each of the four holes. If I had the tap in the drill or mill chuck I fear it would have broken.

Once the tap is through, or bottomed, remove it and clean out all the chips and the oil. Shop air works well for this. If you don't have a compressor, spray degreaser works well too. You can buy commercial gun degreaser or pick up some Brakleen at one of the 'marts or your local auto supply store.

MODIFYING THE BASE

If you have a scope mounting base designed for 6-48 screws, turn your attention to that next. Use a #19 .166-inch drill bit to drill the through holes on the base larger to accommodate the larger 8-40 screws. Make sure the base is level and the holes are aligned with the drill press before starting, so it cuts straight and true.

▲ This shows the modifications to the base screw holes.

▲ Drilling the base.

Switch to a Fillister counterbore for #8 screws to cut the holes in the mount larger to accommodate the larger diameter of the 8-40 screw heads. (All these drills and tools are available from Brownells or included with the Brownells Tactical Scope Base Conversion Kit.) Set the stop on the drill press or milling machine so that the counterbore kisses the bottom of the existing hole, just enough to leave shiny metal all the way around.

MOUNTING THE SCOPE BASE ON THE RIFLE

If you are building a gun and preparing the action, mounting the scope will be one of the last jobs you do after the rifle is completed. If you are upgrading the mount on an existing rifle, now is the time to install the base. Either way, the barrel should be installed in the action before mounting the scope base.

Tighten each of the screws for the base one at a time to make sure they lock the base tight and do not bottom out. Then loosen that screw and tighten the next. With luck the front screw will bottom out before it locks the base tight, which is good. If it locks the base tight and does not

bottom out on the barrel threads, it's too short and should be replaced with a longer screw.

The front screw takes the most abuse and because it's so short, it is the one least capable of handling it, so it needs to be a perfect fit. If it bottoms, it must be shortened a little bit at a time until it will lock the scope base tight to the gun without contacting the barrel threads. Cutting the screw to the exact length needed gives you a custom screw that uses every available bit of thread in this short hole.

Double-check that it's not bottoming out by coating the bottom of the screw with a felt-tipped marker or with Dykem. (Dykem Layout Fluid is a gunsmith's best friend. Make sure you have some in your shop.) It's possible that the screw is locking the base tight to the action, but is still contacting the barrel threads. If the screw bottoms out and contacts the barrel threads, the Dykem or marking from the felt pen will be smudged or scraped off. The screw must be shortened a little bit more. As I said, this front screw is very short and it takes most of the stress, so you want every single bit of thread you can get without contacting the barrel. Take some time and get this right.

Make sure none of the other screws are projecting into the rifle's action. Pay close attention to the screw over the bolt's locking lugs as it can impede the bolt function. It's important that there is no contact as the bolt is worked.

Make sure the screws go all the way to the bottom of each hole so that you have the full strength of every single thread available. This will probably require making all the screws by custom cutting them to exactly the right length. With a Torx head or other screw style with a head that has parallel sides, I do this by chucking the screw in my drill press and using a file to shorten the screw one thread at a time. Add a slight chamfer to the edge of the last thread with the file, so it will start easier. This works well, but unless you have done a bunch of them, sometimes getting the exact length is a hit or miss deal. I'll also note, for safety, always have a handle on the file you are using.

The screw checker/shortening jig that comes with the Brownells screw kits is more precise, as it lets you set the exact amount of thread to remove. Put the screw in the

▲ This Brownells tool is very useful for shortening screws.

jig with what you want removed projecting. Clamp the jig in a bench vise and use a file to shorten the screw down to the level of the hardened jig. It takes a bit longer than using a drill press, but it usually gives better results due to the control it allows. Also, the screw will be square on the bottom. Brownells also sells these as a standalone product.

Degrease all the screws and the holes with a spray degreaser that dries without residue. Put some blue #242 Loctite on the threads of each screw, tighten them to 30 inch-pounds of torque and the base is mounted and done.

If you custom fit these screws and then take them out to continue the build with the intention of installing the base at a later date, put each screw in an individual envelope and label for the hole it was fitted for.

BOLTING IT DOWN

The action has two master parts—the receiver and the bolt. At this point we can turn our attention to the bolt.

Let me take an aside here. Gunsmiths are an adaptive bunch and can be very innovative. We often find ways to work with what we have to get the job done. We love our tools and gadgets, but it would be easy to go broke buying every tool out there. So, we make do, adapt, overcome, and find another way. I am big on that and pride myself on figuring out ways to get the job done with the tools I have on hand. When it comes to working on Remington bolts there are ways to do that, but they will have one undeniable effect on your attitude. You may invent swear words with creativity you didn't know you possessed.

As I work through this chapter, I'll talk about the "Towsley" way and the better way. There are a few tools here that just make life easier. They are not horribly expensive and if I convince you to buy them, you will thank me every time you use them.

The first step is to take the bolt apart. Remove the firing pin and the ejector.

▲ This tool works much better than a quarter in a vise.

There are two ways to remove the firing mechanism from a Remington bolt. The first is the "conventional" way. Put a quarter in a bench vise, hook the notch on the firing pin head over the edge of the quarter, then pull and twist. The end result is often punching yourself in the face or tearing essential skin off your knuckles. I can tell you from experience that while blood is a decent short-term lubricant, it does not make this job go any easier.

Or, you can buy a Remington bolt disassembly tool from Brownells. I stalled on getting one of these for years and now fully understand how stupid being stubborn can be. If you buy nothing else I suggest in this book, buy this tool. It makes life so much easier.

This takes the firing pin assembly out of the bolt. Next you need to remove the ejector. That is the little plunger in the face of the bolt. If you look on the side of the bolt you will see a small roll pin, which holds the ejector in place under spring pressure. Using the correct size roll pin punch, drive out this pin while you are careful to catch the ejector and the spring. They are under spring pressure and will fly away to places you can't possibly imagine if you fail to stop them, so pay attention.

Reassembly is the reverse, except it requires three hands and the ejector is even more prone to taking flight. Where there is a will there is a way and gunsmiths learn to adapt. I have installed a lot of ejectors by clamping the bolt in a vise and pushing down on the ejector with a large punch or an empty cartridge case until I can insert a slave pin (another punch the same size as the hole for the roll pin). Then I tap the roll pin into place as it pushes the slave pin ahead of it. It all sounds easy, right? Trust me, this is when you need three hands. All too often the slave pin pops out of the bolt, and the ejector and spring sprout wings.

When I was working on the 6mm Creedmoor "Brownells" rifle this happened. Larry Weeks was the marketing guy for Brownells for a century or two before retiring and turning the job over to the very capable Roy Hill. Larry and I became friends and shared hotel rooms at 3-gun matches a few times. He had a saying that, "A gunsmith spends more time on his knees than a cheap hooker." No doubt Remington ejectors account for a good bit of that kneeling time.

With my 6mm Creedmoor, I heard the spring bounce off the wall and then hit the surface grinder behind me, so I knew where to look and found it rather quickly, but the ejector was gone. I looked for hours before giving up and robbing the ejector from the bolt out of another Model 700 rifle in my vault so I could complete the build. The idea was I would buy a new ejector from Brownells. They are only a few bucks, so I figured to get a couple of extras. I know if I buy extra parts in anticipation of losing another one, it will never happen again, so this is the best insurance you can find. To an accountant-type that would appear to be wasting money, but most gunsmiths understand the voodoo here and that it's karma or whatever that makes sure if you buy a spare part you will never need it.

Anyway, I got caught up in finishing the build and didn't get around to ordering the new ejector for a week or so. Then one day my wife came out to the shop and seconds later bent over to pick something up off the floor. "What's this?" she asked. It was the lost ejector, of course, sitting in plain sight in a place where I had looked at least a dozen times.

I do have a point to all this. As I was writing this chapter and looking at the Brownells website to get the correct name for the Remington bolt disassembly tool, I stumbled onto a tool called the Sinclair Remington Ejector Spring Tool. This thing compresses the ejector and then you turn it to lock on the bolt lugs to hold it in place while you insert or remove the roll pin, depending on if you are taking it apart or putting it together.

▲ This LaBounty Bolt Fixture is a must for replacing the factory extractor with a Sako or M16-type extractor.

It's my new best friend.

I can't tell you how stupid it was struggling with the ejectors all these years when this simple and inexpensive tool was on the market.

On a Remington bolt, you may want to leave the extractor if you are planning on using it. The riveted extractors are difficult to remove without damage and even harder to replace. The non-riveted extractors can be removed and replaced if you are careful not to spring or bend them. If you are going to modify the bolt to take an M-16, Sako or other replacement extractor, go ahead and remove the existing extractor regardless of the style.

If you are planning on changing the extractor you will need a LaBounty Bolt Fixture (from Brownells) to hold the bolt while you do the lathe work (all explained later in the section on replacing extractors). If you have this tool, it's not a bad idea to true up the bolt locking lugs front and back while you have it in the lathe and before you lap the lugs. Some gunsmiths, like Mark Bansner, also use this fixture to square the face of the bolt.

▲ ▼ My new best friend, "Buddy."

The bolt is placed into the tool which is then dialed into center using a 4-jaw chuck on the lathe. Once you have the bolt trued to center, you can make a light cleanup cut on both sides of the lugs. Coating them with Dykem first lets you know when you are done. Take just enough to clean them up.

Lapping the lugs to the receiver ensures there is a perfect mating of the surfaces and that there is full contact with both lugs. For the best accuracy in any rifle, the bolt's locking lugs must seat evenly and completely in the receiver. (Lapping also smooths up the feel of the action.) Lapping ensures the lugs are supporting the bolt equally with no room to flex under pressure when the gun is fired.

You know that cliché, "where has this thing been all my life?" That was my thought as I stopped what I was doing (writing this chapter) and ordered the tool. That's it in the photos shown here.

I named it Buddy.

If you don't have the LaBounty Bolt Fixture tool to true the lugs first, lapping might take a little longer, but the end result is mostly the same.

PERHAPS THE GREATEST BARGAIN IN THE BROWNELL'S CATALOG

There is one more process in disassembling a 700 bolt when you need a little help. The firing pin assembly you removed is not yet fully disassembled. You may want to remove the firing pin and spring. There are lots of reasons, but the main one here is so that the bolt shroud is free so you can sandblast it and recoat with a much cooler spray-on coating.

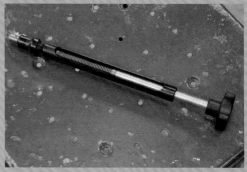

This tool compresses the firing pin spring.

The firing pin is spring-loaded and held in with a pin that must be driven out with a punch. You can see it by putting the firing pin against the bench and pushing on the bolt shroud. See that round metal piece? Look close and you can see the pin that needs to come out.

Now try and get it out alone, I dare you. It requires at least two men and even then it's about impossible.

Have you tried it yet? Yeah? Good. Are you bleeding? No? Damn liar, you are too.

Let me tell you something that will make me a god in your eyes. I have removed and replaced this pin all alone, with no tools other than a punch, a hammer, and a vise. Oh yeah and a set of vise grips. That one is important.

I compressed the spring and clamped the vise grips on the extended metal part to hold it while I removed the pin. Putting it back together was a bit more of an issue. I managed to compress the spring and insert a slave pin. Then I compressed it further and clamped the vise grips in place.

Once the firing pin spring is compressed, it's easy to remove the retaining pin.

It worked great, except the jaws of the vise grips gouged the hell out of the part; so much that it would not go back in place. I had to pull it apart and clean all the burrs off the metal, leaving some horrible scars. I tried padding the jaws, but they would not hold against that powerful spring.

That's redneck gunsmithing. Sometimes it's necessary, but it's never good.

I discovered a better way.

Brownells sells a simple tool called the Sinclair Remington Mainspring Tool. Here is their description:

> *"Our Mainspring Tool for Remington bolts is an easy to use spring compressor which allows you to disassemble the firing pin and mainspring from the bolt body. Our tool has an anodized aluminum body, steel lead screw and a large comfortable handle. This tool in conjunction with the Sinclair Firing Pin Removal Tool is a must to change firing pins or springs safely, without damaging the bolt or bolt parts."*

This description is too modest. This tool was invented by angels and will salvage the eternal soul of any gunsmith.

You simply screw the bolt shroud into one end of the tool with the firing pin inserted inside. Then you turn the handle on this tool to advance the spring compression screw and push the firing pin against the spring. When it's compressed enough to access the pin, place that end on a bench block and drive out the pin with the correct size punch. Then back the compression screw off to release the tension. Unscrew the shroud and all the parts are free. Reverse the process to put it back together. Simple, easy, no blood and nothing gets damaged.

At this writing in early 2018 it's less than $30 for this tool. I think its value is incalculable.

LAPPING IT UP

When lapping, it's important to keep pressure on the bolt. You can make a tool to do that as detailed in *The Complete Illustrated Guide to Precision Rifle Barrel Fitting.* Or you can use the Brownells Bolt Lapping Set, which is fairly inexpensive. Making your own tools is very cool, but, by the time you buy the materials and spend hours making a bolt lapping tool, the price of the Brownells kit looks like a pittance.

▲ The Brownells bolt lapping tool is a must have.

That said, I didn't have the threaded sleeve to fit a Mini Mauser action when I was building the .223 Ackley Improved, so I made one. This served two purposes. I now have the tool forever and making it was very good practice to learn the machining skills I needed before I started building the rifle. In this case the thread is metric, so there were some special techniques used when cutting the threads on the lathe. Of course, I decided to do this more complicated rifle first, so I had an adventure or two, most of which I have written about in this book. Well, to be honest, there are a few things I left out and I'll never tell anybody. A man's gotta keep a little dignity.

No matter if you buy or make it, the tool screws into the front of the receiver and has a spring-loaded plunger that contacts the face of the bolt to keep spring pressure against the bolt lugs as you lap them into contact.

A light coating of Dykem layout blue or felt-tipped marker should be applied to the rear surface of the locking lugs on the bolt as well as the corresponding surfaces of the receiver locking lug recesses. Put a little 600-grit silicon carbide abrasive on the mating surfaces of the receiver. Use just a small amount of lapping compound and be careful that it's only on the surfaces being lapped. You don't want it grinding away at something else while you work.

▲ Mark Bansner uses a syringe to apply lapping compound with precision.

Install the bolt, move it into the locked position and screw in the fixture until the shoulder contacts the action's shoulder. Adjust the plunger so there is strong spring pressure on the bolt face.

Lift the bolt handle approximately 45 degrees and then return it to the locked or down position. Do this several times. I think the directions say 50 cycles, but I rarely count and that's sometimes too much for a tuned action on which you squared all the surfaces. If I had to assign a number, I would say check after 20 cycles. Don't allow the bolt to move far enough to let the lugs move out of contact. That can lead to removing metal from the angles that lead the bolt into closing, which is not a good idea.

▲ Mark Bansner lapping the bolt lugs.

Remove both the bolt and the Bolt Lapping Fixture and clean up the lapping compound. The rear of the locking lugs on the bolt and the locking lug recesses or seats in

▲ This lug has 100 percent contact. Note the polished area on the bolt body from the lapping compound migrating. In this case it will be covered when the bolt is finished, so it's not a problem.

the receiver can then be examined to determine the extent of contact that is being achieved. This is indicated by the area where the Dykem or felt pen markings are worn off, showing contact.

Most texts say that the goal is 95 percent contact of the bolt lugs to the receiver, but, when building a new rifle, I try for 100 percent contact on both lugs. If you laid the groundwork, aligning the receiver lugs with the Manson Receiver Accurizing System and truing the bolt lugs in the lathe, they will almost be there anyway and will require very little lapping, unlike some actions I have lapped without doing the prep work. I remember one when I had 100 percent mating on one lug and about 10 percent on the other. It took a long time to get that second lug into contact. In contrast, if the surfaces have been trued there will usually be close to 90 percent contact on both lugs to start and lapping them into 100 percent contact happens very quickly.

After lapping the lugs, be sure to clean up every speck of the abrasive lapping compound from the bolt and the receiver. I keep a big jar of Brakleen on my bench and swish them around in that. Then I use a spray degreaser to get into all the nooks and crannies while I work with a cotton swab and a dental pick on the built-up spots. Repeat until it is 100 percent clean. Don't blow the lapping compound off with shop air as that can drive it into places it should not be. Remember, this stuff is very abrasive, that's its job. Don't let it misbehave by getting into places it doesn't belong.

FACE-OFF

The bolt face should be trued. If it's not pushing evenly on the base of the cartridge the cartridge will be out of alignment in the chamber. When it fires, the case head will not have an even, square surface to push back against. All this can be detrimental to accuracy.

The easiest way to true the bolt face is to use the truing tool made by Manson and available at Brownells. This tool has a piece that threads into the receiver and squares

▲ The bolt face after truing.

against the front ring, very similar to the bolt lapping tool. There is a precision hole through the center and three different size carbide cutters with precision ground shafts that fit in the hole. You can make the holder if you like, but you will need to buy the cutter(s).

If you left the Remington extractor in place, care must be taken to work the edge of the cutter under the extractor. If you do not, the cutter can cut away the extractor, making it useless. (I know this all too well from experience.) If the extractor is the non-riveted style it's easy to remove it from the bolt and it's highly recommended that you do so before truing the bolt face. If it's the riveted style, work the cutter under the extractor and be very careful.

Once everything is aligned, flood the area with cutting oil and use a handheld cordless drill to turn the cutting burr. Always run clockwise and never reverse the direction as that can damage the cutter. The cutter is designed to work slowly, but if you have a good bolt it should not take long to true up the face; although that's not always the case. For example, the 6mm Creedmoor "Brownells" rifle cleaned up very quickly and was done the first time I checked. The .300 Winchester "Training Rifle" took forever, so long I thought I would never get it finished. I even called Dave Manson to see if I was doing it wrong and that is how I know the cutters are designed to work slowly to keep from ruining the bolt.

Another note here about what has happened since writing this chapter. I replaced two of my cutters, the .308 "standard" and the magnum. Both were cutting extremely slowly. The new cutters are much faster and I am now of a belief that my first cutters, including the one used on my training rifle, were defective. Now it takes just a few minutes to face off a bolt.

The bolt face may be blued. If not, you should have coated it with Dykem before starting. Once you have the entire bolt face shiny, it's done.

The cutting burrs are available in three sizes, .223 is for any bolt used for that size case head. Next is .308, which

▲ I made the holder, but used a Manson cutting burr for this Mini Mauser bolt.

covers all the .30-06 family and Magnum to fit magnum bolts. These are also the same three sizes that you can get in a Remington Model 700 bolt.

When I was building my .223 Ackley Improved there was no tool for this, but the bolt lapping tool I made had the same shaft diameter. I kept it as precise as possible using a boring bar and, as it fit the .223-size burr, I was able to true the bolt face.

If you want to stop here, you are ready to fit the barrel and build an accurate rifle, but you can do more to the bolt if you like.

EXTRACTION PLAN

For years the extractor on a Remington 700 has been subject to brutal criticism from just about every direction. The dangerous game hunting guys and the tactical guys all claim it's a huge problem that will get you killed in the "real" world.

I'll be honest, it looks like it should be a problem. It's a fragile looking little thing. But the truth is, I have been a fan of the Model 700 rifle for all of my life. A quick check of my records shows that in the past decade I have owned, or had here to test for magazine articles, 31 different Model 700 rifles and about a dozen of its relatives that use the same extractor system, such as the Model 788, Model Seven, 721, 722 and the like. I bought my first one, a Model 788, in 1968 and I have been writing about guns for about thirty-five years, so, if you extrapolate, that's a lot of rifles. I might also note that this extractor style has been used by Remington going back to at least 1948, with the 721 and 722 model rifles.

According to my buddy John R. Fink, who was the Director of Product Management for Firearms with Remington, *"Remington is approaching 7,000,000 rifles with this style extractor. It is actually stronger than a Mauser extractor. If a case is stuck, the extractor is more likely to pull through the brass before the extractor lets go."*

So there are about seven million of these rifles out there with the "horrible" extractor and yet there are virtually no reports of them failing during a critical time and getting somebody killed.

If we followed up on most of the reports of extractor failure, we would find that an overpressure handload was stuck in the chamber and somebody beat the hell out of the bolt to remove it, which is gun abuse. The truth is I have done that myself back before I knew better and I still have never had an extractor fail. I have seen the bolt handle break off when a guy was beating on it with a chunk of firewood to extract a stuck handload and still the extractor held.

I am sure they wear out like any other piece of machinery and that they break now and then, but I just can't find any evidence that the Remington extractor is a true problem.

I say this with the full understanding that it will almost certainly get me blackballed in the gun guy circles. The bottom line is that there are certain "facts" in the gun world that lazy gun writers, loud-mouth range rats and incompetent gun store salesmen just keep repeating as truth and as far as I can tell, "Model 700 extractors suck" is one of them.

I probably have used guns with the 700-style extractor more than any other style of rifle. I have trusted them on dangerous game on multiple occasions, including Cape buffalo, grizzly and brown bears. I have carried a Remington on some very extreme hunts from Alaska to Africa and I have put thousands and thousands of rounds through Model 700 rifles in just about every imaginable cartridge, yet I have never seen an extractor fail from normal use or from shooting the rifle. I know it happens, but either I am very lucky or it happens far less than all the hysteria would suggest it does. Sure, I have replaced a few, but those I have replaced were all damaged by abuse, not use.

Like I said, it is a fragile looking little thing, and replacing it on a rifle that "must not fail" such as a dangerous game rifle or a tactical rifle makes sense, at least from a mechanical engineering point of view. Besides, for a hobby gunsmith, it gives us an excuse to make some chips and spend time with concrete under our feet.

Let's look at some of the rifles I built during the writing of this book using a Remington action. On my 6mm Creedmoor "Brownells" rifle I left in the Remington extractor. On my "Training" rifle, the .300 Winchester, I replaced the Remington extractor with an M-16 style. On the "Father & Son" .308 rifles Nathan and I built, we left in the Remington extractors, mostly due to time constraints and budget. My "Magnum Opus" rifle was fitted with a Sako style extractor. I left the Remington extractor in both of the 9.3X62 rifles. Tony Kinton has one of them and has already whacked a nice Cape buffalo with the rifle. He trusts the Remington extractor just fine.

In the end, the rifles have all run fine and without issues and I have seen zero empirical evidence that any one extractor style works better than the other. They all pulled the empty case from the chamber and allowed the ejector to spit it out of the gun.

Actually, that's not 100 percent true. The "Training" rifle had some problems that puzzled me for a while, even with the M-16 extractor. It didn't eject at first, which was my fault. I was all caught up in the "precision" aspect, thinking that the closer the tolerances I was cutting to, the better machinist I was. As a result, I made the inside diameter of the bolt face too tight, which didn't leave any room for the cartridge to tilt as it ejected. So I stripped the bolt, chucked it back in the lathe using the LaBounty tool and opened the I.D. up just a little bit. I also added a bit more bevel on the front edge. I put it all back together and it functioned just fine.

I set the gun aside and worked on some other projects, making a big mistake. I had degreased the bolt after working on it and forgot to put any oil back on to protect the steel. It gets very humid in Vermont in late summer and when I tried the gun the next time, it would not eject. I was puzzled and about to do something stupid like put it back in the lathe and start cutting again, when I noticed the ejector was stuck. I took it apart and found it was full of rust, enough to stick the ejector and spring down in the collapsed position, enough, in fact, that I had a hard time getting them both out of the bolt.

Feeling foolish, I cleaned it all up and put it back together, remembering this time to add a drop or two of oil. It ejected just fine after all that.

I was shooting photographs of every step of this build, which takes time, so by the time I had the receiver and the scope mount modified for the 8-40 screws and mounted on the gun, it was a week or so later. Just for giggles I shot the gun into my Snail Trap and, again, it wasn't ejecting.

It worked fine running it slowly enough that I could watch the brass leave the gun, but when I ran it fast, it jammed. The ejector was working fine this time. I double-checked all my dimensions, rechecked the location of the extractor and messed with the rifle until I thought my head would explode.

Then I noticed the brass marks on the bottom of the one-piece scope mount base rail. The mouth of the empty cartridge was hitting the scope base rail when I ran the action fast and was bouncing the case back into the receiver. I ground in some relief on the base mount and once the gun was ejecting properly, I pulled the rail and coated it with black Aluma-Hyde II. When it was dry I put it all back together, tested it again and it ejected just fine.

I stuck a scope on the gun and put it in the vault, ready to range test. The scope was one I keep here for testing new AR and precision rifles for magazine articles. It's a Vortex Viper 6-24X50. When writing about guns I feel a strong responsibility to provide as fair a test as I can, so I like to do the accuracy portion of a gun test with a powerful scope to eliminate as many variables as possible. I keep this scope in a quick release mount to use for those tests. Because it fit the rail on this gun and was just sitting there, I put that scope on the rifle as a temporary optic for the initial test.

This rifle has a 1:12 twist barrel, which means it needs lighter bullets than are normal for a .300 Winchester Magnum with match ammo. The gun sat around until I had time to handload some ammo, so by the time I got to the shooting range I was really anxious to see how well my creation would shoot. To my surprise and my joy it shot ½-MOA groups with the first handload I tried using Sierra 168-grain MatchKing bullets. But the damn thing would not eject again.

I started to get mad, thinking this gun was cursed. Then I realized that the empties were clearing the modified base rail but hitting the AR-15 style scope mount. Once I got the gun finished and mounted a scope properly in conventional rings, it was good to go.

I guess I have a few points about this rant. One is to

maybe make you laugh a little and realize that this gunsmithing thing does not always go as planned. Also, anytime you change things, it changes things. One thing can affect another thing and often the problems are not coming from where you think they are. If you start having problems, stay calm. Don't do rash stuff. Work it out. The answer is there. You just need to find it and it's not always what you expect.

Remember if you start cutting away metal, it's gone. You can't put it back. If you know in your heart you have everything done right and it's still not working, think it through before you start cutting or grinding. The answer might be someplace other than where you expect it to be.

One other piece of advice. After you degrease, put some oil on the metal. The feeling you get in the pit of your stomach when you find rusty parts on the rifle you have spent weeks building really sucks.

The final point? None of this was directly related to the M-16 extractor I had installed. It worked perfectly and as it was designed. Yet, that was the change I had made to the rifle before all the problems started. So that was where I kept going back to while looking for the source of the problems, while not seeing the real issue. I kinda got stuck on stupid and got tunnel vision for a while.

In the end, all these guns have ejected just fine (at least from the perspective of which extraction system they are using) and while they are all pretty new, nothing has broken, just as none of my other Model 700 extractors have ever broken. However, there are times when I do think a bigger, stronger extractor is a good idea. I am a huge fan of over-engineering and over-building most things. It means far fewer problems in the future if you build well past the minimum design parameters.

Just ask my family. What started out as stairs to my shop fifteen years ago turned into a set of steps, several walks, multiple terraces, and a patio big enough that my pilot son said he thought he could land a Cessna on it. The whole thing is so overbuilt I have no doubt that some future archeologist will do a dig on the location that used to be my property a thousand years from now and say out loud, "What the hell?"

Overbuilt? You bet, but it does not give me any more problems. The first time I completed the construction, it did. I am not a landscaper, so I bought a bunch of books and I built it the way the books said it should be done. Whoever wrote the books clearly lived in the south. The frost from our brutal Vermont winters destroyed everything in two years.

I talked to all the contractors and landscapers I could find in my area, but none of them had a clue what to do or wouldn't tell me if they did. So, I rebuilt it my way. That is to say it's a bit "over-engineered." Where the books said to use compacted gravel, I used reinforced concrete and lots of it! I tied everything together with rebar, wire mesh, and spikes. It's one giant connected unit now that probably weighs as much as the rock of Gibraltar. Like that famous boulder, it has not moved. It has survived several brutal, deep-frost winters without a wiggle. Overbuilt? It's a matter of perspective. It has one job that it now does it without fail, no matter how bad the conditions. I say it's built just right.

Making something too strong is rarely an issue if it means it does its job without problems. That applies to guns as well as walkways. Based on that philosophy, there are times when it makes lots of sense to replace the Remington extractor. For example, if you have plans to use your tactical rifle for defense, it's never a bad idea to overbuild. If you are going to use the rifle for competition and put thousands of rounds through it under tough conditions and where a failure means the loss of money and time invested in the match, by all means change the extractor. If you simply plan to shoot the living hell out of the rifle (which is why we build them, right?), a larger extractor might be a good idea.

I am building a dangerous game gun for a buddy to take to Africa for Cape buffalo and that one will get a new Sako style extractor. I will leave nothing to chance there, because he is my friend and I want him safe. He is also my taxidermist and I have some buffalo heads he needs to finish, which he can't do if he gets stomped.

I know the argument is that a DG rifle should be a controlled round feed. In reality that is another one of those "gun myths" that keeps being repeated by people who lack critical thought or experience. I have shot a bunch of dangerous game with push feed rifles including Cape buffalo, hippo, leopard, brown bear and more. Despite what all the "experts" say, I survived.

I will concede that, at least in theory, a controlled round feed should be more reliable and it's not a bad idea to build a DG rifle with a CRF system. However, my friend is a Remington man to the core and would hear no other argument.

Another point. If you picked up an old beater rifle to act as an action donor for the project and you have no idea of the rifle's history, it makes sense to replace the extractor. You can, of course, put in a new Remington extractor. But where is the fun and adventure in that?

If you are going to modify the bolt face for a larger cartridge, a new extractor is pretty much a must, as recutting the groove for the Remington extractor is difficult and it's much easier to use a Sako or M-16 extractor.

The bottom line in following with the theme of this book is to ask the question, "Why not replace the extractor?" Modifying and improving guns is what this is all about, right? It's about the journey as much as the destination and installing an extractor upgrade is a fun project that will call on your machining skills with the lathe and the milling machine. That alone may be the best argument for changing the extractor; we get to play with the machines, make chips and have fun. All while making good guns even better.

Isn't that really the point?

THE BANSNER FIX FOR EJECTION PROBLEMS

Mark Bansner is well known for building some of the best hunting rifles in the world. He is most famous in sheep hunting circles for his very accurate, lightweight rifles. In fact, Mark is an avid hunter and has a Grand Slam of sheep to his credit. Lately, he builds a lot of precision, long-range rifles as well.

This is a Remington Model 700 bolt after being modified by Mark Bansner. Note the new location for the ejector. You can clearly see the old location, which has been plugged.

He is a longtime friend who has built several rifles for me over the years. He showed me how to blueprint an action and fit a barrel when I visited his shop in Pennsylvania a few years back. He has been one of my advisors about gunsmithing for a long time. He was a tremendous help on *Gunsmithing Made Easy*, as well as this book, and he has fielded more than one late-night panicked call when I got into trouble.

He and I were talking about my ejection problem after replacing the extractor.

"It's a big issue with these new huge scopes with big turrets that the long-range guys use," Bansner told me. "After installing an M-16 or Sako style extractor, often the empty case will hit the turret, scope or mount and fall back into the action, jamming it all up. So, I move the ejector and the problem is solved."

This operation is performed after the new extractor is installed and the bolt ring is machined to its final inside diameter.

The ejector is held into the bolt against spring pressure by a roll pin fitted into a precision reamed hole. The trick is to move the ejector position so that it remains captured by that pin. The ejector on Remington 700 bolts and many clones is off to one side of the retaining pin, on the right edge of the bolt lug when looking at the bolt face with the ejector at the top. Bansner simply moves the ejector to the left edge of the bolt lug as far as possible while still maintaining position with the locking pin. This moves the ejector closer to the extractor and changes the angle of the empty case as it is pushed out of the gun.

Mark says that the bolt must be held very rigid and that a milling machine should be used for this operation. It goes without saying that the bolt is disassembled and the ejector, spring and retaining pin are removed. Bansner has a jig he made to hold the bolt standing on end in the milling machine vise. V-blocks work. In fact, Mark did lots of bolts with commercial V-blocks before he made the jig by modifying a set of longer V-blocks for more support.

If you modify the Sako Extractor Installation Jig from Brownells as detailed elsewhere in this chapter, you can use it to hold a Remington 700 bolt. The key is to hold the bolt correctly indicated into place and rigid.

This is a staged photo, to show the ejector still in the bolt. It illustrates the drill and V-blocks used with the milling machine to make a new extractor hole.

Locate the new hole so that it clears the bolt ring, but is as close as you can get to it (see photo). Mark uses a 60-degree tapered pin in his mill. He finds the center of the old hole and then moves the table on the X axis until the pin is over the location for the new hole. He inserts a tight-fitting punch into the retaining pin hole and visually checks to be sure the new hole will be oriented so that the retaining pin will come to the center of the ejector. The new ejector hole should also be close to the edge of the bolt face ring, but not touching it.

Use a new, sharp, high-quality 9/64 or #28 (.140-inch) drill. Bansner uses new, top-quality cobalt drills and makes only five holes before replacing them. A carbide drill is too brittle and the chance of it breaking is too high. However, he recommends keeping a carbide drill bit on hand to drill out any broken cobalt drills.

The hole should be 1.24 inches deep. Be very careful not to drill too far as it will destroy the bolt if you drill through into the larger hole in the bolt body. If you are a bit short, that's probably okay. Just shorten the spring, but never drill too deep.

Set the stop on the milling machine spindle so that it will drill to that exact depth. Drill the hole, taking care to do a nice clean job. Go slowly and "sneak up on it" with a series of careful steps.

Fill in the old ejector hole with a piece of .140-inch drill rod and silver solder it in place. Before inserting it, grind a relief on it so that the retaining pin can be inserted without interference and make sure that relief is oriented correctly before soldering the plug into place. A Dremel works well for this chore. Bansner suggests inserting a long piece into the hole and using a small scribe to reach through the retaining pin hole and mark the location to grind. Do not try to insert the plug and then drill through the retaining pin hole. The drill will be cutting on one flute, which is a recipe for disaster.

After grinding the relief, cut the plug to length. The plug should be left long enough that it sticks out from the bolt face just a few thousandths. It must then be faced off flush with the face of the bolt. You can do that in a lathe or, if you have one, the Manson Bolt Face Truing Cutter works well for the final step in this job.

The ejector, spring and retaining pin can now be fitted into place and function tested. The rifle should eject cases out of the ejection port without interference from the scope or mount.

Mark Bansner
Bansner & Co. LLC Riflemakers
261 E. Main St.
Box 839
Adamstown, PA 19501
mark@bansnerandcompany.com
www.bansnerandcompany.com
610-587-7547

MY .300 WINCHESTER "TRAINING" GUN

Every one of us will have a gun like this one sometime in our gunsmithing career. It's a gun we use to work out how to do the processes and one that will endure a lot of mistakes. Sometimes though, the end result will make you smile.

This was my first attempt at building a rifle on a Model 700 action and it was, to say the least, an "interesting experience."

It was the first action I blueprinted using the Manson Kit. Other than the trouble fitting the bushings as detailed in the action section of this book, it went fine. The Manson Kit is pretty much idiot-proof.

I fitted the bolt with an M-16 extractor, which is also detailed in the section on actions. The extractor fit went well, mostly because I practiced a bunch using brass rods before making the cuts, although there were some

▲ An oversized bolt knob is a nice custom touch.

peripheral issues as I detailed in what I think is one of the more humorous sections of the book.

I added an oversized bolt knob without any problems.

The barrel was one that my friend John Fink at Remington sent for me to practice on and practice I did! For some reason the belted .300 Winchester gives me fits when I am chambering a rifle. I always seem to go too deep. It's a learning process (at least that's what I kept telling myself!).

Well, I had plenty of learning experience with this one. Each time I ran the reamer in too far I would set back the shoulder. Then I would use a boring bar to make the bolt recess deeper and I would face off the threaded shank to make that correct. That's a lot of processes when you are learning and every time it seems I did one of them wrong.

So, I would start over again, cutting all these different points and again something would go wrong. Rinse and repeat until the entire thing was one big, ugly mess.

Finally, it reached the point of absurdity. I cut off the threaded shank and started over again. This time, I of course ran the reamer too deep once again, not having learned from the multiple other times I had done that. This was back when I was trying to "cut to the numbers" and do the final depth on the lathe. The problem was I

didn't fully understand the process in those early days and I proved that point over and over. (I have a much better understanding today.)

I finally fixed the last chamber problem by putting the recoil lug on a surface grinder and making it just a little thinner. After that, all the numbers looked good, which came as a total surprise.

I wanted to put a brake on the gun, but, as this was a practice rifle, I wanted to keep the cost down. I found a brake on an old barrel that had been taken off a European-made hunting rifle. With the application of heat and torque, I managed to get it off the barrel. The thread was some kind of oddball, presumably metric, but nothing that matched up with any data I had on metric threads. I suspect it was something very unique to the rifle it came off from. It did, however, fit a U.S. thread pitch pretty closely, though with a diameter that was not standard to anything I could find. I figured out the numbers and threaded the muzzle. I had it a perfect fit when my wife called to say dinner was ready. My mistake was removing the tooling on my lathe, thinking I was done.

I went back to the shop after dinner and the brake would not thread onto the barrel. I have no idea what happened, gremlins I guess. It fit fine before I left and to this day it is still a mystery.

I read up on how to pick up an existing thread and like a dummy tried to do it late at night when I was tired and frustrated. Anyway, that ended with cutting the threaded portion off the end of the barrel before calling it a night.

The barrel was getting shorter from both ends. Before long I would have a .300 Winchester carbine!

Starting fresh the next day, the threading went well and I installed the brake. It's a goofy looking thing, way too small in diameter for the bull barrel.

I coated the barrel with Brownell's Aluma-Hyde and finally things were going well. I stepped back to admire one of the best jobs I have ever done with a spray-on coating only to watch a giant bug come through the open door and land on the barrel. Parts of him are still there.

Sometime later I decided I didn't like the color and because this was a practice gun, I sprayed the barrel with flat black rattle can paint. It looked really good, until I shot the gun. The barrel heated up and cooked the paint until it started flaking off. No matter, as I keep pointing out, I was not going to keep this barrel anyway.

I fitted a Timney trigger and put it all into an H. S. Precision stock that had been lying around the shop for a decade. I had a magazine extension from Brownells that had also been lying around for years. It fit nicely and gave me a five-round capacity.

I fitted it all up with a scope and made up some handloads with 168-grain bullets to match the 1:12 twist of the barrel. (The barrels were designed for a .308 varmint rifle, not a .300 Winchester.) Nothing fancy with the load,

▲ This brake looks goofy.

just picked one from the Hodgdon book. Then, with great trepidation, I headed to the range.

As I keep saying, my plan all along was to use this as a learning project and at some point to put another barrel on the action. With all the problems I had encountered, I wasn't expecting much.

Then I shot the rifle. First time out the groups were under ½-MOA. That's five shots into half an inch at 100 yards. Not just once, but every time I shot the gun.

I have to admit, it looks like it was designed and built by a committee. This thing inspires giggles with its Rube Goldberg appearance, but it shoots so well I hate to mess with it.

Sometimes you just get lucky.

Or maybe the moral of the story is "if at first you don't succeed, try, try again." Which is what I did, again and again and again.

The barrel is several inches shorter than planned, the brake looks like a child designed it and the paint is less than perfect, but the damn thing really shoots!

Isn't that what matters?

Sometime between finishing the initial writing and doing the edits this rifle had another adventure. I received a new, adjustable comb stock from Bell & Carlson designed to solve the problem of eye alignment from the high mounting position with most of the new generation of long-range scopes.

The trouble was I didn't have a rifle on hand to fit it properly. So, I decided it was time I learned to contour a rifle barrel.

I took the learner gun apart and the first thing I did was check all the dimensions. I was both happy and a little shocked to see they were spot on.

I cut that foolish brake off the barrel and turned the barrel to fit the dimensions that Bell & Carlson sent for their stock. I finished it with Aluma-Hyde in black. As you

▲ This is the final version of the "Training Rifle" in .300 Winchester Magnum after turning down the barrel contour and cutting the muzzle brake off. Note the Bell and Carlson stock with adjustable cheekpiece.

can see in the photo it's a much different looking rifle now, and it still shoots great.

A PAIR OF ACES

There are two basic styles of extractors that most gun-smiths use for replacing a Model 700 extractor. The first is the "Sako" style, named for its use in Sako bolt action rifles. The other is the M-16 extractor from the M-16/

▲ The bolt in the back has an M-16 extractor and the front bolt has a Sako extractor.

AR-15 family of rifles. Both are larger, stronger and, at least in theory, more reliable than the Remington extractor. Several manufacturers offer kits, but there seems to be no standardization. As a result, there is some variation in dimensions from brand to brand, so I will not attempt to provide any dimension information here. Make sure you have a print and instructions that are correct for your specific extractor and make the cuts to the dimensions shown on that print.

SAVING FACE

With both extractor styles, you will first need to modify the bolt face. Assuming you have already stripped the bolt, remove the Remington extractor. Remington uses at least two different extractors in their Model 700 bolts. One has a rivet to hold it in place and the other does not. With either one, slip something underneath it like a dental pick or a tiny screwdriver and pry it out until you can grab it with pliers. (I always keep old or damaged screwdrivers around for jobs like this so that my good screwdrivers don't become old or damaged by misusing them.)

If it is the free-floating type you can easily remove it without damage. If it's riveted, don't worry too much about damage to the extractor; the odds do not favor salvaging it for future use, so just grab it and pull. If it won't come free you may need to grind or drill out the riveted section. Sometimes you can use a center punch on the rivet to break it free eliminating the need to drill or grind, which can risk damaging the bolt.

The first time you try to remove a fresh, new extractor on a new Remington bolt you will begin to appreciate the genius of design and how strong that little dude really is. As I write this on a Monday, I worked on a rifle build over the past weekend. The thing that stands out in my mind most is the difficulty I had removing a riveted extractor from the new Remington bolt. Anything that fights that hard to stay in place must be tough.

Once the extractor is removed, mount the bolt in a LaBounty bolt fixture and install the fixture in a 4-jaw chuck in the lathe. Dial the bolt to run true to center. The problem I have encountered here is knowing where to run the indicator on the bolt when you are dialing it into center. The Remington Model 700 uses a two piece bolt, so clearly you want to index on the front or head section, as that is where you will be doing the work. Many of the references I checked said that the best place to run your indicator is on the bolt head, just behind the lugs.

▲ ▼ Dialing a bolt in with a 4-jaw chuck.

That makes me question some of those sources. Almost every time I have tried that I have encountered out of round bolt heads that gave me fits trying to dial them in. What works better is the short section in front of the lugs. You will get a bounce from the divot where the extractor was riveted in place, so ignore that.

You can also attempt to run a test indicator on the inside ring in front of the bolt face. I have even heard about somehow using the firing pin hole. I tried that using a snug fitting drill bit as a gage pin and it worked acceptably well. With a true precision ground gage pin that may be an option, assuming the hole is in the center of the bolt. In the end, running the indicator on the short section in front of the bolt lugs seems to be the best option more often than in the other locations. With a problem bolt, you sometimes need to try more than one location before you find one that works for that bolt.

No matter where you decide to indicate the bolt to center, it's been my experience that you need to pick one spot and stick with it. Dialing in one location and then attempting to verify it at another location will lead to bulging eyes, primal screams, and a desperate need for alcohol. So pick a location, preferably just in front of the lugs and use an accurate indicator to dial the bolt into center.

If you don't already have the lathe tools for this project, Brownells sells a kit called the High-Speed Steel Cutting Kit that has everything you need. It comes in both quarter-inch and 3/8-inch sizes and you will want the bigger of the two.

The boring bar alone is worth the price of admission. I use mine all the time for things I never expected, like cutting an 11-degree crown on a rifle barrel. When trying to cut a crown, none of my other tools had enough clearance and the tool holder would hit the barrel, which made it balk and bind and generally be a pain in the butt. Of course, I can grind a tool for this job, which is what most of the texts I consulted suggested. But, when we were building his rifle, Nathan decided to use the boring bar from the Brownells kit and it worked great. I have used it for that chore ever since.

Well, I did until I got a piloted 11-degree cutter. Now I just run that tool in a Manson floating head to cut the crown. The cutters might be a little expensive, but they cut the work time by half or more.

A word of caution about the boring bar in the Brownells kit. It's a bit of a delicate little thing, so go easy. I broke the

▲ The bolt face has been machined as part of the process for a different extractor.

first one I had the very first time I used it with my ham-handed lathe technique. (That was early in my learning curve; I am much more refined now. I still break stuff, just not as often and rarely as spectacularly.) Take small cuts. Be gentle, be kind and this tool will make you look good.

Once the bolt is dialed into center, use the boring bar to open the inside of the bolt face recess until you clean up the groove from the old extractor. I run my compound parallel to the work piece and set zero for the bolt face. That lets me control the depth of the cut so I can cut to the bolt face with a nice clean shoulder.

If you don't know how to do these machining operations, I suggest you buy some books on basic machining and then practice on scrap metal until you feel comfortable. You might look for classes near you on basic machining or watch videos. Or find a crusty old machinist who is willing to teach you some tricks of the trade. I have run into some retired machinists who miss their trade. They are happy to be able to make chips again and will help set up a machine and teach the new dog some old tricks just for the opportunity to be back working metal. There are many ways to learn. Find one that works for you.

There is no shame in stopping your gun build right now and practicing on scrap metal until you feel confident. I made more than one trip to the metal supplier to pick through their scrap bins for short sections of steel round stock to use for practice. I have even paid full retail for some brass rods to practice with as that was much less expensive than messing up a rifle bolt. The brass is soft and a bit more forgiving to mistakes so it doesn't dull or break your tools as quickly while you are learning.

Bottom line: If you are not comfortable with this or any other machining process, before you start cutting on expensive gun parts, practice, practice, practice.

(I am a type A person who does not listen to his own advice and I have paid the price by messing up a bolt. Do as I say, not as I do and practice until you have it down cold. It's not only expensive to make a dumb mistake, it beats you to a pulp psychologically.)

Once the recess in the face of the bolt is machined you will need to make a ring of steel to fill it back to the size needed for the cartridge you will be using. The common material to use for this is a piece of rifle barrel. You do save all those ends you cut off, right? If not, any high-quality steel will work, including, perhaps, some of the practice pieces you have.

I much prefer to switch to the 3-jaw chuck on the lathe for this part of the process. It is much faster than trying to dial in a 4-jaw and turning the material will bring all your cuts to a common center anyway.

Measure the inside diameter of the bolt after you have machined it to remove the extractor slot. The outside diameter of the piece you are making should be .002 inch smaller than the inside diameter of the bolt recess. The

▲ Measuring the inside diameter of the bolt in preparation of making a filler plug.

▲ Measuring the depth of the bolt face.

ring you are making will need to be at least .010 inch longer than the depth of the recess in the bolt face.

Face off the work piece so that you have a clean, square, and finished surface. This faced off end will be the bottom of the piece when it's in the bolt. It's helpful to add a small radius on the outside edge to make it easier to insert into the bolt and to eliminate the sharp edge. Hit the spinning edge with a file held at an angle and break the edge on the corner so it will not be sharp when you insert it into the bolt.

Always use a file with a handle on it when working on a lathe. Files without handles can have amazing penetration on the human body if they are launched by a chance encounter with the chuck.

Cut the inside diameter of the ring to .010 inch smaller than your final dimension. That will be determined by the cartridge you are using. For .308 or "standard" size cartridges that have a .472-inch rim diameter, the final size will be .475 with a -.003 tolerance. No plus tolerance. For a magnum case with .523 rim diameter, the ring will be .536 -.003. If you have other cartridges, you should refer to the print with your extractor kit. In fact, always refer to the print anyway; think of this this as just a general guideline.

Drill the hole as close to the diameter as possible by using a series of progressively larger drill bits. Then, switch to the boring bar. Clean up the surface and stop .010 inch short of the final inside diameter.

Once the ring is complete, check it for fit before you cut it off the work piece. It should slide into the recess you machined in the bolt easily, but with very little clearance. It should not be tight, but it must not be loose either. If it's good, cut it off and clean up any burrs. Now, try it for fit in the bolt again. Take note if the ejector plunger is going to clear, keeping in mind you will be removing another .010 inch from the inside diameter (.005 inch per side) after installing the piece in the bolt. If the ejector will not clear you must mill or grind a clearance cut. It's best to mill, as it looks better, but you can do it with a Dremel grinder and have a good result. It's easier to do this clearance cut now, before the part is installed in the bolt.

It's common in shooting circles to badmouth the Dremel tool, but those critics are wrong. Any tool is only as good as the person operating it. The Dremel is a wonderful tool for any competent gunsmith. Those who think it's the Devil's invention, designed only to ruin guns, are not competent gunsmiths. Never blame the tool for your failures.

You should now have a ring that is an easy slip fit into the bolt face, measuring .002 inch smaller than the I.D. of the bolt face recesses. The ring should be at least .010 inch longer than the recess so it protrudes past the leading edge of the bolt. It should also be at least .010 inch smaller on the inside diameter than what the prints calls for as the final dimension. It should sit square against the bolt face, which should have a square junction between the side and face.

SOLDERING ON

The next step is to solder the ring into place. All the parts that will be soldered must be clean and free from oil or oxidation. The oil should be removed with a good degreaser

▲ The ring is a good fit. Time to solder.

like acetone or Brakleen. You have just machined them, so the oxidation part should be fine since you have fresh clean surfaces on the metal, but it's never a mistake to hit them with some sandpaper after you degrease them. If they have sat around for any length of time, you must refresh the surface with a little sandpaper or emery cloth.

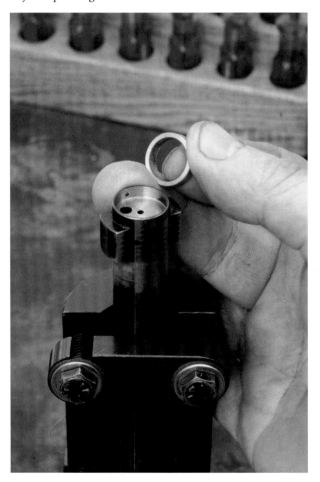

▲ The final ring ready for soldering.

▲ Heat Stop.

The bolt lugs are heat treated for hardness, so you want to preserve that and protect them from excess heat. Brownells sells a product called Heat Stop. This is a paste that absorbs heat to protect the metal it's covering.

It's so good, Brownells says you can heat one end of a rod red hot and with Heat Stop in the middle you can hold the other end with a bare hand.

▲ The drill plugs the ejector hole and the goop protects the bolt lugs from excessive heat.

Put the bolt in a vise and cover the outside, including the lugs, with this paste. Don't use a thin film; instead, goop it on the outside, as you need some volume to make it work right. Be careful not to get any on the surfaces you will be soldering.

Plug the ejector hole with a drill bit of the correct size to prevent solder getting inside. You might also do the same with the firing pin hole just to be sure.

▲ Tin the ring.

Tin the outside of the filler ring you made by covering it with flux and then heating it until solder will melt and flow to cover the entire outside diameter of the ring with a thin coating.

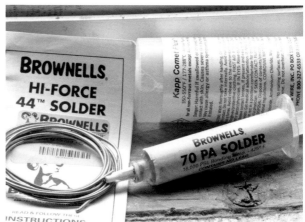

▲ A low-melting-point solder is important.

Hi-Force 44 solder is a good choice, as it flows at the low temperature of 475 degrees Fahrenheit, minimizing the possibility of heat damage to the bolt. Use this solder with a good flux like Knapp Comet Flux (I got them both from Brownells). Other solders have a flow temperature as high as 1,200 degrees, which is too high to preserve the hardness on the bolt lugs.

My friend James Darst suggested another option, Brownells Homogenized solder. The 70PA Solder has a 16,000 psi tensile strength and bonds at 425 degrees Fahrenheit. This solder uses a special homogenizing process that blends both solder and flux into a paste. It comes in a syringe for easy application. Having tried it, I found it more difficult to work with than wire solder. That's probably because I am more experienced with using the wire solder. After using the paste on my Magnum Opus rifle, I switched back to Hi-Force 44 wire solder for future projects. That said, the end result was fine with the paste, so I encourage you to explore the options and find what works best for you.

Once you have the ring tinned, coat the inside of the bolt with flux and insert the ring. If it will not go, that's fine. Start it and then apply the heat as you put pressure on the ring with something flat, square, and resistant to heat. Fingers are not a good option.

Just sayin'.

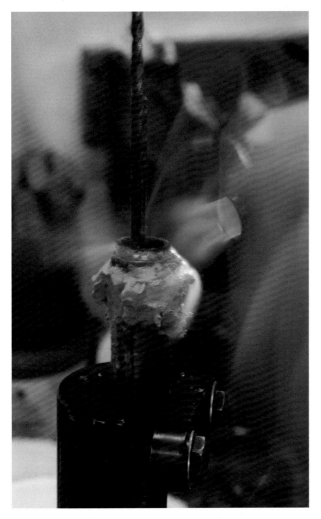

▲ Sending the heat. Because I had to keep the heat moving or risk damage to the bolt, this was a hard photo to capture.

Heat evenly with a Mapp gas torch until you can easily push the ring into position. I use a small brass hammer to tap the ring around its circumference to be certain it is

seated. This must be done, of course, while the solder is in a liquid form, so do it under heat. Run a little more solder into any obvious gaps, keeping the heat on, until the entire ring is soldered with no gaps. If you have extra solder on top, that is fine, as you will be facing off the ring in the lathe anyway.

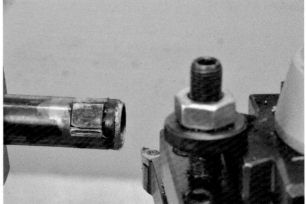

▲ After soldering in the ring, the bolt must be put back in the lathe and the ring brought to final dimension.

Once everything has cooled off, clean up the bolt, put it back in the LaBounty fixture and dial it into center using a 4-jaw chuck on the lathe. Face off the ring until it's to the dimension on the print for the extractor type you will be installing. Use a boring bar to open the inside diameter to the correct dimension for the cartridge you will be using and to clean up any solder that flowed into places it should not be. Add a chamfer to the leading edge of the ring as dictated in the print. Usually it will be 45 degrees and .025 inch.

You may also want to clean up the face of the bolt with the lathe, although I prefer to use a Manson Bolt Face Truing Cutter to lower the risk of things going wrong. Check and re-check all the dimensions before you remove the bolt from the lathe. It's a lot of work to dial in a 4-jaw chuck so make sure you have everything correct before you remove the bolt.

I like to put the bolt back in the receiver and kiss the face with the Manson Bolt Face Truing Cutter. Coat the face with Dykem and just kiss it enough to remove the blue and show shiny metal all the way around. This ensures there is no warpage and that no solder has migrated to the bolt face.

EXTRACTING METAL FOR THE EXTRACTOR

The next steps for either of the extractor styles will be done on a milling machine. Before starting you must make sure the milling machine is adjusted correctly. That means that you will tram the mill head so it's perfectly square with the table. Then, check to make sure the vise is square to the spindle on the milling machine. That ensures your cuts will be correct at the start and at the finish and that the

▲ Using an indicator to square the milling machine vise.

▲ After I used a surface grinder to face off the top of the milling machine vise jaws, I was able to use that surface to tram the vise and ensure it was 90 degrees to the spindle.

cuts follow the line you expect them to follow. If the mill is all out of whack, the cuts can vary in depth and direction and will not be square with the centerline of the bolt.

Both extractor types will require a jig to hold the bolt at the correct orientation in the milling machine.

▲ Note the modified Sako Extractor Installation Jig, so the screw heads are below flush.

▲ With the modified jig, it can be turned 90 degrees to allow drilling the pivot pin hole for the M-16 extractor.

The Remington 700 Sako Extractor Installation Jig from Brownells works fine.

I modified mine to use with the M-16 extractor. For that installation, the bolt has to be turned exactly 90 degrees to make the hole for the pivot pin to hold the extractor in place. If you turn the tool in the milling vise the screw heads are in the way, so I used a 9/32 end mill to deepen the holes enough that the screw heads are well below the face of the tool. Then I cut enough off the other end of the screws so they don't stick out the back side. Now I have nice clean surfaces to clamp to in the milling machine.

When using the jig for the M-16 extractor, it's important that it be square and the edges parallel. Install the bolt,

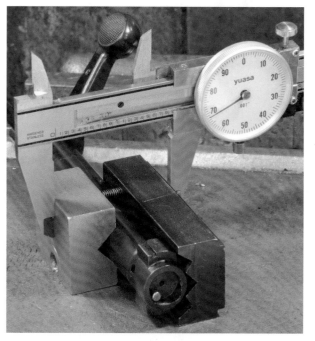

▲ Measuring the sides of the jig to make sure it's square.

then use a micrometer to measure both sides and adjust the screws until they are exactly the same, meaning the two edges are parallel to each other and the jig is square. You can double-check using a machinist's square to be certain.

THE SAKO-STYLE EXTRACTOR

The Sako style is probably the easier of the two extractors to install, as it does not have the cross pin hole that must be precisely located. That said, it's the one I screwed up on my first attempt, so I guess "easy" is relative.

▲ The Sako extractor installed in a Remington 700 Bolt.

Again, it's very important to follow the print with your kit. Be aware that the dimensions will vary with the cartridge you are using. For example, the kit I use most is from Brownells. It is made by Harris Gunworks and is the larger size. The smaller size is for .223-size cartridges and the larger is for everything else. If the gun is chambered for a .308-size cartridge head, the depth of the cut is .166 inch deep. If it's for magnum cartridges it is .136 inch deep. Always check and double-check every aspect before you start cutting. If you rush into removing metal you may regret it. *(I know this from painful experience!!!!)*

▲ Making the first cut for a Sako extractor.

Fit the bolt into a Remington 700 Sako Extractor Installation Jig from Brownells. True the jig to the spindle in your milling machine and lock it into the vise. There are two grooves on the edges of the underside of the jig that fit a pair of thin parallels used to support the jig at the correct height in the vise. If the vise is correctly trammed to the spindle, using the parallels should position the bolt correctly and square to the spindle. Always use an indicator to verify the position before you start cutting metal.

▲ An edge finder with the bolt.

Use an edge finder to locate the center of the bolt by locating one edge and adding half the measured diameter of the bolt. Use the edge finder to locate the front edge of the bolt to manage the length of the cut for the extractor. If the print dimension is from the face of the bolt, you will need to use a depth micrometer to measure the distance from the front edge of the bolt to the face and adjust the math accordingly. Make sure you know if the measurement is from the front of the bolt or from the face, which is where the cartridge will contact the bolt.

This is critical information and I can tell you from painful experience you need to be sure. I once installed an extractor that said the cut depth was measured from

▲ Zero out the mill dials before starting cuts.

▲ This shows the finished bolt cuts for a Sako extractor.

▲ Drilling the hole for the stud.

▲ Drilling the hole for the spring.

the bolt face. Naturally, I assumed it was the face where the cartridge contacts. Imagine my surprise when my final cut was too deep, by exactly the distance from the face to the front of the bolt. Don't assume when it comes to nomenclature. Check, double-check, and check again.

For the Sako type extractor a single long cut is made. The Harris Gun Works kit calls for a .235-inch-wide cut. Brownells sells several extractor milling cutters that are sized for these kits. For this one I used a 15/64 cutter with a slot width of .231. The slot is, of course, too narrow, so a .002-inch cleanup cut on each side will fix the problem.

Next, drill a hole at the rear of the slot for the extractor stud to fit. For this one, a #9 .196-inch drill is used. Follow the dimensions on the print, use an edge finder to locate the front of the bolt face and drill this hole in exactly the designated location, as it controls the position of the extractor. Do not mess this up. Again, don't ask me why I know what happens if you do, just trust me, get it right. You will sleep better at night. It's my job to make these mistakes so you won't have to. At least that's what I tell myself to ease the pain.

(Ok, I'll 'fess up. In this case, I drilled on the previously mentioned bolt, assuming the cut was correct. When I discovered that the cut was too deep, I also realized that the hole was positioned incorrectly. It was fixable, but far from pretty in the end result.)

It was a lesson that was hard learned and well-remembered for future installations. I am happy to say that I only made that mistake once.

Next, the bolt is turned up on end to drill a small hole for the spring and plunger. The print calls for a flat bottom hole. Brownells recommends using a Solid Carbide Drill to finish the hole. This tool is made for drilling very hard steel and is not recommended for soft steel. Rather than use it for the entire depth of the hole and risk breaking the very expensive drill, I predrilled the hole using a standard twist drill and then cleaned up the bottom to make it square with this tool.

The problem is that this is still a drill and it has a taper on the point. To be honest, if I had to do it over I would not order this tool. The only thing I know of that can make the hole perfectly square on the bottom is an end mill. A 1/10-inch end mill with a long cut would probably work. However, I asked Wes Harris, the guy who makes the kits and he said if you don't have something to make the base of the hole square, it's probably not a big issue.

Harris Gunworks suggests that if you have not opened the bolt face and filled it with a soldered ring of steel as covered elsewhere in this section, fill the extractor groove with JB Weld to prevent the cartridge rim from catching in the groove. Of course, this applies if you are keeping the same cartridge head dimension the bolt was originally designed to use. While that is obviously not as good an end result as using steel, it is a much easier way to go than with all that lathe work. If you do not have a lathe or the LaBounty jig for your lathe, this is a viable option to allow installing a Sako extractor using just the milling machine.

Assemble the extractor per the instructions, making sure to orient the leg on the spring-loaded pin correctly so it will lock over the bottom of the extractor.

I found that the little screwdriver that comes with an eyeglass repair kit works very well to slide in the slot on the extractor and compress the spring for removal of this extractor.

THE M-16 EXTRACTOR

One primary difference with the M-16 extractor is that it's held in with a cross pin that allows the extractor to pivot against a spring. The hole for that pin must be located perfectly for the extractor to work properly. Making the hole requires that you first mill a flat with a 1/8-inch end mill, then make the hole with a drill and finish with a chucking reamer. Also, this extractor requires a plunge cut with the mill, in the rear of the main cut to create clearance for the extractor to pivot.

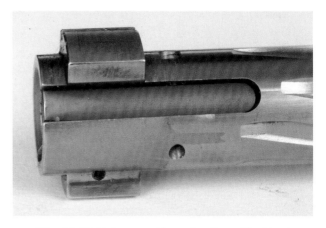

▲ The M-16 Extractor. Note the flat milled in the bolt to allow drilling for the pivot pin.

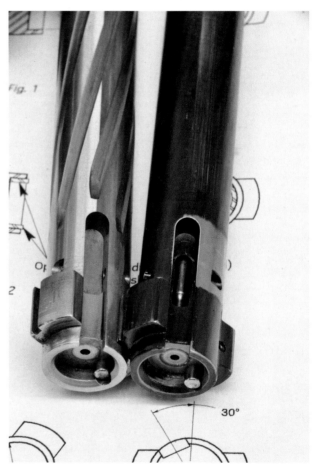

▲ These bolts show the mill cuts for an M-16 extractor. One goes all the way through, the other does not. They were done by two different gunsmiths and both say their way is the right way.

So, measure twice and cut once. Check that; measure a bunch of times. Check and double-check before you start removing metal. If you do that and make your cuts and holes with precision, the end result will be perfect.

In contrast to my rather disastrous first run at a Sako extractor, my first attempt at installing an M-16 extractor went very well, even though I did the M-16 first. The difference? Probably because I made several practice runs using brass rods that I machined to be the same as the bolt.

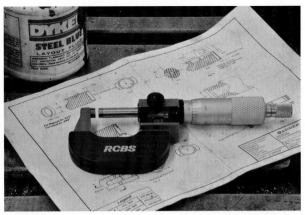

▲ Read the print that came with the extractor kit.

The cut will be the depth and length as specified on the print that came with your extractor kit. I used a carbide four-flute end mill that cuts on the bottom as well as the side. Like almost everything else I needed for this book, I got mine from Brownells. A bottom cutting end mill is necessary to do the plunge cuts. With the extractor kit from Badger, a .255-inch-wide cut is called for, so I used a ¼-inch end mill. The required .255-inch is slightly larger than the .250-inch cut of the quarter-inch mill, so you will need to open the slot a little bit. Remember, if you widen the cut, take half off each side so you maintain the center of the bolt. In this case, take two and one-half thousandths from each side.

There are two mill cuts needed for the M-16 extractor. Make the first long cut, then plunge and make the deeper pocket cut as indicated on the print.

▲ ▼ Practice, practice, practice.

Once you have a few extractor installations under your belt it becomes much easier, but that first time you start cutting a bolt can be confusing and a bit intimidating, so practice before you cut on important parts.

Install the bolt in the jig and clamp the jig in the milling machine that is trammed and the vise squared. The jig positions the bolt at a 30-degree angle. When the cut for the extractor is made at top dead center, the edge of the cut will just clear the bottom bolt lug. Use an edge finder to locate the center on the bolt. Find one edge and add half the measured diameter of the bolt. That's the location for TDC. Also, use the edge finder to locate the leading edge. If the print dimension is from the face of the bolt, you will need to use a depth micrometer to measure the distance from the front edge of the bolt to the face and adjust the math accordingly. Again, make sure you understand where the dimension for the cut is starting from. It might be the front, leading edge of the bolt or it might be from the bolt face. It is critical that you understand that the *terminology* on the print might not be correct.

▲ Measuring the depth of the primary cut with a dial caliper.

When the cuts are completed, the bolt is turned 90 degrees in the vise. I read about various ways to do this, including using a square. But, if you modified a Remington 700 Sako Extractor Installation Jig from Brownells as detailed earlier in this chapter and shown in the photos, you can attain a perfect 90 degrees with the jig and the mill vise.

The jig is a V-block, so one side can be tightened more

than the other, tilting the top. It's important that the jig is adjusted exactly square, so use a micrometer or dial caliper and adjust the screws until both sides are equal thickness and the front and rear faces of the jig are parallel to each other. Verify this with a machinist's square. Now, clamp the jig in the vise and you should be 90 degrees off the first cut. This sets up for the cross pin to hold the extractor in place.

▲ This shows the flat cut into the radius of the bolt to allow drilling and reaming for the pivot pin.

Using an edge finder, locate the edge to determine the location of the hole based on the dimensions on the print. Use a 1/8-inch end mill to make a flat. Be very careful and work slowly. You are cutting against a radius and if you put too much force on the cut it can break the mill. Once you have the flat, switch to a #0 center drill to spot the location for the hole.

The instructions call for drilling with a #43 drill. Be very careful when you break through the bottom of the bolt so as not to break the drill or elongate the hole. Use a 3/32 chucking reamer to finish the hole. I didn't have

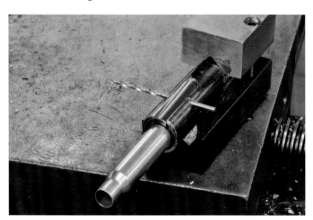

▲ The drill is serving as a slave pin to make sure the M-16 extractor is going to work. This is a brass practice piece. Once I perfected the technique using brass rods machined to simulate a bolt, I did the installation on my rifle bolt.

a reamer the first time I did this so I drilled with the #43 then finished with a new carbide coated 3/32 drill. Sometimes you need to use the tools you have and in this case the result was just fine.

Of course, it's better to use the reamer and I ordered one for future installations. Actually, I bought two. If I bought just one, I would break it at a critical time. But, with a backup waiting in my toolbox, I'll never have any issue with the first one. Don't ask me why, that's just how it works.

Clean up any burrs and break any sharp edges with a hand grinder and a Cratex polishing stone. Install the extractor per the instructions and check for function. If you made all the cuts correctly it should fit and work fine.

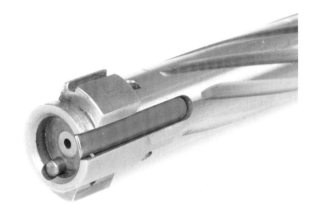

▲ The installed M-16 extractor on a Remington 700 bolt.

With this M-16 extractor you will need to open the bolt body counterbore recess in a Remington Model 700 barrel to allow clearance for the extractor to pivot and work. The dimensions will be on the print. Keep this in mind as you are fitting the barrel and do the work at that time. If you are using something like the Manson Bolt Body Counterbore Cutter, covered in the section on fitting a

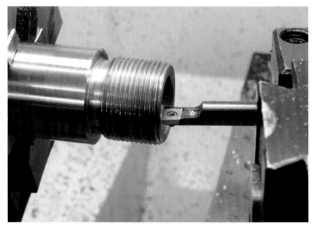

▲ Using a boring bar to open the bolt body counterbore on a Remington 700 barrel.

barrel, you will need to go in with a boring bar and open the bolt counterbore recess wider.

GET A HANDLE ON IT!

Give your tactical precision rifle an oversize bolt knob for faster operation and to spread envy among your fellow shooters.

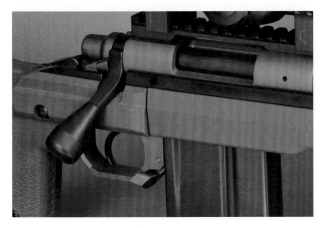

▲ A tactical rifle has to have an oversized bolt handle.

Your bolt action rifle might be able to drill the eyes out of a bug at 1,000 yards, but it's not a "precision rifle" unless it has all the right bling. One important option, for a multitude of reasons, is an oversized tactical bolt handle. A big knob has a practical use, of course, making it much easier to run the bolt fast. But it also makes a statement that says, "This is a specialty rifle, a 'tacticool,' long-range precision tool."

Fortunately, installing an oversized bolt handle on your rifle is a pretty easy project. Most aftermarket bolt handles are threaded, so the real task is cutting down the existing bolt knob and threading the shank of the bolt handle to accept a new knob.

There seems to be several options for doing this. I saw a video for Badger Industries where the bolt was set in a jig and milled on all four sides. Then a center-cutting mill was used to form the shank. It looked fast and efficient.

I suppose this process is only restricted by your ingenuity. I have heard about grinding the old bolt handle down using a belt sander until it will go into a threading die. In fact, that's more or less what is on the instructions that came with the Brownell's oversized bolt handle I used on my Magnum Opus rifle.

You can grind the bolt handle with a belt sander, getting it close to the right shape and dimension and then finish it with a file. Clamp the resulting mess in a bench vise and thread it by hand. Even if you don't get it exactly right, if you have enough metal to cut a decent thread, it will be fine. The thread only needs to be strong, not pretty, as the bolt handle will cover the threads and any mistakes.

It's recommended you glue the bolt handles on with epoxy anyway.

I suppose that gets it done, but I am trying to avoid promoting that kind of redneck gunsmithing in this book. As I have stated more than once, I recognize that you can't always afford to buy the tools suggested and that part of being a good gunsmith is the ability to improvise and use the resources you have on hand to accomplish the job. Sometimes you get a very good end result using shade-tree tactics, but here in this book I am trying to promote the "correct" way of gunsmithing your rifles.

Of course, if you don't have a lathe, don't buy one just for this job. If you do have one, the right tools are a good investment because you will get a much nicer end result. In that light, Pacific Tool and Gauge is the source for the tools used to remove the bolt handle and prepare it to be threaded for a new oversized handle. PTG makes several tools for this chore and are pretty much the singular source for tooling for fitting oversized bolt handles. One they offer is a jig to use in a milling machine, but most are lathe related.

One of the tools PTG offers is a cutter called the Slugger that is like an end mill with a hollow center. I know that Jim Majoros from Viktor's Legacy Gunsmithing likes to use the Slugger in conjunction with the Phase III bolt jig. It's faster and time is money for a working gunsmith.

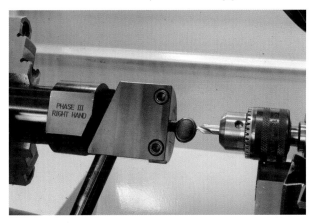

▲ This jig makes installing oversized bolt handles an easy job.

The best option for most of us and the one I like most is the Phase III bolt jig because it works with a wide range of bolts. I have used it with Remington bolts and found it lined it up perfectly. I have an earlier version of this tool for which I had to dial in my bolt and found it difficult, *check that*, almost impossible, to get it exactly right. This new Phase III jig positions the bolt handle perfectly.

Of course, you can make a jig. As I keep saying, part of being a hobby gunsmith is innovation, but it's a lot of work and the materials will be expensive.

Another option is to trade work for tools. If you have

several buddies who want bolt handles, have them split the cost of buying the jig and you do the work. It's a win-win. They get bolt handles, you get a great tool and you get to spend time making chips. Which, for the record, is a lot more fun than mowing the lawn.

This approach works well for hobby gunsmiths. Say one of your shooting pals wants a re-barrel job in a cartridge you don't have the tools for. Trade your work for the reamer and headspace gauges. He gets a rifle, you get the tools and everybody wins except the IRS.

Since the projects here are mostly geared to the Remington 700 rifle action, the following steps are specific to the Model 700. They may also apply to other models' angled bolt handles with a different insert for the jig.

The first step is to remove the existing bolt knob. That means either cutting it off, or making it smaller. Some instructions recommend cutting off the knob and threading the remaining shank. However, that leaves the handle too short, so I always turn down the existing bolt knob. This basically adds length to the shank; the handle on the finished bolt is actually longer with the new knob installed. If this makes the handle too long for your taste, it's easy to cut it shorter. But once the knob is cut off, it is much more difficult to replace the length if the handle turns up too short.

I dug up an old article I wrote for *Shooting Illustrated* magazine about doing this project to see if I could use some of it here. Back then, I used the old style jig where I had to index the bolt handle before locking it down. With the odd shape and nothing really to measure from, it was a difficult chore. I just deleted 500 words from that article describing how to index the bolt in the fixture.

Here is what I replaced it with:

"Clamp the bolt in the Phase III jig with the appropriate insert and clamp the jig in the lathe."

▲ Supporting the bolt with a live center.

So I guess you know where I come down to on this tool. It eliminates the single most aggravating chore of using the earlier version.

A 3-jaw chuck works fine. Use a countersink drill in a Jacobs chuck in the tailstock to make a 60-degree tapered hole in the end of the bolt handle to accept a live center and help support the bolt when making the cuts.

▲ The bolt handle removed and ready for threading.

Now, turn the bolt handle knob to size. Because of the shape of the Model 700 bolt knob, this is an interrupted cut for much of the operation, which can be hard on tungsten cutters. I found that out the hard way by chipping a couple while turning my first bolt handle. These cutters were the style where the carbide is brazed on a steel shank. I switched to a tool-steel cutter and have not had any more problems.

That was with my old 1941 South Bend lathe. The new Grizzly lathe has a different size tool holder and I didn't have any tool-steel cutters I could make work. So, I used a replaceable insert carbide cutter. I picked the largest, toughest one I had and if I am careful to make small cuts and run the RPM relatively slowly, it works fine.

This is a good place to use your older inserts that are nearing the end of their useful life anyway, so that if one is chipped it's not a huge loss. The work is not extreme precision and the steel used on the bolts never machines all that nicely anyway. The finish is always rough, so just run your old cutters and don't worry about it, at least to rough it out. If you want to switch to a newer, sharper cutter once you have a round piece with no interrupted cuts, it will give a nicer finished product.

I have found that if you grind some of the bolt handle off before starting, getting it close to round, it eliminates a lot of the interrupted cuts on the lathe and speeds up the process by quite a bit.

Run at low RPM, as the big bolt sticking out the side can create an imbalance at high speed. Also, be very careful. You have a bolt sticking out to the side and whipping around, just waiting to smash your hand. Be very aware and very careful.

Before you turn on the power, make sure you have plenty of clearance by running the tools to each extreme at the ends of the cut and turning the chuck by hand to check for clearance. The first scar I put on my new lathe was when a bolt hit the cross slide table. The bolt was fine, a testament to their durability, but it marred my baby. I cleaned it all up with no harm done, but there is a scar to remind me of my mistake. Be very careful. Check and double-check before you turn on the power to the lathe.

Always check the thread size before cutting anything. Most knobs use a 5/16-24 thread, so the goal is to turn the old bolt knob down until it is round and measures 0.3125 inch, which is the diameter needed to make that thread.

You can find the correct dimension for any thread you are cutting in the *Machinery's Handbook*. This book is a wealth of information on just about anything you will be doing with your lathe or milling machine.

In this case, I found the 5/16-24 thread and the major diameter of 0.3125. So I turned to that size, the length of the removed knob. End it with a square shoulder for the bolt handle to butt against. (If your new knob has a different thread size, of course you must adjust accordingly.)

Once you have the bolt handle turned to the proper size, remove the live center, and face off the end. Adding a slight radius on the edge with a file will help start the threading die. Shut off the lathe and use a small file to clean up the shoulder, as there will probably be a few burrs.

You can single point cut the thread using a 60-degree threading tool and following the threading instructions with your lathe. However, as this is not as critical a thread as, for example, a barrel thread, it's much faster and easier to use a die for the threading operation.

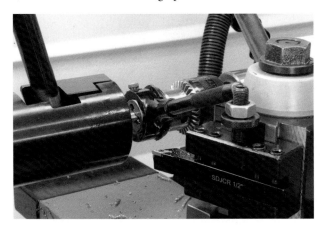

▲ Threading the bolt handle with a die.

Turn off the power to the lathe and take it out of gear, so you can turn the chuck by hand. Install a 5/16-24 threading die in a die handle. Take the live center out of the tailstock and use the flat end of the tailstock to hold the die handle square against the bolt handle. In my case, the diameter of the tailstock was too large, so I put in my Jacobs chuck and used that. The idea is to hold the die holder square against the bolt so the threads start correctly. Adjust the

tool holder on the lathe so the die holder handle will rest on it and prevent the die from turning.

Flood the area to be threaded with plenty of cutting oil. Then turn the chuck by hand while applying continuous light pressure from the tailstock on the die holder until it has cut several threads. If you wish, you can then slide the tailstock out of the way. Continue turning the chuck until the shank has threaded to the end, or you can lock the chuck and turn the die holder by hand, whichever is easier for you.

Back off the die and reverse it in the holder so the cutting threads now extend all the way to the edge of the die. Run the die back onto the threaded shank and use it to cut the final few threads the tapered "starter" side of the die left undone.

▲ The threaded bolt with the handle.

Before removing the bolt from the jig or the jig from the lathe, make sure the new knob will completely screw onto the shank. If the threaded shank bottoms out before the knob hits the shoulder, it might be necessary to remove a few threads from the end of the shank, using the facing tool.

▲ Make sure the bolt knob fits. This is with my older jig.

Once the knob fits properly, remove the bolt from the jig. Clean all the oil and metal chips off the handle and bolt. Degrease the threads.

A lot of gunsmiths glue the bolt knob in place, but that permanence seems a bit of overkill. What if a new, much cooler bolt knob hits the market and I want to change the bolt handle? Heat overcomes most glue, but, at least on my rifle, I like the idea of being able to remove the handle if I want. Also, heat will probably destroy any spray-on coating you might put on the handle. I prefer to put a few drops of blue #242 Loctite on the threads and install the new bolt knob. That way I can remove it later. If you prefer a more permanent installation you can glue the knob to the bolt with Marine-Tex, Acraglas gel, or even epoxy.

Before you glue anything, though, place the bolt in the rifle. Check make sure there is ample clearance between the knob and the stock and between the knob and the scope. If it's all good, do the final installation with glue or Loctite.

Finally, take the rifle to the range where you can mock your buddies for their continued use of inadequate, undersized bolt handles.

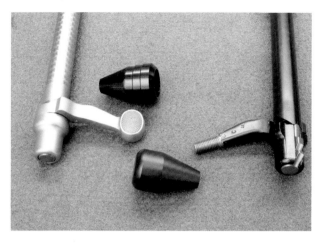

▲ Oversized bolt knobs.

MY 6MM CREEDMOOR "BROWNELLS RIFLE"–HOW I FINALLY ACHIEVED NIRVANA IN GUN BUILDING

I wanted to build the most accurate rifle I could using parts available from Brownells. Like everybody else in the shooting world at that time, I was thinking about a 6.5 Creedmoor. The trouble was that I already owned two of them, a custom rifle and a Ruger RPR.

My friend John Snow is the shooting editor for *Outdoor Life* and he had worked with Hornady to develop the 6mm Creedmoor. He talked me into that cartridge just as I got some insider information that Hornady was going to take it mainstream. The good folks at Hornady provided me with a chamber reamer drawing which I sent to Dave Manson to have a reamer made. When I started the project the cartridge was still a wildcat, but by the time it was finished it was the hot new darling of the long-range shooting world.

My "Brownells Rifle."

From Brownells I ordered:

Remington Model 700 short action with bolt
A 6mm 1:8 twist Shilen, Select Match Barrel in #7 contour
Kinetic Research X-Ray Chassis
Brownells oversize tactical bolt knob

Other parts I used that are available from Brownells include:
Timney trigger with a 1.5 pound pull
Badger Ordnance FTE Muzzle Brake
Holland Gunsmithing recoil lug

I blueprinted the action, changed the scope mounting screws to 8-40 and fitted an oversized bolt knob. Then I threaded and

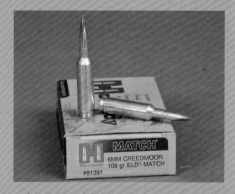

When I started this project, the 6mm Creedmoor was a wildcat. By the time I finished, Hornady had factory ammo.

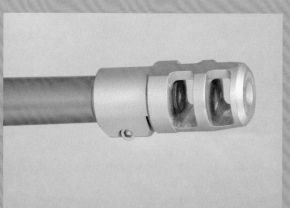

This brake requires a little extra machining.

Indicating the brake into a 4-jaw chuck.

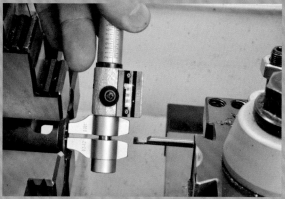

Measuring the final hole in the brake. Note the tiny boring bar used to true up and finish the hole.

This little boring bar ensures the hole through the brake is correct.

chambered the barrel. I used a Holland oversized recoil lug and modified the action to allow pinning the lug in place. This all went without a hitch, which kind of spooked me.

The Badger FTE muzzle brake requires threading the barrel and then machining a section of the barrel .9 inch long and .8745 inch in diameter for the brake to clamp onto. This allows easy clocking of the brake and easy removal.

The bore through the brake comes undersized, so it has to be opened up to fit the bullet diameter. I dialed the brake into center on a 4-jaw chuck, then drilled it to the closest size and finished with a small boring bar to

(continued . . .)

true it up at .265 inch. It's recommended that the final size be .020 inch larger than the bullet diameter. With a .243 bullet, I added .020 and rounded up.

I finished the action, trigger guard, muzzle brake, bolt shroud and a few other parts in Cerakote H series Burnt Bronze. I didn't have a large oven at that time and I wanted to experiment with Cerakote air-dry coatings so I did the barrel and bolt with C series in Graphite Black.

I fitted a Talley rail with 20 MOA elevation built into the rail. Then, using Talley 34mm rings, I mounted a Kahles 6-24X56 Tactical Scope.

The finished "Brownells" rifle.

This gun is a beast. The 27-inch barrel alone weighs more than seven pounds and the finished gun with the giant scope is 16 pounds. I built it for one use: shooting very accurately at long range.

The first time at the range using Hornady factory loads, it averaged .6 inch for five, five-shot groups. With handloads, that average dropped to .46 inch. Later, as the gun broke in and I got to know it better, I shot several groups at .25 inch and even smaller. The limitations seem to be mine, as I think the gun is capable of consistent sub .2s if the shooter (me) does his part well. My home range is 500 yards and this rifle holds ½-MOA easily at that distance. Some five-shot groups are well under two inches at 500 yards.

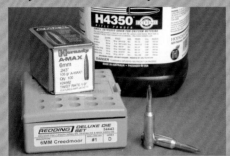

Handloading usually produces the best accuracy.

The last time out we hung a tennis ball (2.6 inches in diameter) on a wire at 500 yards and once I dialed in the right elevation, I hit it 10 times straight.

After building this rifle, I felt like a gunsmithing god.

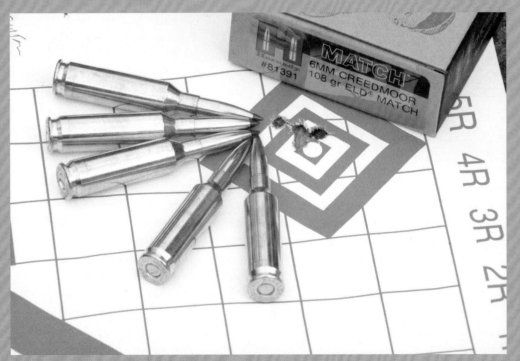

The first 100-yard group with the new rifle.

CHAPTER 15

MAKING IT YOURS

THREADING A RIFLE BARREL

This is the moment of truth, when you finally turn the blank into a barrel. Or at least the start of it. It's a bit daunting the first time or two when you put that expensive, precision piece of pipe into something designed to remove steel and start cutting off metal. Until that moment, it is all about the barrel maker and his precision and expertise. But the second you remove that first chip, it all transfers to you. It's both terrifying and wonderful, but either way, you own it. This is when you really start to feel like a gunsmith and begin to believe that anything is possible.

It could also be remembered as the defining moment when you were forced into lifelong therapy.

Start this project when you are fresh and clear thinking, go slowly and remember, it's all going to turn out great.

For somebody anyway: you, the guy selling you another barrel, or the therapist.

PRACTICE—PRACTICE—PRACTICE

If you have not already mastered the machining arts, including single point threading on a lathe, this is no time to learn.

Remember the old joke about the guy lost in New York City and carrying a violin case? Needing directions, he asked a local, "How do I get to Carnegie Hall?"

The guy looked at the violin case and replied, "Practice, practice, practice."

Same deal here. Before you cut on your barrel you should practice, practice, practice. Do all you can to understand and learn all the machining skills needed before you put an expensive barrel in your lathe.

Before starting any project with expensive materials you should have some lessons, either from a machinist or in some sort of self-taught program. I work best teaching myself and I have found plenty of information in books and on the web. Just remember books have editors, the web does not. While there are some good videos on the web, there is a lot of trash as well, so be careful. If there are any local trade schools that teach basic machining, sign up.

To my thinking, the best way to learn is to get the basics and then spend some time in front of your lathe making chips. You will make mistakes and break some stuff, that's part of the process. The key is to make most of those mistakes on cheap materials. For the record, a new rifle barrel blank is not "cheap material."

POINT IT AT THE JEEP

There was an old joke at my family deer camp, back when

lever action rifles were popular. To unload one, the hunter had to work every cartridge through the action, so the potential for an unplanned discharge was higher than with a magazine-fed rifle.

When a hunter was unloading his rifle after the hunt, some wise guy always yelled out, "Point it at something cheap." In other words, if you gotta damage something with a mistake (such as an accidental discharge while unloading) make it something cheap. The problem was, one old deaf guy thought they kept telling him to "point it at the Jeep," which ain't cheap. Thankfully, somebody noticed before he blew away their 4X4 transportation.

So, before you work on an expensive barrel, "point it at the Jeep" and practice on some cheap stuff. Go to the steel-yard and buy some practice pieces. At my local dealer they have a cutoff box where the scrap ends go and I can pick through that box and find practice pieces for a pretty reasonable cost. Just remember to bring some leather gloves or a lot of Band-Aids to deal with all the sharp edges and burrs. Gloves are better. If the guys at my local place are any indication, metal salesmen get unreasonably grumpy when you bleed all over their stock.

TO TURN OR NOT TO TURN

The best approach for any gunsmith, regardless of skill level, is to use a pre-contoured barrel. That means the barrel maker has contoured the barrel and in most cases stress relieved it after contouring. It's possible to buy a straight, cylindrical barrel blank and contour it yourself, but why? Every gunsmith I know uses pre-contoured barrels. They may make a few small modifications to the contours, but they all let the barrel makers do the heavy lifting.

Many gunsmiths will, however, turn the straight section over the chamber to reduce the metal diameter and to true it up with the bore. Mark Bansner is a big advocate of this as he believes it results in a much more professional looking end product. I would never argue with his professionalism, as the rifles he has built for me have been flawless.

▲ Turning the straight section over the chamber.

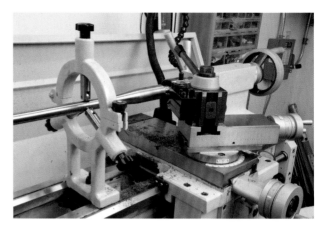

▲ The setup to turn the barrel. Note the use of the steady rest.

▲ This shows the lathe dog clamped on the barrel. Note the tape to protect the finish.

I am not sure what to call this part of the barrel as I think that every barrel maker I checked has designated this section of barrel differently in their dimension schematics. The bottom line; it is the large, usually straight, section at the rear, or breech end, of the barrel. It's the section where the chamber will be.

Some barrels come extra-large at the chamber with the idea that they will be turned down, but leaving options to allow for different cartridge diameters. For example, you could turn this section to a much smaller diameter for a .223 Remington than if you were chambering that same barrel for a .223 WSSM. Not that there is much reason to build the latter these days, but the point is valid.

One issue is stock fit. If you are fitting and bedding the stock completely, then the barrel diameter is not much of an issue as you can adjust the stock to fit the barrel. Some synthetic stocks come as blanks and require the entire barreled action be fitted. In that situation, make sure the barreled action will fit properly in the stock, then use bedding compound to do the final fit.

If you are into self-torture, you may want to hand fit a

wood stock. I understand there are those craftsmen who enjoy this process. I also understand there may be Bigfoots and unicorns. I don't pretend to understand any of them.

I admire their talents (the stock makers, not Bigfoot, it takes no talent to grow big feet) but I learned long ago that making a wood stock from a blank is "not my thing." If it is yours, you can make the barrel any diameter you wish and then spend hours and hours tediously scraping away the wood until it fits.

I put that talent in the same category as guitar playing. I have studied the basics and even some advanced techniques (at least with stock work). I have spent time watching some of the best in the world practice their craft and I still cannot make my hands do the right motions.

I know, it's just like Michelangelo said:

"I saw an angel in the stone and I carved until I set him free."

The best see a graceful stock in the wood and carve until they set it free. Me? I carve until the angel's wings are on the floor in the scrap pile and then I curse and order a new blank.

Clint was right, "A man's got to know his limitations." Mine are often found in wood. If you are a renaissance gunsmith who loves working with wood, you have my admiration.

I am not, nor likely will ever be, a stock maker, so most of the time I use a pre-contoured production made stock; wood or synthetic. I try to get the stock to match the barrel contours as close as possible before final fitting, but sometimes these large diameter rear sections can be difficult to fit into a pre-contoured stock, so turning the barrel to fit is a good idea.

When building the two 9.3X62 rifles mentioned in other chapters I used E. R. Shaw barrels that had a rather large diameter over the chamber. At his request, I left it full size for Tony Kinton's rifle as he wanted the extra weight. For mine, I turned it down a little, mostly to be different and to explore the options.

In the end, I can't see a bit of difference in the performance of the rifles. They both shoot very well and they both look just fine. But I did discover a few little things, at least from a gunsmith's perspective.

The pro side was it was much easier to fit my barrel to a pre-contoured rifle stock after I reduced the diameter of the chamber section. These stocks are usually designed to fit a common factory rifle barrel contour and when you deviate, they must be hand-fitted.

We had quite a bit of time into fitting Tony's to his wood laminate Boyd's stock. On the other hand, when we were doing it we were tired and out of time, which always makes this kind of work tedious and aggravating. We simply did not have the option of waiting, as he was flying home to Mississippi the next day with the rifle, so perhaps it seemed worse than it was.

On the other end of the time spectrum, even though we spent quite a bit of time fitting the stock, leaving Tony's barrel full size required a lot less time in setup and machining the barrel, so it's probably a wash in terms of work hours.

My stock was a Bell & Carlson synthetic and Wade Dunn had warned me that if I didn't turn some metal off the chamber area on the barrel there would be a fair amount of fitting needed.

I did turn the barrel and while the principal of fitting the two stocks was exactly the same, mine required a lot less time scraping material away to fit.

I didn't try to match the stock, as I didn't have it in hand when I started. I just turned metal until I thought it looked good. In the end, I spent a few minutes with a barrel channel scraper and it fit perfectly. If I had taken another .020 inch off the metal, that would not have even been needed. Sometimes planning ahead is a good thing, but this willy-nilly approach is a lot more fun.

The best approach, of course, is to know what barrel contour the stock is designed around and try to match that if possible.

Another important aspect of this was pointed out to me recently during a phone call with Mark Bansner. The bushings on your barrel vise must fit this flat on the barrel. Probably the most sensible approach is to turn the chamber section on the barrel to match the bushings you have for your vise.

I will note (and this is my fault) in finishing and smoothing out the contours on my barrel after turning it down, I contacted the barrel with the corner of my file. As I smoothed the angles with the barrel in the lathe, I focused on the area where I was working and lost track of the rest of the file. A corner contacted the barrel and left some deep scratches and I did a poor job of removing them. I had lots of opportunity to correct the problem and in fact I did fix most of it, but I did not do as good a job as I should have. I wanted the rifle finished in time for a hunt and got a bit lazy. My fault, but if I had not turned the barrel, it would not have happened.

On the other hand, this is a classic case of transference, trying to shift attention from the real problem, poor craftsmanship. The truth is simple: it was me, not the process.

I am not even sure why I put this in here, except it is bugging me to no end. So consider it a warning and a caution that each new process can have unintended consequences. Be prepared to deal with them properly rather than taking the easy road of lazy craftsmanship, something I detest. Particularly when I do it myself.

To beat the drum some more on a recurring theme, please learn from my mistakes. This time I made a mistake and then I got lazy about fixing it, which is the much bigger sin. It is probably not even noticeable to most people, but it bugs the hell out of me every time I pick up the rifle. If there is a lesson here, it's that this kind of perfectionist attitude will drive you crazy, but there is nothing in the world better for continuing to improve your craftsmanship.

REDUCTION PLAN

If you are going to turn the outside of the barrel over the chamber, it's probably best to face off both ends of the barrel and put a 60-degree bevel on the bore at each end, using a center drill.

Suspend the barrel on centers. Use a live center on the tailstock and make sure you have the tailstock precisely aligned as detailed elsewhere in the book. You can use a dead center in the lathe with a faceplate and a lathe dog, but it is much easier and simpler to use the technique outlined in the section on blueprinting an action to make a center and true it with your 3-jaw chuck. You will need a lathe dog to hold the barrel and turn it. Wrap some tape on the barrel to protect it from the lathe dog as it clamps tight.

Mark uses a live center on the chamber end and simply

▲ Mark Bansner's setup for turning the outside of the barrel.

clamps the last inch or so of the muzzle end in a 3-jaw chuck. He will first support the muzzle end with a live center and true up the outside to the bore. Then the 3-jaw is clamped over this trued section to turn the chamber section. That part of the muzzle end is cut off when the barrel is cut to final length.

Make your cuts small, light, and smooth, starting at the breech end of the barrel and letting the power feed run until the cutter is past the tapered contour and no longer cutting. Set the feed rate to give a nice finish. Remember to keep the RPM level low when using a lathe dog as it creates a weight imbalance.

Measure often, until you have the diameter you previously decided as your target goal. You may want to smooth out the transition where the taper to the smaller barrel diameter starts, as the edge can be pretty abrupt after machining. Use a file, but be very careful, because as you turn the file to follow the taper, the edge of the file can contact the barrel and scratch the hell out of it, just like mine did. Pay attention, that's all I am saying. Watch everything, miss nothing.

Also, be careful about where you remove metal with the file, as you do not want to create a dish shape in the barrel. Only remove enough metal to smooth out the transition from straight to taper on the barrel.

If you use a barrel spinner against a belt sander, you can do the contouring and smoothing and not risk the file causing damage. If you are going to use a spray-on coating you will need to sandblast the barrel at a later point. This hides a few small flaws, but not the deep ones. Bluing hides nothing, so the finish must be perfect. The key is to not introduce the flaws to start with and if you do, spend a little more time to completely remove them.

You can, of course, do this work with the barrel spinning on the lathe. If you decide to use sandpaper or emery cloth to smooth, contour or polish the barrel on the lathe, it is imperative you protect the lathe ways from the abrasive that comes off the paper. Cover all the ways and be careful removing the coverings so that you do not spill any of the abrasive. If this stuff gets imbedded in any part of the machine it can cause premature wear. Even if you use a cover, it's a good idea to perform a very thorough cleaning of the lathe before using it again.

Of course, if you are a coward, you can avoid all of this and simply thread and chamber the barrel just as it comes out of the shipping tube.

CUTTING EDGE

Now you are ready to thread and chamber the barrel. Most gunsmiths and barrel makers recommend you cut a little off both ends of the barrel before finishing them. That helps set back into a clear section of the rifling that has never been touched by tooling. If your barrel maker has it in their instructions, it's always best to do what they suggest.

I recommend that you cut the chamber end off now, but not the muzzle. Leave the barrel longer to allow better control while doing the machine work on the back end. If you cut both ends you may wind up short when trying to fit the barrel through the headstock and spider. The barrel must be long enough to hold the muzzle end in the spider and if it's too short, you will encounter difficulty supporting the muzzle while working.

If you have not done it already, it's not a horrible idea to put the muzzle end into the lathe and face it off to clean up the edges. However, don't make any major cuts. Just face it off clean and perhaps put a little bevel on the front of the bore with a center drill to allow easy access to the bore with the tooling, such as gage pins, that you will use to dial it into center.

You can cut off the back end of the barrel with a parting tool in the lathe, if you are into self-torture. That is one tool that is wonderful when it works and will make a strong man weep when it doesn't. Predicting which will happen takes witchcraft and black magic more than any machinist's skills.

▲ Cutting off a barrel with a band saw.

In my never humble opinion it's much faster and easier at this point to put the barrel in a vise and use a hacksaw, or use a power band saw to cut off the back off the barrel

▲ I don't like to cut off much on the breech end.

close to the final length. Leave enough to face it off in the lathe to true it up. Remember, the saw cut will probably not be square, as it's difficult to hold a tapered and contoured barrel perfectly square in a vise. Leave a little extra length, maybe a quarter inch, so when you face off the barrel to correct for the less than perfect cut, you have a final length that is correct. Even if it's still a bit long, you can remove metal with the facing tool until it's correct. But as always, once it's gone you can't put it back, so always favor the side of caution.

I have seen recommendations for cutting off more than an inch, but I think that's a lot for the breech end. I usually cut a half inch or even less, depending on how the barrel looks, how long the large chamber section is and what I want for a final product. It's important to have enough parallel section over the chamber for the barrel vise to hold when you mate the receiver and barrel. I cut most of this parallel section off on one barrel and had quite a time figuring out how to hold the barrel while I tightened it into the action.

▲ None of the inserts for my barrel vise would fit, so I made my own.

None of the inserts for my traditional barrel vise would work, as they slipped on the tapered shape of the barrel and none were sized to fit the smaller diameters. I finally used a hardwood block that was drilled to a slightly smaller diameter and split into two pieces. Wood itself does not grip well, so I coated it with powdered rosin and fitted the blocks in my milling machine vise.

Try fitting the barrel into your stock and match where the barrel best fits in the contour of the stock. I like to spend a little time putting the action, barrel, and stock all together like a jigsaw puzzle, just to see what is going to be a good fit. As with anything, you can always cut more off, but you can't add it back, so use caution. (I know this is repetitive, but it's important.)

If I am going to use a chassis or am planning on completely fitting a stock later where the placement of the barrel contours is not important, I leave the large, straight, chamber area as long as possible. If nothing else, if you shoot out the barrel someday, there may be enough material to set it back to clean rifling and start over, saving the price of a new barrel. In the end, I just hate cutting away anything I might need later, so I am pretty cautious about how much I chop off the end of the barrel without a compelling reason.

Remember, in the breech end you are removing the first few inches of rifling anyway, so it's not as important that the rifling be perfect as with the muzzle end. At the muzzle you are using the rifling, at the breech you are not. So, even if there is a little damage from manufacturing tooling in the chamber end, you are going to cut that away. Besides, the muzzle usually loses inches when you are fitting to the final barrel length, whereas the chamber end is often cut off just to clean things up. So, again, use caution.

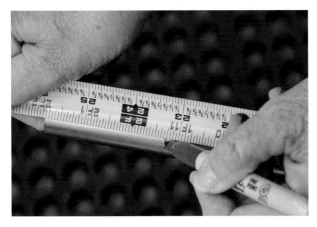

▲ Marking and cutting the barrel to its final length is best left until after you have the chamber end all machined.

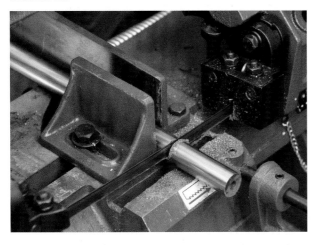

▲ Cutting the barrel to length is best left until after all the threading and chambering work is completed.

In some of my rifles I removed nothing more than to face off the breech end of the barrel. With barrels like Bartleins that have all the technical details stamped on the back, I cut off a medallion and keep it as a souvenir.

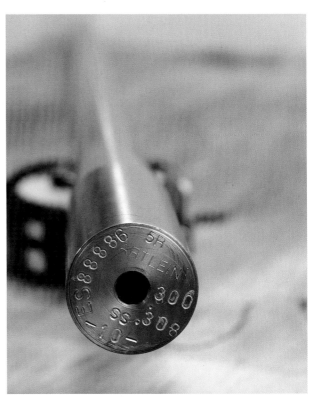

▲ Bartlein Barrels stamps a lot of info on the end of the barrel. I cut this off and keep it as a souvenir.

TO THE LATHE

Open the spider and the 4-jaw chuck to accept the barrel and carefully insert the barrel in your lathe. Use some soft metal shims to place between the jaws and the barrel. (The spider should have brass-tipped screws.) The shims do a couple of jobs. They protect the barrel from marring from the steel lathe jaws and they allow the barrel to move and flex just a little as you dial it into alignment. Brass seems like a good choice. It is soft enough not to mar the steel, but will still grip it well to hold it while working. It's also tough enough that it won't become malleable and flow under pressure, which could cause problems as you work. If the shim metal were malleable enough that it flowed as you were working, the barrel would lose center and your work would be inaccurate as a result.

I made my shims from empty brass .50 BMG cases. They are fine, but were a lot of extra work to get them just right. I had first thought I would leave the case heads to butt up against the lathe jaws, thinking that would look cool in the photos with the .50 BMG headstamps showing. But, the brass tapered too much up close to the case head and I had to move further up the case to find brass with less taper, which meant removing the case heads.

The shims I made work and I have used them on a lot of rifle barrels. But, as with any tool, you will always see some room for improvement over the first set you build. If I ever make another set of shims, I'll use flat stock rather than a cartridge case. I'll also make them large enough to hook over the top of the jaws to help hold them in place. My biggest complaint is that the shims can be difficult to keep in place when trying to do the initial setup. A design that will hold itself when the chuck jaws are loose would be a good idea. I have used thick grease on the shims to hold them in place on the chuck jaws. This works, but the grease is a little difficult to clean up after the work is done. That said, I continue using these shims, cussing when they fall out and making no attempt to replace them, so I guess I am pretty happy with their performance.

LONG OR SHORT

Many of the older texts about threading and chambering a rifle barrel show it being done with a steady rest out far away from the headstock and chuck. This is probably due to a couple of things. Many older lathes did not have a large enough spindle hole through the headstock to pass a large rifle barrel through. Often, the headstock was so long that some barrels would not pass out the other end enough to be supported. Even if one did, there was no way to support the muzzle end on those old lathes, as they did not ship equipped with a spider.

Many gunsmiths using an old lathe, including me with my old South Bend lathe, made "spiders" to mount on the outside of the headstock to support the muzzle end of the barrel, which solved one of the problems. This is one of the great features of the Grizzly gunsmith lathes, they come fully equipped with a spider to hold and adjust the muzzle end of the barrel. This feature is critical to the modern method of threading and chambering a rifle barrel while working close to the chuck. The Grizzly gunsmith lathes also have a large spindle hole and a short headstock.

Another, less mentioned issue is that many of the old, used lathes bought by amateur gunsmiths had worn ways near the chuck from years and years of use. If you moved down the ways to a less worn area and used a steady rest to support the barrel in that location, you could work with

more precision, at least in terms of having less need to compensate for wear on the ways.

I encountered all of these issues with my first lathe, an ancient South Bend that was made in 1941 and shipped to the Department of the Navy. By the time I acquired it, that old workhorse was pushing seventy years old and had some history behind it. It's a grand old lathe and still sits with honor in my shop. I learned a lot about running a lathe with this old classic, but, when I started to get serious about building precision, accurate rifles, I decided to upgrade to a newer machine. Much of this decision was because I wanted to start using modern techniques, which means doing the machine work on the barrel as close to the chuck as possible. The new Grizzly lathe has all the features I needed and zero wear on the ways.

It's important to have the barrel as tight to the chuck as you can and still have clearance to do the work. That means you need to know how long the shank will be. To get that measurement, clamp your blueprinted action into a vise with soft jaws or put it in an action wrench and clamp that into a bench vise. Insert the bolt, set the recoil lug on top of the action, and use a depth micrometer to measure from the top of the recoil lug to the front edge of the bolt lugs. That distance, minus a little clearance of about .010 inch, more or less, will be your final barrel shank length. For working on the lathe, I like to add at least another .030 inch as a cushion. The shank will be cut to the final length before chambering.

Place your barrel in the 4-jaw chuck, using the barrel shims. Check to make sure you can do all the work with plenty of clearance for all your tools. Run the tool holder to each extreme with the lathe shut off and turn the chuck by hand to make sure nothing will collide. I like to have at least one half inch of extra clearance to allow for slow reactions and other mistakes.

Clamp the barrel lightly and hold the muzzle end lightly with the spider. Turning the chuck by hand with the lathe turned off and in neutral will allow you to visually center both ends as best as you can.

INDICATING DIFFERENCES

There are two types of indicators that most gunsmiths will use the most, a dial indicator and a test indicator.

While there are a lot of differences between the two, the primary one is that dial indicators use a plunger-type movement that is straight in and out. Test indicators use a lever that moves on a pivot. Most gunsmiths will find that they need both.

Dial indicators tend to be larger and have a much greater range of motion than the test indicators. They will measure over several revolutions of the dial, usually with a second, smaller dial inset that indicates the multiple

(continued . . .)

revolutions. Dial indicators use a straight plunger motion, so they will return to the same point of contact even if the piece is moved up or down.

The longer range of motion means that a dial indicator is the obvious choice to measure movement over distance. For example, the cut for an M-16 type extractor on a Remington Model 700 rifle bolt is 1.26 inches long. If, like me, you do not have digital readout on your milling machine, a good approach is to use a two-inch range dial indicator to measure the progress of the cut. Many gunsmiths use a dial indicator to measure the progress of a chambering reamer. There are hundreds of other uses for a dial indicator and it's one of the most useful tools a gunsmith can have in the tool box.

A test indicator uses a lever that pivots to measure movement. They tend to be smaller than dial indicators and have a much smaller range of motion.

A dial indicator top, test indicator bottom.

The angular motion of the test indicator's lever allows the contact to ride easily over irregularities on surfaces. A dial indicator does not do that well, as its plunger can bind and push sideways against the contact.

A gunsmith will use a test indicator for many processes, but the most common use will probably be dialing a barrel into center in a lathe.

A test indicator.

When dialing a barrel into center, measuring off the bore, a test indicator can not only reach inside the barrel, but it will ride over the lands easily, allowing you to rotate the barrel and measure off the grooves.

Test indicators are smaller than dial indicators. The dial on a test indicator is small, compared to those on dial indicators, and a bit harder to see well. They usually have higher resolution than a dial indicator, but a much shorter range of measurement. Typical resolution for test indicators is .0001 inch to .00005 inch. For dial indicators it is .001 inch to .0001 inch. Dial indicators usually have a total measurement range of at least .250 inch, but are available up to two inches and perhaps more. The measurement range of test indicators is a lot less, usually between .008 inch and .030 inch, which is not a lot of movement.

Mark Bansner uses a dial indicator to dial in a rifle barrel.

One reason for the limited range of motion is that test indicators have only one revolution of the pointer around the dial. Most dial indicators allow 2.5 revolutions or more.

As a rule, test indicators are more expensive than dial indicators. No matter, don't cheap out with either of the indicators. You don't have to spend several hundred dollars on top of the line, but at least look for something in the middle range. Remember, these indicators are in charge of precision and the better the indicator, the more precise the result.

A hobby gunsmith starting out with a limited budget would probably be best served with a dial indicator, but plan to buy a test indicator as well just as soon as the checkbook allows. You will find both indispensable.

A test indicator left, dial indicator right.

ROUGHING IT IN

Start with the chamber end. You will need a point of reference to visually rough the barrel into center. I use a dial indicator that fits into a tool holder and position it off the barrel so it is not quite touching at the highest point. Anything that gives a visual point of reference is fine, even a parting tool or cutting tool. I like the parting tool as it has a large leading edge that is easy to see and works well for a visual reference.

Position the reference so that it just clears the barrel when the barrel is at its closest position as you turn the chuck. Then, turning the chuck by hand, you can visually see how the barrel is out of center and what adjustment is needed to correct. Keep the visual checkpoint close by moving it in as the barrel moves closer to center. Be careful to not make contact, as it can damage the tools and the barrel. Once I am close, I use a dial indicator on the outside of the barrel near the breech end to get the barrel centered in the chuck.

Now do the same on the muzzle end. The cover over the gears on my Grizzly lathe is alloy so a magnetic chuck will not stick. For a long time I removed the cover, which allows the magnetic chuck to clamp to the gear box and give easier access to the spider, but this exposes the turning gears and is a safety hazard. So I could work with the guard in place, I used double-sided tape to fit a piece of steel on the guard that allows me to use a magnetic base for an indicator. I use an indicator without contacting the barrel as a visual aid to rough it into center. When it's close, I run the indicator on the outside of the barrel to fine tune.

GETTING CENTERED

For the next step, which is dialing the barrel to exactly center, there are many options and many opinions about how to do it.

One of the popular theories today is that the bore is never straight in the barrel and that the barrel should be dialed into center and aligned with a short section of the bore just in front of the chamber. This is a bit more complicated when setting up the barrel in the lathe and will require the ability to measure the bore in at least at two locations deep inside. The spider and the 4-jaw chuck are used to align the barrel to this section of the rifling inside the barrel by measuring off each end of the chosen section.

This requires measuring deep in the bore. To do that, you will need a very long arm on a test indicator or you must use one of the specialty rods designed for this technique. They are available from Pacific Tool and Gauge, Dave Manson Precision Reamers or from Grizzly Industrial.

They are called Grizzly Rods or Gritters Rods after gunsmith Dave Gritters, who developed the concept. The rods are designed to be fitted with a bushing that is bore size. The rod is held in a Jacobs chuck in the tailstock and

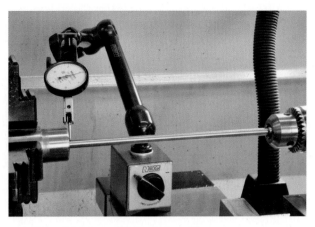

▲ The Grizzly or "Gritters" rod in use.

the bushing end is inserted to the desired location inside the bore. An indicator can be used on the section of rod projecting from the barrel to measure the center of the bore at the location where the bushing is fitted. The chuck and the spider are used to true a section of the barrel just in front of where the chamber will end. Then use a boring bar to pre-cut the chamber, truing it to that center.

The technique is detailed in much greater depth in the DVD available from Grizzly Industrial and titled *Chambering a Championship Match Barrel*.

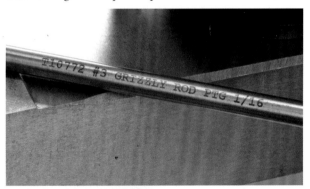

Many gunsmiths believe that centering both ends of the bore, that is, the chamber end and the muzzle end, will produce an accurate rifle. It was the gold standard before Gritters developed his concept.

This technique is easier to master for a new gunsmith and has worked well for me. My theory is that if I use a piloted reamer installed in a floating reamer holder, then the reamer will follow the bore and should be aligned correctly when the chamber is completed. This is likely the most common approach and is probably used by the majority of gunsmiths.

Is one approach better than the other? Who knows. Unless you could do a scientific, side by side accuracy comparison with multiple rifles it would be hard to prove, but both methods have and will continue to produce accurate rifles.

I encourage you to explore all the options and find one that works well for you. Here are the techniques I have used with success.

DROP A PIN

Perhaps the simplest way to center the barrel is to run a test indicator into the bore and let the ball of the arm ride on the rifling. Using only the grooves, or the low points for the indicator, dial the barrel into center. You must watch the indicator, as it will bounce as it passes over the lands. Take the readings only off the grooves. One potential issue is that, with some types of rifling with an odd number of lands and grooves, there are no opposing grooves. The adjustments on a 4-jaw chuck are made from four locations; it's necessary to use opposing measurements for centering the barrel.

Many gunsmiths use tapered indicating rods called Range Rods by PTG. Range Rods are caliber specific and require a fitted pilot bushing. The rods have a tapered section to center in the bore. To insure precision, it is suggested the gunsmith first cut a bit of the bore with a 60-degree center reamer with a fitted bushing. The problem with this approach for a hobby gunsmith is the cost adds up fast. By the time you buy the Range Rods, bushing(s) and reamer, it's pricey.

Perhaps the easiest approach is to use gage pins. These are precision ground steel pins that come in specific diameters. The standard pins are two inches long. They can be purchased in sets or as individual pins from most industrial supply catalogs.

The idea is to use the pin that fits tight in the bore so there is zero wobble. By pushing the pin most of the way into the bore you can run an indicator on the short, quarter-inch or so portion left sticking out of the barrel.

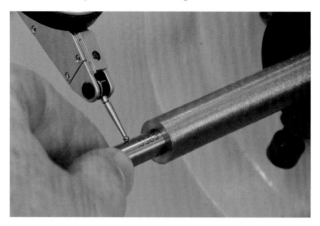

▲ Using a gage pin in the muzzle to dial in the spider.

▲ Using a gage pin in the bore to dial the barrel into center in a 4-jaw chuck.

Usually a pin the same diameter as the SAAMI specification for the land diameter for the barrel will be a good fit. However, the pins are not horribly expensive, so I ordered a few extra in half-thousandth increments for insurance. Even if it turns out they are not needed for the current job, they might be for a future barrel.

There are different classes of pins as well as plus and minus designations. Those designations are tolerance levels and they are important when the pins are being used for very precise gaging during some manufacturing processes. In this situation, we are just looking for a pin that is a good fit in the barrel. If it's a snug fit with zero wobble, it really doesn't matter if it's a class XXX or ZZ or if it is a plus or a minus. It just has to fit snugly in the bore.

For example, for a 30-caliber barrel, the SAAMI specification for the land diameter is .300 inch. (The one exception I found in a quick look at the *SAAMI Rifle Specifications* book is the .300 Weatherby, which for some odd reason is listed at .3005 inch.)

▲ Gage pins for a 30-caliber.

If you are building a 30-caliber rifle and feel lucky, just order a gage pin that is .30 inch. Or you can go in .001 increments and buy three, .300, .299 and .301. I did that with good luck for several barrel installs.

In my later builds, I ordered the pins in groups of five in half-thousandth increments to ensure an even more precise fit. Recently, I had occasion to be glad I did with the barrels for the 9.3X62 builds. The specifications for this European cartridge are not as clearly defined as those listed by SAAMI. While I expected to need a .357-inch gage pin, I wound up using a .358-inch gage pin at the chamber end and .3585-inch at the muzzle. The barrels were only tight in the last couple of inches at the rear. That part of the rifling was reamed out for the chamber and the barrels were very consistent for the remaining bore. The issue here is that I needed two different gage pins to dial in the barrels on the lathe. I'm not sure why the ends of the barrel were slightly different, but I was glad I had ordered the extra pins.

I will admit that this was cause for a little concern when building the two rifles, but both turned out to be excellent shooters, producing groups well under our target goal of 1 MOA. In my rifle, some factory loads shoot to half that, which is outstanding for any hunting rifle. I have expectations that handloads will be even more accurate, I just have not had time to test any at this writing.

So, for a 30-caliber barrel (which makes an easy example size to work with here) I would buy gage pins in .300, .3005, .301, .299 and .295. All five pins will run something less than $20 at 2018 prices, plus shipping. The shipping will be the same for one or five anyway, so a few extra bucks ensures you will have the exact pin you will need when you start the build.

SAAMI BORE DIAMETERS

The following is for the most common American cartridges. There may be variations, particularly with older cartridges and European cartridges.

CARTRIDGE	BORE DIAMETER IN INCHES
.17	.168
.204	.200
.22 Hornet	.217
.22	.219
.24 (6mm)	.237
.25	.250
.26 (6.5mm)	.256
.27	.270
.28 (7mm)	.277
.30	.300
.31 (7.62X39)	.300
.32	.315
.32 (8mm)	.311
.338	.330
.35	.349
.36 (9.3)	.354
.375	.366
.416	.408
.44	.424
.458	.450
.470 NE	.4587
.500 NE	.500

DIY GAGE PINS

Using a homemade gage pin to dial in the muzzle end in preparation for threading for a muzzle brake.

Homemade gage pins are a custom fit.

For several rifle builds, I made my own pins by machining brass rods that can be found at any hardware store. I custom size them for tight fit in the bore, like a gage pin. These rods are very inexpensive and come in long lengths, so for a few bucks you have material to make multiple tools.

Making your own gage pins is good practice and will help build your machining skills. It also gives you options. For example, you can make a long rod with a bore riding section on the end to use like a Grizzly Rod for dialing in at a location deep inside the barrel. Making these can be time consuming, but the result is good and there is a certain satisfaction in doing it yourself.

DIAL UP IS STILL COOL

The first time I dialed in a 4-jaw chuck it took me all afternoon. At the end I was frustrated, grumpy and convinced it was probably impossible. Then, for no discernable reason, it all came together. My mood improved and I was ready to start the lathe.

The point is, don't get too frustrated with your early attempts. It's a time consuming job even on the best days, but it's important that you get it exactly right. Dialing in a 4-jaw chuck is an acquired skill and I promise, it will get easier.

While a plunger type dial indicator will work, a test indicator is a far better choice for dialing in a barrel. They can be used to indicate directly off the bore and if nothing else, the lever action of the indicator is a bit more forgiving about placement on the pin or rod if you use one rather than indicating directly off the bore.

Buy a test indicator that measures at least to .0005 inch. That is one-half of one-thousandth of an inch. By watching the indicator needle you can dial into a fraction of that measurement. Look for little or no movement in the needle as you turn the chuck by hand. If you get that, you are on the way to building an accurate rifle.

They make indicators that measure to one ten-thousandth of an inch. They are much more expensive, but I am never one to discourage more precision. If you can dial in for no needle movement with a .0001-inch reading indicator, you will have nailed the center line. Fair warning though, dialing to, as they say, "one tenth" or less, is difficult. Also, little things like temperature changes can affect the reading and drive you crazy. If you spring for the better indicator and have the temperament to fight for the last fraction of one ten-thousandth of an inch, go for it. Precision is never a mistake.

Make sure that the barrel, lathe and all your tooling are temperature stabilized and have been for several hours. To save on heating costs, I keep my shop at 50 degrees in the winter on the days when I am not out there working. But, if I am going to be doing machine work of any kind, I turn it up to 65 degrees, my preferred temperature for a work environment, at least a day ahead of time. It's a good idea to run the lathe for a bit to warm up the bearings before inserting the barrel and getting started.

If you are ready to thread and chamber a barrel, then you should already have developed some machining skills. That should include how to dial in a 4-jaw chuck, but I'll cover some of the basics here anyway.

Remember that you are working with opposing jaws. When adjusting the barrel you will work with odd and even numbers. I numbered each of the jaws on my 4-jaw chuck using a paint pen so I can keep track.

Shut off the power to the lathe and put it in neutral. Turn the chuck by hand to align a jaw with the indicator. Then check the opposite jaw.

To make the adjustments, move both, one in and the other out. Split the difference on the indicator. For an easy example, if jaw #1 shows high and jaw #3 reads low, tighten #1 (the high side) half the distance between them. Loosen #3 the same. Repeat until the indicator shows the same number for both.

Now repeat for the #2 and #4 jaws. Just remember that moving the odd-numbered jaws will have an effect on the even-numbered jaws and vice-versa. That's the frustrating part. You get one set dialed in perfectly and then adjust the other set, only to go back to find the first set all out of kilter again. It's enough to make a bishop curse.

When you are very close, sometimes you can tighten the high jaw just a little without loosening the opposite jaw. This is for very small changes only.

Keep the faith, it does get easier. After you do it a few times, you will develop an intuitive feel about the process and it will go much faster. Like I said earlier, my first time took all of a long afternoon. Now I can do it in fifteen or twenty minutes on a good day. I have watched Mark Bansner dial in a 4-jaw in about five minutes, the damn show-off.

After you have the 4-jaw dialed in, move the gage pin and the indicator to the muzzle and repeat using the spider. The spider is not gripping the barrel against the machining stresses, so it does not need to be as tight as the 4-jaw chuck. Keep the screws snug, but don't tighten so much it flattens the brass ends. There is no need to ask me how I know this can happen.

After centering the muzzle, go back and check the breech end again. Don't be surprised if it's no longer centered. Moving one has an effect on the other. Re-center the breech, then repeat on the muzzle. Keep alternating until they are both running true and there is no bounce on the indicator as you turn the chuck for either end of the barrel.

Make sure that all the jaws on the chuck are tight and that all the screws on the spider are snug. This is a process and it can take a while, but there is an end, I promise. Often you will be surprised when all of a sudden everything is running true. Check and double-check, of course, before you start machining. Be fussy about this, as every cut you make from now on will be on the center of rotation you provided. If you keep the center of rotation exactly the same as the center of the bore, you should have an accurate rifle. Remember, everything is round with rifles: the bore, the bullet, and the cartridge. If you keep them on the same center, accuracy follows.

BANTERING WITH BANSNER

Mark Bansner suggested a few ideas about setting up barrels in the lathe. He will true the outside of the barrel over the breech. He runs the barrel on centers and takes a clean-up cut over the chamber area of the barrel to true it to the bore. He will often turn the diameter down smaller here to reduce weight and produce a more finished end product.

This surface can be used to rough in the barrel in the 4-jaw chuck. Then finish dialing in to center with one of several options, including those covered elsewhere in this book.

Mark did suggest two unique approaches. If you don't have a rod or gage pin to fit in the bore, use the expandable mandrels that come with a lot of bore-sighters. They work very well for dialing in the spider end of the barrel and in a pinch can be used for the chamber end.

Using a dead center to dial in the bore as described by Mark Bansner. The indicator should probably be a little closer to the barrel.

Another approach is to face off the breech end of the barrel, then use a precision ground dead center with the point in the bore and the back end fitted to a live center in the tailstock. Of course, the tailstock must be perfectly aligned, but that goes for any of these operations. See the section on how to align the tailstock elsewhere in this book.

Run an indicator on the precision ground taper on the dead center, as close to the barrel as you can get. This will true to the centerline of the bore. You can double-check and/or fine tune by running a test indicator inside the barrel and indicating off the grooves.

SHANKIN' IT

Face off the back of the barrel. Mark the length of the shank. I use a machinist's scale (ruler) and a medium felt marker to mark the location, with the rear edge being my initial cut-to goal. Marking with a felt marker is hardly precision, it's just a visual guideline, so make sure you are generous. If the shank is too long, it's not a problem. It's always easy to cut metal off with a facing tool. However, if it's too short, that is a problem. In fact, plan on it being too long for now. You will cut it to a precise length later in the process.

▲ The line from the felt marker is a guide.

I try to cut to the leading edge of the mark with my first pass. It's fine to cut into the mark just a bit with each successive pass, but never go past the back edge and remove the mark. You must always maintain it as a visual marker.

Turn the shank down to the correct diameter for your barrel threads. Remember, if you used the Manson kit to blueprint the action, the threads will be .010 inch oversized, so the shank should be to .010 inch larger than it would be for a standard thread.

The *Machinery's Handbook* states that a 1-1/16-16 Class 3A thread will have a major diameter of 1.0625 inch. When fitting a barrel to a Remington Model 700 receiver that has been blueprinted and trued using a Dave Manson Precision Reamers Accurizing System, the instructions recommend a diameter for the shank of 1.075 to 1.072 inches.

I always strive for the larger number, for a tight thread and to give me a bit of leeway if I make a small mistake. At the risk of sounding like a broken record, you can always take more metal off, but you can't put it back once it's gone.

Make sure your cutting tool is adjusted so that you can finish with a 90-degree shoulder. On the last cut, make sure you move into the shoulder enough to clean it up as you back the cutting tool away from the barrel.

Double-check that the shank diameter is correct and that shank length is slightly longer than the final number indicated. The amount is not critical, but don't go overboard. Something like .010 inch is plenty. If it is much too long, as may be the case because you were using a non-precision felt

▲ Measuring the shank diameter with a 1–2 inch micrometer.

marker, remove some by facing off the end of the barrel until it's .005 inch to .010 inch longer than your final length. Too short is, of course, a problem, but, if it's too long, it can cause problems when threading as well.

GETTIN' GROOVY

The next step is to cut a relief groove for threading. This is a groove between the thread and the shoulder and it allows a couple of things. First, it allows the thread to end properly, so that the barrel will tighten correctly into the action. It also gives you a little space to stop the advance of the threading tool. The idea is to let the tool cut the thread until it passes the edge of the groove and is no longer cutting. Then, before the tool can pass the groove and contact the shoulder, the lathe operator stops the forward advance.

There are tools designed for grooving, or you can use a parting tool. Make sure the tool holder is perfectly square to the machine axis. I do this by using a 1-2-3 block against the face of the chuck and then squaring the tool holder against the other end of the block. Also, as with any cutting tool used on the lathe, it should also be cutting on center.

▲ Cutting the groove.

I have several parting tools that range in thickness from .090 inch to .135 inch and have tried them all for a threading relief groove. For the threading tool I use, I found a 1/8-inch wide (.125-inch) groove works fine on a barrel shank. As long as it's narrower than the recoil lug, the width is not all that critical. However, it's not a bad idea to keep it as narrow as you can. This allows leeway to move the shoulder back if you run the chamber reamer in too deep, which is easier to do than you might think.

I prefer to run the parting tool so it is not quite contacting the shoulder. Some say it's okay to create the shoulder with the parting or grooving tool and that may be fine, but I much prefer to cut it with the same indexable turning cutter I use for turning the shank. Since the shoulder is already machined, I prefer not to mess with it at this point. So, when setting up for the relief groove, I think it's best to keep the tool out of contact with the shoulder.

▲ A cigarette paper is almost exactly .001 inch thick.

At least .001 inch off. That just happens to be the thickness of a Zig Zag cigarette rolling paper. Use the paper as a feeler gauge to adjust the tool to the shoulder. Just keep in mind that it is paper and subject to crushing or cutting from the tool. Adjust for a slip fit and it should be fine, crush or cut the paper and you may be contacting the shoulder.

Coat the shoulder with Dykem or with a felt marker to give a visual indication in the event you contact it with the tool. If that's the case, it will need to be cleaned up later, after completing the threading operation. The truth is, often you will need to clean it up anyway, because the threading tool made contact at some point, but I try to make a nice clean shoulder and not damage it in any way. I don't always succeed, but it gives me a goal and keeps me on my toes while machining and threading the shank.

I love the looks I get when people see the Zig-Zag papers in my toolbox. Of course, I didn't want anybody to think I was a stoner, so I had my wife buy them for me.

Run the lathe at its slowest setting and use plenty of cutting oil. The bottom diameter of the groove must be slightly smaller than the minor diameter of the thread. The *Machinery's Handbook* lists the minimum, minor diameter for a 1-1/16-16 Class 3A thread as .9880 inch. If you add .010 inch for the oversize thread, that makes it .9980 inch. It is fine for the groove to be deeper than the minor diameter, but not acceptable for it to be larger. If it's larger, the threading tool will continue to cut along the bottom of the groove and the barrel may not tighten to the action correctly, so cut the groove deeper than the thread. In this case, a Remington 700 with oversized threads from blueprinting the action, I make it .980 inch to .975 inch. Of course, you will need to adjust accordingly for any other rifle you are building.

▲ Measuring the depth of the relief groove.

The beveled end of most dial or electronic calipers should fit into the groove to measure the diameter.

START A NEW THREAD

You should know the basics of threading long before you started on a rifle barrel, but I'll cover some of them here as they apply to fitting a barrel to a blueprinted Remington Model 700 action.

Make sure you have the proper thread cutting tool to make a 60-degree, 16 thread per inch (tpi) thread. Set the lathe to cut the correct thread pitch. There should be a chart on the lathe and/or in the owner's manual for the settings. Check, recheck and double-check that all the settings are correct. For my Grizzly lathe, there are multiple gears, dials and levers that must be adjusted and if even one setting is not correct it will screw up the thread.

▲ There are multiple settings for each thread.

The compound should be set to 29 or 29.5 degrees. Most sources say this is not critical, as long as the angle is less than half the included angle of the thread, which is 60 degrees. So if you set to 29 degrees instead of 29.5, it should be fine. The idea is to be slightly less than half the included angle, but never more.

▲ Do not use the scale on the Grizzly lathe to set the compound for threading.

Remember that on a Grizzly lathe, or at least on mine, the scale on the compound is 90 degrees off for this chore. If you set it to 29.5 on the scale it will be wrong. I know this, because I cut a bunch of really horrible looking threads before my son Nathan figured it out.

I had called all my "Help, I am in deep doo-doo" friends, I had rechecked every book I had and I surfed the web until I about wore it out. They all said the same thing: 29.5 degrees should be perfect when cutting a 60-degree

thread. The scale on my compound was very clear and I had set to 29.5, yet the threads looked awful.

Nathan is a machinist and an engineer and when he was home for Christmas that year my gift to him was the parts to make a rifle. When we started cutting the barrel thread he was smart enough to stop after a few passes. He recognized that something was wrong, so he reset the compound to zero, which is an option and finished the thread for his rifle. It turned out very nicely by the way and it's a very good shooter.

Later, we got talking about what was going on and he realized we were using the wrong axis. The scale on the lathe is relative to the axis of the work. The 29.5 degrees so often used in threading is relative to the face of the chuck, or 90 degrees off from the scale on the lathe. Once we realized that, everything fell into place.

To correctly align the compound you can use this simple trick: Loosen the locks and turn the compound so that the feed wheel is pointed at you. This should put it at 90 degrees to the axis of the work piece and/or the lathe axis. Now rotate the compound counterclockwise 29.5 degrees. This is the correct location for cutting a 60-degree thread. If the scale on the Grizzly had a 60.5-degree mark, that is what it would read, but it stops at 60 degrees, so the indicator will be just past that.

▲ Using an adjustable protractor to confirm the angle is correct for the threading tool.

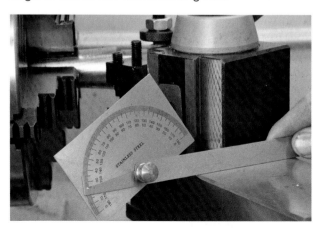

As there were no marks on my lathe to locate the correct position, I used an adjustable protractor to measure from the face of the chuck to make sure I had the angle correct. On my lathe the correct setting puts the locator off the chart on the compound, so I made a small mark that I can return to each time I have to cut a new thread.

▲ Using a 1-2-3 block to adjust the threading tool.

Once the compound angle is set correctly, square the cutting tool to 90 degrees to the work. If you are using an indexable cutter, setting it square is easy with a 1-2-3 block. Put one edge against the flat on the face of the 4-jaw chuck and adjust the edge of the tool holder against the opposite end of the block. Tighten the tool holder in place.

▲ Using a fishtail gauge to square the threading tool.

Another method to square the tool is to use a fishtail 60-degree center gauge. These tools are inexpensive and can be pretty handy. Place the gauge against the work and use one of the 60-degree notches to align the thread cutting tool. If you are grinding your own threading tool or using any sort of tool that is not locked into the tool holder precisely, this is probably the best method. Using the 1-2-3 blocks squares the tool holder, which is fine if the cutting tool is correctly located. Using a 60-degree center gauge actually aligns the cutter itself, which is a sure thing.

You can use a Zig Zag cigarette paper to touch off the cutting tool. The paper is about .001 inch thick and can be used as a feeler gauge to set the cutter. With the threading cutter just touching the work, adjust the cross slide and the compound feed wheels to zero.

▲ Set both wheels to zero before threading.

Back off the cross slide and run the tool back to the start position, which is a small distance off from the end of the work. Return the cross slide wheel back to zero, which puts the cutter back to the starting position where it is just flush with the work piece. With the wheel on the compound, feed a very small amount forward, just a few thousandths of an inch. The cutter should be advanced just far enough to make a deep scratch on the work surface.

▲ Use the compound to advance the thread depth.

When cutting a thread, the half-nut on the lathe is engaged at a specific point as determined by the numbers on the threading dial. The correct number(s) for your thread will be marked on the thread chart for the lathe. With an even number thread like the 16 tpi we are cutting here, there are multiple options. Again, as a hobby gunsmith, I take a cautious approach.

Even though a 16 tpi thread can use several numbers, to avoid confusion I use #1 on the thread dial each and

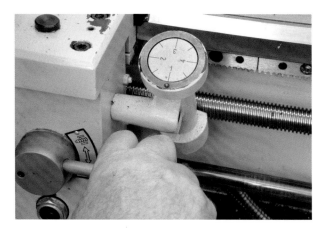

▲ Engaging the half-nut to start the threading process.

every time. It's a bit slower as I am often waiting for it to come around, but it allows some control. It also gives me a little time to think about what I am doing, which helps keep mistakes at a minimum.

Use a very slow setting on the lathe so you have good control. Later, as your skills progress, you can turn up the RPMs a little. Start the lathe and when the correct number is aligned with the mark on the threading dial, engage the half-nut. This starts the thread cutter moving down the work piece at a speed that is correlated with the rotation speed perfectly to make a 16 tpi thread.

The thread cutter should be making a visible but shallow scratch cut. When the cutter passes into the relief groove, disengage the half-nut very quickly to stop the advance. Shut off the lathe. Back the cross slide out and run the cutting tool back to the start point. Then reset the cross slide to zero.

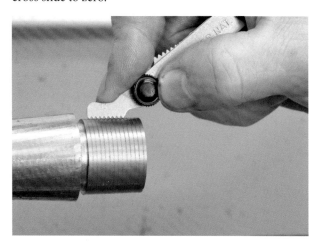

▲ Checking the first "scratch" pass to make sure the thread pitch is correct.

With a thread measuring screw pitch gauge, measure the scratch cut using the 16 tpi blade. The marks should line up perfectly with the teeth on the gauge. If not, recheck all the settings.

Once you are satisfied the lathe is cutting the correct pitch thread, you can start threading.

Use plenty of cutting oil at all times. Feeding will be with the compound, never the cross slide. The cross slide wheel is used to back the tool out to allow it to run back to the starting point. Then the cross slide wheel will go back to zero. This brings you back to the last point where you made a cut. Advance the compound feed a small amount for a deeper cut and make another pass on the thread. Again, I think it's best to use the same number on the threading dial every single time, so wait for #1 on the threading dial to engage the half-nut.

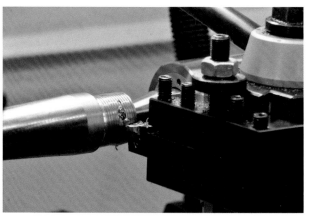

▲ Cutting a thread on a rifle barrel. Always use plenty of cutting oil.

It's always better to make multiple small cuts and a lot of passes. On every fifth pass, do not advance the compound before starting the cut. Simply leave it at the same setting as the last pass. This will clean up the thread and compensate for any spring back.

As the thread begins to take shape start checking with the receiver to see how close it's getting to fitting on the thread. Each time you check, clean the threads with a wire brush before stopping the lathe. Use a file with a handle to make a small bevel on the start of the threads. Stop the lathe, move the tool out of the way and attempt to thread the receiver onto the barrel. At first it won't go, but sooner or later it will start on for a thread or two.

From this point on, work very carefully. Take only a few thousandths with each cut and check the fit again after each pass. As the thread is cut deeper, the receiver will begin to screw onto the barrel a little bit further each time. The goal is to reach the point where the receiver will screw onto the barrel easily and without interference, but with a tight fit that allows little or no wobble. You do not want to force the threads, so, if it resists, cut the thread a little bit deeper.

Of course, each time you check the threads on both the barrel and in the receiver they must be clean, free from any chips and well lubricated. The goal is to cut the thread just to the point where the receiver screws onto the barrel with minimal torque and is smooth and even for the entire thread. If it starts binding near the end, you need another small cut with the threading tool. Remember, though, that the barrel will not thread all the way into the receiver without the recoil lug in place. Also, the shank is still too long and the thread may be longer on the barrel than the threaded portion of the receiver. Do not be fooled by any of this into thinking you need to cut the thread deeper.

As you approach the last few passes run a file *lightly* over the top of the barrel threads to remove burrs and clean up the top of the threads. Also, use the file to put a larger taper on the end of the threads. This allows easier starting.

▲ The completed thread.

The thread is complete when you have the barrel thread matched exactly to the receiver thread and the two fit together smoothly and without interference. This is a custom fitted thread that is mated perfectly to the blueprinted receiver. When you screw them together with the recoil lug in place the receiver should come to a hard and sudden stop with a "clunk," as everything tightens up.

It's not uncommon to hit the shoulder with the threading tool, causing minor damage. Or you may have contacted it with the grooving tool. It's important to clean it up and bring it back to a precision, square shoulder. I use a long, diamond shaped indexable carbide cutter which will fit inside the clearance groove. After carefully adjusting the cutter, start at the bottom of the groove and cut slightly into the shoulder. It will clean up as the cutter is slowly backed out. Take off just enough to clean up the shoulder and no more. Marking the shoulder with Dykem before cutting allows visual confirmation that it is fully machined.

CUTTING THOSE "FOREIGN" THREADS

Cutting a metric thread on a Grizzly lathe (and probably other brands as well) is a little bit different than cutting an inch-based thread. The inch base threads are called American Standard Unified Screw Threads. For this thread, the machinist can use the thread dial and half-nut on the lathe to ensure the thread is picked up correctly by the thread cutting tool for each pass. That method allows disengaging the half-nut so the thread cutting tool can be backed out and the carriage moved back to the start position for another pass. To start the next pass the half-nut is engaged when the correct number on the thread dial is aligned with the fixed marker and that ensures the thread cutting tool will engage the thread correctly.

If you are cutting a metric thread, that method will not work. Once it's engaged, the half-nut cannot be disengaged.

Make sure the work has been turned to the correct diameter, that you have the proper thread cutting tool installed and that it is correctly aligned. Find the correct thread pitch on the metric thread chart on the lathe or in the owner's manual for the lathe. Set all the switches, dials, gears, and gizmos to the indicated setting for the thread pitch selected, just as you would for an inch-based thread. Most V-threads are 60 degrees, even for metric, so setting the compound to 29.5 as described above is still correct.

The main difference between inch-based and metric threading is that when cutting metric threads, the half-nut lever must never be disengaged. That means that at the end of each pass, the machine must be stopped and then run in reverse to move the cutting tool back to the start position.

At the end of the pass, as the threading cutter enters into the relief groove, use the foot brake to stop the machine. If you try to stop the machine with the power switch or even the red safety switch, the momentum will allow it to continue enough for the cutting tool to collide with the shoulder on the barrel. This results in a lot of bad things like broken cutters, damaged barrels, and a gunsmith with a nasty attitude. The foot brake stops the machine instantly and turns it off. It means you have to turn the machine back on before you can use it again, which takes a few steps and a few seconds.

After stopping the machine, back the cutting

(continued . . .)

tool out of the thread, using the cross slide just as you would for an inch-based thread. Then run the lathe in reverse to move the threading tool back to the start position. This time you can use the power switch to stop the machine.

Use a metric thread measuring screw pitch gauge to make sure the first cut is the right pitch.

Reset the cross slide, adjust the compound for the next cut and start the machine in forward. Because the half-nut has remained engaged, the thread cutting tool will correctly pick up the thread for the next pass. Repeat this process until you have a finished thread.

▲ Measuring the bolt counterbore diameter with an inside micrometer.

▲ Measuring the bolt counterbore depth with a depth micrometer.

ENDING IT

The finished shank proper final length is the measurement made from the receiver face, including recoil lug, to the top of the bolt lug, minus the clearance. For a precision rifle I use .005 inch clearance, for a hunting rifle .010 inch clearance. Obviously, there is a tolerance here. The bolt should never contact the barrel, but if you are off a thousandth or two it's fine. This is a clearance, not a part fitting dimension, so it's not as critical. Just do not make the gap too small because dirt, crud, fouling, carbon, or heat expansion could cause the bolt to bind against the barrel. It also should not be too big, for safety reasons.

▲ Ready to cut the bolt counterbore recesses with a boring bar. The relief cut at the start of the threads is a bit too large on this barrel.

The famous Remington "three rings of steel" design requires a recess be cut into the back of the barrel for the front, or nose, of the bolt to fit into. You can do this with a small boring bar. In fact, I encourage you to do a few barrels that way to learn the process and so that later you will appreciate the genius of Dave Manson.

▲ Nathan Towsley cut this bolt counterbore with a boring bar.

For this approach, first face off the end of the shank to the final length. The counterbore must provide clearance for the leading edge of the bolt. The diameter of a Remington bolt is .700 inch, so the diameter of the counterbore should be .705 inch to .710 inch. That is, unless you are going to install an M-16 or similar extractor. In that case the counterbore must be larger to allow the extractor to pivot. The exact diameter should be included in the instructions with the extractor kit. For example, the print that comes with the Badger Ordnance M-16 extractor kit shows the diameter of the counterbore as .785 inch.

The depth should be enough to allow clearance so the bolt lugs do not contact the back of the barrel and they have a sufficient clearance. I measured a new Remington bolt and from the front to the bolt lugs is .145 inch. Of course, this might change just a bit if you faced off the lugs to square them when prepping the bolt. Either way, a depth of .155 inch should work fine.

If you wish to fine tune the fit by measuring the bolt and allowing for the clearance already built into the barrel shank, leave at least .010 inch clearance.

▲ The Manson Bolt Body Counterbore Cutter. Note the Dykem to show when the cutter is deep enough to start cutting the shank.

start the pilot into the bore of the barrel. Using a lot of cutting oil, slowly feed the Bolt Body Counterbore Cutter into the barrel using the tailstock quill. Watch carefully until the facing cutter just removes all of the dye from the Dykem or felt marker. Continue feeding for another .003 inch.

▲ This Bolt Body Counterbore Cutter shows the genius of Dave Manson.

It's much easier to use a Bolt Body Counterbore Cutter from Dave Manson Precision Reamers. The first time you use it, you will fall in love. What will take a lot of time with a boring bar, the reamer does in a few minutes. It really is a "must have" tool for building rifles.

The Bolt Body Counterbore Cutter cuts the counterbore to .705 inch inside diameter and a depth of .155 inch and faces off the end of the barrel shank, all in one operation.

To use it, face off the shank with a carbide facing tool, leaving it .005 inch longer than the final length. Mark the end of the shank with a felt marker or coat it with Dykem.

The Bolt Body Counterbore Cutter uses a replaceable pilot, which should be fitted to ride in the bore, so make sure you have the correct diameter pilot installed. You can use your gage pins to measure the land diameter and subtract .0005 inch.

This tool works best in a floating reamer holder, which is a tool also useful for both chambering and cutting the crown. It is a great investment for any gunsmith.

Set the lathe to its slowest speed, turn it on and carefully

▲ Measuring the final shank length with a depth micrometer.

Stop, clean everything, and carefully measure the shank length, which should be within .001 inch of your target. Again, this is a clearance number, so just make sure you have enough clearance between the barrel and the bolt lugs as noted before. If it's a few thousandths too short, that's probably okay, but, if the shank is too long, feed the reamer in a little more until you hit the target length.

Now you are ready to chamber the barrel.

MIRROR IMAGE RIFLES

It was January and we were 60 kilometers north of Budapest, Hungary, which puts the latitude somewhere close to Quebec City's. I had not dressed for the weather and I was so cold I almost wasn't ready when a huge European wild boar broke cover.

He was surrounded by a dozen howling, darting dogs and I had to watch carefully through the trees for an opening that was both dog and brush free. This boar looked as big as a grizzly and at the shot he staggered, turned, spotted me, and charged. I had to wait for him to clear some brush before I got off the next shot. When the bullet struck, he dropped, skidded down the steep hill a few feet, and stopped close enough that he sprayed snow on my boots.

When I start to waver in my arguments with those who somehow think it's a heroic thing to hunt with a small cartridge, I remember that day and genuflect once more at the altar of big bullets.

I had wanted a 9.3X62 since I first saw one while hunting in Zimbabwe decades ago. After this boar, I knew I had to have one and that was only reaffirmed during a few more European boar hunts.

My buddy Tony Kinton shared the same longing, so we decided to build a couple of rifles in 9.3X62. Tony flew from Mississippi up to my Vermont home and we spent several days building his rifle. Then we headed to Vermont's Northeast Kingdom for a little woodcock hunting with my friend Bob Rose and his Old Hemlock setter, Fionn. A day later, Tony and his rifle headed south, while I started building my rifle the following week.

The guns are mirror images, as Tony's is left-handed and mine is right-handed. I am a lefty, but I shoot right with long guns. The reason (I think) is that nobody taught me to shoot. When I was a kid, they just turned us loose with our BB guns. Those were different times, that's for sure. As long as we got home for supper and no cops showed up, nobody much cared what we were doing. (For the record, I was not able to keep the "no cops" part of the bargain.) Everybody else shot right-handed, so I did too. By the time I figured it all out, it was too late to change. I took up handguns later in life, when I was in my teens, so I shoot handguns left and long guns right.

Tony and I had matching, mirror-image Remington 700 actions. I blueprinted them with the Manson kit and modified the receivers to take 8-40 scope base screws.

Then I fitted E. R. Shaw barrels. We were both on a tight budget and the E. R. Shaw barrels are relatively inexpensive and provide an excellent bang for the buck. (Pun was intended.) Another big reason is that E. R. Shaw had 9.3 barrels in stock and there wasn't a long wait for delivery. My barrel is 25 inches, while Tony's is 26 inches. I like to cut my barrels to odd numbers, just to be different. Tony is pretty

My 9.3X62 rifle.

This is Tony's left-handed rifle.

The author lapping the bolt lugs on Tony's rifle. Note the orderly work bench.

Bob, Fionn, and Tony.

conventional. The 9.3X62 cartridge responds well to these long barrels and measured muzzle velocity usually is a bit higher than the published velocity for a given bullet weight.

I finished both barrels with an 11-degree crown. I used a Holland oversized recoil lug on both guns, modifying the receiver to allow using the alignment pin that comes with these recoil lugs as detailed elsewhere in this book.

We had big plans to hunt whitetails and hogs in Mississippi, in early 2018, but, as they say, the best laid plans, yada, yada, yada. Or as another old saying suggested would happen, "God laughed at our plans."

The first blood from either of the rifles was when Tony whacked a big Cape buffalo in May 2018. One shot dropped the bull where he stood. Tony provided a second insurance shot even though it was not needed. The old truth with Cape buffalo is that, "it's the dead ones that get up and stomp you" so a smart hunter sends insurance.

Both rifles are finished in Cerakote Elite in Smoke color, which is a unique and different look that I really like. Tony's rifle is fitted with a Boyd's laminated wood stock. Mine is in a Bell & Carlson synthetic stock. Both are fitted with fully floated barrels and with the action glass-bedded to the stock.

Both rifles have Timney triggers. Yes, Timney makes a left-handed trigger for the Model 700 with the safety in the correct position.

Tony reported groups right at MOA with Hornady factory loads and handloads using Barnes TSX bullets.

My first time at the range, I shot Norma 232-grain Oryx factory loads, which I planned to use for deer and hogs. The three-shot groups averaged right .6 inch, which put a smile on my grumpy face.

I have shot this rifle a bunch more and it shoots everything well and some ammo extremely well. It is capable of ½ MOA with several factory and handloads.

Tony Kinton with a Cape Buffalo shot with his 9.3X62 rifle. Barnes 286 grain TSX bullet.

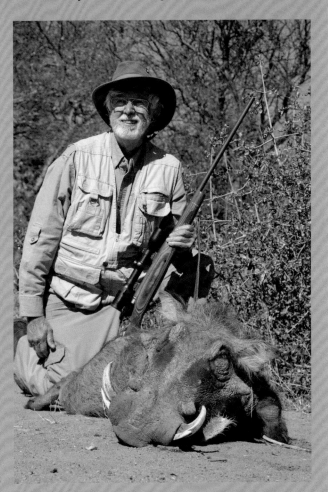

Sam Valentine borrowed Tony Kinton's 9.3X62 rifle to shoot this warthog. Reports are it was like a semi-truck was dropped on the boar and he simply quit without argument.

CHAPTER 16

CHAMBER OF HORRORS?

Maybe not.

Chambering a rifle barrel would seem to be one of the most daunting tasks a hobby gunsmith can tackle. It's filled with mystery, intrigue and, many would have you believe, a deep dose of black magic.

There is so much information and misinformation out there you might think that only those who belong to the Secret Society of Master Gunsmiths and have risen to the 32nd Degree of Grand Masters can do this properly. It's enough to scare a lot of would-be gunsmiths off to the nearest church to ask for forgiveness for even thinking about chambering a rifle.

When I was teaching myself how to do this I consulted with a lot of other gunsmiths, both professionals and hobby guys. I have also talked with the people who make the reamers and other tools and of course I have read most of the books and watched some of the videos. (Nobody could watch *all* the stuff on YouTube and remain sane.)

I have discovered that there are a lot of differing opinions about how to chamber a rifle barrel. I have talked with some big name guys who claim their method is the only correct approach to chambering a rifle, while the next big name guy is just as adamant about his much different approach being the only way to success. They can't all be right or all be wrong. The odd thing is that they all build accurate rifles. That's because all their secret formulas pretty much end up in the same place. Sure, there are a few subtle things that probably make one slightly better than the other, but in the end if the gun shoots and groups tight, you got it right.

Like most things in gunsmithing there may well be more than one "right" way to chamber a barrel. The one thing I am sure of is that chambering a barrel is not magic or voodoo. I'll admit, it's a bit tricky, but so what? There are a lot of machining processes used in gunsmithing that are tricky. Those are the challenges that make this hobby so interesting.

Rest assured you won't need to draw a pentagram with Speedy-Dry and garlic around your lathe to ward off evil spirits. No need to burn candles or chant when you are chambering a rifle. (Still, if you wanted to, I can't see that any of it would hurt anything.)

This is a simple machining job, removing metal, nothing more, nothing less. Take your time, stay focused, use good tools and you will be rewarded with a fine-shooting rifle. Cut corners and you end up with something else.

There are some differences between hobby gunsmiths and the pros. Mainly, the pros will build multiple rifles in a given time span, while a hobby gunsmith will only build a few guns. The pros do it for a living, so time is money and they must turn out the work to pay the bills. We hobby gunsmiths do this for recreation and have all the time needed to finish the project.

That difference is reflected in several aspects of chambering a barrel. I am going to explain the system I have developed that works well for me. Frankly, some of the pros will scoff and laugh, but this works. I have run it by several professional gunsmiths like Mark Bansner and Jim Majoros and with reamer maker Dave Manson. They have all pointed out that it's a bit slow and meticulous as an approach for a professional trying to make a living. They have also agreed that this method will result in a very precise rifle chamber.

First is the issue of reamers. They are expensive, so a lot of pros use a roughing reamer to start the chamber and remove the bulk of the metal. This is to save wear and tear on their finish reamers. Mark Bansner has a set of high-quality drills he uses to remove much of the metal in the chamber before finishing with a reamer.

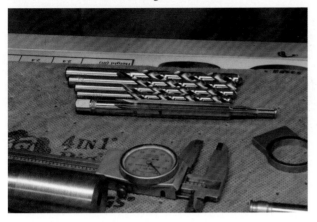

▲ Bansner uses a series of drills to pre-cut the chamber.

I was wrestling back and forth with which technique to use and called Dave Manson to talk about buying a roughing reamer for my first gun build. What I got was some honest advice and Dave actually talked me out of spending more money with him.

Dave suggested that the best approach for a hobby gunsmith is to simply use the finish chambering reamer to cut the chamber, start to finish. For the pros, that means the job takes longer and the reamer wears out or gets dull and needs to be sharpened or replaced much sooner. The thing is, a hobby guy may only build a few guns in a given cartridge and doesn't have to worry about such things. Dave suggested that a gunsmith could easily chamber 10 or a dozen rifles using this method before a reamer needs attention. While that's a good week or a busy couple of days for a lot of professional gunsmiths, it's most likely a lifetime of use for a hobby guy.

If you are like most hobby gunsmiths, you will build a rifle for yourself and maybe a few more for friends with any given cartridge. Then you will move on to the next project and next cartridge. That reamer may come out of retirement once in a while, but it will never see the kind of use it would with a high-volume professional gun builder. In a popular cartridge, a custom gun maker may build dozens and dozens of rifles and reamer wear is a very important aspect of cost control. With hobby gunsmiths, reamers are more in danger of rusting than being worn out.

Another advantage of using the finish reamer start to finish is that the reamer, particularly one with a removable pilot that can be precisely fitted to the bore, will be guided by the pilot right from the start. If you first remove metal

from the chamber by any method, it's possible that the finish reamer will start cutting before the pilot is inside the bore and under control. This can lead to chatter and/or misalignment of the reamer. By using your finish reamer start to finish, it is guided by the pilot the entire length of the chamber.

There is much attention given in any instruction about chambering to the chamber being aligned with the bore. It seems to me that if you use a correctly fitted pilot to guide the reamer it will follow the path of the bore pretty precisely. Of course, you must take great care to have the barrel dialed into center in the lathe. I also use a Manson Floating Reamer Holder that allows the reamer to shift and move, so it can follow the path of the bore as guided by the pilot. If the reamer is held rigid in the tailstock and the bore is not straight, the tailstock not perfectly aligned, or the barrel not dialed exactly into center, the result can be an oversized or misaligned chamber.

▲ Starting to chamber a .308 Winchester Barrel. Note that you can see the shoulder just inside the chamber. This one has a long way to go.

After threading the barrel and before starting to cut the chamber, I check to make sure the barrel is still dialed into center. As explained earlier in the chapter on threading the barrel, I use a tight fitting gage pin and check both ends of the barrel to ensure nothing has moved during the threading process. Sometimes I need to tweak the adjustments just a bit to bring the bore back to the exact center of the axis.

The biggest problem with chambering, at least for me, is to control the depth. The pros often "cut to the numbers." That is to say they use the headspace gauge to measure the depth of the chamber, usually from the barrel face. Then they measure the action to the bolt face and do the math to figure how much further they need to cut. Most also add in a .002-inch to .003-inch crush factor for the threads to tighten up and "crush." Then they set up the final cut and run the reamer to the number they selected. The depth is measured with a digital readout (DRO) or a dial indicator to keep it very precise.

I have seen Mark Bansner use this method, run the reamer into the barrel the exact amount of his calculations and hit the headspacing dead nuts every time. But, he does this every day and is a master at the process. A hobby gunsmith may only chamber a few guns a year. That means skills can get rusty, or may never be fully developed.

CUT TO THE NUMBERS

Here is how to cut a chamber "to the numbers," as explained by Mark Bansner. This is to be employed once you are very close to the final depth of the chamber.

Make sure that the bolt does not have the firing pin, extractor or ejector installed. Place the bolt in the action and close it fully. Using a depth micrometer, measure the distance from the end of the action to the front of the bolt face where it contacts the head of the cartridge. On a Remington, you will need to include the recoil lug, so simply set it on top of the receiver before measuring. Or you can measure the recoil lug with a micrometer and add in that dimension.

Write the number down as the first measurement.

Now measure the distance from the shoulder on

This is Mark Bansner's setup when chambering. He uses the dial indicator to cut to the numbers.

the barrel to the end of the barrel threads. Subtract that barrel thread shank length from the receiver to bolt face measurement and write down the number.

Make absolutely sure that the chamber in the barrel is clean and then place a go gauge in the chamber. Measure the distance from the back of the gauge to the back of the barrel. Subtract that number from the last number you wrote down. The difference is how much you need to lengthen the chamber. The two numbers should match before installing the barrel.

Actually, Mark likes to subtract .003 inch of "crush factor" when installing a new barrel. So, the number should be .003 inch *more* than equal before installing the barrel. That makes the chamber .003 inch too deep, but when the barrel is tightened to the receiver, the threads "crush" and make up the difference.

Start the lathe and use a dial indicator or DRO to measure the advance of the reamer and simply cut to the number. Screw the barrel to the action, check the headspace and it should be tack-on.

This is how most professional gunsmiths chamber a barrel. It is no doubt a good way to go, much faster and just as precise.

If you don't mess up.

In the immortal words of Mr. Eastwood, "Do you feel lucky?"

If you do, go for it. It will save you a lot of time over my method.

Or it will make you howl at the moon in frustration.

TROUBLES NO MORE

No doubt, this is a great way to chamber a rifle barrel and some would argue it is the correct way. I do not disagree, but it's a little tricky for new gunsmiths learning the skills and for those who do not do it often enough to keep their skills razor sharp.

If the chamber is short it's not a big deal, you just need to ream it a bit deeper. But, if you go too deep, then you have a problem. It can be fixed, but it's not easy. For me, the error is never on the short side and I have "repaired"

all too many barrels with the chamber cut *just a little bit* too deep. It has taught me to slow down and be a lot more careful.

For example, with a Remington style barrel if you cut the chamber too deep you will need to set back the shoulder enough to fix the chamber depth issues. That's fine, as long as you don't make the relief groove wider than the recoil lug, as the lug needs some threads to keep it aligned properly. However, you would need to screw up pretty badly for that to happen.

The trouble now is the shank must also be shortened and the bolt counterbore must be cut deeper. The shank is easy, just face off the end until you have the correct length, but the bolt counterbore is not.

If you did the initial bolt counterbore cut with a boring bar, then you know what to do to make the adjustment. This is an important skill you should learn on the first few builds. Then, do yourself a huge favor and buy a Bolt Body Counterbore Cutter from Dave Manson Reamers. You will no doubt decide it's one of the best tools you ever bought. However, if you mess up and go too deep on the chamber, this tool is no longer your best friend.

The cutter requires a bore riding pilot and you have removed the bore with the chamber reamer. The counterbore tool now has nothing to guide it as it cuts and if you try to make the cut without the pilot, it will chatter and not cut correctly. I speak from experience here. The result looks horrible and you risk damaging your reamer.

Dave Manson told me he can make a custom pilot to fit the chamber you are cutting, but they are cartridge-specific. I suppose if you are a production gun builder and you find you are doing a lot of guns in a single cartridge it's not a bad idea to have one on hand, but most hobby guys will not be doing multiple guns in a single cartridge. At least not enough of them so that the occasional mistake is common enough to need a custom pilot.

The cheaper solution is to set up a small boring bar and correct the depth of the bolt counterbore. This takes time, which is money to a production shop, but it is just a chance for a hobby gunsmith to have a little more fun. Or at least that's what I tell myself when it happens.

One other piece of advice, if you are a hot headed, type-A personality like me. Add a cooling off period between discovering the mistake and starting the correction. It certainly helps my brain function well if I stop and do something else for a bit before I start cutting metal again.

Another, less desirable option is to use a surface grinder to make the recoil lug thinner to adjust for the overage in the chamber depth. I have an old surface grinder and I have used this method with good results, but not many hobby guys have a surface grinder in their shops, so this is usually not a viable option unless you have a machine shop nearby that can do the work for you. Do not attempt to thin the recoil lug without a surface grinder as the edges must remain precise and parallel, which is all but impossible to maintain by hand or even with a milling machine.

STOP RIGHT THERE

The best approach, of course, is to avoid all this trouble to start with. I found that using a reamer stop keeps me from doing stupid things. You can buy one that has micrometer adjustments from Pacific Tool and Gauge. They offer a couple of different options.

▲ PTG reamer stop.

▲ Setting the chamber reamer stop.

Of course, you can chamber a barrel without a stop, by using careful measurements with digital readout (DRO) or a dial indicator, but the stop is a wonderful tool for idiot-proofing the process. I have done several barrels both ways and have become a huge advocate for a stop. Not so much for the finished product as you will see, but to keep me out of trouble as we get down to the final cuts.

▲ Reaming a rifle chamber with the stop installed.

You can make a stop to fit your reamer, but it will be just a simple tool that will stop the reamer from advancing at one location. From there you must remove the stop and use your DRO or a dial indicator to measure the advancement of the quill and control your remaining depth of the chamber.

The "store bought" reamer stops have threads that are 40 threads-per-inch, just like the micrometers used for measuring. The spindles on the stops sold by PTG are marked in .001-inch graduations so you can actually dial in the exact depth the chamber reamer needs to move. If you are new to this, be careful. It's easy to dial in too much, as I know all too well. Any tool is only as good as the operator using it and for a newbie doing their first chamber it all gets a bit confusing. Slow down. Measure often. Cut little.

MICROMETERS

Any gunsmith will need a few micrometers. Just one note, a micrometer is a very precise measuring tool, not a C-clamp or a wrench for removing nuts from bicycle wheels as my youngest brother Scott used mine for when he was six years old.

While a good dial caliper is an essential tool for any gunsmith, it cannot provide the level of precision that can be obtained by a micrometer.

You will need both a one-inch micrometer and a two-inch (1–2 inch) micrometer. At some point, you will probably also want to buy an inside micrometer that can measure inside diameters.

For example, when cutting a bolt recess on a barrel for a Remington 700 you will need to measure the diameter inside the recess.

I find that electronic micrometers are more trouble than they are worth. You must reset them to zero all too often and the batteries always seem to be dead. I much prefer a conventional mechanical micrometer. The most precise also have a Vernier scale on the micrometer so it can read down to one ten-thousandth of an inch.

One feature I really like is a mechanical digital counter on the micrometer. This reads out the numbers much faster. For a final precision reading, you should still use the scale on the body of the micrometer, but the digital is great for fast readings.

One place I think this feature is indispensable is in a depth micrometer. The depth micrometer is different because instead of having two anvils, one fixed and the other moving, it has a stem moving in and out from the bottom of the micrometer. It's designed to measure the depth of a hole. A gunsmith will use it often to measure into the action to figure out important dimensions when fitting a barrel. It's also used to measure the length of the barrel threads and for a multitude of other jobs when working on guns.

The problem with a depth micrometer is that in essence you read it backwards from a conventional micrometer. This is not a big issue if you work with them every day. My son, Nathan, uses one all the time and laughs at me when I struggle with reading my depth mic.

Left to right, top: Depth micrometer, digital 1 inch, mechanical 1 inch, inside micrometer. Bottom, 1–2inch micrometer.

A 1–2inch micrometer in use.

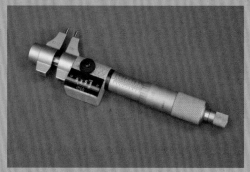

A micrometer for measuring inside.

However, as hobby gunsmiths, we may not use one for months. Smarter people than me are probably fine, but I am sometimes confused when using a depth micrometer after a long layoff. It's easy to make a mistake in a critical measurement.

Recently, I switched to a Starrett depth micrometer with a mechanical digital readout. What a difference. Upon seeing the digital readout, the numbers on the body of the micrometer become much easier to understand. To have the most precision you still need to use the scale laid out on the barrel of the micrometer of course, but it programs your brain to read that by also having the digital readout giving you the numbers. When you are ready to buy a depth micrometer, I highly recommend the Starrett mechanical digital model.

The Starrett depth micrometer. The digital readout is a huge help in reading these "backwards" micrometers.

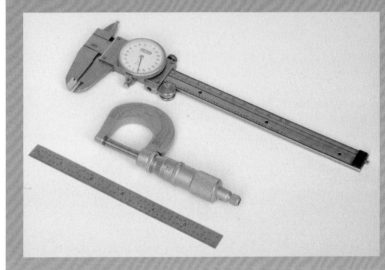

Three measuring tools a gunsmith will need, a dial caliper, micrometer, and a machinist's scale.

TOWSLEY'S IDIOT-PROOF WAY TO CHAMBER A RIFLE BARREL

I have developed an almost foolproof approach for a hobby gunsmith. I set up the reamer stop short of the required chamber depth. I do this visually with a no-go gauge side by side with the reamer, using the shoulder, rim, or belt as a guide. I want the reamer to stop .030 inch or .040 inch short of my final chamber dimensions. That way I can make the cuts needed to form the chamber without fear of going too deep.

I use a Dave Manson floating reamer holder to fit the reamer to the lathe tailstock quill. The floating holder allows the reamer find its own center and to follow the bore riding pilot and cut the chamber in line with the bore. There are lots of other methods of holding a chamber reamer, but in my never humble opinion, the floating holder is well worth the price.

The tailstock should of course be locked in place. Before starting, you should also have verified that the tailstock is correctly aligned as detailed elsewhere in this book.

Turn your lathe down to the slowest setting. That is

70 RPM on my Grizzly. Use lots and lots of cutting oil on the reamer. Later, as you develop skills, you can turn up the RPM to make this job go faster. Slowly start the reamer into the barrel and advance it using the tailstock quill.

▲ "Feeling" the reamer.

Keep your left hand on the floating reamer holder so that you can "feel" how the reamer is cutting. Work the reamer into the barrel very slowly as you develop a "feel" for how it is cutting. It needs a certain amount of "load" to work correctly, so you should not use too slow a feed. You also don't want to go too fast and start jamming things up.

Back the reamer out often and clean off the chips. It depends on the reamer, but a good guideline is to clean the chips after two revolutions of the quill advance wheel. I use a small paint brush for this chore. You can use compressed air, but be careful about using compressed air around the lathe as you do not want to force a chip under the apron where it will scratch the ways.

That's why you never clean the lathe with compressed air. I have machinist friends who tell me that is a firing offense in most machine shops.

That said, careful application of compressed air can help clean the chips off the reamers. Turn down the air pressure. I like to catch the chips with a rag or paper towel. It goes without saying that you must always wear eye protection. Make sure it fully protects your eyes and that there is no way debris can enter under, over, or through the sides of the glasses. Tight-fitting goggles are best. Or just use a paint brush, which is much less troublesome. I keep a coffee can of acetone around to clean the brush as needed.

Slather more cutting oil on the reamer, squirt some into the barrel and insert the reamer back into the bore. Make sure the lathe is turning as you start cutting again. Do not allow the reamer to make contact unless the lathe is turning. Advance the reamer a bit more and repeat.

When the reamer has hit the stop, back it out and clean everything up. Shut off the power to the lathe to prevent any accidental restart.

I use an air hose to blow out the chamber while holding a rag over the muzzle to catch the chips that are blown out. Then I wipe out the chamber with large cotton tipped swabs to ensure it's clean. Clean the threads and install the action and recoil lug.

▲ Using a large, cotton tip swab to clean the chamber.

It's best if the bolt is disassembled, with the firing pin, extractor and ejector removed, but if you have properly blueprinted the action, that's all done anyway.

▲ Using a feeler gauge to see how much deeper the chamber must be cut. Note this is with a Mini Mauser action, so there is no recoil lug as with a Remington action.

Put the go gauge into the barrel and the bolt into the action. Install the recoil lug and carefully screw the action onto the barrel until it bumps the go gauge with the bolt face. Just tighten until it stops; do not apply a lot of force. Push the recoil lug tight against the barrel and measure the distance from the recoil lug to the front edge of the action. This is a measurement of how much further you need to go, more or less. If the gap is large, you can measure it with a dial indicator. If it's smaller, feeler gauges work best.

In theory, you could just dial in that number and cut the chamber, but I am cautious about this and like to sneak up on the end result. Reset the stop on your indicator so that you will ream to half the remaining distance. Then ream again to the stop or, if you are not using a stop, when your indicator says you have reached the correct depth. Stop, shut off the lathe, clean everything and install the recoil lug and receiver again. Insert the go gauge and tighten until the bolt contacts the gauge. Do not overtighten, just go until it stops. Again, measure the gap between the recoil lug and the front of the action. If you did this right, it will be half what it was the last time. Repeat until you are close, say about .015 inch to .020 inch out.

These steps take time, but they slow you down and help you make sure you are not making any huge mistakes. Like I said, it's best to sneak up on the final dimension. As your skills develop you can modify this approach to something that is faster. For now, take it easy. You have a lot of time, money and work invested into your project, so why risk the outcome by rushing? Relax, enjoy the process. Remember this is a hobby, not a job.

Set your stop or indicator to stop .010 inch short of the number indicated with the go headspace gauge when you measure from the recoil lug to the face of the receiver. Remove the action and ream to the stop again.

Clean everything very carefully, particularly the chamber. Also clean the go gauge, all the threads and all contact surfaces such as the recoil lug and the shoulders on the receiver and the barrel. A chip will screw up your measurements. Put the action and the recoil lug on, insert the go gauge and tighten until it stops. Again, if you did this correctly, the gap should measure .010 inch. If you are confident, you can simply set the stop on your dial indicator, adding .001 inch to .003 inch for crush, ream .012 inch to .013 inch deeper, and just cut the finished chamber.

▲ Headspace gauges for a .308 Winchester. Note the broken rim on the go gauge from dropping it on a hard object. It was replaced after this job.

I am the first to admit, this rarely works for me. I am never sure what went wrong, a math error or simply reaming too deep. So, I take a very cautionary approach from now on. The issue is simple, we hobby gunsmiths do not do this every day like gunsmiths in a production shop. Our skills never will be as finely tuned as theirs and skills at any level grow rusty when we don't use them. Most of us just don't do this often enough to get cocky. On an important job like fitting the chamber I prefer to spend more time to get it perfect. Again, if I were doing this for a living this approach might not be profitable. I do this for fun, so I don't mind taking a little longer and using a very cautious approach to getting the headspace set correctly.

I know this is starting to sound like a broken record, repeating the same thing over and over, but that just means you should listen. Learn from my mistakes here. This is what I have developed as a nearly idiot-proof approach to making a perfect rifle chamber. It's not *100 percent* idiot-proof, as this idiot has beat the system and screwed things up a time or two. That only happens when I am not paying attention or I am trying to cut corners and speed it up. When I stick to the plan, it usually goes pretty well.

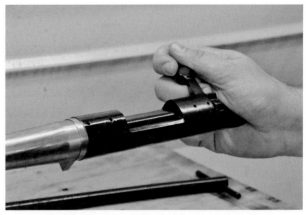

▲ The bolt still will not close on the go gauge. The chamber must be reamed slightly deeper.

▲ Now the bolt will close all the way on a go gauge. This means the chamber is done.

Remove the go gauge and tighten the action as much as possible without stressing the lathe or causing slippage in the chuck jaws. This of course is not going to be as tight as the final fit, but it's close enough for this process.

▲ Using a T-handle with a chamber reamer to make the finishing cut in the chamber.

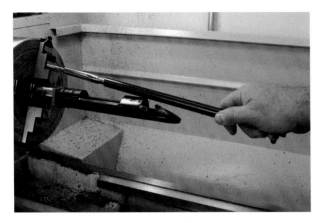

▲ The chamber reamer in the T-handle.

Insert the reamer into a Clymer Rifle T-Handle (available from Brownells, of course!). This tool allows you to cut the last part of the chamber by hand.

Insert the reamer into the chamber and turn it a little. Go slowly as you develop a feel for how it cuts. Use plenty of cutting oil.

Remove the reamer, clean the chamber, and try the go gauge. The bolt should not close on it. Repeat this process until you can just feel the go gauge as the bolt closes.

▲ This action is tight on the barrel and the bolt will close with no resistance on the go gauge.

Again, remove the gauge and the bolt and insert the reamer with plenty of cutting oil. Take a light easy turn. The idea here is to make a very light cut; you only want to remove about .001 inch. Often, a partial turn is enough. Clean everything and try closing the bolt on the go gauge again. If you can feel the gauge, take another small cut. Do this until the bolt will close without feeling the go gauge. The idea is to get just about a thousandth of an inch past contact with the go gauge. This gives you a minimum-spec chamber.

One word of advice. Remove the no-go gauge from your work area. Put it back in the tool box so there is no possibility of picking it up by mistake. Again, learn from my mistakes. It's easier than you might think to insert the wrong gauge and wind up cutting too deep. If you ask me how I know this, I'll just tell you a lie.

▲ Polishing the chamber.

Remove the action and recoil lug. Polish the chamber and break the radius on the edges, using emery paper. Of course, the lathe ways must be protected from the abrasive. I use the same piece of plywood to cover the lathe ways that I use when changing chucks. I have one side marked as "up" so that I always put the clean side against the ways. Be very careful, as anytime you go hands-on with a turning lathe you can get hurt if something catches.

Use 320-grit emery cloth. Put it on your finger and carefully break the sharp edge on the entry to the chamber and at the back of the bolt lug recesses. Move your finger to form a nice smooth radius on both of these edges. Then polish the inside of the chamber with 400-grit wrapped around a pencil or wooden dowel to polish the inside of the chamber walls. You don't want them highly polished or smooth. The fired case must grip the chamber walls when under pressure. If it's too smooth the case won't grip properly, but you also don't want it rough or to have any machining marks so that brass grips the chamber enough to stick when the cartridge is fired. Move the polishing tool in and out to create a crosshatch pattern. Go very lightly on this, just enough to change the sheen of the chamber walls without

▲ This barrel is finished, chambered and ready to fit to an action.

removing any amount of metal. Make sure you get up on the shoulder of a bottleneck case. You can feel as the dowel advances to the shoulder.

Remove the barrel from the lathe, clean the chamber and install the barrel in a barrel vise. Put some anti-seize grease on the barrel threads and a little on each side of the recoil lug and install the lug and action to the barrel. Don't

▲ ▼ Using an action wrench and barrel vise to tighten the barrel to the action.

worry at this point about the recoil lug alignment, let it point where it wants.

Use an action wrench to torque the action to the barrel. Brownells sells a conventional action wrench which is excellent. This grips the outside of the action and is tightened with two big bolts. When you do the final tightening, there is a cut to align the recoil lug on the wrench. Presumably this is for factory Remington recoil lugs as it never seems to fit right with aftermarket lugs. I use the feeler gauge method mentioned in the sidebar on recoil lug fitting to align the recoil lug. This wrench is excellent for both removing and installing actions to the barrel as you can really get some force on it. If you can only afford one wrench, this is the one to get. The down side is that it's a bit slow to install and can mar the finish on the action. For a final fit after I have finished the action and barrel, always wrap some protection between the wrench and action. I usually use brown packing paper, but, after reading about using sheetrock seam tape, I tried that on my last gun and it worked very well. Another down side of this wrench is that it will not work with a torque wrench.

Lately, I have been using Darrell Holland's wrench that fits inside the Remington 700 action. This is fast and easy to use. It also allows the easy application of a torque wrench, because the wrench is in line with the threads and the back has a 7/8-inch hex to fit a socket. Opinions vary on how much torque to apply, but I torque to at least 80 foot-pounds and often to 100 foot-pounds.

After torqueing the action and barrel, check again with the go gauge. If you can feel the gauge again, use the reamer and extension until the bolt will just close on the go gauge without feeling it.

I used to think that if I could just feel the go gauge it would be better because the chamber would be tight and therefore more accurate. However, I have found I get much better accuracy by reaming until just past where I can feel the gauge.

Now check with the no-go gauge, which should not allow the bolt to close. In fact, the bolt handle should remain high if you have the chamber to minimum spec as planned.

That's it, the rifle is chambered, the "dangerous" part of building your rifle is over and you can breathe again.

REMOVING CHATTER: DAVE MANSON PRECISION REAMERS

This is edited for length. The full version is on the Dave Manson Precision Reamers' website. I urge you to log on and read the entire article, as it has a lot of information on chamber reamers.

The thought of reamer chatter during chambering strikes fear in the heart of even the most experienced gunsmith. This condition can ruin an expensive barrel and add unnecessary cost to what should have been a profitable job. With many possible causes of chatter, it's not unusual for several to be present at one time.

What can you do if chatter starts while you're chambering?

First thing—stop as soon as you suspect there's chatter. Don't continue to cut deeper with the same parameters, thinking it will go away. Unless you're extraordinarily lucky, it will only get worse—can you make a washboard road smoother by driving on it?

The general machining rule of thumb if something chatters is to reduce the spindle speed, increase the feed-rate, or both. By doing this, you're loading the reamer more heavily and the tool is less likely to be able to vibrate (chatter). Check your reaming "system" for possible sources of vibration that may be inducing chatter and tighten or eliminate any looseness. Sometimes a little hand pressure on the barrel as it turns can cause the reamer to smooth out—this is a sign you're close to a vibration node that might be eliminated by changing feed rate and/or spindle speed. When experimenting with different spindle speeds, recall that our reamers can be run as high as 300–350 RPM without damage.

Check the fit of the pilot to the bore; there should be very little play. If using pilot bushings, select one that will fit the bore with a very slight drag. It should turn on the reamer's spindle smoothly, with virtually no play.

If you're lucky enough to have a second reamer in the same caliber, try it—often another reamer will have teeth spaced sufficiently differently that it will remove chatter caused by the first and continue to cut smoothly.

Some gunsmiths recommend using a boring bar to remove chatter before attempting to cut the chamber deeper. This removes the chatter, but, if taken too deep, will keep the pilot from being engaged in the bore when the shoulder of the reamer starts to cut.

A technique that works quite well is "the patch trick." This involves using cleaning patches on the reamer to damp vibration while chatter is gradually cut away. Different versions of this technique employ greased paper or other materials, but follow the same concept.

Assuming a 30-cal reamer has chattered, choose a number (six to twelve) of thick cleaning patches about 1.25 inches square and poke holes in their centers large enough to allow the patch to slip over the neck of the reamer and lie against its shoulder.

Using cleaning patches on a reamer to correct chatter.

Note, for smaller bore sizes, use proportionately smaller patches; if patches are thin, use two at a time. Slide a patch on the reamer so it lies against the shoulder and resume cutting the chamber again under power.

While cutting, hold your left hand on the reamer or holder so you can feel when the reamer cuts through the patch and starts to engage the chatter—you'll feel the reamer "tug" when this happens. As soon as you feel the tugging, pull the reamer out of the cut, replace the patch, and repeat the process. You may have to repeat this a number of times, but the chatter should slowly be removed from the chamber. Once it's gone, continue cutting to proper headspace; if the reamer continues to want to chatter, keep using patches until the chamber is complete. What you're doing with all this is gradually cutting the peaks of the chatter until the surface of the chamber is the same height. The patches serve two purposes—they damp vibration caused by the chatter and fill the low points of the chatter during reaming.

In conclusion, I'd like to paraphrase an old saying: "There are those who haven't experienced chatter but will, and those who have experienced chatter . . . and will again!"

BUY OR RENT?

I am a tool junkie, so I like to own my reamers. If I am building more than one rifle, for example as I did with the 9.3X62 rifles I'll ask the friend getting the other rifle to share the cost as my price for doing the work. In that case, Tony Kinton and I split the expense. We both got a new rifle built and I kept the reamer and headspace gauges.

Buying your reamers not only builds on your tool collection, it ensures you have a brand new, high-quality reamer to build your rifle. It also means you know the entire history of the reamer and how it's been used.

There are companies that rent reamers and from what I can see, you will save half or more over the price of buying a new reamer. That's a pretty large incentive to rent a reamer for a one time rifle build.

I have no experience at all with renting reamers, so I really can't form an opinion. However, I did talk with a few guys who have rented with very mixed results. One professional gunsmith said he tried it three times and each time the reamer was dull, chipped, or broken. He stopped renting and now buys all his reamers. Another well-known custom rifle builder said he has had good experiences with renting reamers. I have a gun writer friend who rented a reamer to have a rifle built and was happy with the result.

I will put the option out here in an attempt to keep my readers as informed as possible. All I can say is, be careful. Anytime you rent anything you are dealing with the history of that object in the hands of past "renters." The old saying "beating it like a rented mule" has some insight. You may be fine; in fact, you probably will be, if you work with reputable companies. It's also possible that you will be the first person to rent the reamer, but you also may be the twentieth. There is really no way of knowing for sure.

Here is my way of thinking about renting. By the time you buy all the components to build a rifle and spend all those hours in the shop to build it, does it make sense to risk the outcome by rolling the dice on rented cutting tools?

Only you can answer that question.

MAGNUM OPUS

I wanted to build a serious long-range rifle in a serious long-range cartridge, one that hit with authority at long distances, but was still manageable both in recoil and ammo cost.

This is my "Magnum Opus" rifle.

The new wave of long-range cartridges use mild mannered short action cartridges designed for high ballistic coefficient bullets. They are great for punching targets, but lack serious stopping power down range. (Yes, in spite of what Tactical Timmy may have said on the internet, stopping power is a real thing.)

The long-range fad now sweeping the nation often forgets its roots. The .300 Winchester Magnum was once the darling of the long-range shooting society and it held a lot of 1,000-yard records. Times have changed, but ballistics have not. The .300 Winnie is still a superior cartridge if you are streaming much past 1,000 yards. It also will bring a lot more power to the target at any range than the "tiny" cartridges in vogue today.

My rifle started with a Remington Model 700 Long Action. I blueprinted the action with the

(continued . . .)

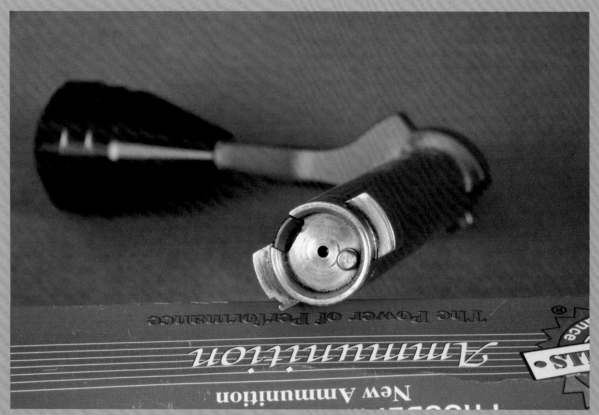

The bolt is fitted with a Sako style extractor.

Manson kit, changed the scope mounting screws to 8-40 and drilled the front ring to work with a Holland pinned recoil lug. I installed a Sako style extractor in the bolt and fitted an oversized bolt knob. Then, I polished up everything so it ran like the bolt was on oiled bearings.

The trigger is a Timney Calvin Elite Custom set so light that when I am ready, I just think about shooting and it reads my mind.

The barrel is a top of the line Bartlein with a 1:10 twist rate and is 27 inches long as installed. The muzzle brake is a Precision Armament M11, 30-caliber, sold by Brownells. The fitting of this brake is unique, as Precision Armament sells a package of washers of varying thicknesses. To install and time the brake, you simply select the washer that is the right thickness so the brake is positioned where you want it after it is torqued tight. There are a lot of ways to fit muzzle brakes, but I think this is one of the most ingenious and one of the best.

The rifle is fitted in an Accuracy International AX AICS chassis system. This chassis has a folding buttstock, so I can fit the gun into conventional carrying cases like the Holland Signature Series Rifle Case I use to transport this beast. The chassis also

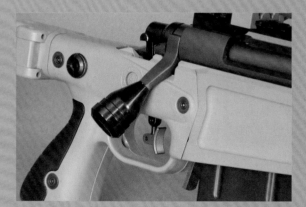

The oversized bolt knob and the Timney trigger show this is a serious precision rifle.

The Bartlein barrel is fitted with a Precision Armament M11, 30-caliber muzzle brake. This brake uses different thickness washers to time the brake.

takes AI magazines for rapid reloads. As rifle chassis systems go, I think it may well be the best of the best. I have another on a custom built 6.5 Creedmoor and was so happy with it I would consider no other for this build.

I fitted a Talley Picatinny rail base with 20 MOA of elevation built in. The scope is a Vortex Razor HD 4.5X27, 34mm tube scope in Talley rings.

I finished the barrel in Cerakote Elite Earth color. The action and bolt, except the knob, are in Cerakote Elite Smoke color. I left the Holland Recoil Lug uncoated to create a transition between the colors. With the Pale Brown color of the AI Chassis it makes a striking looking rifle.

With handloaded Sierra 190-grain MatchKing bullets this gun is easily capable of sub ½-MOA on a good day, which is code talk for "when the shooter is running in good form."

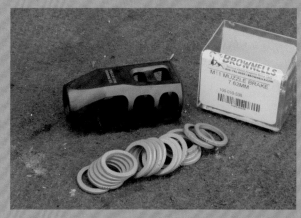

These washers are different thicknesses. Install the brake with the washer that allows it to be positioned correctly.

This rifle gathers a crowd at the range and is rapidly became a long-range favorite with my shooting buddies (particularly if I am supplying the ammo!). The other cartridges ring steel at long range, this one makes it dance!

I made this rifle for target shooting and as a long-range rifle to defend Camp Towsley against the zombies if the world falls apart.

It's a heavy brute, checking in at 17.75 pounds with the big Vortex scope, so I doubt I'll use it sheep hunting, assuming my brutalized knees even have another sheep hunt left in them. But, I would not hesitate to take it to a deer stand where a long shot is a probability.

The Accuracy International AX AICS chassis system of course accepts AI-style magazines.

CHAPTER 17

MUZZLE END

 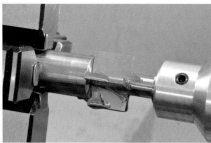 

▲ Using a piloted 11-degree cutter in a floating reamer holder to finish the muzzle and crown.

The muzzle end of the rifle will require one or possibly two operations after it is cut to length. The muzzle must be crowned and often threaded for a brake or suppressor.

Put the barrel in the lathe just as you did for cutting the threads and chamber, but reversed so the muzzle is in the 4-jaw chuck side. Dial the barrel into center using the same methods detailed in the section on barrel threading. Face off the end of the muzzle until it's nice and square.

THREADING

If you are going to thread the muzzle for a brake or suppressor it's a good idea to do that first. This allows you to use a live center to support the muzzle while you work.

Use a center drill to make a 60-degree bevel on the front of the bore to use with the live center to help support the barrel while cutting and threading. This will be removed after completing the threads and before crowning the muzzle, so make sure that you add enough length to the thread to allow for cutting back the barrel to remove the 60-degree taper.

Cutting threads on the muzzle for a brake or a suppressor is pretty much the exact same technique as cutting the barrel threads for the action, but on a smaller scale.

The first step is to discover the thread pitch you will be using and the length of the thread. For example, 5/8-24 is a common thread for a lot of muzzle brakes. The final thread length should be long enough to fill the threads inside the brake, without sticking out from them. Don't forget to add length for the crush washer or other spacer used for indexing the brake.

Cut a shank for the correct diameter, ending at a square shoulder. Information on the shank diameter for any

▲ Measuring the shank before threading for a muzzle brake.

▲ Use cutting oil when machining the shank.

common thread can be found on line or in the *Machinery's Handbook*. Use the Major Diameter of the thread.

Because this is a smaller thread I like to make a thinner relief groove using a thinner grooving tool. Brownells sells a kit with multiple thickness grooving tools called the 3/8 Cutoff Groover RH Kit. The 1/32 size groover works well here. Use the same threading technique as outlined in how to thread the receiver end of the barrel. Of course, you must adjust the lathe to the thread being cut, using the chart on the lathe to set all the gears and dials.

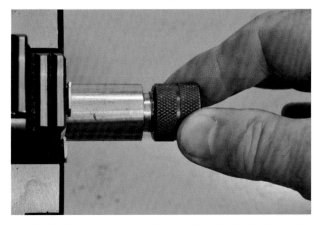

▲ This thread protector is used to check the threads.

Use the brake or suppressor adaptor to test the fit of the threads, just as you used the action on the other end. Stop when the thread allows the brake to turn on and off easily with a minimum of wobble. This makes for a custom fit thread to keep the brake precisely aligned. It's important to have a square, clean shoulder for it to butt against.

CROWNING GLORY

Now it's time to cut the crown.

Of course, if the rifle is not going to have a threaded muzzle, you would jump right to this process and skip over the threading process.

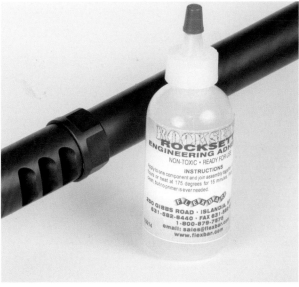

▲ When installing the break, Rocksett works well to lock the threads, as it's not heat sensitive. This is a Little Bastard II Brake from American Precision Arms.

Face off the muzzle. If you added a 60-degree bevel for using a live center, face off enough to completely remove that.

The one that all the hip and happening kids are using for accuracy is the 11-degree crown. Set the compound on the lathe for 11 degrees or 79 degrees depending on which axis you are working from. On my lathe, I use an adjustable protractor against the face of the chuck to verify that the compound is set to the correct 11-degree angle.

I have found that none of my indexable cutting tools work. The tool holder hits the barrel, making a mess of everything. For this operation, you need a small cutter that can extend inside the bore of the barrel. I know that a lot of gunsmiths grind a special cutting tool just for this job, but I found that a small 3/8-inch boring bar works just fine, at least for the muzzles I have done so far. Other bore diameters may not be compatible. However there are some small boring bars on the market that should work with almost any diameter bore.

Always start the cut from inside the bore to prevent forming a burr and cut out toward the edge of the barrel. Take very light cuts with each pass. You can watch the edge of the 11-degree crown move out on the barrel diameter with each cut. Keep going until it's all the way to the outside edge, or stop any time the look of the crown catches your fancy.

A much easier and faster way is to use a crown cutting tool. There are a wide range of piloted tools on the market. Brownells sells several to use with brass pilots, either as a standalone or in a kit. I don't have a floating holder for

▲ This nice 11-degree crown was cut on a lathe using a boring bar.

these, so I use the hex adapter that comes with the kit. I put it in my Jacobs Chuck and leave the chuck slightly loose so the reamer can float and follow the pilot. The front of the jaws will push against the adapter to apply pressure to the reamer. I use a wrench on the hex adapter to prevent the tool from turning in the chuck.

I also like to use a reamer from PTG that uses removable pilots, the same pilots I use on the chamber reamers. This tool will fit into my Manson Floating Reamer Holder.

Run the lathe at the lowest speed, flood the barrel with cutting oil and slowly feed the piloted reamer into the muzzle until you achieve the desired crown. I end by feeding the last few thousandths very slowly and then holding the final position for several revolutions of the lathe. This seems to give a nice, clean looking crown. You can polish the face of the crown with emery cloth for a finished look.

You can tweak the crown with a brass lap, but most gunsmiths I know think it's unnecessary. I have to admit, I was not sure until I started shooting a few rifles that are simply cut to 11-degrees without using the lap. The accuracy has been outstanding.

The last step is to use a file to put a radius on the outside edge of the muzzle.

ACKNOWLEDGMENTS

Special thanks to Jim Majoros, Jamey Majoros and Mark Bansner. Those guys spent a lot of time and treasure making sure this book became real.

Many thanks as well to Ken Kelly, Dennis Amsden, Karl Sokol, Darrell Holland, Wade Brown, Tom Mercier, and many others.

This is my gunsmith posse. Without their help, this book would not have happened. They have fielded questions and checked manuscripts for errors. They have all taught me how to do a million different things and bailed me out when I got it wrong. Most of them have spent hours on the phone, walking me through the difficult projects. They are the brain trust of this book, but any errors in this thing are all mine.

Thanks to my son, Nathan, who has shown me the way in machining and for answering all those technical engineering and machinist's questions.

Without my wife, Robin, this book would look like a kindergartener wrote it. If you can't spell, it's a good idea to marry somebody who can. She has proofread every word (some of them many times) I have written in the thirty-six years I have been writing professionally and has not tried to kill me even once.

Many thanks to Jay Cassell, my editor at Skyhorse, for all his patience. I know he dreads the calls begging for yet another deadline extension and I am sure he hates me, but he hides it well.

The good folks at Brownells, including Roy Hill, have been an incredible help in getting this done. Thanks to Pete Brownell for the Foreword; he lends a lot of credibility to this book with that.

I much appreciate all the help from Shiraz Balolia and Melinda Sweet from Grizzly Industrial. Without them, the second half of this book would not have happened.

If I forgot to mention you here, I am sorry. This is the end of the largest writing project I have ever attempted and it's been an exhausting process.

ABOUT THE AUTHOR

ryce M. Towsley published his first magazine article, about hunting with handguns, in 1982 in the *Vermont Sportsman* magazine. In the years since, he has published thousands of articles and photos in most of the major outdoor and gun magazines and on multiple internet sites.

Towsley's wide ranging writing includes technical articles on firearms, gunsmithing, reloading, optics, and shooting. His hunting writing covers the spectrum from technical how-to articles to adventures in wild places. He also writes mood and humor pieces and is working on a collection of those for a new book. He wrote an opinion column for several years that won multiple awards.

Towsley has written and published 10 books and has contributed to several others, most are about hunting or guns. Another, *The 14th Reinstated*, is an action/adventure novel. This is his second gunsmithing book. The first, *Gunsmithing Made Easy,* is one of the best-selling gunsmithing books ever published.

Towsley is an avid hunter with more than fifty years of experience, taking his first whitetail in Vermont in 1966 at the age of eleven. Since then, he has hunted extensively throughout the United States and Canada, as well as in Mexico, South Africa, Zimbabwe, Tanzania, Namibia, Argentina, Russia, Australia, and several countries in Europe for a wide variety of game.

He has been to all fifty states, all but one Canadian province and every continent except Antarctica. He has competed in several competition shooting disciplines and currently is active in 3-gun shooting and USPSA.

Towsley has been reloading for fifty years. He has several wildcat cartridges that he created and hunted with. He wrote the majority of the text in the Barnes #5 reloading manual and has contributed to other reloading manuals, including Lyman, Hodgdon, Nosler, and Berger Bullets.

Towsley enjoys shooting, hunting, fishing, reading, and riding his Harley Davidson motorcycle. He is an accomplished gunsmith and builds many of his own firearms for hunting and competition.

He lives in Vermont with his wife Robin and a couple of dogs. His children Erin and Nathan are grown and doing well in the world.

Check out his website, www.brycetowsley.com.

INDEX